DEMOCRACY, LAW AND GOVERNANCE

Studies in Modern Law and Policy

Series Editor: Ralf Rogowski,
Professor of Law, University of Warwick

Also in the series

Judicial Accountabilities in New Europe
From Rule of Law to Quality of Justice
Daniela Piana
ISBN: 978-0-7546-7758-1

The European Social Model and Transitional Labour Markets
Law and Policy
Edited by Ralf Rogowski
ISBN: 978-0-7546-4958-8

The Changing Law of the Employment Relationship
Comparative Analyses in the European Context
Nicola Countouris
ISBN: 978-0-7546-4800-0

Property in Work
The Employment Relationship in the Anglo-American Firm
Wanjiru Njoya
ISBN: 978-0-7546-4587-0

Contract and Control in the Entertainment Industry
Dancing on the Edge of Heaven
Steve Greenfield and Guy Osborn
ISBN: 978-1-85521-561-0

Labour Law in the Post-Industrial Era
Lord Wedderburn, Max G. Rood, Gérard Lyon-Caen,
Paul F. van der Heijden and Wolfgang Däubler
ISBN: 978-1-85521-644-0

Democracy, Law and Governance

JACQUES LENOBLE
Université Catholique de Louvain, Belgium

and

MARC MAESSCHALCK
Université Catholique de Louvain, Belgium

Routledge
Taylor & Francis Group
LONDON AND NEW YORK

First published 2010 by Ashgate Publishing

2 Park Square, Milton Park, Abingdon, Oxon OX14 4RN
711 Third Avenue, New York, NY 10017, USA

Routledge is an imprint of the Taylor & Francis Group, an informa business

First issued in paperback 2016

British Library Cataloguing in Publication Data
Lenoble, Jacques, 1950-
Democracy, law and governance. -- (Studies in modern law and policy)
1. Political science--Philosophy. 2. Democracy--Philosophy.
I. Title II. Series III. Maesschalck, M. (Marc)
320'.011-dc22

Library of Congress Cataloging-in-Publication Data
Lenoble, Jacques, 1950-
Democracy, law and governance / by Jacques Lenoble and Marc Maesschalck.
p. cm.
Includes bibliographical references and index.
ISBN 978-1-4094-0395-1 (hbk) -- ISBN 978-1-4094-0396-8 (ebk) 1. Law--Political aspects--Philosophy. 2. Political science--Philosophy. 3. Democracy. I. Maesschalck, M. (Marc) II. Title.
K487.P65L46 2010
340'.11--dc22

2010000631

ISBN 13: 978-1-4094-0395-1 (hbk)
ISBN 13: 978-1-138-26071-9 (pbk)

Contents

List of Tables

Introduction[1]

The context for this book is a crisis in democratic political systems interpreted as consisting essentially of a major failure in collective regulatory methods for the market economy. There has flowed from this a generalized crisis of confidence in politics, reflected in the search for new forms of "resistance" to power and in the effort at establishing new forms of counterforce. And yet, however radical this crisis may appear to be, it does not represent a challenge to the major principles of the democratic ideal. Rather, what is manifested is the felt need to redefine the conditions for fulfilment of the democratic ideal and to change the forms of democratic organization, which actually confirms the success of the democratic ideal. Thus, as P. Rosanvallon (2006: 9) recently wrote, "the democratic ideal prevails unchallenged, but nearly everywhere, the regimes that profess to subscribe to it are eliciting vigorous critique." It is undoubtedly significant that this crisis has arisen during the continuation of a period of intense reform in methods of governance of the welfare state and an effort to "modernize" or redefine the conditions for building public interest policy. The issue is first and foremost a problem of the effectiveness and relevance.

Thus, this crisis and this requirement for change reflect neither a rejection of the democratic ideal, nor a challenge to the basic beliefs which this ideal is understood in the sphere of modern political philosophy to embody: the belief in the sovereignty of the general will, self-government, and the common good. Rather, they reflect the recognition of the inadequate way in which applied democratic theory has conceptualized the conditions for its own fulfilment, that is, the conditions that will allow for a collective action to produce a form of common life that meets the normative expectations of its members. For, rightly understood, applied democratic theory is in fact a theory of collective action, that is, a theory that allows for determining the conditions that a collective action must satisfy in order to guarantee, to the extent possible, the fulfilment of its participants' normative expectations.

Although it is true that the concept of democracy is more usually associated with the principle that the people are the sole legitimate basis of power, or, as J. Cohen (1989) has recently pointed out, with "the notions of autonomy and the common good", there are many benefits to framing it in terms of an applied theory of collective action.[2] Framing it in these terms makes it possible to take a fresh look

1 This research has been supported by the Sixth European Framework Programme in Research and Development and by the Interuniversity Attraction Pole Programme (IAP)—Belgian State– Belgian Science Policy (BELSPO).

2 D. Cefaï's studies provide good evidence of the helpfulness of this perspective in understanding the role played by new forms of collective action in what he calls the "public

at political philosophy and understand the reasons for the inadequacy of current democratic theory. It brings to light the consequences for democratic theory of its own failure to attend to the concept of action it deploys and nevertheless inevitably presupposes. In fact, the hypothesis we will defend here is that, because of this "failure to attend", the existing approach to democracy has remained dependent on an inadequate conceptualization of collective action. This, we maintain, is the case at two levels of analysis: that of the construction of the legitimacy of public authority and that of the mobilization of the actors concerned with the application of norms.

This inadequate conceptualization results in a twofold analytic blind spot, or, as we call it, blockage, in current theorizing about democracy, including the most recent efforts at reformulation. It is these two blockages in current political thought that this book seeks to analyse and overcome by engaging with them point by point across the book's two main parts. As a preliminary to this detailed analysis, we identify the two blockages in this introduction. In so doing, we hope to make clear to the reader the specific nature of our approach to the political; the nature of the intellectual shift we propose; and the outline of our contribution to the debate. Each of the two blockages relates to an aspect of the social production of the generality of power, understood both as a capacity specific to the institutional mechanisms of public authority and as a capacity of collective actors themselves to participate in establishing this authority through social participation.

The First Blockage in Democratic Theory

The first blockage in current democratic theory relates to the institutional mechanisms by means of which the legitimacy of public authority is thought to be guaranteed. We refer to this blockage as the "representationalist belief" that persists in applied democratic theory. It takes the form of the ascription of self-sufficiency to the reference to public authorities. Thus every drive to broaden the conditions for respecting democratic legitimacy has been translated into the expansion of the "rights" that may be legally opposed to the authorities' sway, the creation of a new power granted to the authorities, or the creation of a new authority. Although democratic theory has thus in effect progressively increased the number and scope of the conditions that must be fulfilled for a public action to be "rationally acceptable", it has always been understood that the conditions for fulfilment of the normative operation itself (that is, of the effective determination of the new norm) reside solely in the final say-so of the public authorities. Thus, the process of social transformation has always been understood to take adequate shape through the actions of the public authorities themselves. Let us see if we can better grasp the nature of this first blockage as it relates to institutional reforms.

The first analytic blockage relates to the fact that political philosophy has usually focused on the question of the "legitimacy of the norm", that is, on the

arenas" of democracy (Cefaï 2007).

question of the conditions that must be respected in order for a norm adopted by a public authority to be rationally acceptable. The underlying presupposition is reflected in the prevalence, at the heart of traditional democratic theory, of a political model that privileges a representative form of democracy. The idea assumed to be self-evident and left unexamined is that the action by which the group acts upon itself—that is, the action by means of which the group adopts norms for shaping and transforming reality in the light of its own objectives—is performed exclusively through the established public authorities. Let us try to pinpoint the implications of this idea.

Political inquiry has worked hard to define the conditions that a democratic theory requires for "establishing" "legitimate" public authorities and accordingly for guaranteeing the legitimacy of those authorities' normative actions. Three main forms of condition have thereby been successively identified.

(1) First, the concept of democratic legitimacy has been defined by reference to electoral mechanisms, the notion of universal suffrage, and the progressive extension of the franchise to all categories of citizen (with debate continuing in our day as to whether it should be extended to non-citizens). Thus, the representative form of democracy was, in the first instance, reduced to its "electoralist" version.

(2) Next, without abandoning this electoralist perspective, political inquiry expanded the conditions for political legitimacy by broadening the bases of the rights that must be respected by public authorities. The concept of representation could not be limited solely to the rights implied by the electoral representative mechanism. In association with the liberalism-socialism debate and the more recent debate initiated by the communitarian critique of liberalism, the question of expanding the basis for rights beyond the civil and political to the socioeconomic and the "cultural" (thus allowing for the guarantee of respect for the cultural conditions for moral autonomy) has been increasingly studied.

(3) Last, it is possible to identify a third type of expansion of the conditions for democratic legitimacy. As has been suggested by P. Rosanvallon, this consists of engaging with the position of impartiality and the reflexivity of the mechanisms that back up the actions of the public authority. This type of change has flowed from the concern to better ensure the presence of the conditions necessary to social representation by rethinking the institutional frame for the practices that enable the production of the "general interest". The establishment of the welfare state had already led to a change in the balance among the various public authorities, especially the balance foundationally established between the legislative and executive branches. It would appear today, however, that even a "true administrative power" (Rosanvallon 2008: 12) based on competency is not sufficient to guarantee the adequate substantive framing of the general interest, as was seen in the cases of the public service model in France and the rational-administration model in the USA (Rosanvallon 2008: 12, Lenoble 1994: 7–32). The truth is that the idea that a bureaucratic force can ensure fulfilment of the general interest continues to rest on a "substantive" presupposition. During the second half of the twentieth century, applied democratic theory saw a decline in this perspective. Alongside

that trend, new methods for "achieving the social generality" were developed that corresponded to new forms of democratic legitimacy;[3] yet, in our view, the analytic blockage we have identified persisted.

One new method for achieving the social generality is that of the legitimacy of impartiality (Rosanvallon 2008: 18), whose clearest manifestation is in the development of surveillance and regulatory authorities. These authorities' legitimacy derives from their ability to demonstrate their impartiality. In an irreducibly fragmented world, the project of a positive identification of the general interest no longer makes sense. Power must take its distance from individual interests and transcend them, by appropriating to itself the locus not of a higher interest but of an "empty place" (Rosanvallon 2008: 157). With this expression, P. Rosanvallon (2008: 157) (who borrows it from C. Lefort) conveys not so much the idea that power cannot be "hijacked by just anyone". Rather, the expression conveys the idea that the social subject in which the indivisible property of power resides "remains ever virtual; it is never substantially single: it is always traversed by the divergent nature of interests and opinions" (Rosanvallon 2008: 158), whence the need for a constant reminder of this incompleteness and for organizing the production of a social generality in a "negative-procedural" form.

A second new method of achieving democratic legitimacy consists of the reflexive "shaping" of the expression and construction of the popular will. This P. Rosanvallon terms "reflexive legitimization". Whereas legitimization through impartiality aimed to embrace the impossibility of a completed substantive determination of the "content" of the general interest, here incompleteness relates to the conditions for the expression of the general will. It's a question of becoming free of the old myths about the possibility for an immediate expression of the popular will. The "social generality" can only be the outcome of a reflexive process.[4] The idea is that the social will must somehow be organized to "enter into dialogue" with itself, with the requirements it rests on. Its meaning cannot be considered to have been "exhausted" by any one of its representations. The most definitive expression of this form of legitimization is observable, as P. Rosanvallon shows, in the recent opening up of the accepted role of supreme courts. Contrary to what is usually maintained, the opening up of the area of control of supreme courts (or constitutional courts) is not so much the logical unfolding of the consequences of the regime of the rule of law for the public authorities subject to it. Instead, the specific meaning of a development of this kind is above all that, through these

---

3 P. Rosanvallon identifies three such forms of legitimacy: impartiality, reflexivity, and proximity. We will initially focus on the first two, which are associated with the institutional blockage. The third will be addressed when we come to deal with the second blockage (the actantial blockage, that is, the blockage concerning the actors' capacity to act) in current political thought.

4 As used in this instance by P. Rosanvallon, the term "reflexive" must be understood in a comparatively non-technical sense—in the ordinary sense of involving "dialogue with the self". As will be seen, in this book we assign a more technical meaning to "reflexiveness".

constitutional courts, a "reflecting third party" (Rosanvallon 2008: 213) is set up, by means of which the social will is organized for ongoing assessment of the norms adopted, and the actions taken, in its name, in the light of the "principles" that define it. By means of this control, a twofold reflexive task is accomplished: not only does the body social evaluate its concrete choices on the basis of the principles that define its axiological horizons; but through this very control, it also continuously redefines the meaning of these axiological requirements. R. Dworkin, whose thought we will examine more closely in Part II, has given clear expression to this role of the supreme court as a privileged agent of a social hermeneutic.

As evident, then, from this brief overview of the evolution of democratic theory, the very concept of representation has significantly broadened in meaning and in so doing has led to an increasing complexity in those conditions that must be respected in the organization of the public sphere in order to ensure that the current understanding of representation is adequately fulfilled. Nevertheless, with every increment in the inclusiveness of the concept of representation, the idea persists in the background that, beyond these limitations imposed on the legitimacy of normative actions, the actions of the group upon itself can be reduced to the norms adopted by the established authorities. The group need only place itself in the hands of the established authorities in order to "advance" the cause of the social, that is, in order to translate into normative actions the objectives for social change that lie behind the collective action.

Our discussion of the first blockage in terms of the "representative" approach to democracy is intended, then, to reflect the existence in current political philosophy of this underlying belief. The belief in question is manifested in the self-sufficient nature of the reference to the established authorities, which in turn flows, as we have just shown, from the self-referential nature of this conception of how social authority is guaranteed. The reference to authority is an expression of the unending dialogue with itself of the social group, as it undertakes analysis of its own divergences and resistances. *The conditions for fulfilment of the democratic requirement are thus thought to be subject to formalization and integration into an institutional arrangement of the "reflexive" or self-referential representation of the sovereign will of the group members.* It is a belief of this nature that accounts for how rearrangements in our democratic regimes have usually been conceived of in terms of the extending of rights to be granted to individual citizens or groups of citizens (groups marginalized by virtue of their culture, their gender, their sexual orientation, and so on), or else in terms of the creation of new public authorities. These rights expansions and institutional innovations are thought to be able to "resolve" the democratic incompleteness they seek to engage with.

In our view, it is an assumption of this nature that constitutes one of the two blockages in existing conceptions of democracy and that undoubtedly accounts for the recurring search for new forms of "counter-power" observable in democratic regimes today.

To substantiate this diagnosis and present its foundations, we dedicate Part I to a critical analysis of the concept of law. Rightly understood, the representative approach to democracy—in the sense we have just given it—rests in the last analysis on a specific conception of the meaning of "law". This conception assumes that, as the positivist theorists believe, law is determinable based on the social practices of the public authorities alone.[5] Thus, without taking cognizance of the fact, political philosophy endorses the definition of the concept of law that is advanced today by positivist theory. We will show that defining the concept of law in this positivist manner, by exclusive reference to the practices (often defined in terms of the "rule of recognition") of the public authorities, is problematic and theoretically incomplete. It does not allow for an account of all the conditions for possibility required to provide the foundations of the operation by which members of a social group determine obligatory rules. The hypothesis we will present has three components. In one of these components, we are in agreement with current thinking and in the other two we diverge from it.

(1) *The point of agreement.* First, like all the leading current authors in the field, we share the perspective well expressed by H. Kelsen: the conditions for the definition of law are internal to social practices and thus cannot be defined by an assumed substantive definition of a reality "external" to a given social convention, such as (to take one example) the ideal of justice. The perspective we adopt is thus purely conventionalist and internalist. The conditions for possibility of the normative operation are internal to the social practices by virtue of which the operation is carried out. As will be seen, those authors who are most representative of current research in philosophy of law, be they positivist (for example, H. Hart and J. Coleman) or critical of positivism (for example, R. Dworkin) subscribe to this epistemological requirement. Nevertheless, the implications of this internalism remain to be clarified. And it is here that our twofold divergence from the current state of research arises.

(2) *The first point of divergence.* The first aspect of this divergence relates precisely to the issue of taking account solely of recognition by the public authorities in determining what constitutes law within a given social group. We will show how other authors conceive of this practice of recognition and, in that light, how little relevance there is to the hermeneutically based critiques of it, foremost among them R. Dworkin's. We will also show, however, that the mere fact of recognition by the public authorities is not sufficient to account for the obligatory dimension characteristic of normative practices. On this score, it could be said that our argument is in accord with a critique made by H. Kelsen. As he discerned, the mere fact of recognition by a public authority—even when correlated with the legal system's effectiveness as a whole—cannot "on its own logically account for the normative operation". Such a way of understanding the "conditionality" of the normative operation—that is, the ability to produce the norm's normativity, its validity or obligatory nature, its nature as a necessary condition for something

5 See Part I for a more explicit and rigorous articulation of this positivist thesis. In reality, this thesis does not exclude reference to citizens' behaviour. But this reference is conceived solely in terms of a general habit of obedience.

else—is incomplete. Reference to the practices of the public authorities requires turning to something external to them, in a sense a second-order recognition. As H. Kelsen demonstrated with rigorous logic, a "condition cannot be identical to what depends on it".[6] True, being a good Kantian, H. Kelsen then conceives of this "exteriority" along the lines of an "assumed norm", which he calls a "basic norm". But this solution is easily seen to be problematic: whence comes it that the assumed norm circumvents the stipulation H. Kelsen has himself just articulated, namely that a "condition cannot be identical to what depends on it"? By assuming that the "hypothesis of a transcendental logic" is always-already given within a social group, he "mentalizes" this second-order conditionality.

Positivist authors subsequent to H. Kelsen grasped the difficulty associated with this mentalization of the internalist requirement. To speak in terms of an "assumed" norm (and thus one that is always already inscribed in the "heads" of the social group's members) is to err in regard to the internalist project of conceiving the conditions for carrying out a normative operation in terms of a social operation, a social practice that must be organized. Thus, those authors sought to correct H. Kelsen's position and reinterpret the hypothesis of a fundamental norm in terms of a practice of recognition. Moreover, they progressively increased the complexity of their account of this practice of recognition of criteria for legality by the public authorities. On this score, as will be seen, the contribution made by pragmatist philosophy has proven crucial: the practice of recognition must be analysed as a cooperative practice.

Our own hypothesis (which is internalist and genetic) will allow, as will be seen, for fulfilling both the requirements[7] that the positivist position would thus appear unable to accommodate simultaneously. Besides reference to a cooperative practice of recognition of criteria for legality by the public authorities, the existence of law also requires, as we will show, a condition of "practical acceptance" by the norm's citizen-addressees. *A norm's normativity does not depend only on its compliance with a norm of recognition that results from a cooperative practice by the public authorities charged with its application. It also depends on its being recognized and practically accepted by the citizens who constitute its "private" addressees.*

(3) *The second point of divergence.* The second point of our twofold divergence from current thinking flows directly from the first. The first point of divergence makes it possible to see how the concept of law includes in itself a "normative" requirement that the positivist approach contributes to obscuring. True, as was said above, this normative dimension is not to be understood along the old lines of the "substantive" approach to a given ideal of justice. The debates of the past about

6 "Eine Bedingung kann mit dem von ihr Bedingten nicht identisch sein" (Kelsen 1960: 219).

7 Let us recall the two requirements. The first is that reference to the practices of the public authorities necessitates turning to something external to them, that is, it entails a second-order recognition. The second is that of avoiding the "mentalist" trap implicit in the hypothesis of a fundamental norm.

natural law have, in that sense, been definitively laid to rest. But what is revealed by a reconstruction of the conditions for possibility of the collective action by which the members of a social group aim to regulate themselves and adopt obligatory rules is that such an operation carries within itself the requirement for "attention to the necessary practical acceptance" of the norm in process of adoption, by those who are to be its citizen-addressees. The norm's "end purpose"—its "regulatory" aim, its internal teleology—thus necessitates that there be inscribed within the rule's development attention to the forms of cooperative action by which the norm's addressees will be able to cooperatively construct their normative expectations and thus to participate in the shared construction of this norm. Thus, the concept of law bears within it a requirement that makes it possible to measure, depending on the level of attention paid to the condition of practical acceptance, the capacity of a normative operation to fulfil its "internal teleology", or, put in more familiar terms, its capacity to satisfy to the extent possible the normative expectations of the actors concerned.

This second point of divergence has important consequences. We will mention two that are of direct concern at this point.

First, it makes it possible to grasp why inquiry on law must incorporate inquiry on political philosophy, that is, open itself up to the question of the conditions for organization of cooperative participation by the norm's addressees in the norm's construction.

It also makes it possible to grasp, however, how important it is for inquiry on political philosophy not to stop—however great the gains already made—with inquiry into the investigation into the conditions for "rational acceptability" of the norm, that is, with the various conditions that democratic theory has progressively illuminated in defining the conditions that action by public authorities must fulfil if those public authorities are to be deemed legitimately representative of the public will. And with this we arrive at the second blockage in current political thought.

The Second Blockage in Democratic Theory

The second blockage in current democratic theory relates to the other aspect of the production of the social generality, namely, recourse to citizen participation in order to guarantee the acceptability of norms. P. Rosanvallon defines this mode of production of generality as that of legitimacy through proximity. In this context, participation is now a means of government (Maesschalck 2008: 182–94). The dynamic at work is that of an effort to improve society's "reflexive" power by improving the task of interaction between power and society. From here on in, the question is not so much that of challenging the governing with a view to replacing them to the extent possible with the governed. On the contrary, the issue is based on the assumption of the need for a governed-governing duality and consists of how to enhance the quality of the interaction between governed and governing parties.

Judged by its engagement with "participation", recent political philosophy has not remained wholly the prisoner of the "representative" approach to democracy. True, as we have just seen, the process of going beyond the electoralist frame has been largely dominated by the belief that it was sufficient to create new institutions to ensure better respect for the requirements of the democratic project. But it was not limited to this belief. Since the 1990s, the will to organize more direct relations between citizens and the public authorities has been manifested: "[A] flowering of original initiatives—establishment of neighbourhood committees, experiments with citizen juries, consensus conferences, public forums, public inquiry procedures, participatory budgets, etc.—has given rise to an imperative in this vein in many countries" (Rosanvallon 2008: 319).

The democracy of interaction is not limited, however, to these new forms of participation and deliberation, whose actors are essentially from "the activist world of associations, whose movement traces out a kind of cooperative and contradictory double of power" (Rosanvallon 2008: 329). It also includes the development of more diffuse forms of democracy associated with the "multiple more informal or more individualized manifestations of involvement in the life of the city".[8] What is important to note, however, is that in these two forms (formal innovations to enable participation and diffuse citizen involvement), the emergence during the 1990s of this democracy of interaction cannot be viewed as the resurgence of traditional demands for the narrowing or the abridgement of the distinction between the governed and the governing.

Thus since the 1960s, the will has been manifested to raise anew and in a transformed version the old critique regularly levelled, somewhat quixotically, by advocates of direct democracy against the "representative" strand of democratic theory. But the more recent development of new participatory and deliberative forms of democracy are distinct in two ways from the "self-management" and "participatory" demands made, in the USA as well as in Europe, by the student and activist movements of the 1960s.

(1) First, the development of these new forms of "governance", unlike those older demands for "self-management" and "direct democracy", does not aim to "increase the influence of citizens at institutions' and parties' expense" (Rosanvallon 2008: 323). The participatory innovations developed since the 1990s aim essentially either to facilitate the handling of new, controversial sociotechnical

8 "The interest in public issues can also be measured in terms of newspaper readership, interest in political programming on radio and television, discussions with friends and colleagues, information searches on the internet, and contributions to associations. One of the rare studies on the subject, conducted by the Electoral Commission of the United Kingdom (Bentley 2005: 31), did suggest the importance of this form of involvement, estimating that close to 15 million political conversations are held daily in that country. The forms taken by what might be called *diffuse citizenship involvement* merit attention however" (Rosanvallon 2008: 327).

issues[9] or to "organize better developed information-gathering channels to facilitate decision making in a universe where the potential for blockages is multiplying" (Rosanvallon 2008: 324). "That is why the terms governance and functional democracy are probably those best suited to designating what is happening" (Rosanvallon 2008: 325).

(2) Then, the development of a "democracy of interaction" precisely reflects a dynamic at play at an entirely different level than the more traditional one of the effort to "narrow" the gap between the governed and the governing. What is at issue with the advent of a democracy of interaction consists precisely of no longer focusing on the question of the "mandate" under which the "representatives were simply the extension of those represented" (Rosanvallon 2008: 328), and instead on enhancing the quality of the interaction between the represented and the representatives.

In this light, it could be said that this reflects a sort of recognition of the first blockage we identified. The idea is emerging, both in the transformations that affect the reality of our societies and in political thought about democracy, of the need to strengthen the forms of citizens' participation in the exercise of power. Often, however, the purport of the term "participation" is left vague. Moreover, even when analysis is more precise, the requirement the term points to remains more of a black box than a theoretically constructed operation. This defect in theoretical construction not only accounts for what we have identified as a blockage; it also justifies the detour we will take in Part II via current social-scientific research into "theory of governance" in order to better grasp the requirement for participation and its limitations, so that the theoretical implications of the hypothesis we are presenting may be better understood.

In effect, on the view usually adopted in political philosophy, it would appear that everything happens as if the generalizability of the "social" were always-already given, that is, as if the mere summoning together of groupings or even individual citizens as individuals could instantly give a "form and substance" to society in its task of reflecting on itself. The reflexivity that would be thus expressed through the process of interaction presupposes as given the two parties to this task of interaction; that is, it presupposes that each of the terms placed in interaction with each other—society and power—is transformed by the sole fact of their having been brought together.

In other words, the question of the conditions for generating this "social whole" is not posed: it is assumed to have been resolved by the mere bringing together of either the "activist" actors involved in the associative process that is part of the new forms of participation or of the diffuse and informal expressions of citizen involvement. But whence comes it that we can assume this bringing together immediately enables the construction of this collective expression? Thus, things appear to unfold as if the mere summoning together of the actors, their

9 "The 'hybrid forums', or citizen conferences, set up to explore possible responses to issues surrounded with radical uncertainty (as in the case of GMOs, nuclear waste, and health problems with no precedent) have this role" (Rosanvallon 2008: 323–4).

multiplication or mere aggregation, sufficed to ensure the production of the most adequate possible representation of the social interests at the table and thus, by the sole effect of an encounter with power's propositions, to ensure, through a kind of spontaneous reflexive capacity, the ever-evolving construction of the collective representation of the common will. What is at work here is a kind of ontological presupposition according to which the conditions for the construction of the social are always-already given, that is, according to which the issue of the necessary construction of the capacity to construct the common will could be assumed to be always-already resolved. This presupposition must, on the contrary, not be presupposed but be examined by research. It is this presupposition that constitutes the second usual blockage in democratic theory, leaving beyond reach the conditions for the internal transformation of society and of power that is necessary to the interaction of society and power.

This "un-thought-through" element of democratic theory accounts for that theory's "indifference" to, and relative misapprehension of, the internal debates of which current social-scientific research on theory of governance consist. Rightly understood, the true impact of this current research is to open up a black box, that is, to construct a "theory of collective action" and better define the conditions necessary for the generalizability of the social—that is, the construction of an action that allows for "maximizing to the extent possible" the normative expectations of its members.

While, as P. Rosanvallon has written, it is true that, for all the considerable volume of the works published over the past 20 years on the question of governance, there remains "a feeling of a certain residual conceptual vagueness", the value of these works is not to be sought in their ability to delimit a field of inquiry or define a typology of regulatory practices.[10] The real issue of interest in these works goes

10 However, there is no doubt that the issue termed the issue of "governance" is broached in our day in diverse ways depending on the disciplinary tool being used (economic, legal, political scientific, etc.) and the analytic level of the question addressed. In fact, it is striking to observe that the studies in this area are difficult to incorporate into a homogeneous inquiry, the questions examined being so diverse and occurring at such distinct levels. How are we to integrate economic analyses of the reform of the management of common goods with analyses by political scientists or jurists of "multilevel governance" or with analyses of new modes of governance inspired by the theories of deliberative democracy? Thus under a single rubric—that of research in common on the question of governance—may be observed an aggregation of studies that are highly divergent as to both the kinds of questions examined and the methodological approaches used. Besides this, however, even when these studies deal with similar questions, dialogue appears to be impossible because the disciplinary approaches have often been designed in ignorance of research on governance based on other approaches. That is, no interdisciplinary dialogue is being organized with regard to the theoretical models deployed by various disciplinary approaches to the theory of governance. A salient example of this compartmentalization is that of the neo-institutionalist economic approach, which, while it deploys a specific theory of learning, remains under-informed about recent inquiry into theory of learning conducted in the field of political science and above all in research on organizational theory.

beyond the variety of questions of collective organization they broach (reform to the public service, reform in the design of public policy, reform of enterprise governance, reform of market organization, reform of international regimes). The deepest issue in this interdisciplinary social-scientific research on theory of governance becomes clear only if it is interpreted from an "epistemological" perspective on theory of action. True, numerous participants in this research do not themselves define the object of their study in terms of a theory of action. Nevertheless, as we will show in detail, the true implications of this whole area of research as developed in the past 30 years or so are that it brings back to the drawing board the question of a theory of collective action, that is, the question of the conditions for possibility that must be in place for a collective action to "maximize to the extent possible the satisfaction" of its members' normative expectations.

Moreover, in taking cognizance of an inadequacy, as regards this objective, in both the traditional forms of hierarchical regulation by the welfare state and the decentralized forms of coordination by the market alone advanced by neoclassical economists, this research on theory of governance takes as its point of departure a position contrary to that of the presupposition at work in current political thought. As has already been said, the idea that the question of the construction of the social cannot be assumed to be a given underlies this research. Thus, the task is to open the black box of the conditions that must be set up in order to construct the common will. To assume, as is usually done in political thought, that merely summoning together associations and individual citizens ensures the construction of the collective subject whose "reflexive" encounter with power will guarantee the self-adjustment of our normative expectations is to err as regards of the conditions for possibility required for the "success" of this operation of construction.

That is why it appears to us necessary today to incorporate into any inquiry on political philosophy a detour via this current social-scientific research on the question of governance. The question of theory of action cannot be ignored or left un-thought-through in this context. To engage, then, with this second analytic blockage in political thought, we seek to provide an overview reconstruction of current discussions of governance in the social sciences. And in so doing, although we share the view that democracy requires reflexive governance of collective action, we here propose, in order to avoid the "conceptual vagueness" that continues to surround "reflexivity", speaking of a "genetic approach" to governance. The shift suggested by this expression is directly linked, as will be seen in detail in Part II, to the lessons yielded by the process we have used to reinterpret current debate in theory of governance. This process consists of examining the "background theory" of the various positions taken and comparing the different theoretical approaches to collective action deployed, often only implicitly, by research in different disciplines.[11] This reconstruction of the theoretical presuppositions about the theory of collective action contributes to three theoretical findings.

---

11 Recall how we understand a theory of collective action: it is a theory of the conditions that the organization (that is, the provisions for governance or regulation) of a

(1) The first finding is that this reconstruction brings to light a shared presupposition of the various trends in current social-scientific research on governance, despite their apparent differences. As will be seen below, it is at the level of this presupposition that we situate the "reflexive" dimension that must characterize any organizing of a collective action to guarantee the best possible satisfaction of its members' expectations.

(2) The second finding is that this shared advance in current social-scientific research, because it often remains obscure and under-illuminated by the various current trends in theory of governance, is not the object of sufficient "attention" in this research. Now if a proper reconstruction of current debate on theory of governance brings to light a shared awareness of the need for the "reflexive" organization of governance, it also brings to light a different approach to this "reflexivity". That is, any advance in theory of governance entails the elucidation of the question of this reflexive dimension on which the "success" of a collective action depends.

(3) A third finding is that, in reconstructing the various current approaches to theory of governance from the perspective of how they conceive reflexivity, one observes that the differences among these approaches are less reflective of deep divergences or antagonisms than of the growing recognition of the need to progressively expand the conditions that must be set up to ensure the success of this reflexive operation. It could be said that the main theoretical currents that make up the core of recent research in theory of governance[12] are in fact complementary with each other and reflect the increasingly acute recognition of the precise nature of the conditions necessary for the success of this operation. Our own research, which brings attention to bear on this dimension that has too often been left in the shadows by current debate on governance, even suggests a way of deepening the most recent findings as to the success of this reflexive operation.

The reconstructive method we adopted to engage with current debate in theory of governance has thus resulted in two decisive advances in how reflexive governance can be conceived. The first consists of bringing to light the point of integration that unites the four approaches to reflexive governance. This is the commitment, found in all four approaches, to expanding the conditions for success of learning operations in such a way as to guarantee those operations' effectiveness as a normative process from the perspective of the expectations of the actors concerned. The second advance consists of the identification of a specific issue which, on one hand, is obscured by attending to the requirements for expansion of the conditions for success in learning, but which, on the other hand, only emerges on the express condition that this point of integration on which attention is focused is brought to light. This issue consists of the persistent indeterminacy surrounding

---

collective action must fulfil in order to ensure the best possible satisfaction of its members' normative expectations.

12 In Part II, we identify four such currents: neo-institutionalist, relational-collaborative, pragmatist, and genetic.

the role that reflexivity is to play within the collective action itself. On this score, one minimalist option consists of viewing reflexivity as a property by which we can identify mechanisms designed to favour and incite the use of collective learning capabilities that are viewed as already given. The maximalist option consists of "dementalizing" the approach to the operation of reflexivity in order to isolate its genetic features and discerning therein a specific type of operation on collective capabilities. This operation would make it possible to articulate, in the process of action, the potential for a return along the trajectories of action already described, along with the needed projection of new positionings. The result of our reconstruction consists of showing that all the approaches that differentiate themselves from the minimalist option have no choice but to progress towards the maximalist option if they are to envisage their conditions for fulfilment in a fully coherent manner.

The meaning we give the term "reflexive governance", and the meaning we give the genetic perspective for which we wish to provide the foundations in order to allow this epistemological option for reflexivity in collective action its full scope, are to be understood in the light of this reconstruction. The expression "reflexive governance" does not in itself designate a unique and specific form of governance. Often the expression is used in an ambiguous manner. This ambiguity consists of defining reflexive governance (rightly) through reference to the idea of learning but of allowing it to be believed that, so defined, it consists of a specific and determinate form of governance that allows for precisely determining the forms of institutional organization that a collective action must take in order to best satisfy "public interest".

Such a definition, while not inaccurate, risks giving rise to more indeterminacy than precision. It hinders seeing what differentiates the four main current approaches to governance—in Part II, we will term them "neo-institutionalist, relational-collaborative (or deliberative), pragmatist, and genetic"—from each other, once recognition is given to their common commitment to avoiding the fallacious assumption of a process of natural selection that guarantees ongoing adaptation of our collective actions towards a "social optimum". And what differentiates them from each other is precisely their conceptions of the learning operation (and thus of the reflexive operation implied by any learning operation). A comparison of the main approaches to governance as regards their conception of the learning operation reveals, as we will show in Part II, a gradation. What emerges is that these four approaches reflect an ever more "expansive" conception of the conditions that must be set up to ensure the success of learning operations. When they are examined through the prism of the learning operation, it appears that these four approaches reflect four stages of a single inquiry, with each successive stage working to broaden and expand the conditions needed so that the mechanism of governance can allow the actors to produce the best possible solution to the problem of collective action they are working to solve.

This is why we can speak of a furthering and progressive "expansion" in the conception of the conditions for success of the learning operation that the governance mechanism must take into account if optimal satisfaction for the actors involved in the learning operation is to be guaranteed. When taken separately, the three first main approaches to reflexive governance betray a pragmatic inadequacy. It is in order to take account of this pragmatic inadequacy that, with our genetic approach, we propose to expand the conditions for success of the learning operation. What is at stake in this expansion is the aim to go beyond the taking account only of actors' "ability-to-do", as with approaches centred on actors' enablement, and to subordinate this enablement to the self-transformation of the resistances that lead the actors to repeat past blockages. In this way, the genetic approach puts forward an epistemological shift from one type of attention, a rational attention focused on actors' "ability-to-do", to another type of attention, which could be called "geneticizing", focused on actors' "collective identity making". The idea is that such a capacity for "collective identity making" depends on a specific operation: it requires the identification and transformation of resistances to take place through the construction of a relation with exteriority by means of a type of "terceisation" (Maesschalck 2009: 19–36).

Only this operation makes it possible to prevent the change in representation associated with learning during a process of reflexive governance from remaining the prisoner of a kind of "unconscious repetition". Such an "unconscious repetition", through the "defensive strategies" that are its traces, restricts the field of the shifts required for solving the problems the actors face. Lacking an engagement with the need for this "self-enabling" operation, the three first main approaches to reflexive governance are unable to surmount the twofold analytic blockage in current conceptions of democracy. Neither through external reference to new government processes that are more "impartial" and more "reflexive", more "responsive", nor through internal reference to greater proximity to the actors concerned through increased participation and even social experimentation in the search for solutions, does this dual movement of "enablement" succeed in guaranteeing, on its own, the real self-transformation in the identities of action in the democratic space or in the conditions of access to new role production that are integral parts of the process of the social generalizability of the collective interest.

PART I[1]

Beyond Hermeneutic and Pragmatist Approaches: Toward a Genetic Approach to the Concept of Law

Introduction

Philosophical inquiry, J. Coleman[2] recently observed, is an exercise that develops austerely and modestly, like a variation on a familiar theme rather than like the chimerical construction, often too prized today, of a new system for its own sake. But this does not prevent advances and shifts. To pursue the musical metaphor, the quality of the variations becomes evident when, on the basis of a familiar theme, they open up to stimulating and even sometimes destabilizing interpretations[3] and thereby reveal an unknown face of the seemingly over-familiar.

Of course, this observation also applies to philosophical inquiry into law. In fact, it may even take on broader significance here. A brief look at the history of philosophy of law during the last century seems indeed to attest that those "variations" that are generally considered to have been truly "inspired" are the work of authors who have been especially aware of the necessity to learn, not only

---

1 Part I is an extensively modified and augmented version of two earlier texts. The first was presented at the colloquium of the Italian Association for the Philosophy of Law held in September 2004 at the University of Catania and was subsequently published under the title "Teoria della norma e teoria della governance nella filosofia del diritto: al di la dell'attuale dibattito tra ermeneutica e pragmatismo" (Lenoble 2006). The second appeared as "Beyond the Judge: From Hermeneutic and Pragmatist Approaches to a Genetic Approach to the Concept of Law" (Lenoble 2007).

2 "Real philosophers not only learn the history of their discipline; they internalise it. They are not embarrassed by the fact that there is an important sense in which nothing is new in philosophy. They are not embarrassed working and reworking familiar themes What distinguishes good philosophers from others is not that they invent new paradigms" (Coleman 2001b: ix–x).

3 "Great blues players first make it clear to us that they are playing a blues … then they go off, play around and through the familiar, connect dots in unusual, sometimes awe-inspiring ways, then bring us back to the familiar again, thus deepening our understanding and showing us the extraordinary possibilities inherent in what we already know" (Coleman 2001b: x).

from the history of their own discipline, but also from a discussion conducted in the background: the meta-theoretical discussion of epistemological inquiry.[4]

There are many indications that a favourable moment is approaching for the emergence of such a new variation. It would be linked mainly to the debate prompted by the revisiting of traditional issues in legal theory in the light of the recent pragmatist[5] revival in epistemology.[6]

One of its most representative and fully developed expressions is J. Coleman's project of "pragmatic conceptualism"[7] and his proposal for what might be called a pragmatist turn in the philosophy of law. We will therefore take it as the starting point for our own reflections. Of course, this proposal for a pragmatist turn is

---

4 To mention just two of the last century's most influential advances in legal positivism, recall the significance of the links forged by H. Kelsen with logical positivism and with the late nineteenth century neo-Kantian revival, and those forged 30 years later by Hart with the philosophy of ordinary language.

5 The term "pragmatist" is often the object of less than rigorous usage in the legal literature, especially that of the USA. It is often used to refer to the "sceptical" or instrumental analysis of law, as in R. Dworkin and several contemporary writers who make allusions in passing and in an exegetically problematic way to R. Rorty's pragmatism. This is not how "pragmatist" is used in the present text. J. Coleman (2001: 6, note 6), one of the main initiators of the project of a pragmatist approach to legal theory, says, "[L]egal academics typically draw, for their understanding of philosophical pragmatism, upon the work of Richard Rorty, John Dewey, and William James (and the latter two are themselves often seen through Rorty's interpretation of them). These are not my roots or my sources. The sources I draw from include, most prominently, Wilfrid Sellars (especially his view of semantic content as inferential role), W.V.O. Quine, Donald Davidson, and Hilary Putnam". In the "holistic" (that is, internalist or pragmatist, to use an expression more directly related to H. Putnam) perspective opened up by these authors, the meaning of a concept is analysed "in terms of the inferential role it plays in the variety of practices in which it figures"; and at the same time, these "inferential roles our concepts play reveal the holistic web of relations in which they stand to one another, and it is this web that determines a concept's content" (Coleman 2001b: 7). For a fuller development of this point, see Chapter 2, 59–65.

6 Perhaps one of the earliest expressions of this movement was the debate initiated by B. Leiter and J. Coleman with H. Putnam and published in the inaugural issue of Legal Theory 1 (1995: 5–80); see also Chapter 2, 59–65 for an analysis of H. Putnam's position in this debate. Besides B. Leiter's and J. Coleman's work, that of such authors as S. Perry, S. Shapiro, and B. Zipursky can be placed within this movement, although explicit references to epistemological discussions or the pragmatist approach are not always found there, despite the existence of certain differences in their methodology and hypotheses. See below for references to some of this work.

7 This is the excellent expression proposed by B. Zipursky (2000), which seems to be explicitly endorsed by J. Coleman (2001: 10, note 12); recall however that this methodological approach is not shared by all the authors who, to different degrees, participate in the movement identified here. For instance, on the differences between this form of conceptualism as proposed by J. Coleman and B. Zipursky and that proposed by B. Leiter, see (Lenoble and Maesschalck 2003: 296–ff).

not without predecessors. The interpretivist or hermeneutic turn that governs numerous recent studies in philosophy of law itself reflects the will to respect a form of epistemological internalism which anticipates the project for a pragmatist approach to legal theory. Similarly, beyond the sphere of philosophy of law, the anti-foundationalist trend which has characterized a significant part of American legal scholarship since the 1960s anticipates the pragmatist turn, although in a still more implicit and less developed way. Certain features specific to the pragmatist turn, however, augur the fruitfulness of this approach.

First, the project for a pragmatist turn (and more broadly the movement of which it is a privileged expression) has introduced a salutary clarification to current debate in legal theory. Thanks to a patient rereading of current findings in positivist research on law (and of certain elements of the background to these findings that help in gauging their import),[8] it has been possible to reinterpret the theoretical significance of the theses in question and thus assess the issue at stake in several current debates. As we shall see, it allows in particular for an understanding of why the interpretivist or hermeneutic turn in philosophy of law, and more generally the central place assigned to the judge in current inquiry into law, do not yield the critical exposure of legal positivism that their supporters still too often continue to credit them with.

However, this first feature reflects a second, deeper one. Of course, simply listening attentively to the lessons of the past helps place the purported advances of much current inquiry into law in perspective. It does not suffice, however. The advance made by the pragmatist turn consists mainly of its reformulation of the lessons of the past (and the questions underlying them) in the light of a meta-theoretical, that is, epistemological, inquiry. As the term indicates, the pragmatist project, by deploying the theoretical clarity of recent epistemological discussion in analytic philosophy, leads to the restoration[9] of an essential link between legal theory and a theory of judgement. Elucidating the concept of law comes down to understanding the practice by which a social group produces shared normative meaning. Such understanding necessarily presupposes a degree of understanding of the process by which meaning is produced in (social) reality. This is the issue at the heart of any theory of judgement: it aims to inquire into the conditions for possibility of the operation (that is, the action, the practice) by which judgement

8 Besides J. Coleman's, B. Leiter's, and S. Shapiro's works on H. Hart's theory, the importance of B. Leiter's work on legal realism, which has led to a reinterpretation of its epistemological significance (see Leiter 1995: 481–ff., 2001: 278–301), and of S. Perry's works on O. Holmes (see below, note 40) must not be overlooked.

9 "Restoration" because a careful rereading of the legal and political philosophical debates in German Idealism (especially those between I. Kant and J. Fichte) reveals, against the usual reductive interpretations, an analogous will to "link" the analysis of the conditions for possibility of governance by law with an analysis of the conditions for possibility of the operation of judgement.

produces meaning effects.[10] In reconstructing the conditions for the process of implementing (that is, the process of applying) a judgement, epistemological reflection provides a necessary and privileged means of revealing the conditions for possibility of the practice by which a social group produces and recognizes a normative authority, that is, a means of revealing the conditions for the possibility of governance by law. The pragmatist turn, advanced mainly by J. Coleman in philosophy of law, leads to the elaboration of the discussion surrounding these presuppositions and to its analysis in the light of critiques of mentalism (associated in particular with the work of W. Quine and H. Putnam) that embody the main trends in current epistemological thought.[11]

It is the explicit insistence on this epistemological requirement that accounts for the fruitfulness of the pragmatist turn proposed by Coleman. Certainly, as already indicated, for some time now many authors had been revisiting the traditional questions of inquiry into law in the light of the instruments developed by the philosophy of language, W. Quine's and L. Wittgenstein's[12] holistic approaches included. The internalist approach R. Dworkin has attempted to develop on the basis of his hermeneutic perspective is one revealing example.

But, as will be seen below with regard to R. Dworkin, the advance inherent in the pragmatist turn as proposed by J. Coleman is due to the effects associated with the explicit invocation of epistemological arguments. This explicit invocation not only makes it possible to reformulate the fundamental question of theory of law as the question of the conditions for emergence of a given social practice (be it interpretive or other) of adherence to a shared normative meaning. It also reveals the twofold conceptual weakness of current theories of law. First, the weakness of hermeneutic theories,[13] which, though they seek to expose the inconsistencies of positivist theories with regard to a holistic approach to meaning, are themselves incapable of making explicit the requirements of such an approach and respecting them. Second, the parallel weakness of current representations of legal positivism,[14] which, in spite of their accurate insight into the need for a conventionalist approach to law, remain incapable of adequately inferring all the conditions for emergence of such an approach.

---

10 Thus *epistemological reflection* refers here to a theory of judgement rather than having the more methodological, reductive meaning of "inquiry into the method to follow in order to produce scientific knowledge", which it is sometimes assigned in the philosophy of science.

11 On J. Coleman's presentation of these main trends, see below note 17.

12 For some representative references to this work, see below note 6.

13 And (to go beyond the strict boundaries of philosophy of law) the weaknesses of the anti-foundationalist approach of American legal scholarship.

14 Note that, in reframing the true implications of recent versions of legal positivism in epistemological terms, authors associated with the pragmatist turn are also clarifying the exact nature of the arguments that must be addressed by anyone who (rightly) wishes to expose the weaknesses of positivist legal theories, at least as they stand at present.

This is where the central issue in our own inquiry emerges. While highlighting the significant gains made by the process that the pragmatist turn has launched in theory of law, we nevertheless wish to extend it in the name of the epistemological requirement that this turn is working to enact. In relying on the especially highly developed version of the pragmatist turn that J. Coleman has provided us with, we shall seek to apply to it the movement that H. Putnam (1988: xii), in the figurative terms he uses to explain his analysis of the limitations of cognitivist theories, has described as "the trick attributed to adepts in jiu-jitsu of turning an opponent's strength against himself". In other words, we wish to show how J. Coleman's explicitly epistemological project contains within itself requirements that make it necessary to deepen and indeed modify his proposed pragmatist reformulation of current theses in legal positivism. These modifications relate to the way that the conditions for possibility of the conventional social practice by which a group produces and recognizes normative authority must be understood. We will show how a non-mentalist approach to the operation of judgement entails extending the requirement of what H. Hart has called "the internal point of view" specific to this practice of recognition beyond the officials responsible for applying the rules (that is, mainly the judges). Our hypothesis is that an exact understanding of these requirements of the epistemological holism called for by the pragmatist turn entails revisiting a presupposition shared by the positivist and hermeneutical approaches, namely the conception of the operation of the production of normative authority mainly through the operation of judges' production of law.

We will specify below the exact content of these modifications and its twofold consequences: first, an epistemological consequence that reveals the normative meaning of the concept of technical law; and second, a consequence related to the need for the theory of law to reconnect with political philosophy and open up to the current debate in the social sciences about the question of governance.[15] The

15 This discussion is linked to the search for mechanisms for regulating collective action better suited to "maximizing", to the extent possible, the satisfaction of the normative expectations of participants in the action (For an overview of this debate and a philosophical analysis of it, see (Lenoble and Maesschalck 2003) and below, Part II. The renewal of this research approach during the 1960s, which took place essentially in the USA, is reflected in particular in the use of the notion of "governance" to refer to what was traditionally called (in economics and political science) "regulation" or (in law or in political philosophy) "government". As R. Mayntz (2002: 15–27, 21) has said, "governance is the type of regulation typical of the cooperative state, where state and non-state actors participate in mixed public/private policy networks". This new orientation in the approach to questions of "regulation" has so far relied on recognition of the weaknesses of both traditional forms of hierarchical control (command-and-control regulation) and that kind of self-regulation that is based exclusively on recourse to market mechanisms (coordination of collective action exclusively by aggregating for individual preferences in a competitive manner). It was mainly developed in economic science, albeit in a close relationship with research in social psychology on bounded rationality. However, it was not without an impact in the field of inquiry into law. In effect, inquiry into the necessary transformation of the mechanisms of

latter consequence is also implicitly introduced by the pragmatist turn, although inadequately. This is the case not so much because J. Coleman and B. Zipursky have used as their point of departure for their reflection a confrontation with the "law and economics" approach; nor is it because S. Shapiro and J. Coleman borrow explicitly from theories of action whose significance in current reflection in social science is well known. Rather, it is the case because from the very heart of the pragmatist reformulation of H. Hart's rule of recognition there emerges the notion that an adequate understanding of the conditions for possibility of the form of cooperative activity by which law is produced results in an inclusion of the need for specific institutional mechanisms. The opening up of the concept of law to the neo-institutionalist reflection at the heart of current debate in the social sciences is,

---

governance found in our social democracies began developing in the 1950s in the USA in relationship with the weaknesses of the institutional mechanisms set up by the New Deal for ensuring effective fulfilment of fundamental rights. To correct these weaknesses, it was initially proposed that recourse be had to judges in order to ensure better effective respect for fundamental rights. Under this approach, the judge takes on the role of therapist to the regulatory process and creates the conditions necessary for the effective fulfilment of the respect due to those rights. In order to dispose of the necessary means for this new style of judicial activism (inaugurated by the celebrated Supreme Court judgement in *Brown v. Board of Education* in 1954), judges equipped themselves with methods of intervention that resulted in a significant transformation of both the judging function (creating "public law litigation"; on this, see (Chayes 1976: 1281–316, Fiss 1979: 1–30, Marcus 1988: 647–57) and the administrative function. The idea is that the rationality of public policies developed by the administration must depend on the possibility given to all concerned interest groups to enlighten the authorities and take part in the development of regulatory compromises. This would lead the judge to subordinate the legality of administrative intervention to respect for all the procedural conditions that guarantee such participation (Stewart 1975). This initial response to the perceived need to improve and transform our mechanisms for coordinating collective action has thus been of concern to jurists, because it put the exercise of the judging function in question. This accounts for the fact that in American theory of law, it came to be reflected in an intense critical inquiry into legal process theory and the synthesis that the latter sought to put forward to resolve the weaknesses of both Ch. Langdell's formalism and the realism of the 1930s in dealing with the operation of the judge (H.M. Hart and Sacks 1994) and some forms of a recent effort at critical synthesis (Rubin 1996). Parallel to this, there also developed numerous trends in a sociological and, indeed, economic and political-scientific perspective seeking to interpret the transformations of law produced not just by this initial response to the crisis in our social democracies but also by subsequent responses prompted in social science research by critiques of the initial reform. In the latter case, legal inquiry reflected a closer tie with the discussions then current in the social sciences on the theory of governance. Many legal studies sought to import into legal thinking theoretical models developed by the social sciences. These included the thinking of neo-institutionalist economists in the tradition of R. Coase, that of sociological theory on self-regulation, that of the communicative theory of J. Habermas, and "experimentalist" approaches in deliberative democracy as currently expounded by J. Cohen, M. Dorf, and C. Sabel. On this, see below Chapter 2, 59–85, and in particular notes 44 and 52.

however, only sketched out. It does not result in a revisiting of the usual postulate in current approaches in philosophy of law, consisting of "inoculating" analysis of the concept of law against other analyses pursued by theory of governance (or political philosophy).

Our hypothesis, in contrast, is that an inoculation of this kind must be critiqued for epistemological reasons. Under this same head, we will present our idea of the "normative dimension" that any complete approach to the concept of law must include. Let us here present a brief overview of our argument. It covers four points:

(1) As will be seen in detail below, an in-depth analysis of the social practice by which citizens express their respect for the decisions made by the authorities responsible for issuing and applying legal norms requires that the way the positivists describe this practice be specified and redefined. As we know, the positivists are satisfied to refer to this practice as a simple, objectively observable fact that manifests on its own the overall efficacy of a legal system.[16]

We will show that every general and customary habit of obedience is definitely the result of a shared judgement by which citizens make this obedience depend on the expectation that the public authorities will satisfy their (the citizens') normative expectations to the extent possible. This practice thus presupposes a form of shared intention, that is, the shared adoption and acceptance of *a form of life in common assumed to be able to respond to its members' expectations to the extent possible.*

(2) A redefinition along these lines does not just constitute a more fine-tuned description. If that were all, the advance made would be of little interest. On the contrary, such a redefinition brings with it significant theoretical and practical consequences. Before proceeding to sketch them out, however, we must first highlight an initial advance yielded by this redefinition. This is the fact that this redefinition results from the outset in reformulations of two positivist theses (as well, as will be seen below, as hermeneutic theses).

The first reformulation relates to the matter of the question. As has already been mentioned, the analysis of the concept of law is usually considered to aim at an understanding of the conditions for possibility of the social practice by which a group produces and recognizes normative authority. The redefinition we have given above helps show how this question can be reformulated in "teleological" terms. Recognition of normative authority includes a dimension of "end purpose", a "teleological" dimension. The ability of a legal system to act authoritatively, that is, to ensure its "regulatory" capability, flows from its ability to "meet the normative expectations of the social community". Put another way, recognition of a legal system's normative authority must be analysed as the result of an operation

16 As was explained in the Introduction, H. Kelsen argues that the efficiency of a legal system constitutes a sine qua non of its existence: "Eine Rechtsordnung wird als gültig angesehen, wenn ihre Normen im großen und ganzen wirksam sind, das heißt tatsächlich befolgt und angewendet werden" (Kelsen 1960: 219). Along with most positivist authors, H. Hart and J. Coleman endorse a similar position.

of "teleological" judgement. On such an operation of "teleological" judgement depends law's "potential for social governance", that is, its "social destination", its ability to meet the normative expectations of its addressees. Accordingly, the question of the conditions for possibility of a social practice of recognition of normative authority can be formulated as that of a *pragmatic* (operating) frame capable of *inferring* the ability of the normative system to meet its beneficiaries' normative expectations.

The second reformulation relates to the distinction made by theory of law between two categories of addressees concerned by the application of a norm. On one hand, there are the public authorities (often referred to as "officials") in charge of applying norms. On the other hand, there are the citizen-addressees responsible for adjusting their behaviour (and thus their normative expectations) to what is prescribed by the norms imposed by the authorities. As we will show in fuller detail below, the positivists often express this distinction in H. Hart's terms, those of a difference between an "internal" and "external" point of view. The internal point of view is that of the public authorities, who, when they apply the norm, respect it themselves, because they recognize its validity, that is, its obligatory nature as "a model and a reason for action". By the same token, the existence of a legal system within a social group does not (according to the positivists) require the "internal point of view", which is demanded of the authorities responsible for applying the law, to be manifested among citizens. It is sufficient for citizens' behaviour to reflect a customary and general practice of obedience to the law (that is, the adoption of a simple "external point of view").[17] A better analysis of the form of judgement that governs this general practice of obedience results, contrary to this view, in expanding the requirement for what H. Hart calls the "internal point of view" specific to the practice of recognition beyond the public authorities responsible for applying the rules.

(3) But how does this dual reformulation help in understanding the deeper consequence of such a redefinition of the type of behaviour required of citizens so that the internal teleology of any legal system can be fulfilled? The consequence in question is that this invalidates the positivist assumption that it is sufficient to refer to citizens' general practice of obedience to assume that the condition for citizens' acceptance, which is one of the two conditions that guarantees a legal system's ability to ensure its regulatory role, has been fulfilled. Why so? First, because this shows that the judgement that justifies this general practice of obedience is a judgement of the "maximization of normative expectations". But above all,

17 For H. Hart, external judgement has to do solely with an observer outside a legal system, as opposed to those who, from within it, recognize its validity. The observer outside a legal system is the one who "without himself accepting its rule of recognition, states the fact that others accept it" (H. Hart 1994: 103). It will be observed that H. Hart uses this same distinction between external and internal judgement to differentiate the kind of attitude that the existence of any legal system requires of citizens on one hand from that required of the officials on the other.

because, if the analysis of this operation of judgement—which, in current theory of law, remains a black box—is not opened up, this general practice of obedience is postulated to reflect the rational outcome of the operation of judgement. And it is because of this postulate that it is assumed the public authorities have only to rely on the fact of the customary and general practice of obedience to their decisions to be assured that citizens accept their (the public authorities') normative authority and that citizens' normative expectations will adjust to any new decisions the authorities decide to impose. Once a social system appears to have been stabilized through a general practice of obedience,[18] the judgement that officials would have to exercise regarding citizens' acceptance of their authority can be analysed as a "postulate".[19] It would suffice to assert by a simple formal rule of judgement that what is observable does indeed correspond to a general form of behaviour necessary to live within a given legal system. Thus, this postulate is assumed to be rationally acceptable solely based on an observable fact and is considered to be able to be determined, as regards the authorities, by a simple formal rule of judgement (in this instance, the axiomatic generalization of the observable behaviour deemed to be adequate). But such an assumption is invalid in two ways.

First, if on the contrary one observes that this practice—and therefore this acceptance by citizens—is an activity of judgement exercised through an intention, an end purpose (the effort to fulfil normative expectations), the preceding line of argument is tenable only if such an intention, such an end purpose, is also "formally able to be determined". It is necessary, in effect, to assume that the meaning of this "intention", that is, the condition for its fulfilment, must be formalizable, that is, able to be determined independent of its context of use. As will be seen, this is an assumption in which the pragmatist turn has already enabled us to detect epistemological inconsistency, because it entails mentalism. An intention cannot be identified with a rule stored in the mind. That is why, indeed, we argue that the pragmatist turn that philosophy of law has recently taken will only achieve its full impact if we revisit a distinction that the pragmatist approach to the concept of law unluckily wishes to maintain, namely a purely externalist approach to the condition for citizens' acceptance of the authority of the law.

Second, this conclusion is confirmed by a "logical" analysis of the judgement that governs a citizen's acceptance of a normative authority. That is, opening up the black box of the operation of judgement that justifies a general practice

18 Note that analysing the practice of citizens in terms of a simple general practice of obedience results in the situation that in any social system (setting aside the rare scenario of "revolutionary" social situations and transitory anarchy), this condition can be assumed to be always-already fulfilled.

19 Thus we can understand why, from this perspective, law in effect depends essentially on the sole deliberative activities of the authorities called upon to negotiate the rule of recognition. Of course, as will be seen below, the way of conceiving this type of activity varies according to author. But both the positivist and the hermeneutic approach (an example of the latter being R. Dworkin's) result in this type of reductionism.

of obedience results in a coming to awareness about the pragmatic inference harboured in this judgement: such a judgement always-already assumes its own verification in order to be accepted. Thus the very thing by which I seek to define the satisfaction of my normative expectations (acceptability) already refers to the possible fulfilment of my own judgement of satisfaction (acceptance). In other words, the relationship of conditionality that is being forged between the public authorities and their acceptance by citizens features the logical characteristics of the kind of function traditionally known as "recursive". This will be examined in detail below. We will show, in fact, that this relationship is even more complex, because the dimension of recursive reference (that is, as will be seen, a dynamic of crisscrossing anticipations and crisscrossing postulations) places citizens simultaneously in relation to each other and in relation to the authorities.

Without going deeper into the matter here, we will merely emphasize that, just like the conclusions drawn from the argument based on the impossibility of treating intentionality in a mentalist manner, what we have here is the impossibility of assuming that the analysis of the condition for citizens' acceptance of the normative authority of "officials" can be reduced to a simple formal rule.

The only way to get around this mentalist trap and the belief in an illusory "formalist" handling of the condition specific to citizens' acceptance of authorities' normative authority consists of conceiving of "verification" as a kind of learning relationship between the two groups (citizens on one hand and the authorities on the other). That is, conceiving of it as a kind of cooperative activity within which a trust relationship is built and at the end of which citizens' normative expectations are adjusted. This adjustment remains dependent on the conditions that citizens themselves plan to impose in order to go ahead with the proposed transformations. From this perspective, it could be argued that officials' postulation of acceptance of their decisions should be analysed not as a postulate but merely as a postulation, that is, as an act that requires the implementation of an operation of adjustment whose conditions can only be defined within a cooperative activity that must be set up between the norm's beneficiaries and officials. This learning process must first of all allow for the inference that the authorities responsible for applying norms will display behaviour capable of incorporating the requirements entailed by the normative expectations of the norm's addressees and the transformations associated with them. This ability will, in turn, generate an increase in the authorities' ability to elicit citizens' adherence to their decisions. Thus, the learning process is designed not just to increase the capacity for adherence inferred by officials' commitment; it would also refer this commitment to an external position that shifts it as regards its specific requirements for legitimacy (entailed by H. Hart's rule of recognition) and place it in relationship with the requirements for transformation entailed by the normative expectations that determine the social destination of officials' action.

Thus we are led to a new way of envisaging the conditions for existence of a legal system. Theory of law has traditionally identified two conditions, each of which has been thought of as the requirement for a specific and independent attitude on the part of two differentiated social groups (citizens on one hand and officials on the other). Our analysis, on the contrary, leads us to emphasize that the fulfilment of the end purpose internal to any legal system necessitates a form of collective organization that organizes the reciprocal influence of these two groups. Thus the two groups influence each other through their behaviour to a much greater degree than the degree to which they differentiate themselves from each other.

To discuss these two conditions, one can, if one wishes, pick up the "internal/external" distinction that H. Hart and the pragmatists deploy (as will be seen), but only if we assign it a different significance[20] from the one they give it. The "internal/external" distinction concerns the internal limitation of rational activity in general, that is, the impossibility for reason to transcend its own usage and assume the givenness of the rules for generating that usage, to which it could submit. Thus the formal conditions for possibility of rules of rational activity are always internal to that activity's conditions of usage. In other words, the formal conditions cannot recognize themselves as internal except by referring to the external order of the implementation of the rational activity that has been internalized as usage. This splitting of the internal and the external found in the internalist perspective on reason is especially clear in H. Putnam's expression "internalist realism". The internalism of rules of usage always assumes an internalized reference for an external order of implementation as the pragmatic condition of its usage. When it comes to the judgements made by social groups with respect to the normativity of legal norms, the consequences of such pragmatic internalism are significant to the extent that the judgement formed by each group—whether the authorities or citizen-addressees—assumes the internalized reference to the external order of implementation constituted by exo-groups (that is, the citizen-addressees for the officials, and, inversely, the officials for the citizen-addressees). It is this immanent relation of the internal to the external that, in our view, constitutes the genetic condition for a legal order of social normativity and that determines the necessary meaning of an exo-group learning process as part of the process of generating social normativity.

Thus the internal/external distinction no longer reflects only the formal idea of an incompleteness specific to each act of judgement, that is, the idea that reason could find within itself (the internal dimension) the conditions for its implementation. On the contrary, it expresses the idea that reason could not find within itself—as simply given—the conditions for its implementation. And indeed, that is what

20 This other significance was discerned, as pointed out in the Introduction, by H. Kelsen when he wrote that a condition for something cannot be identical to what is dependent on it. He thus pointed to the formal incompleteness of any handling of the question of the conditionality of law, that is, of any judgement about the fulfilment of the internal teleology of any legal system. No matter that H. Kelsen restored a form of mentalism with his belief that the dimension of externality that characterizes the incompleteness of any formal condition is to be found in the hypothesis of "basic norm" (*Grundnorm*). We will just note that this restoration of mentalism results from the fact that H. Kelsen continued to formulate his theory of incompleteness in logicist terms and thus persisted in believing it was possible to turn this incompleteness into a new rule.

pragmatism reveals in exposing the impossible mentalism of the approach of intentionality of action. It is, as will be seen, this necessary rejection of mentalism that accounts for the pragmatist reformulation of H. Hart's rule of recognition in terms of cooperative activity. However, it is necessary to go farther than this pragmatist reformulation of the conditions for existence of a legal system. In fact, if we want to avoid reformalizing the conditions for the operation of judgement that governs the general practice of obedience (that is, if we want to avoid treating this collective practice as a "pure coordination game", as game theorists say—see below), we must reconstruct, on a genetic basis, the internal/external distinction inherent in judgements of authority and obedience and organize the reciprocal "encroachment" of these practices at the level of the condition specific to the construction of the rule of Recognition. Because of the encroachment between the two conditionalities, neither can be satisfied except by organizing and integrating within itself the relationship of reciprocal conditionality that constitutes them. Concretely, this means that the judgement of the public authorities assumes its own confirmation on the basis of citizens' *external* belief in the social potential for implementation, and that this external judgement cannot develop its culture of law as a possible way of life except by itself relying on the mediation of a capability internal to the organization of the legal system. The necessary crisscrossing of these two forms of teleological judgement thus shows that it is impossible to isolate the group "officials" from the group "citizen-addressees". It is necessary instead to envisage a process of mutual adjustment by the two groups' judgements about the fulfilment of the law.

This conclusion accounts for and justifies the need to call into question what we called the first blockage in political thought, which was based on the idea that the mere production of law by procedures *internal* to the institutional system of public authorities could, provided its design was adequate, ensure the satisfaction of normative expectations.

In our view, these features—of teleology internal to the legal system, of inter-group relations, and of the learning process—give full potential to the impact of the pragmatist turn initiated by J. Coleman. By inciting us to better construct the epistemological requirements for the analysis of the social practice by which a social group produces normative authority, the pragmatist turn decisively opens up the road to its own furthering and to a renewed understanding of the conditions for possibility of governance by law. In so doing, it arrives at the justification for opening up the analysis of the concept of law to current debate in the social sciences, that is, to the normative matter of the desirability of restructuring our modes of production of norms.[21] And this last idea represents the final stage of our argument.

21 Both H. Hart's positivist theory (including the pragmatist reformulation of it by J. Coleman) and R. Dworkin's hermeneutic theory focus on the authorities responsible for applying the law, that is, essentially on judicial authorities. Clearly, our own reformulation of the question of the judgement of citizens' acceptance of officials' authority automatically entails extending the coverage of the term "officials" to all public authorities, including those

(4) This fourth stage, then, relates precisely to the matter of the organization of the social-learning relationship between the group of officials and the group of citizen-addressees. This learning relationship entails some form of negotiated, cooperative participation by the citizen-addressees in the production of norms. And that is precisely the issue that is at the heart of current inquiry in theory of governance. That is why our reformulation of the question of the conditions for fulfilment of the teleology internal to the concept of law opens logically onto a reconstruction of the discussions within the social sciences about the conditions that are necessary if a collective action is to "maximize to the extent possible" its participants' normative expectations. But first, a clarification.

It could be objected that such a reformulation leads to a highly problematic result. How do we qualify the normative systems of societies within which the "ideal" conditions assumed to allow for such maximization are not respected? Would we be precluded from calling these normative systems legal systems? Clearly we cannot allow such a result. Our own view is more nuanced. It consists simply of saying that, absent the establishment of the conditions needed to organize the "inter-group" learning relationship (that is, of a form of cooperative participation in establishing norms while respecting the conditions we will define in Part II), the legal system cannot guarantee the form of "regulatory stabilization" it aims to realize. This objective remains unfulfilled: the form of social stabilization sought by law remains random and dependent on conditions that have not been mastered.

And indeed, is that not just what is revealed by the real condition of our societies?

Doesn't the sought-for restructuring of our public policies result from the felt instability triggered by the perception (whether justified or not) of the inefficiency of the methods of development of many of our public policies? Such, after all, is the implication of what is highlighted (as was seen above) by present-day political thought in shedding light on the current search for new forms of counter-power. Things appear to unfold as if our societies were faced with the diffuse impression of the difficulty of finding adequate conditions for their regulatory capacity, that is, for the form of social stabilization that could provide them with a system of norms that, to the extent possible, match the satisfaction of their members' expectations.

We will proceed with our argument in two stages. First, we will demonstrate how, in the synthetic version provided by J. Coleman, the pragmatist turn appears to pinpoint the inadequacy of both interpretivist critiques of positivism and the presuppositions of the theory of collective action that distort the usual way of

---

responsible for issuing norms. In fact, the reformulation of the conditions for recognition specific to the general practice of obedience necessarily presupposes an expansion of this reformulation to include the recognition of all officials. This also shows, as was indicated in Chapter 6 of *Toward a Theory of Governance* (Lenoble and Maesschalck 2003), that the question of the application of the law must be investigated, not in the restricted form that jurists give it but in the more inclusive sense of the internal application to any normative operation, including that of the production of norms.

formulating the rule of recognition as found in H. Hart (Chapter 1). Second, we will demonstrate the way this pragmatist reformulation of the conventionalist definition of law demands that it be furthered in the direction of a genetic approach to the practice by which a social group produces normative authority.[22] We will also demonstrate the consequences of this furthering as regards the necessary opening up of the theory of law to the question of the desirability of transforming our modes of production of norms. Finally, in so doing, we will show the impact of this furthering on a renewed conception of teleological judgement in the framework for the collective production of normative authority (Chapter 2).

22 As shown below (Chapter 2) and (Coleman 2001b: 96), the point of calling our approach *genetic* is to emphasize the significance of the consequences associated with specific attention to the conditions for possibility of the conventional practice by which a social group produces norms, as well as attention to the epistemological rootedness of those conditions for possibility.

Chapter 1
From a Hermeneutic Critique to a Pragmatist Redefinition of the Rule of Recognition

The main criticism of positivist theses since they rose to prominence within theory of law has usually been based on their inadequate understanding of the operation of the application of normative judgement. Positivist approaches were seen as reflecting an inadequacy associated with an epistemologically defective construal of the operations of judgement necessarily presupposed by any theory of norms. True, often enough these critiques were not formulated with explicit reference to this philosophical background. But we consider their having been presented this way to have two benefits. First, this approach makes it possible to pinpoint the true philosophical impact of the critical insight that has fuelled the regular recurrence of the critique of positivist approaches since the end of the nineteenth century. Second, it offers the benefit of framing the question in terms that make it possible to measure the limitations of the critique while opening up an approach to reformulating the valid insight this critique seeks to express.

That is our hypothesis. While this critique has often correctly perceived the inadequacy of positivist interpretations about the operation of the application of normative judgement, it has remained riveted to a restrictive interpretation of this operation. This critique therefore missed its target and was open to a valid rebuttal by positivists. In contrast, *a shift in emphasis* in the way of construing the question of the application (or implementation) of a judgement and an *enlarged conception* of the epistemological levels at which this question is posed within the theory of norms would allow for a clearer view of the direction in which the positive approach to law needs to be extended. This working hypothesis strikes us as being all the more fruitful for being imbricated with the dynamics of the discussion internal to present-day legal positivism.

The most recent reformulations of the positivist analysis of the concept of law—more specifically, the pragmatist reformulation of H. Hart's rule of recognition—implicitly reflect growing recognition of the need for greater respect within theory of law for recent advances in theory of action. While this pragmatist reformulation has itself remained tied to an incomplete construal of the conditions for possibility of action, the advance it has facilitated in current philosophy of law must not be underestimated. Besides making it possible to deepen the internal dynamics of positivist research, it has initiated its own extension by shedding light on the usefulness of a broadened examination of the conditions for possibility of the social practice by which normativity is constituted. This is the project that defines our own hypothesis, as will be seen in Chapter 2. However, before analysing this "pragmatist" reformulation of H. Hart's rule of recognition and the extension it calls for, we must conduct a rapid review of those critiques of legal positivism that bear on its inadequate understanding of the operation of application internal to any normative judgement.

As indicated above, this critical current, which has lasted until the present time, conceives of the question of the operation of the application of a norm in somewhat restricted terms. That is, the critique often levelled at positivists is associated with the way the latter conceive of the operation of judgement. The operation of application internal to any normative judgement is conceived on the model of judicial operation.[1] This critique has taken two successive forms, the first of which we call the realist critique and the second the hermeneutic critique. While most readers will be familiar with them, it will be useful to summarize them briefly. This reminder will help to better understand the reasons for a "pragmatist" corrective to H. Hart's concept of law.

The Realist Critique

The realist critique essentially stemmed from work in the sociological and realist theory of law and sought to expose the lack of scientific precision in the positivist definition of law. As formulated by N. Bobbio, this definition is based on the following assessment of the facts: "It is true that law as presently in force consists of a set of rules of conduct which, whether directly or indirectly, are formulated and validated by the state" (Bobbio 1961: 61–2). The realist and sociological critics point out that this assessment is inaccurate as a *question of fact*, because it underestimates the 'creative' power of the judge in applying these rules. Critiques of this kind have been very legitimately rebutted. As L. Green (2003: 2) reminds us, they are:

> the product of confusion; lawyers often use "positivist" abusively, to condemn a formalistic doctrine according to which law is always clear and, however pointless or wrong, is to be rigorously applied by officials and obeyed by subjects. It is doubtful that anyone ever held this view; but it is in any case false, it has nothing to do with legal positivism, and it is expressly rejected by all leading positivists.[2]

1 On this, see Chapter 2, 70–77.

2 In the same vein, L. Green notes elsewhere that although the earliest positivists, that is, J. Bentham and J. Austin, had, in their approach to the nature of law, emphasized the idea that law is "the command of a sovereign backed by force, by the mid-twentieth century … this account had lost its influence among working legal philosophers; its emphasis on legislative institutions was replaced by a focus on law-applying institutions such as courts, and its insistence on the role of coercive force gave way to theories emphasising the systematic and normative character of law" (Green 2003: 1).

Besides this, however, these critiques are fallacious in logical terms.

It is worth reviewing two relevant arguments at this point.

One counter-argument is succinctly stated by N. Bobbio. As he points out (Bobbio 1961: 67–8), and as we have just seen in citing L. Green:

> The creation of law by the judge … is a reality … that ethical arguments come up against like arrows shot against a wall. Even the most faithful and orthodox partisans of legal positivism have been unable to do other than come to terms with this reality: the "mechanistic" theory of interpretation has been abandoned by nearly everyone. H. Kelsen himself set the example.[3]

However, N. Bobbio then observes that this fact does not in itself negate the positive theory of the sources of law according to which law is reduced to rules. We must choose one of two possibilities. Either, as many authors propose, we restrict the label "sources of law" to the facts that the legal system recognizes as productive of generally constraining norms. And, if so, even if through judges' decisions "the law in force in a given country is changed, is supplemented, is adapted to new situations, this does not authorize us to include decisions among the sources of law (where, of course, the institution of precedent does not exist)". The judge's decision in effect constrains only the parties involved. If it takes the form of a general maxim that tends towards becoming obligatory through the practice of the courts, "then the source of law in this instance is custom and not the judge". Or else, as advanced for instance by H. Kelsen, we extend the compass of sources of law to include individual norms, in which case, judicial decisions clearly do constitute a source of law. But "this elevation [of the judge's decision] is not dependent on a discovery of the creative power of the judge, because a sentence is an individual norm, both when it is the product of the judge's power and when it consists purely of an application of a general norm" (Bobbio 1961).

H. Hart presented another counter-argument in *The Concept of Law* in 1961. It is well known that H. Hart shed light on the fact that the creative power of the judge results from the impossibility for any rule to lay out the cases for its own application. This argument definitively negates any theory of law that, under the pretext of extreme conceptualism or formalism, would deny or minimize this source of indeterminacy in order to restore a mechanistic concept of interpretation. However, H. Hart observes, we must also reject the position at the other extreme, which, in the form of sceptical theory, would have it that "talk of rules is a myth, cloaking the truth that law consists simply of the decisions of courts and the prediction of them" (H. Hart 1994: 136). It is not just that a perspective of this kind must itself acknowledge at the very least the existence of organic secondary rules of the court and other legislative authorities. As well, and most important,

3 N. Bobbio (1961: 68) also embraces a position expressed by Fr. Carnelutti in 1951, according to which it is necessary to recognize, as do sociological theories, that "the decisive moment in the life of law is the judgement".

this perspective does not take account of a second dimension that the theory of language has been effective in revealing, which rests on the distinction between "mention and usage".[4] The fact is that what is specific to the behaviour of those who make use of the "norms" of law, whether as their ultimate addressees or as public authorities in charge of applying norms, relates to the fact that these norms "are *used* as rules not as descriptions of habits or predictions" (H. Hart 1994: 138). In reducing norms to predictions, we fail to take account of what emerges through our way of using them when we apply them. True, this does not negate the fact that judges often reason purely intuitively, but the sceptical perspective fails to differentiate between two distinct things: "the question whether a person, in acting in a certain way, thereby manifested his acceptance of a rule requiring him so to act" on one hand; and on the other hand, "psychological questions as to the processes of thought through which the person went before or in acting" (H. Hart 1994: 139–40).[5]

The Hermeneutic Critique

A second kind of discussion succeeded the first critique based on the judge's creative power. As we have already seen, no theoretical argument opposed to an understanding of law in terms of "rules" can be inferred from the so-called sociological and realist approaches to law or the new light they shed on the functioning of the operations of judgement. But according to some present-day theorists, the insight that produced these approaches remains valid, provided it is reformulated and shifted.

The question is in fact not that of the creative power of the judge—which in any case no one seriously doubts. The fact that this power exists does not *in itself* invalidate recourse to the notion of the rule as a way of accounting for the concept of law. According to these theorists, the question is rather that a more powerful analysis of *the way* judges exercise this discretionary power entails an invalidation of the way that current positivist theory of law defines the concept of law.

The best known representative of this recent critique is R. Dworkin, although the fullest developments of the justifications and philosophical extensions that it entails have not always been expressed by R. Dworkin himself.[6] His argument

4 On this, and on the way this distinction, which emerged from the philosophy of ordinary language, made it possible to deepen the distinctions that H. Kelsen sought to establish (in particular between the point of view of causal explanation and the constructivist point of view that the science of law must embrace), see (H. Hart 1983).

5 H. Hart is judicious in pointing out that the fact that our behaviour is often intuitive (and is therefore not the result of an explicit calculation performed in light of the rules) does not prevent it from constituting a true application of a rule. The proof of this is that when our behaviour is challenged, we seek to justify it by referring to the rule.

6 Among the most interesting approaches within this recent effort at a critical destabilization of the analytical positivist approaches deriving from H. Hart are certain

is very simple: Judicial practice shows that alongside rules in the strictest sense, judges often use "principles" (which may or may not be expressed as written norms). Of course, use of these "principles" constitutes one way of applying "rules" in the broad sense. But the importance of these principles (that is, the power to neutralize rules, in the strict sense, that their use makes possible) and their mode of operation lead, as R. Dworkin points out, to the putting into question of our usual understanding of what law consists of; that is, the conditions for its identity or existence. Thus clearer understanding of the way judges exercise their power of interpretation (that is, how they identify the "meaning" of law) reflects back on our understanding of the question of the validity of law; that is, the conditions for its definition.

Thus, as R. Dworkin argues, the dominant theory of law is tainted with "the semantic sting":

> [P]eople are its prey who hold a certain picture of what disagreement is like and when it is possible; they think we can argue sensibly with one another if, but only if, we all accept and follow the same criteria for deciding when our claims are sound, even if we cannot state exactly, as a philosopher might hope to do, what these criteria are (Dworkin 1986: 45).

However (still as R. Dworkin argues), not all our disagreements can be reduced to this model. For example, there are certain words we use to confer what are often controversial interpretations on a social practice in which we participate. According to this hypothesis, our agreements and disagreements can be explained not by our obeying shared rules but by our shared or divergent interpretations of the same material. The example of "rules" of courtesy within a given society is particularly illuminating. The way members of a social group determine what is required by courtesy is a function of an "interpretive attitude" (Dworkin 1986: 47), which subjects these requirements to ongoing reinterpretation in light of the values that they must serve. "Law is an interpretive concept as courtesy in my imagined example" (Dworkin 1986: 87). In effect:

> [L]egal philosophers are in the same situation as philosophers of justice and the philosopher of courtesy we imagined; they cannot produce useful semantic theories of law; they cannot expose the common criteria or ground rules lawyers follow for pinning legal labels onto facts, for there are no such rules; [theories of law] are constructive interpretations: they try to show legal practice as a whole in its best light, to achieve equilibrium between legal practice as they find it and the best justification of that practice; so no firm line divides jurisprudence from adjudication or any other aspect of legal practice (Dworkin 1986: 90).

Wittgensteinian analyses. See (Patterson 1988, 1990, 1996); see also, for a less critical perspective, (Bix 1993, Coppens 1998, Endicott 2000).

If law is thus an "interpretive concept", it follows, as R. Dworkin argues, that not only the positivist approaches of J. Austin (reduction of law to an imperative) and H. Kelsen (the normativist perspective), but also their more recent and subtle reformulation advanced by H. Hart in his work on the rule of recognition, would prove to be unacceptable. For H. Hart, as is well known, law can be explained in terms of social facts. These are of a particular kind: law is effectively made possible by a kind of convention or social practice that consists of agreement by the officials in charge of applying the law as to the criterion for the identity or existence of law. This practice can itself be formulated in terms of what H. Hart calls the "rule of recognition". It is this conventionalist approach to the criterion for legality, as framed in terms of the rule of recognition, that R. Dworkin wishes to critique and prove invalid. Such a conventionalist approach, he argues, would lack two defining features of legal practice.

First, the practice by which the law of a social group is identified is of an interpretive nature. It follows, argues R. Dworkin, that not all the criteria for identification can be formally defined in terms of "rules".

Then, this interpretive practice reflects the necessary link between law and morality, and consequently invalidates the positivist conception of a science of law that would be descriptive rather than normative. Law, R. Dworkin says, can be identified, whether by judges or scholars, only by means of the interpretation of the requirements of the political morality of the social group:

> Hard cases arise for any judge, when his threshold test does not discriminate between two or more interpretations of some statute or line of cases; then he must choose between eligible interpretations by asking which shows the community's structure of institutions and decisions—its public standards as a whole—in a better light from the standpoint of political morality (Dworkin 1986: 255–6).

According to R. Dworkin, then, the interpretive practice regarding what law consists of itself refers us back to the normative requirements of an institutional morality that is simultaneously immanent in the community[7] and the subject of ongoing reinterpretation.

As L. Green (2003: 6) accurately points out, R. Dworkin rejects positivist theses:

> [H]e denies that there can be any general theory of the existence and content of law; he denies that local theories of particular legal systems can identify law without recourse to its merits; ... a theory of law is for Dworkin a theory of how cases ought to be decided and it begins, not with an account of political

7 Of course, this new form of the doctrine of natural law in no way reinstates belief in an *a priori* definable moral content or any sort of moral intuitionism, which in our day has little epistemological acceptability. On the other hand, it is also clear that any judgements about this political morality must have a claim to objectivity. If this condition is not satisfied, R. Dworkin's theory cannot maintain coherence.

> organization, but with an abstract ideal regulating the conditions under which governments may use coercive force over their subjects.[8]

This hermeneutic critique of conventionalist approaches to law in terms of the "rule of recognition" is itself nowadays the subject of definitive critiques which have made possible a productive deepening of legal positivism.

Law and Social Recognition: A Pragmatist Reformulation of the Rule of Recognition

From among the many objections levelled at this hermeneutic critique of legal positivism and more precisely at the version developed by R. Dworkin, we will address here only the one formulated by J. Coleman, which to us appears definitive. Clearly, J. Coleman has no intention of challenging the descriptive contribution made by hermeneutic approaches to the operation of judging. On the contrary, it could be said that J. Coleman achieves the same shift with respect to the hermeneutic approaches to the function of judging as these approaches themselves had effected with respect to the sociological and realist critiques of legal positivism. Recall that these critiques had erroneously purported to expose the reduction of law to a set of rules by pointing to the "creative power of the judge". It soon became apparent that a critique of this nature, whatever the evidence on which it relied, resulted in an impasse.

Nevertheless, the hermeneutic approach had shifted and reformulated the perception of an inadequacy in formalist approaches, namely the reduction of the concept of law to the idea of the "rule". Clearly, R. Dworkin does not deny that the law consists of norms (rules and principles) which impose reasons for action. Rather, he proposes that a better understanding of the operation of judgement entails abandoning a positivist thesis that defines the criteria for the "validity" (that is, for the existence) of norms in the terms of a "rule of recognition". Thus, his critique bears on the definition of the concept of law in terms of "rules".

J. Coleman's undertaking is to expose the inconsistency of R. Dworkin's critique (1). At the same time, however, he reformulates the notion of the "rule of recognition" in such a way as to definitively deny this critique any relevance (2). Let us take a closer look at each of these features of his argument.

(1) The objection levelled at R. Dworkin is as follows. Not only does R. Dworkin wrongly believe that defining law in terms of a rule of recognition presupposes a "semantic" approach to the criteria for validity of norms, he also falls victim, in his approach to the operations of application in law, to an excessively formalist approach to law.

8 As R. Dworkin (1986: 96) writes, "arguments of legal theory are best understood as arguments about how far and in what way past political decisions provide a necessary condition for the use of public coercion".

As was just recalled, according to R. Dworkin, the interpretive dimension of the law invalidates the positivist project of reducing the conditions for the validity (or for the identification) of law to a rule of recognition, that is, to the way that judges determine the necessary and sufficient conditions for a norm's membership in a given judicial system.

According to him, a reduction of this kind effectively presupposes a semantic conception of law, that is, the idea that the criteria for membership (the condition for the identification of law) can be framed in a propositional form that corresponds to the content of the convergent behaviours of the officials in charge of applying law. An approach of this kind is tainted with the semantic sting because it assumes that formal criteria exist for applying the term "law"; that is, for identifying norms likely to be considered legal. Consequently, argues R. Dworkin, such an approach is incompatible with the idea of law as consisting of moral principles that are by their very nature subject to controversial interpretations.

J. Coleman points out that R. Dworkin's error is in overlooking the fact that the "rule of recognition" need not necessarily be interpreted in semantic terms. It is, in fact, open to being conceived of in a pragmatist manner. In other words, R. Dworkin is right to reject any semantic interpretations of the concept of law (that is, the idea that the meaning of the term "law" could be formally defined in a propositional statement).[9] Indeed, as J. Coleman points out, this rejection was already well framed by L. Wittgenstein in his discussion of rule-following.[10] But R. Dworkin gives the rule of recognition a restrictive interpretation. He supposes that for H. Hart, the rule of recognition consists of judges' convergent practice that, in and of itself, defines a given group's criteria for legality. Moreover, according to such an interpretation, the rule of recognition must be understood as a "source thesis": that is, on this view the rule of recognition defines the "social and conventional sources" that make it possible to identify the content of law.

9 J. Coleman (2001b: 171–2) observes that, "like Dworkin, the pragmatist believes that all legal standards and rules are in principle revisable—what they require or demand of us [is] subject to change". This amounts to one more way of acknowledging the impossibility of reducing meaning to propositional content and the interpretive nature of judicial norms and of law in general. From this perspective, says J. Coleman, "if we look at Dworkin's theory of legal content as instead an account of how judges should [and do] revise the law rationally when the law needs to be revised, then it is ... a perfectly attractive and sensible theory".

10 "A related point, articulated first by Wittgenstein in his discussion of rule-following, is that the grasp of a rule—the ability to go on—cannot be exhaustively articulated in propositional form. Saul Kripke has explicated this point forcefully, showing that even the apparently hard-and-fast rule for our practice of addition cannot be stated in such a way that it uniquely determines what we all know to be the criteria of correctness for that practice. There is always the possibility of interpreting a propositional expression of the rule of addition in an indefinite number of non-standard ways. Since in fact we all converge in interpreting it in the same way, our understanding of the practice must go beyond propositional knowledge" (Coleman 2001b: 81).

A thesis of this kind does not need to be linked to a conventionalist positivist approach. True, numerous positivists, including J. Raz, maintain this "semantic" interpretation of the rule of recognition and of the definition of the criteria for legality. But it is possible to defend the idea that law is *in fine* defined by judges' social practices (the conventionalist and positivist approach) without subscribing to this semantic interpretation framed in the terms of a "source thesis". A social system can consider that its positive law depends not just on identifiable formal sources but also on its content's compliance with moral requirements. If legality is thus defined not just in terms of its formal and conventional source, but also in terms of its content, it is clear that its identification is a function of interpretations that are subject to controversy. Indeed, this is the view that H. Hart worked to defend and that J. Coleman has in turn adopted.[11]

But if the criteria for the identity of legality can no longer be reduced to propositional content that defines the formal criteria (the formal and conventional sources) for identifying the content of a specific judicial order, what does the rule of recognition mean? In such a case, the rule of recognition can only be defined in a "pragmatist" manner; that is, by referring to the use that is made of it. On this view, the rule would be identified with a "practice" of a more complex kind than one whose meaning could be reduced to propositional content. H. Hart and especially J. Coleman distinguish this practice by virtue of two features. First, this practice is associated not with all the addressees of all the judicial norms in a social group but rather only the officials in charge of its application.[12] Next, this practice must be of such a kind that it respects two conditions: it reflects the "recognition

11 In this regard, H. Hart writes of "soft positivism", W. Waluchow of "inclusive positivism", and J. Coleman of "incorporationism", in opposition to positivist approaches that defend an *exclusivist* interpretation of the rule of recognition and that thus view positivism's *social thesis* as a *social source thesis*.

12 This is a feature that H. Hart takes over from H. Kelsen. If law exists only on the condition that it is practised comprehensively, the "validity" of a rule is not a function of whether it is in effect practised and recognized by its ultimate addressee. It is only a function with respect to the practice of the officials in charge of its application. As J. Coleman (2001b: 78) writes, "While the rule of recognition can impose an obligation on officials (to evaluate conduct by applying all those rules that satisfy the criteria of legality set forth in it) only in so far as it is actually practised, this conventional rule in turn grounds the claims of the rules validated under it to regulate conduct regardless of whether or not those subordinate rules are adhered to". Similarly, "acceptance of the rule of recognition from the internal point of view by officials is a conceptual requirement of the possibility of law; acceptance from the internal point of view by the bulk of the populace is neither a conceptual nor an efficacy requirement. Even if they characteristically do, the majority of persons need not as a conceptual matter adopt the internal point of view toward the behaviour by which officials validate law, nor toward the subordinate rules that are validated under the legal system. Of course, it may be desirable on efficiency grounds that a population treat law as legitimate or obligation-imposing, since fewer public resources might then be required to insure compliance" (Coleman 2001b: 76).

of the obligatory nature" of these criteria for legality with respect to the officials in charge of applying law; and it incorporates the potentially conflictual aspect of interpretations of the contents of the normative requirements.

(2) It is with respect to this last point that J. Coleman deems H. Hart's hypotheses must be reformulated. This is where he broadens the analysis of the concept of law, using the gains made by the pragmatist theory of collective action. The interpretive dimension of the concept of law necessitates avoiding any excessively "mechanical" understanding of the way convergent practice by judges, in relation to what is considered law within a given society, is constructed. If, within a pragmatist perspective, it is accepted that the meaning of the normative requirements (that is, the conditions of existence of law) emerges from the use made of them within practices that attest to their recognition by those in charge of applying them, what remains is to identify the nature of this practice, that is, to define its conditions for possibility.

H. Hart has already successfully revealed the nature of this social practice by pointing out that it is not to be understood as a simple "factual regularity": it is defined by an "internal point of view" which expresses the fact that the performers of this "convergent" practice recognize that they "have an obligation" to comply with these conditions of legality.

But this internal point of view, observes J. Coleman, is not sufficient on its own to account for the existence of the obligation: "[W]hile the internal point of view explains how the rule of recognition can create reasons for acting, this does not yet explain how those reasons can be duties".[13] An understanding of the conditions for possibility of legal regulation thus necessitates as well:

> explaining how a rule can impose a duty; the solution to this problem requires that we return our attention from the psychological capacity to adopt a practice or a pattern of behaviour as a norm, and focus instead on the normative structure of the pattern of behaviour to which we commit; in other words ... we must look beyond the internal point of view that officials adopt toward their practice, and consider instead the structure of the practice that rule governs (Coleman 2001b: 91).

Undoubtedly, H. Hart's insight into this requirement is valid. However, he has failed to carry his analysis of its precise nature sufficiently far. What is the reason for this inadequacy? H. Hart, observes J. Coleman, assumes that this convergent practice (the rule of recognition) results from a spontaneous effort at coordination among judges, as though potential conflicting interpretations in law inevitably and automatically eventuate in the choice of a common conventional solution representing a Nash equilibrium (that is, in the choice of the best possible solution

---

13 "If I can create a reason by adopting a pattern of behaviour as a norm, then it would seem that I can subsequently extinguish the reason that norm provides simply by withdrawing my commitment to it. Yet it is the nature of duties that those bound by them cannot voluntarily extinguish them as reasons" (Coleman 2001b: 90).

or, if we believe, as J. Nash does, that there are several possible best solutions, one of the best possible solutions).[14] A conception of the rule of recognition as a "coordination convention" derives from an analysis of the concept of law based on the conventionalist model of D. Lewis (1969). As S. Shapiro (2002: 391) has justly noted, D. Lewis's model of conventions[15] provides the positivist with a powerful argument in favour of the claim that in every legal system, legal officials follow conventions when determining which authority structure to heed.[16] As J. Coleman and S. Shapiro point out, problems of coordination among (legal) authorities relating to the determination of the criteria for legality are more complex. It would be unreasonable to reduce them solely to the category that game theory labels

14 "While H. Hart was right to identify the normative structure of the practice of officials, he was wrong … to conclude that the rule of recognition represents, in effect, a Nash equilibrium solution to a game of partial conflict" (Coleman 2001b: 97). Recall that we have directed a largely analogous critique against positivist theses, including those of J. Coleman (Lenoble and Maesschalck 2003: 283). The reason is that at the time when we were framing this critique we based our analysis on J. Coleman's works prior to *The Practice of Principle*. Until that publication, J. Coleman had continued to defend an interpretation of the rule of recognition framed in the terms of "coordination convention". He nevertheless had already conceded with respect to his construal in terms of coordination convention, "I do not pretend that any of this is obvious or obviously correct" (Coleman 2001a: 120). It is in pursuing his analysis, in light especially of the work of S. Shapiro and M. Bratman, that J. Coleman (2001b: 94, note 29) reformulated his argument in *The Practice of Principle*. Thus even if the terms of the critique of J. Coleman that we ourselves (Lenoble and Maesschalck 2003) framed in *Toward a Theory of Governance* are no longer usable, it will be shown below (Chapter 2) that its content and epistemological tenor continue to be valid and can be used in opposition to the reformulation for H. Hart's rule of recognition as proposed by J. Coleman in his latest work (as well as by S. Shapiro).

15 S. Shapiro recalls D. Lewis's definition of a convention: "A regularity R in the behaviour of members of population P in a recurring situation S is a convention if and only if, in any instance of S:

1. everyone conforms to R;
2. everyone expects everyone else to conform to R;
3. everyone prefers to conform to R on condition that the others do, since S is a coordination problem and uniform conformity to R is a coordination equilibrium in S" (D. Lewis 1969: 58).

16 The relevant reasoning is easy to follow. "Because (1) the choice of an authority structure is a recurring coordination problem; (2) legal officials manage to solve these problems; and (3) conventions are common solutions to such problems, it is plausible to infer that legal officials solve their recurring coordination problems via conventions … The positivist argument concludes with the attempted demonstration that coordination conventions are able to create obligation. As we have seen, when a convention exists, general conformity to it generates expectations that similar behaviour will continue" (Shapiro 2002: 391–2).

"coordination games",[17] which are solved by adopting "coordination conventions" of the kind analysed by D. Lewis. A telling sign, J. Coleman (2001b: 95) points out, of this irreducibility of the rule of recognition to the convention model analysed by D. Lewis is that:

> [S]uch conventions do not seem to capture well the kinds of reasons officials have for acting as other officials do. While it is true that the fact that judges apply certain criteria of legality can be a reason for any particular judge to do so, it is not simply the fact that others do so that explains the character of the reason that any particular judge has. A full explanation of the character of the reason any judge has to apply the relevant criteria will accommodate the fact that these criteria have been adopted as part of a plan or project (a legal system) that can serve valuable ends.[18]

This means that the conventional practice by means of which the rule of recognition is constructed is of a more complex kind than the one H. Hart had in mind. Accordingly, in illuminating the distinctly hermeneutic dimension of this practice, R. Dworkin, while mistakenly denouncing the conventionalism of H. Hart's positivism, is accurate in his perception of its inadequacy. This hermeneutic dimension entails not, obviously, the abandonment of the conventionalist thesis, but the deepening of the true nature of the operation of construction of this convention. The conditions for possibility of the emergence of this convergent practice cannot be reduced to rational choice of an arbitrary convention, allowing for a quasi-mechanical resolution of the usual problems of coordination, like those that can be resolved by adopting a rule of the road requiring drivers to keep to the right rather than to the left.

17 These games have a specific structure that is usually described using the model called "Battle of the Sexes" or "partial conflict game". An essential feature of this kind of game (as exemplified by a scenario in which a woman and her husband agree to attend an event together but must choose simultaneously and without collaborating, and where the man would prefer to go to a boxing match and the woman to the opera) is that the players have prior preferences such that "the players, although they have divergent interests, have more to gain by agreeing than by disagreeing" (Guerrien 2002: 54). And that agreement must translate into the adoption of an arbitrary convention as defined by D. Lewis. As J. Coleman (2001b: 94) states, "it would place an arbitrary and baseless constraint on our concept of law to stipulate that the social practice among officials necessary for the existence of a rule of recognition must always be representable as a game of partial conflict".

18 As stated by S. Shapiro (2002: 393) (whom J. Coleman cites), "to claim that the choice of an authority structure is a recurring coordination problem commits one to holding that the players will see the solution to the game as arbitrary in the sense just described; but is this assumption plausible? This, I think, is rather doubtful; … in fact, I am not even sure that most Americans would view the United States Constitution as an arbitrary solution to a recurring coordination problem; my guess is that many would believe that they had a moral obligation to heed a text that had been ratified by the representatives of the people of the United States, regardless of what everyone else did".

What, then, are these conditions for possibility? How are we to understand the structure of this collective action? J. Coleman says that it is both necessary and useful to take a detour via discussions in social theory and the philosophy of action. He believes it is appropriate to invoke here the model developed by M. Bratman in philosophy of action and called "shared cooperative activity" (SCA). Naturally, this model of action is not unique to law. But this form of shared cooperative activity "might help us understand the nature of the practice of legal officials" (Coleman 2001b: 96).

The practice of recognition by means of which judges define the criteria for legal normativity within a social group can only be thought as a form of SCA. SCA implies a "shared intention". But, as M. Bratman (1993: 107) rightly observes, such an intention is not an intention found in minds: it is an attitude[19] reflected in a certain mode of organizing cooperative practice. This is where the conditions for possibility of this specific type of action are revealed. M. Bratman points out that for the cooperative dimension that this shared intention calls for, various institutional mechanisms must be put in place. The organization of such cooperative activity requires the implementation of an organizational framework in order to "coordinate our intentional actions", "coordinate our planning", and "structure relevant bargaining". These organizational conditions are designed to make possible the threefold "commitment" (Bratman 1992: 328) that this "shared intention" reflects: mutual responsiveness,[20] commitment to the joint activity,[21] and commitment to mutual support.[22] These various requirements, according to M. Bratman (1992: 339), make it possible to differentiate between a "prepackaged cooperation" boiled down to coordinating intentions and a shared cooperative activity that entails coordinating actions.[23] M. Bratman's way of formulating this in his article Shared Intention (1993: 106) is as follows:

We intend to *J* if and only if

---

19 As M. Bratman notes, "Shared intention, as I understand it, is not an attitude in any mind. It is not an attitude in the mind of some fused agents, for there is no such mind; and it is not an attitude in the mind or minds of either or both participants; rather, it is a state of affairs that consists primarily in attitudes (none of which are themselves shared intentions) of the participants and interrelations between those attitudes".

20 "In SCA each participating agent attempts to be responsive to the intentions and actions of the other."

21 "In SCA the participants each have an appropriate commitment (though perhaps for different reasons) to the joint activity, and their mutual responsiveness is in pursuit of this commitment."

22 "In SCA each agent is committed to supporting the efforts of the other to play her role in the joint activity … These commitments to support each other put us in a position to perform the joint activity successfully even if we each need help in certain ways."

23 "Suppose, for example, you and I lay plans for you to go to San Francisco while I go to New York. We might have a web of intentions concerning this joint activity, a web that satisfies (1) <common intentions> and (2) <common knowledge>. And our activity of prior planning may itself be an SCA <shared cooperative activity>. But if when we each go

1. I intend that *we J* and *(b)* you intend that *we J*
2. I intend that *we J* in accordance with and because of 1*a*, 1*b*, and meshing subplans of 1*a* and 1*b*; you intend that *we J* in accordance with and because of 1*a*, 1*b*, and meshing subplans of 1*a* and 1*b*.

1 and 2 are common knowledge between us.

By following such a rule of engagement, the actors involved make themselves capable of incorporating a form of collective action likely to strengthen the fulfilment of the objectives pursued in common. To foreground this rule of engagement as an integral part of the concept of law is to recognize that the concept of law depends, for its social identification, on a specific way of behaving with respect to rules. But this behaviour should not be accounted for as the result of a judgement of a particular kind about the meaning of the rule; rather, it should be explained as a way of assuming joint responsibility for the fulfilment of the rule through concrete actions. J. Coleman (2001b: 97) concludes:

> [T]he practice of officials of being committed to a set of criteria of legality exhibits these features; judges coordinate their behaviour with one another through, for example, practices of precedent, which are ways in which they are responsive to the intentions of one another.

our separate ways there is no mutual responsiveness in action, our activity is prepackaged cooperation, not SCA."

Chapter 2

From a Positivist to a Genetic Approach to the Conventionality of Law: A Necessary Broadening of the Pragmatist Theory of Law

In this chapter, we wish to show how the arguments presented by J. Coleman as a justification for reformulating the positivist approach to the concept of law impose a shift that is more significant than he himself realizes and open up new perspectives in philosophy of law.

First, note that by reformulating H. Hart's thesis, J. Coleman incorporates in the positivist approach a certain normativity. For the function of law as a guide to be realized, the institutional conditions needed for the success of the cooperative action among the officials responsible for applying the rule of recognition must be respected. The reason is that all forms of cooperative activity entail an intentional element and satisfaction of this intentionality cannot be assumed to be guaranteed by "rules stored in the minds" of participants in this collective action. Surely, this normativity does not resemble the "eternal moral normativity" to which theorists of natural law customarily refer. The present argument is much deeper philosophically: it relates to normativity at the level of the conditions for possibility[1] internal to the social activity by means of which law is produced.

At the same time, however, J. Coleman appears to be proposing that these conditions have been fulfilled since the birth of the modern state. The "normative" conditions for the existence of law would, on this view, thus have always been satisfied. At the moment when J. Coleman appears to recognize that the classical positive approach regarding the conventional nature of law should yield to what we call a "genetic" approach to the "conventionality thesis",[2] he also wipes out its

1 This is why we could also call this kind of normativity "transcendental", in the technical sense that I. Kant and J. Fichte gave the term. In this perspective, however, it is important to point out that these transcendental conditions are not to be understood as "ideal conditions for the producibility of norms" (which is the perspective adopted by I. Kant, who thereby restored a mentalist perspective; on this, see below) but rather what one might henceforward call "empirico-transcendental" conditions. Note, too, that such an approach, based on "empirico-transcendental conditions", addresses B. Zipursky's concern to adopt an epistemological position that "restores a place for conceptualism in law while avoiding the conservative and transcendental tendencies of discredited formalist theories" (Zipursky 2000: 459).

2 By "genetic" understanding, we mean an understanding that takes into account the conditions "for production" of the convention by which law is defined, that is, the conditions

effects. In our view, the reason is his inadequate understanding of the conditions for possibility of the concept of law and his reduction of these exclusively to the level of the classical conditions for organization of the judicial apparatus in the modern state. This inadequacy is clearly the result of a theoretical inadequacy. In our view, J. Coleman's reasoning labours under a twofold limitation which results in two consequences whose recognition makes it possible to gauge the scope of the shift that must be effected in relation to the current debate on the concept of law. The present section will develop the two points in question. First, however, an outline of their key features must be presented.

The twofold limitation that affects the pragmatist reformulation of the positivist thesis is revealed as a function of the theoretical instrument that J. Coleman himself deploys to underpin his own reformulation of the positivist thesis, namely the critique of mentalism in the theory of action.

First, as will be shown below, an in-depth understanding of this critique of mentalism would entail a radical expansion of J. Coleman's understanding—and M. Bratman's, for that matter—of the conditions necessary to satisfying the intentionality inherent in any cooperative activity. This first limitation, though essential for gauging the nature of the improvements that it would be appropriate to make to our system of governance,[3] is nevertheless not essential to an understanding of the main reason for the inadequacy that compromises current approaches to the concept of law, whether positivist or hermeneutic (for instance, R. Dworkin's). Suffice it to point out this first limitation here without going into it further.

Identification of the second limitation, on the other hand, plays a major role in revealing the weakness that affects both classical approaches to legal positivism

---

for possibility of this convention. As we showed above (9–10), these conditions for generation rest on an internalized reference to an external order of implementation, that is, on the mutual encroachment of two orders of conditionality, neither of which can be fulfilled unless it organizes and integrates into itself the relationship of mutual conditionality that constitutes them. Note that this obviously does not imply abandoning the conventionality thesis as such. According to this thesis, "legal authority is made possible by an interdependent convergence of behaviour and attitude: what we might think of as an "agreement" among individuals, expressed in a duty-imposing social or conventional rule (for H. Hart this is the rule of recognition)" (Coleman 2001b: 70–71). Conventionality implies that the existence of the rule of recognition does not depend "on substantive (moral) argument" (Coleman 2001a: 116). This conception of the authority of the rule of recognition also provides the explanation for the question of legality: "The key idea of the conventionalist picture is that this rule [the rule of recognition] provides reasons because it is adopted by individuals in order that it guide their behaviour: guide their behaviour by directing them to apply certain criteria of validity determining the conditions of membership of other norms in the category 'law'—thus enabling those norms to claim a power to provide reasons for acting in virtue of their being law" (Coleman 2001a: 118).

3 In particular, to demonstrate the limitations of deliberative and communicative approaches in the theory of governance. On this, see (Lenoble and Maesschalck 2003) and below, Part II.

and pragmatist reformulations of it (that is, hermeneutic "alternatives"). We will show how the argument J. Coleman opposes to H. Hart's can be turned against J. Coleman himself. Indeed, a broadened analysis of the "fact" of citizens' recognition of the authority of the officials in charge of applying the law reveals that this "fact" is the product of numerous operations of judgement. Moreover, as will be shown below, a close examination of these operations of judgement reveals two essential facts. First, they reflect a search for "a maximization of normative expectations" (intentionality) by the members of social groups. Next, this intentional purpose depends for its fulfilment on the conditions specific to the success of any cooperative activity.

In other words, in contrast to what is understood under traditional approaches to the concept of law (whether positivist or hermeneutic), the conditions for production of the rule of recognition cannot be reflected upon exclusively at the level of the judicial authorities. The existence of law is also a function of the conditions set up to ensure recognition of the norm by the citizens for whom the norm is intended. Otherwise stated, the possibility of law (that is, the possibility for a social group to be regulated by law) is also a function of the way citizens "recognize" their relationship with the "officials"; that is, it is also a function of the way *citizens organize their form of the "representation of authority" in order to satisfy their normative expectations.*[4]

This twofold limitation, and more prominently the misunderstanding of the need to extend the internal point of view—to use H. Hart's terminology—of the rule of recognition to the citizen level, has important consequences. We here present two of these.

First, the recognition of this limitation makes it possible (and this is the first consequence we will examine below) to grasp the extent to which positivist theory, even in its pragmatist version, has been infected by what R. Dworkin calls the "semantic sting". But this semantic sting has a greater significance than R. Dworkin assigns to it. The fact is that, in avoiding recognizing its true philosophical implications, R. Dworkin not only appears unable to respond to the justified critiques of positivists, but also himself yields to this semantic error. Of course, R. Dworkin—and, beyond him, the whole "hermeneutic or interpretivist" trend in philosophy of law—is clearly aware of the need to conceive the concept of law as being "shot through" with an internal normativity that leads law always to "exceed" the formal representations of it. Thus the concept of law invokes "normative expectations" that no formal calculus can foresee: law is thus impossible to "implement" unless it so organizes itself as to respect the necessary "ongoing transformation" in the offing of a continuously renewed exigency. At the same time, however, at a deeper level, R. Dworkin assumes the "capability"

4 This second limitation is thus implicitly tied up with a possible reintepretation of a teleological judgement that is external to officials' perspective, which neither H. Hart nor J. Colcman truly takes into account. We will come back to this point at the end of the presentation of our line of argument.

of the "formal system of social representation" to satisfy this exigency, that is to ensure, "to the extent possible", the fulfilment of the normative expectations and guarantee that they will be continuously adjusted. This is the role he assigns to the judicial authorities, who are thus invested with a presumed capability to address the exigencies internal to the normativity of the concept of law. As regards the organization of the "capability" of the social group to "maximize to the extent possible" the group's normative expectations, the system of formal representation of the modern state is thus assumed, as it is by positivists, to ensure entirely on its own the success of the operation of the social production of law. The pragmatist reformulation of the rule of recognition emerges, by other paths, in the assumption that our formal systems of institutional representation have the same capability of ensuring the fulfilment of the concept of law. Put in more theoretical terms, the pragmatist redefinition of the rule of recognition proves incapable, as in H. Hart, of construing the *pragmatic limitation* of the operation of the application of law, and in consequence, of the necessary extension of the operation of recognition that governs the possibility for such an operation. Now *that* one can call a semantic sting: the assumption of the possible formalization of the conditions for fulfilment of the concept of law.

It is easy to infer the second consequence from the first. Yielding to this semantic error and not taking into account this *pragmatic limitation* of the operation of implementation that is internal to any normative operation, legal thinking, whether positivist or hermeneutic, arrives at an effect of blockage and idealization. On one hand, it does not allow for the incorporation into its agenda of the needed reflection on the institutional means that must be set up to ensure a cooperative activity that allows for the best possible fulfilment of the normative expectations of those for whom a norm is intended when hard cases emerge. On the other hand, by reducing these conditions solely to the establishment of the judicial authorities specific to the modern state and consequently by assuming that they are always-already in existence, the theory of law obliterates the normative conditions that must be respected to ensure law's guiding function, which defines the concept of law. The second consequence is all the more astonishing to note, in that it results in the theory of law remaining hermetically sealed *vis-à-vis* two phenomena that ought to be able to engage with it: on one hand, the recent turn in the social sciences, which have become aware of the need to put the question of governance back on the table (whereas traditionally it was addressed only by political philosophy); on the other hand, the recurring efforts, mainly emerging in American law, to transform the traditional modes of organization of the function of judging. Of course, these efforts continue to focus on the figure of the judges. But, despite any theoretical and practical inadequacies they might have, they highlight, through trial and error in the sphere of public law litigation, the need for the production and application of law to be open to modes of negotiated participation which include the private addressees of the norm. This opening up also entails, in our view, revisiting the kind of teleological judgement likely to guarantee the fulfilment of the concept of law from the perspective of the normative expectations of the social group concerned.

Pragmatist Positivism's Advances and Limitations, or the Requirements of the Pragmatic Turn in Philosophy of Law

Advances Made by Pragmatist Positivism

The pragmatist redefinition of the rule of recognition proposed by J. Coleman offers a twofold advantage over R. Dworkin's hermeneutic position.

Its first advantage is that it clearly reveals the error of the critique of conventionalist approaches according to which they overlook the "interpretive" nature of the concept of law. As J. Coleman observes, an incorporationist conventionalist approach does not overlook this interpretive dimension. By assuming that every conventionalist approach to law necessarily entails a semantic theory of language, R. Dworkin fails to perceive the possible pragmatist understanding of the conventionalist approach. The result, as we have seen, is that his critique of positivist conventionalism misses the mark.

There is more, however. R. Dworkin's inability to correctly formulate, in epistemological terms, the nature of the "semantic sting", and therefore the conditions that a non-semantic approach to the operations of judgement would have to respect, also becomes clear. This inability explains not just, as H. Putnam correctly inferred and as will be demonstrated below, why R. Dworkin himself falls back into the error that he imputes to positivist approaches to law, which he thought he could avoid through his hermeneutic approach. It also accounts for why he fails to substantiate his accurate insight into the inadequacy of legal positivism.

This is where we see the second advantage the pragmatist redefinition of the rule of recognition offers over R. Dworkin's approach. While remaining linked to a positivist approach to the *conventionality thesis*, the pragmatist redefinition put forward by J. Coleman itself embarks on the process of its own epistemological radicalization. What then is the contribution made by this redefinition? By reinterpreting the rule of recognition on the basis of M. Bratman's model of "shared cooperative activity", S. Shapiro and J. Coleman make the existence of law subject to that of institutional mechanisms that enable the implementation of cooperative practice among those in charge of applying law. Not only is law determined exclusively by recognition of it on the part of those responsible for applying it, but, as well, any possible conflicts in meaning entailed by the plural nature of possible interpretations on the part of the officials in charge of applying law cannot be resolved by means of a simple calculus of rational forethought, as in "coordination" games. Establishment of a balanced solution requires a more complex form of collective action: it requires a cooperative activity, in order to define, in common, objectives deemed acceptable. Moreover, this cooperative construction necessitates institutional mechanisms in order to ensure the effectiveness of this "shared intentionality" for constructing a common vision. As M. Bratman says, "shared intention" cannot be understood in a mentalist fashion; it does not consist of an "attitude in the minds". It requires institutional mechanisms designed to ensure its effective fulfilment. Note that this need for institutional mechanisms suitable for enabling the cooperative nature of collective practice in itself reveals the link between the theory of norms and the theory of governance.

The Limitations and Reformulation of Pragmatist Positivism

Right from the outset, there were indications to justify our asking whether this redefinition of the rule of recognition advanced by S. Shapiro and J. Coleman is possibly itself also inadequate and overlooks the epistemological requirement that it implicitly entails. After all, is it not significant that J. Coleman himself states his theoretical project does not entail particular attention to the institutional conditions for possibility of any cooperative activity?[5]

In fact, attention to these conditions—and above all to their epistemological justifications—would have enabled J. Coleman to perceive the inadequacy of his own construal of the link between law and the practice of recognition. We thus arrive at the question of whether the reproach of epistemological inconsistency that J. Coleman levels at R. Dworkin[6] could also be levelled at him. Does not the pragmatist reformulation of the rule of recognition advanced by J. Coleman itself rest on the formalist and mentalist presuppositions that his pragmatist project claims to expose? We believe that this reformulation does indeed need to be extended, in two directions.

To start with, if the rule of recognition consists of a cooperative practice, the institutional conditions required for this cooperation's realization cannot be reduced to those defined by M. Bratman and repeated by J. Coleman. In other words, the understanding (as M. Bratman, S. Shapiro, and J. Coleman present it) of the conditions for possibility of a shared cooperative activity needs, in our view, to be deepened and reformulated. Next, this "shared cooperative activity" that the existence of law depends on does not only concern the officials in charge of applying law (that is, in essence, judges); it also concerns citizens who are concerned by norms. The reason for the need for this twofold extension is epistemological: it results from the accurate understanding of the operations of normative judgement, that is, of the way that practical reason operates at the teleological level. Further, the elucidation of this necessity will enable us to understand that at the epistemological

5 "The particular form of interrelated responsiveness constitutive of shared intentions is not important for my purposes" (Coleman 2001b: 97).

6 J. Coleman's argument consists of refuting the false opposition that R. Dworkin sets up between interpretivism and conventionalism. As we have seen, however, R. Dworkin's difficulty in recognizing that interpretivism is not incompatible with, and indeed implies, conventionalism reflects a deeper logical inconsistency that is of an epistemological nature. This inconsistency J. Coleman unfortunately does not explicate. This inconsistency consists in the fact that R. Dworkin is himself, because of his epistemological mentalism, the victim of the semantic error that he believes he is exposing in positivist writings. We return below (51–5) to this epistemological weakness of R. Dworkin's hermeneutic approach.

level R. Dworkin's hermeneutic approach and J. Coleman's pragmatist approach partake of a shared mentalism and thus present the same difficulty.

Coleman's proposed reformulation of Hart's way of formulating the rule of recognition thus appears to us to demand a twofold extension. First, if the rule of recognition consists of cooperative practice, the necessary institutional conditions for realization of this cooperation cannot be reduced to those defined by M. Bratman and repeated by J. Coleman (see (1) below). Next, this "shared cooperative activity" on which law depends for its meaning does not only concern the officials in charge of applying law (that is, essentially judges); it also concerns the citizens who are concerned by the norms (see (2) below). From this there flows a greater understanding of the teleological judgement that guarantees the fulfilment of the concept of law.

(1) A deepening of the approach to the conditions for cooperative activity Why would the approach to cooperative activity advanced by J. Coleman reflect an inadequate grasp of the conditions for possibility of such activity? What is at issue here is not the point of departure for this approach. On the contrary, we can only agree fully with the proposal that J. Coleman (along with S. Shapiro), following M. Bratman, presents as the foundation for his analysis of cooperative activity. Let us once again quote M. Bratman's formulation:

> Shared intention ... is not an attitude in any mind; it is not an attitude in the mind of some fused agents, for there is no such mind; and it is not an attitude in the mind or minds of either or both participants; rather, it is a state of affairs that consists primarily in attitudes (none of which are themselves shared intentions) of the participants and interrelations between those attitudes (Bratman 1993: 107).

However, if we grasp the full implications of this position, we are led to see consequences that entail not just an extension of the institutional conditions necessary for the accomplishment of such action, but also, and above all, a modification of the customary conventionalist approach that positivists take to the concept of law.

If we grant that shared intention is not "in the minds" of the actors but rather must be embodied in institutional mechanisms that enable its possibility, we can reformulate this position as follows: the resources provided by the capabilities internal to the actors' reason are not sufficient to ensure the realization of the intentionality aimed at by cooperative activity. This comes down to saying that in its realization, this intentionality is a function of an internal limitation, since it cannot find within itself, that is, within the internal capabilities alone of representation of the intentional agent, the sufficient conditions for its implementation. In other words: In social reality, any implementation of such an intentional aim is a function of an externality.[7]

7 See the fuller development of this argument above at 9–10.

This reformulation, however, reveals a deeper consequence of the proposal that shared intention does not exist in minds. It is not sufficient to stop with this latest reformulation in terms of conditions for possibility of implementation of any shared intentional aim *qua* conditions that are *external* to reason. If we make an effort to fully grasp what is entailed by this reformulation, we see immediately that the idea of externality necessarily entails another proposition: No form, no representation of this intentional aim, "exhausts" all possible representations, all possible forms of this shared intention. *Every form (or representation) given to a cooperative activity is merely one possible form among others and none "satisfies" the requirements for the optimal realization of the normative requirement of cooperation.* Or, to put it in other words: the form that is spontaneously given to cooperative activity, even when it respects the requirements of *responsiveness* to participants' "interests, intentions, preferences and actions" (Coleman 2001b: 96) and the "commitment to the joint activity and to mutual support" identified by M. Bratman, still remains a function of the background representation that the various parties have of their own preferences. To assume that the representations *immediately* deployed by the parties reflect an "optimal" representation of the preferences of participants *vis-à-vis* the shared activity would come down to assuming once again that the conditions for realization of intentionality are internal to that intentionality and, in so doing, to overlooking the principle of externality mentioned above.[8] This principle of externality entails that the resources internal to the intentionality cannot suffice, on their own, to ensure the intentionality's implementation in social reality.

Thus, any representation of these preferences and, in consequence, any form that cooperative activity might take constitutes no more than one form among others of the realization of the requirements entailed by the shared purpose of a common goal.

But what is to say that such an observation should imply significant consequences? After all, it could be retorted that it matters little whether such a representation is specific, since the desire to define the conditions for a supposed ideal representation of the parties' preferences and thus of an optimal form of cooperative activity is an illusory goal.

True, it will never be possible to define such an optimal representation, since to do so assumes, as mentioned above, the possibility of a form of intentionality that would contain its capability for self-realization within itself; that is, it supposes the possibility of the absence of judgement's internal limitation. But the true implication lies elsewhere. In truth, does the only alternative to such an impossibility consist of supposing that the "naturally" limited capabilities—that is, natural in the sense that participants have them immediately at their disposal for defining their preferences and interests—are to be assumed to be the only capabilities available? It is an

8 This "principle of externality" represents a way of reformulating what, on the epistemological level of theory of action, we called the "contextual limitation" of practical judgement (Maesschalck 2001: 244–5).

assumption of this kind that underlies the position adopted by J. Coleman (as well as S. Shapiro and M. Bratman) in assuming as *given* the specific representation that the parties have of their interests and references. But how could the fact be overlooked that to assume such a representation is a *given* entails neglecting the epistemological principle by which we are forbidden to assume the intentionality would have within itself the sufficient capabilities for its implementation within social reality?

Even if we accept the possible absence of an ideal representation of preferences and accordingly of an optimal form of cooperative activity, there is a third position, which is the only one that respects this epistemological principle. This position consists of taking into account the fact that the representation of their intentions, interests, and preferences that the agents formulate *immediately* (that is, in the absence of mechanisms specially arranged to help them reconstruct their interpretive frameworks) is only one specific selection among other possible ones and that "attention" to this operation of choice could possibly allow for the construction of other possible selections. This would result in an expansion of the possibilities and thus in an "optimization" of the representations deployed by participants in the cooperative activity, and consequently in "optimization" (which does not mean attainment of the optimum) of the forms of the cooperative activity. This expansion of possibilities would be associated with the implementation not just of those mechanisms already clearly pointed out by M. Bratman, but also of specific mechanisms intended to prompt the actors to revisit their initial perceptions of their preferences and to consider these preferences' possible redefinition through the broadening of the interpretive frameworks *immediately* deployed. There would thus occur the identification of their "specific" representation of the requirements of the common intentional purpose; but this one would have as an "advantage" an advance in "extension" over the specific forms that had not taken account of the internal limitation affecting the representation of the intentionality. It could thus be said that, besides the conditions of *responsiveness* and *mutual support* identified by M. Bratman, incentives aiming to ensure the parties' *reflexive learning* would be necessary in order to allow them to carry out a reflexive revisiting of the background representations that *immediately* orient their judgements.

The proposition according to which a shared intention does not exist "in the minds" of the parties to a cooperative activity thus has an epistemological implication which entails supplementing the way M. Bratman, S. Shapiro, and J. Coleman conceive of the nature of the conditions for possibility for ensuring such an action's realization. After all, it is revealing that the various examples M. Bratman uses to construct his philosophical understanding of the nature of a cooperative activity are all examples in which the meaning of the shared intention is always-already given and takes a comparatively simple form (singing together, painting a house together, and so on). True, M. Bratman's analyses show clearly that the application of this meaning necessitates mechanisms for building in common. But in basing himself on a formulation of shared intentionality that is assumed to be already given, M. Bratman is faced with the difficulty in identifying the radical epistemological meaning of his fundamental principle, as well as in identifying its implications for a theory of intentionality.

The deepening of the analysis of the normative requirements internal to shared intention is not without consequences for an analysis of the concept of law. We will return to this. Nevertheless, at this point we can raise several questions about the use J. Coleman makes of the concept of shared cooperative activity, or SCA, in his theory of the rule of recognition.

J. Coleman appears to assume that the forms of judicial organization developed by all modern states would satisfy the requirements for the realization of an SCA. Certainly, J. Coleman would acknowledge that these forms may have varied in time and space. Nevertheless, they are all assumed to reflect, at a level beyond their diversity, the way of taking into account the conditions for possibility specific to an SCA. Where would this spontaneous capability of collective systems for satisfying the requirement of cooperative organization on the part of the officials in charge of interpreting the criteria for the validity of law originate? If we take into account the dimension of reflexive learning that was mentioned above, it is undoubtedly necessary to be more circumspect about this assumed capability on the part of our systems of judicial organization to satisfy the conditions for an SCA. Note that this caution is strongly in accord with the current social theory that J. Coleman appears (quite rightly) to invoke in support of his own reformulation of the theory of the rule of recognition put forward by H. Hart.

Whatever the limitations of current social theory,[9] it is symptomatic that the whole of its evolution reflects a shared concern increasingly to extend the nature of the incentives and mechanisms that must be put in place in order to realize cooperative equilibrium. Moreover, numerous authors, including C. Argyris and D. Schön, explicitly subordinate these equilibria to forms of reflexive learning, even though their theory of reflexivity fails adequately to construe the epistemological framework that it requires. As well (although this observation is less theoretical than sociological), similar prudence regarding the question of whether all forms of judicial organization "exhaust" all the conditions for possibility for "optimized" (but not optimal) satisfaction of the requirements for realizing cooperation in how to interpret the rule of recognition, would perhaps allow theory to better take into account the dynamic that characterizes these forms of judicial organization. In this perspective, various trajectories reveal the need sometimes felt by judicial actors themselves for a desirable adjustment in their modes of organization. To take just one example, the significant changes linked to the introduction, in American law, of the civil rights injunction following the *Brown v. Board of Education* judgment (Fiss 1978, 1983) could be said to have reflected the need to reorganize certain kinds of trial in order to ensure a better construal of the judge's "perceptions" in litigation related to certain public policies.

But the extension of the SCA approach called for by a more epistemologically based understanding of the conditions for possibility of shared intention entails

9 On this, see Part II.

more significant theoretical shifts than this revisiting—decidedly secondary from a philosophical point of view—of the sufficiently or insufficiently cooperative nature of our forms of legal organization. In order to present this, we must first show that a second extension of J. Coleman's proposed approach to the rule of recognition must be carried out.

(2) A reinterpretation of the relationship between the rule of recognition and citizens' practice in terms of cooperative activity Why is consideration solely of cooperative activity by the officials in charge of applying law too reductive to ensure a full understanding of the conditions necessary for the realization of the form of collective action by which a group regulates itself legally? That is, what is the reason why limiting oneself to that consideration alone results in overlooking a conceptual requirement specific to the guiding function of law?

Once again, the reason for the lack of validity of this reduction is epistemological. Moreover, it is analogous to the justification for the first extension of J. Coleman's approach. As we shall show, a reduction of this kind also rests on an assumed given capability, by the social group, to act in common, but without reflecting upon the conditions for possibility of such a capability. To show how this presupposition operates in H. Hart's and J. Coleman's approaches, we will recapitulate their reasoning step by step.

As we have seen, H. Hart, and J. Coleman after him, postulate that the existence of a legal system within a social group does not require that the "internal point of view" needed by officials in charge of applying law be manifested among the citizens. All that is necessary is that citizens' behaviour reflect a simple, accustomed, and generalized practice of obedience to law.[10] As J. Coleman points out, "the majority of persons need not, as a conceptual matter, adopt the internal point of view toward the behaviour by which officials validate law, nor towards the subordinate rules that are validated under the legal system".[11] In other words, it matters little whether the majority of the population "feels obliged" or considers itself to "have the obligation" to respect the rules of law.[12] Requiring citizens to adopt an internal point of view would, according to H. Hart, come down to requiring "that both [the bulk of the population] and the officials of the system 'accept', in the same explicit, conscious way, a rule of recognition" (H. Hart 1994: 114). A requirement of this sort, notes H. Hart, is unrealistic because in all complex modern states:

10 "So long as the laws which are valid by the system's tests of validity are obeyed by the bulk of the population this surely is all the evidence we need in order to establish that a given legal system exists" (H. Hart 1994: 114).

11 "Of course," J. Coleman (2001b: 76) continues, "it may be desirable on efficiency grounds that a population treat law as legitimate or obligation-imposing, since fewer public resources might then be required to insure compliance."

12 On this distinction, see (H. Hart 1994: 88).

> the reality of the situation is that a great proportion of ordinary citizens—perhaps a majority—have no general conception of the legal structure or of its criteria of validity; ... [The ordinary citizen] may obey [the law] for a variety of different reasons and among them may often, though not always, be the knowledge that it will be the best for him to do so; he will be aware of the general likely consequences of disobedience: that there are officials who may arrest him and others who will try him and send him to prison for breaking the law (H. Hart 1994: 114).

Once again, H. Hart expresses himself explicitly. In a scenario where "only officials might accept and use the system's criteria of legal validity", society "might be deplorably sheeplike; the sheep might end in the slaughter-house. But there is little reason for thinking that it could not exist or for denying it the title of a legal system" (H. Hart 1994: 117).

Of course, it is neither a question of denying that such a system is a legal system, nor of criticizing the elementary observation that the majority of citizens have no comprehensive knowledge of the structure of law or its criteria of validity. Similarly, J. Coleman is right to say that the generalized practice of obedience to law must not be the result of a conscious process of judgement regarding the legitimacy of such criteria. In this sense, H. Hart and J. Coleman (as well as most first-rank positivists, including H. Kelsen) are right to emphasize that the existence of a legal system is not dependent on the nature of the individual motivations that justify its generalized and customary application by citizens. But once again, as with the cooperative activity approach, does an alternative of this kind allow for an adequate construal of the problem and for an identification of the conditions that make such a generalized practice of obedience possible? Let us look again at the scenario H. Hart advances as being especially probative of his own reasoning, namely that of a social group in which citizen members identified with a flock of sheep and even went so far as to allow themselves to be led to the slaughterhouse from pure obedience to a sanctioned order. What must be assumed for such a social group and such a generalized practice of obedience to exist?

Undoubtedly, if we lived on a planet where members of the group were "lobotomized", we would be able to understand identical behaviour consisting of obedience to the orders of authority as simple behavioural responses to an external stimulus. However, absent such a hypothesis of lobotomized individuals, we must deploy other propositions to account for a generalized practice of this kind. In effect, we must assume that members of the group conduct at least three operations of judgement preliminary to their own individual decision to obey and behave "like sheep". First, a group member must anticipate the behaviour of other group members and have sufficient reason to believe that the latter will also behave like sheep, that is, in such a manner that this individual is justified, in "cost-benefit" terms, in submitting to the police or the dictatorship's officials and adopting purely passive behaviour, even at the risk of being led to the slaughterhouse. Further, the individual must anticipate the anticipations of others, that is, assume that other group members will go through a process of anticipation identical to the individual's own regarding the "passive behaviour" of the other members of the group.[13] Last, the individual group member must carry out a third form of anticipation: the assumption that the authority the individual's group (citizen-addressees) has decided to submit to, will itself, in the future, decide to continue behaving in conformity with its present role in relation to this group—that is, continue to assume that the citizens will continue to obey it. In the absence of these anticipations, there could be no "generalized" or "customary" practice of obedience. The implementation of such a practice necessarily implies a dimension of duration and a collective dimension that could not take shape if these three anticipations were not already minimally present. However, if this is the case, we must unavoidably conclude that even in the most extreme form of group members' "sheep-like" behaviour, any generalized and customary practice of obedience presupposes some form of intention; that is, the adoption and shared acceptance of a *form of common life*.

Thus at this point in our reasoning, we observe a kinship between the form of action characteristic of "the officials in charge of applying the law" and the form of action necessarily deployed by any generalized and customary practice of obedience by citizens. To repeat: this kinship or formal analogical structure clearly does not imply that what "motivates" the generalized practice of obedience by citizens is a common reflection on the technical matters entailed by an interpretation of the legal criteria of validity. But the link must be brought to light that exists between this practice of majority respect and the possibility for causing the emergence, within a group, of a common culture of "trust" and of adherence to a way of life instituted by the group's institutional structure. Thus, it is a question of understanding the link that exists between this respect and the construction of a sufficiently common "belief" that makes possible the majority's practical acceptance of the instituted way of life. How are we to understand the operations by which is built up this minimal trust that the members of a social group grant to the officials in charge of determining normative requirements? As was just seen, it is not possible to understand this operation without reference to a condition of belief, that is, a form of practical acceptance of a way of life. Thus the possibility of giving "meaning" to a normative requirement (and thereby to law) in social reality, that is, of "applying" it, of causing it to produce effects in reality, depends on a "will", a "common motivation", on the part of the addressees of this norm, and thus on a common culture among the actors, which is likely to ensure effective realization of the normative requirements. The possibility for "governance by law"

13 Note the analogy of these crisscrossing anticipations with M. Bratman's observation in his analysis of shared intention: "In shared intention the constitutive intentions of the individuals are interlocking, for each agent has an intention in favour of the efficacy of an intention of the other; and the intentions of each involve a kind of reflexivity, for each has an intention concerning the efficacy of an intention of her own" (Bratman 1993: 104). It may also be mentioned here that, as of 1796, J. Fichte had constructed his philosophy of law (*Rechtslehre*) on the basis of such a construal of the crisscrossing reflexivities that underlie any social interaction. On this, see (Maesschalck 1996).

depends on its "practical acceptance" by those in charge of respecting it and thus of ensuring its realization within social reality.

This does not mean there exist two hermetically distinct regimes for understanding the social normativity of the legal system. On the contrary, what should be pictured is, as we suggested at the outset,[14] a process of mutual adjustment of judgements about the fulfilment of the law by the groups of addressees (officials and citizens)—a process that rests on something like "crisscrossing postulations".[15] If the officials' judgement assumes the postulate that the norm's citizen-addressees are able to develop a culture of the law likely to fulfil the law as a way of life, it also assumes that the citizen-addressees hold a correlative postulate: that is, that the authority is likely to adjust to the satisfaction of the expectation that underlies its judgement about the fulfilment of the law. This performative structure of double postulation is what such modern authors as Fichte considered to lie at the origins of the concept of law. The idea is that bringing law into existence requires the organization of an inter-group learning community within the social life that is in process of building a new culture of the law as a way of life in common.[16] The relation between exo-groups reflects, as we showed above, the reciprocal relationship of conditionality—taken up in the form of a double postulation as regards the concept of law—that is constitutive of rational activity in general. In consequence, the judgement made by either group, whether the authorities or the citizen-addressees, assumes the internalized reference to the external order of the implementation of the judgements formed by the other group. The result is a conception of the culture of the normativity of law according to which, on one hand, the judgement of the public authorities assumes it is confirmed by an external belief held by the citizens in the social potential for the implementation of legal norms; and, on the other hand, this external judgement can only develop its own culture of the law as a possible way of life by relying on mediation by a capacity internal to the organization of the legal system. This reciprocal conditionality is, in our view, the key provided by a genetic conception of the culture of social learning made possible by a legal system.

Both H. Hart on one hand and J. Coleman and H. Kelsen on the other prevent themselves from opening the black box that is constituted by the operation which makes possible the emergence of such a culture for law. Moreover, they do not

---

14 See above, 9–10.

15 There is a postulation and a postulation of a postulation. Corresponding to the officials' postulation about the suitable adjustment of behaviours is the citizen-addressees' correlative postulation of an authority that makes such a postulation as the basis for its judgement about the fulfilment of law through citizens' behaviour.

16 This performative structure constitutes a teleological mode specific to a legal system's collective action. We showed above how such a performative structure is based on a more general perspective on reason, and that the construction of the concept of law is one application of this perspective. That demonstration was based on a rereading of H. Putnam's internalist realism in the context of the debate with pragmatism. A similar link, between the concept of law and the theory of science, is found in J. Fichte.

perceive the necessity for this conditionality and the form of *cooperative activity* that it entails. Failing to construe these conditions for possibility of any generalized and customary practice of obedience by the majority of citizens, H. Hart and J. Coleman end up assuming as given a form of spontaneous capability on the part of any social group to erect a form of common life, that is, the capability to form a community. Is it not the case that in so doing J. Coleman falls into the very error he wished to expose in H. Hart, which consisted of analysing the rule of recognition in terms of a "coordination convention"? From the moment when we identify the dimension of shared intention that must necessarily structure any generalized practice of obedience, the question arises of its possible realization, that is, of its conditions for possibility. And thus we come back to the question of the conditions for the realization of any form of shared intentionality, which was analysed above in the specific framework of the practice of recognition by the officials in charge of applying law.

As we have seen, by not questioning further the conditions for possibility of this general practice of obedience and recognition of the authority of officials, J. Coleman presupposes this recognition to be given. By *assuming* it, he does not perceive that it is itself the result of an operation of judgement that is internal to the collective practice of construction of a way of living together. This recognition is itself dependent on the way in which the "common" belief which gives rise to this recognition is constructed. In this sense, the practice of *recognition* by the *officials* itself depends on *an externality* that enables it and on which its concept of social fulfilment depends.

The Dual Consequences of the Limitations of Pragmatist Positivism

The Epistemological Consequence and the Normative Impact of the Concept of Law

The analyses above and especially those concerned with extending the approach to cooperative activity proposed by J. Coleman and S. Shapiro, now enable us to work through a further stage of reasoning. That is, they help us grasp the extension of the epistemological framework that the "pragmatist turn" effected by J. Coleman within theory of law calls for. As we will see, this extension results in an expanded understanding of the reflexivity of all operations of judgement (see (1) below). Consequently, the epistemological extension of the pragmatist approach allows us to look afresh at two key questions in present-day discussion in the theory of law: the question of an assessment of the Dworkinian critique of legal positivism (see (2) below); and that of the judgement of application in law, which, as we have seen, has been, for over a century, at the heart of repeated efforts to expose the inadequacies of the positivist analysis of the concept of law. The second question will also enable us to reinterpret the question of the normative meaning of the concept of law (see (3) below).

(1) The need to go beyond pragmatist epistemology It is one of J. Coleman's merits (and indeed a merit of American philosophers close to J. Coleman; e.g., B. Leiter) that

he constructs his theory of law on explicit and well-considered epistemological bases. This is how we should view his "pragmatist approach" and the four main features that distinguish it epistemologically.[17] It is surely respect for the epistemological requirement specific to the pragmatist approach that accounts for the advances made by J. Coleman's theory over those of H. Hart and R. Dworkin. Closer attention by R. Dworkin and H. Hart to the precise implications of the principles of semantic holism and the revisability of beliefs would surely have made them aware of the inadequacies of some of their theses and the need to put forward better constructed versions of them. R. Dworkin would soon have seen that conventionalism in theory of law is, contrary to what he claims, not at all incompatible with an interpretivist approach to the rule of recognition. Similarly, H. Hart would have been obliged to confront explicitly the question of the form and the conditions for possibility of a collective action (a coordination convention or cooperative activity) likely to produce, among the officials, an identical normative meaning for all. Moreover, it is J. Coleman's pragmatism, and the rejection (associated with it) of all epistemological mentalism[18] that, with the help of S. Shapiro and M. Bratman, enables him to open up the theory of law to the constraints of a non-mentalist understanding of the conditions for cooperative activity. It is here that we see the implications of what has been presented above. The extensions we proposed for J. Coleman's (and M. Bratman's) analysis of cooperative activity points to the need for a similar extension of his "pragmatist method" (Coleman 2001b: 6).

Perhaps our undertaking will elicit surprise. Is it not at first sight curious that reflection on cooperative activity should be deemed transferable to a theory of intentionality and meaning? True, just as it is easy to see that a non-mentalist approach to intentionality can be used to better understand the conditions for constructing shared meaning as part of a cooperative activity (and this is certainly

---

17 These four principal characteristics, J. Coleman (2001b: 6) indicates, drawing support here from the works of W. Quine, W. Sellars, D. Davidson, and H. Putnam, are as follows:

> (1) a commitment to semantic non-atomism; (2) the view that the content of concepts is to be explicated in terms of their inferential role in the practices in which they figure; ... (3) the view that the way in which a concept figures in one practice influences its proper application in all others, and, in this sense, practices are to be viewed holistically; and (4) a commitment to the in-principle revisability of all beliefs

We are not considering here J. Coleman's fifth characteristic (however apt it may be), namely *explanation by embodiment*, which does not seem to us to be as relevant to our purposes as the others.

18 On the link between semantic holism and the rejection of mentalism, that is, of a position which consists of thinking "of concepts as scientifically describable—psychologically real—entities in the mind or brain" (Putnam 1988: 7), see (Putnam 1988: Chapter 1: 1–18, Maesschack 2001: 242–ff).

the process followed by M. Bratman to analyse shared cooperative activity), it could appear puzzling to do the opposite and transfer the lessons from inquiry into cooperative activity to epistemological inquiry into the conditions for a judgement's semantic productivity. But this is not so. If we properly grasp the impact of the pragmatist approach as J. Coleman presents it, we see that the question of a judgement's semantic productivity is quite appropriately analysed in terms of cooperative activity.

Semantic holism and the rejection of mentalism consist precisely of considering that meanings (that is, the intentional purposes of the operation of judgement), far from constituting physical or computational entities that rest in the mind, always depend on the meaning of other factors[19] whose meaning itself cannot be assumed to be fixed and susceptible of determination through the application of formal rules. That is, as was made clear by L. Wittgenstein and H. Putnam, meaning is ultimately a function of usage and this usage necessarily takes the form of shared social practice.

Thus the fixing of meaning—or, to put it in other words, the determination of the effects of meaning produced by the operations of judgement—is a function of a form of cooperative activity within social groups intended to produce common beliefs. At the same time, this turning back of meaning towards usage and the social practices which reflect it also makes possible an understanding of the principle of the revisability of beliefs that J. Coleman has quite rightly placed at the heart of the pragmatist approach. The fact is: practices of cooperative activity by which our common representations (or beliefs) are constructed ensure their own "revisability"; that is, their adjustment in light of the "interests"—the intentionality—that "motivated" us to make use of our judgements.[20]

It is precisely on this score, however, that it proves to be necessary to transfer to J. Coleman's pragmatist approach, the reflections we conducted regarding his conception of cooperative activity. It is certainly the case that the rejection of mentalism that results from semantic holism requires a further examination of the "black box" that J. Coleman leaves unexamined and that relates to the conditions for the "revisability of beliefs". It would appear that, not just with J. Coleman but also with the contemporary pragmatist theorists J. Coleman relies on, such as H. Putnam, everything takes place as if this "collective self-revision" resulted from the immediate play of the competencies inscribed in the minds of actors in any social group. But as was seen above, assuming such "innate or immediate capabilities" for ensuring such revision comes down to making two highly problematical suppositions. On one hand, it means restoring a mentalist approach that conflicts with the holism of beliefs

19 As J. Coleman (2001b: 7, note 7) suggests, we will leave the question "open whether the whole semantic system enters into the meaning of every concept, proposition, and belief".

20 We will also leave on one side the question of the criteria of revisability which could possibly be considered as belonging to the specific (empirical, evaluative, etc.) nature of the various possible representations (Coleman 2001b: 9, note 11).

H. Putnam recognized as being logically linked to semantic holism. On the other hand, and as a result of this mentalism, there is an assumption that any operation of judgement has within itself the capabilities needed to ensure, to the extent possible, the realization of the intentionality that motivates its usage. Certainly, no social group can achieve an ideal "revision" of its beliefs. The capabilities of human reason are obviously limited. But if we do not examine the conditions for operation of the revision of beliefs, we will be led to assume that, within these limitations, the best possible revision of the beliefs of a social group is achieved solely by the immediate play of the competencies internal to the operation of judgement. As was seen above, this assumption contradicts the very principle that underlies the rejection of mentalism that is foundational to pragmatist epistemology.

Thus the rejection of mentalism entails revealing what we might call the *reflexive* dimension of any operation of judgement. This reflexive dimension does not consist, as is generally thought, of declaring the "retrospective" competency of reason to reflect back on its previous representations (that is, "to turn back on itself"). Rather, it aims to state that any "application" of reason rests on ("reflects on") or "self-affects itself" thanks to a background representation for which the operations of reason do not on their own allow a reconstruction. It is this reflexive dimension that justifies the view, expressed above, that the representation that parties to a cooperative activity *immediately* form of their intentions, interests, and preferences (that is, absent mechanisms specially organized to lead them to reconstruct their interpretive frameworks) is no more than a specific choice among other possible choices, and that *attention* to this operation of choice will thus potentially allow for constructing other possible selections. In other words, attention to the *contextual self-limitation* that results from the reflexivity that *affects* any operation of reason (Maesschalck 2001: 241–2) would allow for an extension of possibilities and thus a "maximization" of the representations deployed by participants in the cooperative activity and, thereby, "maximization" (which does not mean achieving an optimum) of the forms of cooperative activity. This expansion of possibilities would be associated with the setting up of mechanisms other than those already identified by M. Bratman. These would be specific mechanisms intended to incite the actors to revisit their initial perceptions of their preferences and examine the possible redefinition of their preferences by broadening the interpretive frameworks *immediately* deployed (Lenoble and Maesschalck 2003: 206–7). In this way, another "specific" representation of the requirements of the common intentional aim could emerge, but this one might have the "advantage" of having attained greater "expansion" than those specific forms that did not take into account the self-limitation that affects the representation of the intentionality form. Thus it would be possible to say that, besides the conditions of *responsiveness* and of *mutual support* emphasized by M. Bratman, incentives designed to ensure *reflexive learning* by agents would be needed in order to enable agents to conduct a reflexive review of the background representations that *immediately* orient their judgements. It is only when we have thus deduced the ultimate "epistemological" consequences of the pragmatist rejection of mentalism, and on that basis identified the conditions for possibility of revisability, that we can state the principle of such revision, that is, that we can assume the normative requirements inherent in the intentionality that guides this requirement for the "self-revision" of beliefs on the part of a social group to have been satisfied. In the absence of this, the principle of revisability remains a "black box" and entails, in an occult manner, the restoration of the form of epistemological mentalism that pragmatism aimed to expose. Before analysing some of the consequences that this "extension" of J. Coleman's pragmatist approach leads to, we will make a brief detour to consider both the advantages and the limitations of H. Putnam's approach, as a way of understanding his point better still.

H. Putnam is without doubt the present-day pragmatist who has most effectively sought to identify the epistemological implications of semantic holism and the rejection of mentalism that it entails. As observed above, he has brought to light the "logical" link between the holism of meaning and the holism of belief that guides the social practices by means of which meanings have their usage. Moreover, H. Putnam has never ceased to draw attention to the fact that this *holism of belief* prohibits formally fixing the procedures for defining the beliefs that govern the usage by which any judgement produces meaning effects. It is precisely in order to avoid exceeding the pragmatic limitations of reason that he postulates that the fixing of shared beliefs can only result in a procedure for common construction through public exchange.

Thus H. Putnam explicitly and illuminatingly perceived the constitutive link that exists between the semantic productivity of operations of judgement and cooperative activity. However, this line of reasoning needs to be taken further.[21] Because, if the reasoning in question is accurate, the reflexivity entailed by this holism[22] prohibits the assumption that the belief governing the meaning effect of what it leads to defining as rational requirements is constructed solely by the play of the formal constraints of discursivity. The implementation of the cooperative culture that governs the adaptation of existing beliefs to those that are entailed by reason thus requires specific conditions for possibility.[23] To assume that the mere play of the formal constraints of the ethics of discussion (that is, the mere formal

21 In this sense, therefore, H. Putnam ultimately restores a schematic approach to normative judgement. See, on this, (Maesschalck 2001: 312, Lenoble and Maesschalck 2003: 304).

22 That is, the fact that the conditions for possibility of reason's being implemented in reality are a function of something external to reason, as required by the rejection of mentalism implied by holism.

23 Thus, as we have seen, M. Bratman's insight about the play of this conditionality is valid. However, since he does not underpin it with the epistemological foundation of the reflexivity of the operation of judgement, he overlooks some of the conditions entailed by the realization of a cooperative activity, including, for instance, the condition that makes possible the "reflexive" return of each player on her or his own perception of the context. These conditions must be reflected upon both as regards the institutional setting, which must guarantee that the mechanism for deliberative negotiation provides for effective integration

play of public discussion) will itself ensure the realization of the cooperative culture that it requires, is to neutralize and disregard H. Putnam's argument concerning the impossibility of formalizing the procedures by which beliefs are fixed. To assume that the mere internal play of the formal constraints of debate ensures the adjustment of beliefs disregards the fact that the possibility for debate is itself only made possible by a shared belief that motivates participants to use it.

The necessity for such a "belief"—which the formal operations of reason on their own are not sufficient to cause to emerge—reflects the *inferentially reflexive*[24] relationship upon which the possibility for reason to make meaning (that is, the possibility for reason to be realized in the world) is dependent.[25] Any rational purpose for meaning can be realized only by submitting to a specific dependency that the formal play of reason on its own is not sufficient to guarantee. To *schematize* this capability for realization means assuming that a rule (one that must be inscribed in the minds of the actors) will guarantee its use. In allowing this assumption, we restore mentalism. The fixing of belief is itself a reflexive operation whose realization can never be assumed to have been "settled" by an assumed capability of the subject. On the contrary, unless mechanisms are put in place aimed to organize the reflexivity of this operation of the common construction of an adjustment of beliefs to the critical requirements entailed by formal reason, nothing guarantees that the application of these formal requirements will ensure the transformation of the world and of behaviours that they call for. Moreover, if this reflexive operation is not taken into account, the specifically teleological dimension implied by the adjustment of beliefs as regards inter-group relations will be missed.

of various perceptions, and as regards the capability of each intentionality of ensuring the adjustment of the perception it deploys.

24 The term "inferential" as used here indicates this reflexivity is not "retrospective" and is not enabled by means of a rule "stored" in the minds of the parties. The reflexive operation is not deductive; rather, it operates in "inferential" mode, that is, as a condition for the possibility of meaning (Lenoble and Maesschalck 2003: 201–2).

25 Determining, by means of one's reason, on an action to be accomplished means wishing to "transform" the world in order to solve a problem, that is, wishing to "rationalize" the world. But, as is immediately intuitively clear, *wishing* to rationalize the world implies an existing "culture", that is, an existing belief or adherence to a *way of life*: a life guided by reason. The transformation of the world that the action to be accomplished implies is only possible because one has accepted that the world can and should be rationalized. As J. Fichte says, any operation of reason causes an experience of shock (*Anstoss*) that derives from the impossibility of its producing effects in reality other than by relying on something that is not it. It is not reason itself that justifies belief in its own capability of transforming reality. Rather, the reverse: the application of reason in the world depends on belief in its potential fulfilment. The implementation of reason relies, in the last analysis, on belief, on insight into the power of reason to transform reality. The power of reason thus refers back reflexively to something external that is not itself.

What does theory of law gain through this "reflexive" furthering of a pragmatist approach to judgement? We will not return here to the renewed approach it makes possible to the conditions for possibility of the social practice by which the "rule of recognition", which is constitutive of the criteria for defining law in a social group and of its inter-group relations, is defined and interpretively revised. We will only mention that this furthering, which took the form of a twofold extension of the redefinition of H. Hart's thesis proposed by J. Coleman, rested directly on a better consideration of the conditions for possibility of the principle of revisability of beliefs and of a better consideration of the cooperative activity that ensures its implementation. That is why we called this analysis a genetic approach to the concept of law: that is, an approach which, in contrast to classical positivism, takes into account all the conditions of "generation" of the convention by which law is defined, in other words, the conditions for possibility[26] of this convention. We wish to show here the advance that is made possible by this 'reflexive' furthering of the pragmatist theory of judgement in comparison with the usual critiques of positivism. The fact is that, though J. Coleman quite rightly exposes their inadequacies, at the same time he risks overlooking the reformulation these critiques require, reformulations that would allow for a validation of the insight the critiques harbour. Two matters, then, merit a brief review: first, R. Dworkin's hermeneutic critique; and second, as shown at the start of this section, how to assess the insight that has driven inquiry into law since the end of the nineteenth century, namely the idea that the inadequacy of legal positivism is linked to an inadequate understanding of the operation of application in law. As we will see, the latter question will allow us at the same time to reassess the false opposition between descriptive and normative approaches to law and introduce the "epistemologically" necessary link between the conceptual analysis of law and the theory of governance.

(2) A reassessment of R. Dworkin's critique of positivism When showing the advantages J. Coleman's work offers over both R. Dworkin and H. Hart, we already identified the twofold inadequacy of R. Dworkin's critique of conventionalist positivism. First, this critique is theoretically inconsistent: contrary to what R. Dworkin believes, an incorporationist conventionalist approach, far from overlooking the interpretive dimension of the rule of recognition, entails such a dimension. It is now clear this entailment is directly associated with the pragmatist principle of the revisability of beliefs. Second, R. Dworkin's difficulty in correctly grasping the pragmatist impact of the redefinition of the positivist thesis reflects his own inability to formulate in adequately epistemological terms the nature of the

26 That is why, as we have already indicated (see above note 45) we could also call an approach of this kind to law "transcendental", in the technical sense that I. Kant and J. Fichte gave this term. Note also the extent to which this shift in relation to the positivist approach constitutes a shift analogous to the one that H. Putnam (1988: 8) identifies as being reflected epistemologically in the "holism of meaning" in relation to the "positivist attempts to show that every term we can understand can be defined in terms of a limited group of terms (the 'observation terms')".

"semantic trap" that he attacks in the positivists. This second inadequacy accounts for the way R. Dworkin himself falls back into the very error that he ascribes to positivist approaches to law and that he thought he could avoid by means of his hermeneutic approach. But it also accounts for the fact that he fails to construe his correct insight into the inadequacy of legal positivism. As has been pointed out above, that is why we argue that a certain semantic inadequacy is common to both R. Dworkin's perspective and H. Hart's and J. Coleman's positivist conventionalism.

Let us return first of all to the question of the "semantic" pitfall that R. Dworkin himself falls into even though he thought he had avoided it through recourse to the hermeneutic model.

At this stage of our examination, we are in a better position to grasp how this semantic error manifests itself. To explain our position, we can do no better than to begin with H. Putnam's critical analysis of R. Dworkin's theses. This critical analysis, which H. Putnam performed at the request of J. Coleman and B. Leiter, is highly stimulating because it seeks to formulate its critique in a directly epistemological fashion. But, while it quite rightly exposes, in other than "deconstructionist or Derridean" terms, the formalist pitfall R. Dworkin falls into, this critique remains fragile and incomplete. Let us go over H. Putnam's reasoning. Doing so will make it possible to show how the reflexive extension of H. Putnam's pragmatism that we investigated above helps deepen and reformulate this critique.

The critique developed by H. Putnam relates to the epistemological presuppositions underlying R. Dworkin's theory of "one right answer". Clearly, the theory of one right answer in no way implies a critical reappraisal of the eminently "controversial" nature of the meaning of law.

H. Putnam grants that, at any rate since *Law's Empire*,[27] "Dworkin now holds that in some cases there may not be a unique 'right answer' (reasons on both sides may be equally strong)". Thus, it is quite true that R. Dworkin has abandoned the principle of bivalence, that is, "the logical principle that a statement is either true or false—tertium non datur". However, H. Putnam rightly points out, "*this* sort of failure of a unique right answer to exist is ubiquitous in language, and has nothing to do with the (unreasonably strong) form of bivalence that R. Dworkin continues to accept". What then is the form of bivalence that R. Dworkin continues to accept? "Dworkin's present position … is that for an answer to be 'right' just is for it to be the answer that is best supported by reasons;[28] if the fact that there may

27 It is true that R. Dworkin's position was less clear in *Taking Rights Seriously* (Dworkin 1977). On the evolution in R. Dworkin's theory of one right answer, see (Coleman 1995: 48–54).

28 Note that this description by H. Putnam of R. Dworkin's position is corroborated by something R. Dworkin (1986: 412) himself says explicitly in *Law's Empire*. Having said that he had obviously never "devised an algorithm for the courtroom", R. Dworkin continues as follows: "I have not said that there is never one right way, only different ways, to decide a hard case".

not be a right answer (in this sense) in some cases (because there may be a 'tie' in the strength of the reasons) meant that the logical principle of bivalence had to be given up, then the fact that there may be no right answer to the question 'Who is the tallest kid in the class?' because two or more kids may be tied for tallest would already mean that bivalence has to be given up!; bivalence would have never been accepted as a logical principle in the first place[29] if *this* sort of thing were a counterexample." But, as H. Putnam (1995: 76–7) points out:

> [W]hat *is* a problem for the principle of bivalence is that it entirely abstracts from—in fact denies—the possibility of what is called "second order vagueness"—that is, the possibility that, not only may there be cases in which there is no determinate right answer, but that it may be *indeterminate which those cases are* (where vagueness ends may itself be vague, in other words).[30]

What H. Putnam is exposing is thus the presupposition of the existence of a rule that would allow us, at some level, to formalize interpretive practice, that is, the operation constitutive of meaning.

Is Putnam's critique accurate? H. Putnam perceives that R. Dworkin, at a certain level in his reasoning, overlooks not the holism of meaning but the holism of belief; that is, the concept that there is no formal procedure for fixing belief. But this epistemological inadequacy in R. Dworkin cannot be formulated in the terms used by H. Putnam. R. Dworkin definitely recognizes what H. Putnam calls the "second order of vagueness". He would be the first to acknowledge that the "controversial" nature of law implies that we cannot determine what the easy and the hard cases are by means of a formal rule. He acknowledges that such a distinction is itself the result of an interpretive practice and consequently not subject to formalization. Thus, it is not at the second level of this "second order of vagueness" that the "reformalization of the normative operation" that R. Dworkin falls victim to is manifested. But, this third level is inaccessible to H. Putnam because, as indicated above, his understanding of the consequences associated with a "non-mentalist" approach to the operation of judgement is inadequate. That is, such an approach makes it impermissible for reason to find within itself

29 That is, the kind of bivalence associated with the thesis "that for an answer to be right just is for it to be the answer that is best supported by reasons" (Putnam 1995: 69–81).

30 This questioning by H. Putnam of the principle of bivalence obviously does not imply his acceptance of a sceptical position. On this score, H. Putnam, while critiquing R. Dworkin philosophically, shares his opposition to R. Rorty, or to what R. Dworkin (1986: 151) somewhat inappropriately calls "legal pragmatism". This shared opposition to a "nihilist" scepticism also explains why H. Putnam makes the following statement about R. Dworkin: "Far from seeing himself as more 'metaphysically realist' than Rorty, Dworkin, if I am right, would see himself as more metaphysically innocent (in a good sense) than Rorty; but Dworkin's innocence is obscured by his almost complete failure to discuss any of the metaphysical issues that Coleman lists", that is, issues relating to the theory of truth.

the resources necessary for its own semantic productivity (that is, necessary for its ability to take effect in social reality). Since H. Putnam himself has restored a mentalist presupposition (in relation to the capability of the social group to "automatically" ensure the revisability of its beliefs) and thus underestimates the extent of the reflexivity of all judgement, he does not see that it is at this pragmatic level that R. Dworkin re-formalizes the operation of normative judgement.

R. Dworkin's hermeneutic approach does try to respect the link formed between meaning and usage, just as it tries to take the holism of usage into account. However, by not construing its epistemological conditions sufficiently, he does not see the reformalization of the operation of reason that his "mentalism" entails. Where does this mentalism manifest itself? As an alternative to the hypothesis of the rule of recognition, R. Dworkin defines the conditions for legality by reference to a substantial morality assumed to be shared by the social group and to an idealized judge who would be able to ensure its ongoing reinterpretation in light of the requirements for adjustment to transformations in the social context. The judge is supposed to be capable of deducing the meaning of the law from the requirements internal to the "institutional morality" of the group to which she or he belongs. R. Dworkin's hermeneutic approach assumes there are given *rules in the mind of the judge* that enable the judge to subsume various specific situations under general categories of institutional morality (principles). That is, R. Dworkin *mentalizes* the normative judgement approach by having those rules inscribed in the judge's mental capabilities that make it possible to deduce the normative meanings of law from the requirements of institutional morality and reflect in those meanings (to paraphrase P. Ricoeur) the injunctions of the real (historically designed).[31]

---

31 See (Ricoeur 1990: 404–5). This re-formalization exists in fact in other forms, which J. Coleman has clearly perceived. As we know, J. Coleman accepts that law has an interpretive dimension. He explicitly acknowledges the descriptive light shed by hermeneutic approaches. R. Coleman points out that R. Dworkin very likely provides an adequate theory of the revision of the meanings of law by judges. But even in connection with the description of the function of judgement, J. Coleman wishes to radicalize the hermeneutic approach. R. Dworkin, J. Coleman says, ascribes to hermeneutics unwarranted powers for determining a single meaning. With his theory of the one right answer, he underestimates the significance of indeterminacy in law. Instead of assuming a holistic rationality in law, as R. Dworkin does, it would be preferable to ascribe to law a simply local or partial rationality. As J. Coleman (2001b: 168) says: "Understanding what the law is or means is not the same kind of project as understanding an individual's behaviour—linguistic or otherwise. In order to attribute content to law, we do not have to treat all the law as consistent or as satisfying all the basic rules of deductive logic. Again, local rationality may be enough. Local rationality certainly fits better with the phenomenology of judging. Even if Dworkin is right that judges must posit the working hypothesis that there are right answers to legal disputes, judges find themselves, more often than Dworkin acknowledges, adopting the view that in fact there is no determinate legal answer to the case at hand". R. Dworkin's description of legal hermeneutic poses still other difficulties,

In still assuming a homogenous substantive morality as given within the social group, along with a judge who is capable of providing for its ongoing reinterpretation in light of the requirements for adjustment to transformations in the social context, R. Dworkin assumes a rule of reason capable of guaranteeing realization of the "right way" by which the meaning of the normative requirements within the social group will be optimized. It is just such a presupposition that H. Putnam hopes to expose as philosophically incorrect. As M. Maesschalck (2001: 179) has shown in connection with H. Putnam's internalist realism, this project in effect implies not only the immanence of interpretive practice within belief, but also the impossibility for interpretive practice to define standard procedures for fixing beliefs. This is just what R. Dworkin overlooks.[32] It is also what accounts for the fact that he *formalizes* the operation of judgement and, consequently, falls back into the "semantic" error that he believed he was exposing in positivist thinking.

It is on this score as well that the advance made by J. Coleman's pragmatist redefinition of the rule of recognition appears. As we saw, this redefinition subordinates the ability of judges to define the rule to the existence of institutional mechanisms that make possible their own cooperative production of a uniform interpretation. Thus, it could be said that J. Coleman tempers R. Dworkin's epistemological internalism by subordinating the assumed capability of the social actors—in this instance, judges—to the externality of the incentive of the institutional mechanisms that guarantee the possibility of shared intentionality.[33] However, as has been seen, this way of understanding the "limitations" of epistemological internalism—and its institutional expression—continues to be insufficiently expanded and therefore reflects the re-emergence of a semantic error. The fact is that J. Coleman's analysis, like R. Dworkin's, also ultimately rests on the "mentalist" assumption of the group's presumed given capability to ensure the conditions for satisfying the requirements of governance by law. A brief examination of this question will enable us to see how our epistemological observations will help better construe the recurring insight within legal reflection that positivist analysis has an inadequate analysis of the operation of the application of normative judgement.

including that of accounting for the role of "authoritative statements", which in R. Dworkin are merely "raw materials for the theory of legal content" (Coleman 2001b: 166).

32 Another way of identifying this epistemological weakness in R. Dworkin is to point to the links between his thinking and W. Quine's theory (to which, in fact, he makes explicit reference at least twice in *Law's Empire* (Dworkin 1986)). As H. Putnam (1990: 283) rightly notes, W. Quine's position ends by ignoring the link between "meaning holism" and "the holistic character of belief fixation".

33 This subordination refers back, as we have seen, to a kind of implicit teleology of the cooperative commitment on which the success of this subordination depends, and which articulates it directly to the other social groups concerned by the promise of fulfilment that guides this commitment.

(3) Positivism and the question of the judgement of application: The normative significance of the concept of law Contrary to what is claimed by critiques of positivism in various forms, whether sociological or, as more recently, hermeneutic, the conventionalist approach in no way implies a denial of the interpretivist dimension of judicial work. And yet, subject to reformulation, a valid insight underlies this recurring critique.

The extension of the approach to pragmatism developed by J. Coleman allows for the exposure of a deeper weakness in the understanding of the operation of the application of judgement than that related to his approach to the operation of judgement. It is symptomatic that in theory of law the discussion of the operation of the application of judgement appears not to notice that the question of the application is not limited to the application of an assumed existing norm. The meaning given to the operation of the application of a rule is reduced to the classical concept of application corresponding to that customarily used in ordinary language when it is said a judge "applies a rule" or there exists a technical problem of "applying" a certain normative guideline deemed to be desirable. The operation of application is assumed to be restricted to the scenario in which the rule, or the normative orientation, is given. But in limiting the question to this formulation, we make it impossible to formulate the problem in more epistemological terms. There is a more fundamental operation of application on which production of the norm (or determination of the normative orientation) itself depends. The choice of norm is in itself already the result of an operation of application. The "form" (representation) taken by the norm results from the "application" of the rational requirement inherent in the activity of judgement that members of a social group have decided to deploy in order to solve a problem of collective coordination. The question raised by this operation of application thus concerns the conditions for possibility of the operation by which reason (the activity of judgement) produces meaning effects in reality, that is, "is applied" or "is implemented" in social reality.

Must we assume that this application is wholly determined, in the last analysis, by the formal rules of rational activity (which would necessarily be stored in the mind)? On this view, the operations of application and of the justification of judgement are governed by *the same resources* and thus exist in a *symmetrical* relationship. It is clear, then, that this perspective is that of mentalism. It should be noted that this position does not prevent the recognition of a degree of autonomy inherent in the interpretive activity specific to the operation of application.[34] Such a recognition of the "reversibility" of the operation of application and the operation of justification does not necessarily entail abandoning a symmetrical approach to the operation of judgement, that is, the mentalist point of view. The hermeneutic theory laid out by R. Dworkin is a good example of this.

34 As we have seen, acknowledging an autonomous dimension to the interpretive activity of the authorities in charge of applying the rules of law (including the rule of recognition) has become a truism to which everyone in the field of theory of law makes obeisance.

Must we then assume, in contrast, as would be entailed by a *non-mentalist* understanding of the semantic productivity of judgement, that the conditions necessary to such productivity (and thus to the application of reason in the world) cannot be reduced to the formal rules of rational activity? If so, it would be understood that reason does not have within itself the conditions for its application within the world, that is, the capability for producing meaning effects. From this second perspective, which is the one opened up by any holistic or pragmatist approach to the activity of judgement, we bring to light the *asymmetrical reversibility*[35] of the operation of reason. While the two operations reference each other, the resources needed for the operation of application are not symmetrical to the formal rules on which the operation of rational justification depends. This "asymmetric reversibility" merely reflects what was called above the "reflexivity" of any operation of reason, which is the sole protector against the pitfalls of mentalist epistemology. That is, the activity of reason "reflects" a "perception" that reason itself cannot justify through its own formal rules, but that nevertheless depends on reason for its implementation, in other words, for the "choice" of following a way of life governed by "reason". Could we then say that reason reflects on itself in the sense that it reflects what it gives "itself", namely the choice of reason as a way of life, the choice of a world understood to be "rationalizable", "transformable" according to the requirement dictated by the formal rules of reason? This reflexivity, laid out above in a speculative manner, is even easier to understand if we translate it into the "concrete" terms of the theory of norms. As will be seen, we come back here to certain views already formulated above regarding M. Bratman's theory of cooperative activity.

A non-mentalist reflexive approach to judgement can only be achieved if we open up the "black box" that has been left unexplored by current theories of norms because of their restrictive approach to the operation of the application of normative judgement. This black box relates to the conditions for realization of the purpose underlying any activity of norm development. This purpose consists, from the outset, of perceiving a problem to be solved, of defining the "rationalizing" of the world required in order to solve the problem according to the conception of the norm held by its authors. Clearly, it has become common sense to point to the limitations of the cognitive capabilities of human reason. But the "contextual" limitation we wish to draw attention to here, which derives from the reversible and asymmetrical nature of the operation of application, is of another kind.[36] This asymmetry, in fact, implies that the application of a norm within social reality

35 This expression was coined by M. Maesschalck (2001: 180 and 244). On this, see (Lenoble and Maesschalck 2003: Chapter 1, 3.1.1: 85–7).

36 Certainly, numerous authors have already incorporated a limit to rationality at that level of formality (for example, Gödel's theorem; procedural rationality in J. Habermas's sense, allowing for an ever possible renewal of the argument; and procedural rationality in H. Simon's sense). But the limitations of the formalism of reason also exist on a second level and take on a meaning different than that of "limitations in cognitive capabilities". To

necessitates the deployment of resources that are not supplied by the formal operations of reason on their own.

Underlying any rational decision or voluntary action are two (not just one, as is usually assumed) operations of selection or choice. There is obviously the choice of the transformation that would appear to be called for rationally (that is, the solution deemed to be most rational in solving the problem). But this choice is itself possible only because it rests on a prior operation of selection related to the way of "perceiving" the "context" in relation to which the problem to be solved will be defined, and the *use* made of the solutions envisaged by the actors called upon to apply them, will be determined. Here, the asymmetry is evident in the emergence of the background that any operation of justification relies on. This second operation of selection—on which the first depends—is not solved by the first. It thus calls for a specific "attention" if it is hoped to fulfil the objective sought, which consists of accomplishing the best rational action possible to deal with the problems that need to be solved. The fact is, no "transformation"—and thus no *effective realization of the intentional purpose specific to every norm*—is possible unless the second conditionality is taken into account and a specific procedure for the adjustment and construction of a common perception of the context is organized. What is at issue is the procedural organization of the adjustment of existing perceptions by the actors involved in order to name the meaning and the nature of the inadequacies to be settled and the problems to be solved.

Thus, two processes that cannot be dissociated from each other, but that usually are confused with each other or wipe each other out, must be articulated.

First, we have to guarantee the necessary consideration of the formal rules on which depends the rational acceptability of the solutions to be implemented in order to deal with the inadequacies of existing life situations.

But determining the meaning effects that the solutions to be constructed will produce depends on what will be selected at the outset as the context on the basis of which the actors involved perceive inadequacies to be solved and solutions to be constructed. To assume this context is given, or that the actors involved will immediately and naturally identify their own interests and the meaning of the new constraints that motivate the search for new solutions, is to overlook precisely the structure specific to every judgement, namely the fact that the adjustment of perceptions does not depend solely on the formal rules of judgement. As well, it cannot be assumed that the "perception of context" is identical among the various authors and addressees of the norm. Nor can it be assumed that their common adherence to the solution deemed to be the most rationally acceptable automatically entails a convergent transformation of their perceptions of the context and, consequently, the harmonization of the motivations for the use they will make of the norm to which they adhere.

---

limit oneself solely to the formal process of the justification for my rule for action is not sufficient to take into account this rule's conditions for semantic productivity.

A second specific activity must thus be organized in order to organize a common perception of the context. This will in turn make it possible to increase the number of "possibilities" on the basis of which the solutions deemed the most rational for dealing with the inadequacies of the "context" will be selected. This second order of the conditionality of action is usually wiped out because it is presented as obvious or assumed to be determinable *a priori*. If we assume as given, this capability for actors in the collective action to adjust their common perceptions to the "requirements of context", problems of governance clearly appear to become less complicated. Such an assumption implies from the outset that the actors have the capabilities to translate their normative expectations into the effectiveness of action through their interactions. The assumption of a *mental capacity* (a *mentalism*) for translating into reality the goals pursued guarantees this equilibrium solution. It is understood that the "content assumed to be given" of the intended goals of the actors in an action will be capable of being translated into the effective content of the action. But to assume such a capability as given consists precisely of overlooking the reflexivity of the operation of normative judgement. In contrast, a better construal of the *theory of norms* entails invalidating this assumption and consequently postulating the need for incentives likely to cause the emergence of this "capability" of identifying normative objectives to be pursued in common. On this capability depends as well the possibility for actors to transform their own teleological relationship with the context and redefine their identity according to other normative expectations.

It is in order to respect this epistemological requirement (which exists within both theory of judgement and theory of norms) that we have suggested extending J. Coleman's pragmatist approach to the concept of law and replacing the positivist approach with a *genetic* approach to the conventionality of law. This would allow for a different way of illuminating both the question of the descriptive or normative status of the theory of law and the analysis by J. Coleman (and more broadly the positivists) of the conditions for the existence of law within a social group. Granted, we cannot consider subordinating the definition of law to some external "normativity", as is suggested by classical natural law theory. No one could seriously contest the impossibility for theoreticians to define "the" rationally desirable way of life. That is not at stake here.[37] Moreover, even in its internalist version, R. Dworkin's critique of positivist "descriptivism" is hard to accept because in itself it fails to take into account the "reconstructive and descriptive" status of its own analysis of the concept of law.

---

37 Of course, this critical challenge is not intended to contest the conventional nature of the social practice by which the "trust" and the "effective respect" accorded to the official authorities in a social group are constructed. It seems to us clear that, for the purposes of the conceptual analysis of law, it is not a question of subjecting law to dependency on some outmoded form of belief in natural law which would seek to define the conditions of legitimacy of the social contract. The issue here is of an entirely different nature.

From this perspective, J. Coleman (2001b: 180) is right to point out, in R. Dworkin, "the confusion between the content of the concept of law and the content of the law of a particular community". On the other hand, however, because of his positivist, non-genetic, approach to the conventionality of law, J. Coleman fails to perceive the normative dimension internal to the content of the concept of law and the irreducibility of this normative dimension to a prescriptive dimension. By "prescriptive" dimension we mean the "distinctive feature of law's governance", which "is that it purports to govern by *creating reasons for action*" (2001b: 71). By "normative dimension" we mean the requirement for procedural conditions allowing for a "maximized[38] and common" reconstruction of the representations deployed by the creation of these "reasons for action".

These conditions, as we pointed out in analysing the conditions for cooperative activity, are associated with the conditions for realizing the common intentionality aimed at by the social practice of recognition that is constitutive of the conventionality of law. Moreover, as we have just seen, an adequately epistemological grasp of the theory of norms entails a proper construal of the nature of the teleological purpose borne by every norm. After all, is it not symptomatic that J. Coleman, adopting M. Bratman's analysis relative to the internal conditions for the satisfaction of the shared intentionality that defines cooperative activity, appears not to adopt M. Bratman's distinction between "prepackaged cooperation" and "shared cooperative activity" (Bratman 1992: 339)? True, M. Bratman does not entirely reconstitute the normative requirement entailed by his own rejection of any mentalist approach to shared intention, but he does preserve the idea of a possibility of realization "in variable and progressive extension" of the requirement entailed by such a form of action. This same idea of "degrees of progressive expansion" is just what we wish to radicalize here in order to show that it is entailed epistemologically and in order to draw from it consequences relative to a normative dimension internal to the content of the concept of law. As may be observed, a normativity of this kind is neither substantive nor procedural in the sense given to these terms by J. Habermas and J. Rawls. The procedural entailment that is inherent in it remains internal to a conventionalist approach to law and results from a "descriptive or speculative" grasp of the conditions for possibility of the operation of judgement by which the rule of recognition specific to any social group is defined and interpreted.

Finally, the highlighting of this normative dimension specific to the "content of the concept of law" (and not of the "content of law of a specific social community") allows for one last extension of J. Coleman's reasoning. That is, it requires an extension of the conditions that H. Hart and J. Coleman define as "conditions" that must be satisfied in order to satisfy the requirements of social regulation by law. At the same time, this makes it possible to renounce the somewhat idealized image that the positivist approach results in, which consists of assuming that, since

38 As was seen above, the maximization, that is, the expansion of representations, does not mean the search for an illusory "optimal representation".

the establishment of the formal structures of the modern state, there were brought together the conditions required for the regulation of our societies. This assumption is clearly linked to the fact that J. Coleman, in line with dominant positivist approaches, considers the existence of law, beyond the "practice of recognition of law" by the authorities in charge of applying it, is exclusively a function of the *effectiveness* of respect for the decisions of these officials by the majority of the population. We will not here repeat our discussion of the weaknesses of the analysis of the "practice of respect for and of adherence to the organization of a way of life" in terms of simple *empirical effectiveness*.[39] But it is interesting at this juncture to highlight to what extent it also contributes to an *idealized* representation of the form of collective action by which a group aims to regulate its behaviours. *Idealized*[40] because the form of empirical effectiveness that H. Hart and J. Coleman (and H. Kelsen) invoke is defined in such a manner that it is assumed to be realized within the very large majority of modern societies. Outside the extreme and transitory case of revolution, the effectiveness of a political power over a territory is understood by them to reflect the coming together at one time, of all the conditions that guarantee the accomplishment of the regulatory function of law. With the exception of crisis situations and times of temporary destabilization, the conditions for satisfying governance by law are assumed to have been brought together from the moment that the institutional structures of the modern state are set up. This is understood to be independent, of course, of the forms of government

39 As was seen above, no majority practice of respect for an institutional structure can be analysed outside the intention and the perception of a form of common life deemed to be rationally acceptable. We are also in a position to see that R. Dworkin correctly perceives this weakness in positivist thinking, even though, because of his own epistemological weakness, he fails to construe it adequately. It is just this weakness of the positivist position that R. Dworkin seeks to reveal when he says that every legal system is a form of institutional morality. In so saying, his aim is quite rightly to point out that ultimately the existence of law does not depend on a factual practice independent of an intended acceptable way of life, a mode of collective action respecting good reasons to act. But in just the same way that it is astonishing for J. Coleman to fail to apply his own model of "shared cooperative activity" to the practice of "effective respect for law by the majority of the population", it is equally astonishing for R. Dworkin to fail to apply his "interpretivist" model to the determination of this institutional morality. R. Dworkin takes as given the institutional morality that it would fall to judges to adjust interpretively in light of the constraints of reality. It is this that accounts for R. Dworkin's somewhat naïve ascription of omnipotence to the judge in the judge's mission of "saying" what the best possible representation of institutional morality in a constantly changing context would require.

40 Note that the idealization characteristic of the positivist approach recalls, for all their differences, the kind of "mentalist" belief that the idealized and illusory omnipotence R. Dworkin assigns to the judge expresses. Moreover, even though our respective arguments follow different paths and end in distinct approaches to the "normative" dimension of the concept of law, the observations made here seem to us to have a certain affinity with S. Perry's insights in revealing a kinship between the "normative" presuppositions of the approaches to the concept of law developed by H. Hart and R. Dworkin (Perry 1997, 2000).

or legitimacy (e.g., whether dictatorial or democratic) that they serve. If this is put in somewhat more technical language, it could be said, with J. Coleman, that:

> regardless of the diversity of their aims or purposes, the shape and structure of mature legal systems are similar in the ways Hart claims they are: that is, as consisting in primary and secondary rules, including especially a rule of recognition, rules of change, and rules of adjudication (Coleman 2001b: 145).[41]

This formal organization of the state is thus supposed to embody exclusively the institutional conditions for the emergence of the culture of law that the fulfilment of the function of "guiding conduct" depends on.

Given that the condition for respect for the decisions of officials by the majority of the population are externalized in the form of an empirical effectiveness, they are not analysed as the meaning effect of a collective action with the purpose of a common perception of the "reasons for action". The possible "constraints" that would result from an analysis of the conditions for possibility of the operation of judgement deployed by this form of collective action are thus not analysed for their own sake. *The result is that the function of regulation ascribed to law is assumed to be implemented independently of any specific institutional mechanism that would organize and make possible, at the teleological level, the production of the norm in order to link it to its final addressees, that is, citizens.* This question of institutional mechanisms is reflected upon exclusively in connection with the officials in charge of the operations of producing and applying the rules. The question of the necessary adjustment of our current mechanisms of government in order to improve the conditions for citizen participation in these operations cannot be posed or understood as resulting from a correct theoretical construal of their conditions for possibility.

Undoubtedly, as has been seen, a "genetic approach" to the conventionality of law and the "normative" dimension of the concept of law entail questioning such an idealized image of the conditions for fulfilment of governance of our modern societies by law. But is our "epistemological" reasoning not supported "sociologically" through the mere observation of the concrete dynamics of our societies? And does an observation of this kind not oblige us to perform a more nuanced analysis of the conditions required for law to be "capable of guiding conduct" (Coleman 2001b: 145)? We are witnessing in many spheres today an effort to reflect on the rearrangement of the procedures for constructing normative solutions to make up for the weaknesses that our accustomed procedures result in. Where would these inefficiencies come from if not the fact that the *use* made by

41 It is not very significant for our purposes here that J. Coleman, without specifying other conditions necessary to the exercise of the conduct guidance function that defines law, postulates (2001b: 146–7) that these conditions do not prevent the rule of recognition from taking an "inclusive" form, that is, a form which includes "political morality" as a condition of legality.

the addressees of norms results in these unintended consequences? Let us put it in other words. The meaning given to norms when they are applied in social reality (that is, when they produce meaning effects) tends to make those norms inoperative or ineffective with respect to the normative objective that the authorities wished to achieve. The whole discussion that has taken place in "theory of governance" over the past four decades (whether in economics, with the purpose of strengthening the mechanisms for market coordination and contractual cooperation, or in political science, with the purpose of strengthening participatory and deliberative mechanisms) has without question emerged from this same necessity to adjust our modes of constructing norms in order to better take into account the representations of these norms by their addressees, and thus the "motivations" on which the use that will be made of them depends. In particular, what this current reflection reveals is that wherever divergences are greatest among perceptions of the problem legal norms seek to resolve, accustomed procedures for constructing and applying norms prove "ineffective" for guaranteeing an adequate solution to the problem. The "capability" of the public authorities to construct the solution and identify the "expected" meaning of the norm is thus itself dependent on a "recognition" of this meaning by the ultimate addressees of the norm. In such conditions of marked dissension, one can understand the emphasis increasingly placed by current theory of governance on the necessity to inquire into the mechanisms best suited to incorporating this "condition of recognition" and make possible the cooperative construction of common meaning. All this makes it clear that the question of "trust" or "recognition by citizen-addressees of law" cannot be reduced to the classic question of the assumed allegiance by these citizens to the officials in charge of applying law (in other words, to the condition for effectiveness identified by H. Kelsen, H. Hart, and J. Coleman). This way of understanding "recognition" by citizens proves reductive and inadequate to take into account the condition of "trust", "motivation", or "perception" on which the operation of a norm's semantic productivity within social reality depends. In contrast, as we have indicated, the teleology inherent in the requirement for norms' normativity assumes that the expandable nature of the reflexivity assumed by the rule of recognition is established, that is, that the practical acceptance of norms by citizen-addressees is taken into account in the organization of mechanisms of governance.

The Second Consequence: The Opening Up of Theory of Law to Theory of Governance

Is it justifiable epistemologically for the conceptual analysis of law to remain sealed off from the "normative" issue of the necessary rearrangement of our mechanisms of governance? Is it justified or not for the philosophy of law to remain autonomous from normative inquiry into the theory of collective action that sits at the heart of present-day research in the social sciences?

It is easy to see that these questions call for a negative response. However significant the advances brought about by recent hermeneutic approaches to the function of judgement and the pragmatist redefinition of the rule of recognition, a "more reflexive" extension of the operation of collective regulation that defines law is clearly necessary. True, legal positivism has sought progressively to adapt its definition of law so that it better takes account of the function of the application of rules. As we saw, in the words of L. Green:

> [B]y the mid-twentieth century, … its emphasis on legislative institutions was replaced by a focus on law-applying institutions such as courts, and its insistence of the role of coercive force gave way to theories emphasising the systematic and normative character of law.

Thus, it could be said that the theory of law, by taking into account the reversibility of the operation of application, has sought progressively to take on board the reflexivity of normative judgement by which a social group seeks to act upon itself in order to regulate its behaviours. In internalizing the Kelsenian basic norm (*Grundnorm*) and emphasizing the reflexive dimension of the rule of recognition, H. Hart brought about decisive advances. Similarly, the pragmatist redefinition of the rule of recognition advanced by J. Coleman is part of the same trend. Moreover, this "pragmatist" turn reflects the will to incorporate into the definition of law, in a rigorous manner, the "holism of use" that R. Dworkin perceives but, as H. Putnam observed, fails to analyse epistemologically.

However, because it retains a symmetrical approach to reversibility, the theory of reflexivity deployed by these various approaches to law always ends, at some point or another, by ascribing to the social body a "capability" of satisfying the rational expectations implied by its regulatory purpose. The traces of this "mentalist" presupposition, which, in the last analysis, is associated with a schematic approach to normative judgement, accounts for the exclusive focus on the function of the application of rules by the judge (or by officials). In his somewhat naive idealization of the judge as an organ that guarantees the self-adjustment of the requirements of the social group's internal moral code, R. Dworkin provides an obvious example of this. But J. Coleman's difficulty in penetrating the persisting black box of the conditionality of the "recognition" of the rules by the members of the social group reproduces an analogous epistemological error.

What is needed is a supplementary conceptual effort. The pragmatist turn initiated by J. Coleman must be extended, because it carries within it a requirement that the positivist approach of the rule of recognition does not respect. In an especially fruitful manner, J. Coleman's pragmatism already clearly reveals that the rule of social recognition harbours more than one mentalist model of belief embodied in a convention. The belief embodied in social conventions is nothing more than a by-product of the climate of trust built up by the kind of cooperative commitment undertaken by the officials.[42] From this perspective, the idea that the formal condition for normativity could reside in a *rule of judgement* followed by a group of actors is no longer in play. Henceforward, what is at issue is conceiving a *rule of commitment* supported by the actors themselves, one that cannot be understood solely as defining roles. Only the practical effects to be expected from this kind of commitment are likely to guarantee the effectiveness of the system in its potential for social governance. The question of the normativity of the law then shifts away from the formal coherence of its semantic content towards its pragmatic potential for governance as a social institution. This potential for governance depends on an effect of collective commitment by the actors involved, which could not be expressed by a mental model of adherence to validity requirements.

It remains to be seen, however, whether, as J. Coleman says, in thematizing this commitment in the form of a rule of cooperation to be applied solely to the joint activity of a specific group in society (the group of officials responsible for applying the law), we manage to allow the pragmatist extension of the concept of law its full epistemological impact. One possible objection, indeed, is that in proceeding thus, we are once again endorsing a mentalist approach that consists of assuming that the function of adjusting behaviours depends solely on the application of a common rule. Recall that this was the mentalism that justified pragmatism's criticism of H. Hart. In conceiving the rule of recognition on the model of a coordination agreement, H. Hart assumed that merely resorting to a mental model (judgement) makes possible the adoption of a rule of behaviour (a coordination agreement). *In opposing this mentalist option, pragmatism passes from the contents of a rule to the practical effects likely to result from a method of action. The difference in approach to the "rule" is key. In a mentalist perspective, the rule is viewed as semantic content. In a pragmatist perspective, the rule is viewed as a procedure for action.* This fundamental difference resides in the role ascribed to the capacity for action. The procedure for action seeks to elicit a capacity for action within collective practice, whereas the semantic rule seeks solely to elicit the implementation of a capability already assumed to be available in individuals' minds.

In line with the "procedure for action" approach to the rule, pragmatists defended the idea in political philosophy that adequate kinds of participation could not be determined in advance, independently of social experiments and the formation of the actors' identities made possible by these experiments.

This, however, is not the position that J. Coleman's perspective arrives at. By limiting the cooperative approach[43] strictly to the officials group, we prevent

42 Judges undertake not solely to act according to the formal rules that guarantee the legal order. They also sign on to a system of cooperation with other judges, in solidarity with these other judges in the maintenance and development of the legal system (Coleman 2001b: 97).

43 Let us be clear: The rule of cooperation put forward by J. Coleman does not really go beyond the usual level of the rules for cooperative search for the truth in deliberativism,

ourselves from broaching the question of the fulfilment of law's potential for social governance in these experimentalist terms. In the "positivist" perspective endorsed by J. Coleman, it is necessary to dissociate the role played by the officials group, guided by informed consent to the rule of law, from the role played by other users of the law, guided by obedience motivated by the possible effects of sanctions. Society can develop the capabilities for governance of its legal system to the extent that a group of officials maintains the system's coherence and its adjustment to social circumstances, whereas the rest of the system's users view themselves as constrained to obey it. This constraint results from a multitude of possible combinations, ranging from widespread confidence in a system that is equitable for all to widespread repression in a system that favours a minority exclusively. From users' perspective, obedience to rules viewed as reliable predictors of sanctions is sufficient. It is not necessary for the user to recognize, by virtue of a capacity for critical acceptance, certain kinds of conduct as models of general behaviour (H. Hart 1994: 115). The predictive judgement alone about the system's expected efficiency is assumed to allow the anticipation of the rules' acceptance. The adjustment in behaviour required by the fulfilment of the normative decisions made by the official authorities is assumed to operate by means of the application of a "semantic" rule, the rule whose content corresponds to the one that justifies the predictive judgement of citizen-addressees. The mere anticipation of the efficiency of the regime of sanctions, the mere observation of the general practice of obedience, suffices to ensure the fulfilment of the potential for governance of the law as determined by the officials.

In contrast, from a radically pragmatist perspective (which we term *genetic*), the existence of the law refers back to a structure for action that challenges law's capacity for social guidance. It is then a question of a set of practices that are to be *tried out*, based on a commitment by a given group in society, with the aim of coming back round to the reflexivity of the society as a whole in relation to involvement in the good governance of the legal system. The internal requirement for good governance implies (entails the inference of) a requirement for social experimentation that is impossible to restrict solely to the officials group. Given this, the conception of the social authority of law must evolve. It can no longer be a question of purely and simply dissociating the world of practitioners, with their informed consent, from that of users, with their assumed capacity for obedience. The capability for cooperative commitment can no longer be understood on the model of the professional-code-based development of a specialized group in society. In the same vein, the capability of users can no longer be reduced to that

even though its content seems open to going beyond that level. Is there anything other, in the rule of commitment of practitioners in the legal system, than a cooperative framework for the search for justice that allows for the strengthening of each practitioner's individual capacity for action? Note that we saw above how, even at the level of its procedural design, the proposed approach to the cooperative action remained flawed from the perspective of a critique of mentalism.

"external" judgement in which respect for the rule is determined by a predictive or accustomed relationship with its power to sanction.

The cooperative commitment that is at issue from now on subsumes all the groups in a society, to the extent that it is the bearer of a strong teleological requirement, that of the capability of trying out the making and recognition of law within a decentralized model of authority.[44] In this model, responsibility regarding the legal system's objectives and mutual support by various roles (from practitioners to users) must be shared and must therefore be capable of adjustment. The process of creating and recognizing the social authority of law must thus be conceived differently. After first being concentrated within the practice of a group, this authority must then broaden out to all members of the society, because the practice of justice entails the inference of a *shared destination* that concerns all members of the society, the destination of a just society.

The pragmatist turn must be viewed in the light of this radical requirement, or else it may not succeed in surmounting the mentalist presuppositions that it set out to expose. Conceiving of the rule as a method of action entails this expanded experimentalist and reflexive approach. It's a matter of experimenting, that is, of taking into account the creation of individuals' capacity for self-destination, of their capacity for commitment and cooperation in a process to establish modes of "good life". The pragmatist turn, when understood in the light of its radical requirements, leads to a tension between the *given*, *implicit* moral "we" and the *potential*, *explicit* "we"—that of the community to be built, which itself requires a power of social creation in order to pass from a centralized social process aiming for adherence to a decentralized social process aiming for the coming together of the various groups in the society. This dynamic of social creation reflects what we call the *genetic* approach, because it reflects the fact that it can only result from a process of action that could never be formalized by the semantic content of a rule that would allow for defining its conditions for implementation. This requirement for experimentation in the inter-group relations entailed by the legal system's destination rests on an inferential conception of the governance of social systems, under which good governance of a regulatory system can only be assessed by reference to an externality, that is, according to the expansion of its potential for governance to untried approaches to inter-group cooperation, thus strengthening real participation in the construction of a democratic order.

Such a genetic approach to the concept of law is the only one capable of engaging with what we defined in our Introduction as the first blockage in current democratic theory, that is, the persisting belief in the notion that it would suffice to transform the public authorities' mode of engagement to obtain a new form of political legitimacy. We have shown that the social operation by which

44 (Cohen and Sabel 1997). We will see in Part II, however, how the form this experimentalist decentralized action must take entails an in-depth elucidation of its conditions for possibility, and how, on this score, the approaches developed by J. Cohen and C. Sabel remain inadequate.

the members of a group arrive at obligatory rules for themselves depends on a crisscrossing relation between *their practical acceptance by citizen-addressees* and *the attention paid by the authorities to the fulfilment of this practical acceptance.* This reciprocal conditionality was established not just from the perspective of the concept of law (the double postulation[45]), but also, and more radically, from the perspective of the rational activity in general (internalist realism[46]). Since rational activity always contains in its internal justificatory structure a reference to the external conditions of its usage, it was necessary to manage to better understand how, in the case also of judgements on the normativity of legal norms, reciprocal conditionality had to be defined in order to understand the genesis of normativity. And it is thus that we succeeded in showing progressively how the judgement of the public authorities assumes its own confirmation by means of citizens' external belief in the social potential for implementation, and how this external judgement could only develop a culture of the law as a possible way of life by itself relying on mediation by a capability internal to the organization of the legal system. This is the position that enables us to take a stand against the idea that the mere production of law by a procedure internal to the institutional system of the public authorities could, provided its design is adequate, ensure the satisfaction of normative expectations. Under our genetic perspective, this notion constitutes the first blockage in democratic theory.

Nevertheless, it is certain that, as we highlighted in the Introduction, certain present-day approaches to law and democratic theory have not remained wholly the prisoners of this blockage. This is so to the extent that they have recognized the need to conceive conditions for governance capable of ensuring expanded forms of reflexivity in terms of citizen participation. From this perspective, both the approaches to economic analysis of law based on R. Coase and O. Williamson, on one hand, and the sociological approaches to self-regulation (which are indeed sometimes referred to as "reflexive") and those based on J. Habermas's formal pragmatics, on the other, had already made an advance in comparison with positivist and hermeneutic approaches to law. This is true even though these last approaches, especially those associated with the discussion raised by analytical positivism, have the advantage of performing a more rigorous construal of the technical issues entailed by an analysis of the concept of law. As well, undoubtedly these various critical approaches of an economic, sociological, or (as with J. Habermas) philosophical kind remain hampered by an inadequate epistemological construal of the theory of reflexivity that they sought to deploy. Indeed, their approach to reflexivity is not constructed in relation to an externality that allows for identifying the decentring inherent in the reflexive movement, a decentring pointed out by our reconstruction of the pragmatist approach. This is very clear when it comes to the economic analyses of law associated with theories of rational choice and the sociological approaches inspired by

45 Cf. above, 46–7.

46 Cf. above, 4–5.

N. Luhmann's theories of self-regulation.[47] But J. Habermas, too, can be charged with reflexive weaknesses, although of a more subtle and complex kind (Lenoble and Maesschalck 2003: Chapter 3).

At least, however, these various "critical" approaches already reflect, whether implicitly or explicitly, the insight that a better understanding of the concept of law requires going beyond the reflexive weaknesses of the positivist and hermeneutic approaches currently available. They also perceive that the regulatory function of law needs for its fulfilment an expansion of the reflexivity of our institutional mechanisms of governance,[48] even if the role of reference to externality through this extension is not highlighted. Recall the critiques addressed to jurists by economists during the 1970s.[49] They consisted of exposing the "reflexive" weaknesses of the technique of governance by "rule" (the so-called "command-and-control" technique of governance) and its inability to take into account the reversibility of the operation of application, that is, the dependency of the effects of a rule on the use that will be made of it by its addressees. This was also the reason why economists recommended more "decentralized" forms of our mechanisms of governance,[50] but without correctly constructing the specifically pragmatist requirements of such a "decentring" in applying the rule.

47 In these "reflexive" approaches to self-regulation, it would appear that everything takes place as if the "capacitation" of actors in a "subsystem" is assumed to exist on its own, and thus assumed to be inscribed within the subsystem, a little like the way G. Teubner, following N. Luhmann, assumes "codes" to be "given". To assume that merely convening existing actors suffices to create the conditions for developing a solution suited to the setting implies that the determination of the solution to the question of "balance" between the subsystem and the context would result in simply applying rules existing in the minds of actors in the subsystem. Such a mentalist approach to action entails a denial of the reflexivity that N. Luhmann's functionalist approach was intended to preserve. For some neo-institutionalist economic approaches, see also (Lenoble and Maesschalck 2003: Chapter 1) and see below, Part II.

48 In the same vein, they also have the merit of taking into account not just the parallel evolution of the discussion in the social sciences, but also the evolution of positive law. Indeed, present-day reflection in the social sciences on the necessary revisiting of traditional forms of coordination by rules has been reflected in significant legal transformations in our way of constructing rules in numerous important sectors where the difficulty of making collective choices is more palpably felt. These transformations are directly associated with the search for legal mechanisms that would provide for better cooperation among decentralized actors. This accounts for recent reflections on the phenomenon of the contract, especially the line of thought opened up by relational contract theory initiated by I.R. Macneil (2000). An exemplary application of this approach may be found in the current restructuring of the regulation of the public sector. On this, see (Freeman 1997, 2000a, 2000b, Vincent-Jones 1999, 2000); see also, for more observations on this literature, Part II, Chapter 6.

49 As was observed above, many American jurists thought that they had found in the renewal of judicial activism a way of compensating for the welfare state's weaknesses in ensuring the "implementation" of the fundamental rights inscribed in the Constitution.

50 This proposal for decentralization does not necessarily result in the valuing of the mechanism of the market on its own. Economists themselves have increasingly become

Similarly, J. Habermas perceives the weaknesses of reducing the conditions of validity of law exclusively to the "cooperative" organization of judges' practice. He perceives that the constraints entailed by the fulfilment of the "function of governance" of modern law require arrangements in our mechanisms of governance that go beyond the mere "cooperative" organization that is specific to the judicial apparatus of the modern state, or the putting into place of the somewhat naive "heroisation" (in J. Habermas's appropriate coinage) of the judge that R. Dworkin's hermeneutic approach results in.[51] According to J. Habermas, the procedures for developing rules must be adjusted to allow for a better respect for the conditions for possibility of the normative judgement revealed by the communicative theory of law and politics,[52] although this theory tends to reduce the requirement for increased reflexivity to deliberative conditions.

While we are not prepared to endorse all of J. Habermas's analyses, it is nevertheless the path of greater reflexivity that should, in our view, be pursued. A better understanding of the conditions for realization of the normative requirement inherent in the concept of law (that is, of the conditions for realization of law's guiding function) requires a critical assessment of the reflexive insufficiency of our current mechanisms of governance, in other words, of our modes of normative production as regards inter-group relations and the reference to externality that they assume. This does not mean that we reject the *descriptivist* project of positivism's undertaking or the positivist exposure of the normative impact of the customary forms of adherence to natural law. Possibly what is indicated is the need to rethink the inevitable link between fact and value and take into account what Putnam (2002: *passim*) calls "the collapse between fact and value".

After all, is it not revealing to note the extent to which the analyses of both H. Hart and J. Coleman's conceptual analyses of law are pervaded by an invocation of the ideal? True, it is no longer a question of ideal governance as with R. Dworkin, however, what is now in play is the functionalist ideal of guidance. As was indicated above, J. Coleman tells us explicitly that, as the result of a kind of process of natural selection or collective learning, our modern legal systems are the result of a "maturing process" that has reached completion. According to

---

aware that this mechanism must often be accompanied by other institutional mechanisms in order to better guarantee effective cooperation by the various actors involved in the collective action needing to be regulated.

51 Or for that matter, in a more communitarian tradition, the "heroisation" inspired by G. Gadamer and advanced by M. J. Perry (1988: 152–ff), who, as J. Habermas (1996: 258) points out, ascribes to "the constitutional judge in the role of a prophetic teacher, whose interpretation of the divine word of the Founding Fathers secures the continuity of a tradition that is constitutive of the community's life".

52 That is, an approach to democratic will-formation that "does not draw its legitimating force from the prior convergence of settled ethical convictions", but rather from "on the one hand, the communicative presuppositions that allow the better arguments to come into play in various forms of deliberation and, on the other, procedures that secure fair bargaining conditions" (Habermas 1996: 278–9).

him, the setting up of our modern legal systems reflects the implementation of the conditions necessary to "satisfying" the guiding function of law. Thus, the idea is that the conditions for satisfaction of the ideal of guidance are already given, even though this state of affairs will now be viewed as the result of social gains or of a lesson learned specifically with the emergence of modern societies. As with R. Dworkin, although in a different way, the conditions for satisfaction of the realization of the ideal are assumed to be guaranteed by a play of a formal rule (in this instance, the rule for a process of natural selection or a social learning operation that has been decisively completed). Our own position is exactly the reverse. In our view, what is at issue, for the sake of a better *descriptive* understanding of the conditions for semantic productivity of normative judgements, is to demonstrate that the conditions for fulfilment of the "ideal" implied by any rule require a *normative and critical* approach to our current mechanisms of governance, that is, our normative modes of production. Thus, what is at issue is not to oppose the conventionalism that J. Coleman rightly adopts in opposition to R. Dworkin. Rather, in the name of a radical understanding of the holism of usage that underlies this conventionalist approach, the issue consists of better understanding the reflexive nature of the conditions for realization of the form of collective action by which a group proposes to act upon itself within the horizon of what it deems to be rationally acceptable, thanks to an operation by which its own attention is decentred by reference to an externality.

The radical interpretation of the pragmatist turn that we have put forward thus leads to the affirmation that fulfilment of the "ideal" harboured by every rule does not assume solely reference to a pragmatic requirement for commitment and for decentralized experimentation within a cooperative activity shared by a given social group. Far more, such fulfilment, far from being able to limit itself to resorting to any established authority, depends on the teleological reference to exo-groups that can serve as the externality likely to elicit the construction of a new way of life. In this way, through our rereading of the pragmatist theory of law, we obtain a pragmatic condition for norms' ability to do in respect of collective action: the requirement for a process of expanding what is possible by taking into account a resisting externality. This requirement concerns the officials group just as much as the citizen-addressees group. If the judgement of the public authorities assumes it is confirmed by citizens' *external* belief in the social potential for implementation, this external judgement can, for its part, only develop its culture of law as a possible way of life by itself relying on mediation by a capacity internal to the organization of the legal system. The reciprocal conditionality of these two forms of judgement shows that a process of mutual adjustment must be envisaged for the concerned groups' judgement about the fulfilment of law. Without such a process of adjustment, democratic theory will remain stymied by the notion that the action by which a social group adopts norms to configure and transform reality according to its objectives is accomplished solely via the established public authorities.

PART II
Beyond Neo-institutionalist and Pragmatist Approaches to Governance: Toward a Genetic Approach to Governance

Introduction

While the first blockage in democratic theory related to the role assigned by traditional political philosophy to public authorities in the construction of democratic representation, the second blockage relates rather to the expected role of citizen participation in governance mechanisms. In seeking to promote a democracy of interaction, current theories have effected a neo-institutionalist and pragmatist turn that consists of no longer focusing on the question of mandates for representation and of privileging; rather, on the cognitive and informational (Rosanvallon 2008: 337) nature of the relationship between governed and governing. Whereas the first blockage arose from a belief in the power of the body social's sovereign action on itself, based exclusively on the legitimacy of the public authorities, the second results from a belief in society's native capacity for conducting reflexive work on itself once the conditions for convening and involving the actors concerned have been enlarged and made maximally plural. In this perspective, the neo-institutionalist and pragmatist turn that underlies the new theories of democratic governance remains, as regards its principle of social experimentation, a "black box". This leads these approaches to overlook the question of the necessary construction of society's capacity to erect, by means of its "reflexive work", a common will and thus to give meaning to a conception of the public interest. This is where what we term "the operation of reflexivity" becomes relevant. The concept of reflexivity refers to the "operation" by which a social group seeks to respond to its perception of the necessity to adjust its capacity for action according to its past experiences (reflectibility) and the projection of its identity of action (destinability).[1]

To address the second blockage in current democratic theory, it is necessary to open up this "black box", that is, to identify all the entailments harboured by this neo-institutionalist and pragmatist turn, from the perspective of the conditions

1 We will explain these concepts when we present the genetic approach in Chapter 6.

for constructing the collective capacity to participate in governance of the public interest. After that, the next step will be to demonstrate the limitations of this "turn" and show how to go beyond the blockage by means of a genetic conception of participation.

First, let us specify the meaning we give to the expression "the public interest" (or "the general interest", "the common good", or "public welfare"). The expression "public interest" is so general that it is often deployed with little rigour. In a recent article, R. Mayntz (2002) has attempted to specify the meaning that the expression has acquired in current research in the social sciences, and more specifically political science. Her work can serve as a useful departure point for our consideration of how to construct the question of "governance in the public interest".

R. Mayntz's central idea is that recent developments in political science make it possible at last to broach the question of public interest while avoiding the trap into which modern theory of society has repeatedly fallen. She emphasizes that this trap lies in the illusion of the spontaneous convergence of private interests and the common interest; it consists of the fact that "no contradiction was seen between the maximization of individual happiness and the public interest" (Mayntz 2002: 16). She further notes that current thinking has grasped that this kind of presupposition is clearly problematic. However, this insight often leads to a sceptical and constructivist position, according to which it is necessary to abandon any claim to a theoretical position about the public interest and by implication any theoretical investigation of the conditions for its satisfaction. And yet, she observes, a second position is possible—one that, while eschewing the illusion of the spontaneous convergence of private interests and the common interest, nevertheless reaffirms the possibility for the *objectivization* of the necessary conditions for satisfying the requirements of such public interest. It is this second position that has progressively emerged from current research in political science.[2] For this to happen, it was necessary for the question of the public interest or the common good to be redefined in terms of "common goods". Thus the question was defined as the search for "two distinct types of collective problem solutions, namely, the solution of common pool resource problems in addition to the provision of formally defined public goods".[3]

2 "Though," Mayntz (2002: 15) says, "it goes back to the arguments of economists trying to specify which goods can be supplied by the market, and which goods it is unlikely to supply".

3 As we know, "public goods are formally defined as goods characterized by non-rivalry of consumption, and non-excludability from consumption ... Common pool resource problems, like the famous tragedy of the commons, exist where there is rivalry in the consumption of a scarce resource, coupled with non-exclusion from consumption" (Mayntz 2002: 19). As R. Oakerson (1992: 42) writes, "Like pure public goods, the commons is shared and unlike private goods, it either cannot be or is not ... divided among separate consumers. Yet like the use of private goods, the use of the commons is characterized by individual consumers who appropriate a portion of the flow of benefits (farmers pump water, cows eat grass) and make the portion unavailable to others ... Unlike pure public

This modification of the approach to the question of the public interest yields, according to R. Mayntz, two methodological gains, which in turn constitute advances in the method of broaching scientifically the question of the conditions that regulation of a collective action must respect in order to maximize satisfaction of the requirements of the public good. As we will see, although we will argue against the first of these methodological gains, we believe it justified to endorse the second.

The *first methodological gain* is said to consist of a redefinition of the problem of the public interest in terms of "common goods". Not only (it is argued) does this approach immediately throw into relief the problems of collective action associated with the production of such goods. In so doing, it also makes it possible to surmount the erroneous presupposition of the usual liberal approaches, according to which a spontaneous convergence occurs between private interests and the public interest. And further, it also offers the benefit that "common goods are defined at a lower level of generality than a comprehensive concept of 'public welfare' which refers to a systemwide end-state … [And] it is conceptually much easier to identify (and measure the achievement of) a single concrete 'good' than an overall state of public welfare defined at the system level" (Mayntz 2002: 19). This position is quite problematic, however. Undoubtedly, it presents few problems when it is applied to the kinds of "physical" goods that do generally serve as the basis for economists' and political scientists' reflections on common goods or public goods. Such a description of "public interest" is, however, quite restrictive, as R. Mayntz (2002: 20) indeed recognizes, although without drawing the relevant inferences. For instance, let us take the case of such "goods" as public freedoms, interethnic tolerance, or the establishment of the institutional frameworks needed for the setting up and regulation of the market. What is problematic in these examples is less that they are in the nature of "immaterial goods" than the fact that, in contrast to the usual examples analysed by economists, they may not be desired by members of a given social group. Surely, in connection with this last example, an economist such as D. North realizes, as will be seen below, that numerous "cultures" do not perceive the setting up of institutional frameworks required by the organization of the market as necessary. Nevertheless, he considers the need for such a setting up to be a given. But why should we assume such a necessity to be an obvious *given*? On the other hand, it is not a matter of adopting the opposite position, according to which research on the public interest is equivalent to research on normative criteria for defining the public interest. R. Mayntz grasps intuitively (without, however, adequately explicating the relevant theoretical basis) the weaknesses of these "normative conceptions of a rational societal discourse à la Rawls or Habermas", which, according to her, amount to no more than a renewal "of Kant's

goods, the commons cannot be shared without limit". Standard instances of public goods are education and the lighting provided in public spaces, while examples of common goods are "forests, fishing grounds, pastures, parks, groundwater supplies, and public highways" (Oakerson 1992: 41).

categorical imperative" (Mayntz 2002: 17). But in assuming that the necessity and justification for such "common goods" are well founded and thus a "given" (whereas, in fact, such a necessity is not currently perceived by numerous social groups), R. Mayntz herself implicitly adopts a theoretical position identical to the one she intends to expose as fallacious. This is the "unthought", and therefore highly problematic, dimension of any reduction of the question of the public interest or the common good to that of common goods. What must therefore be attained is a point of equilibrium between the rejection of a sceptical position and the identical rejection of a normative position, whether explicit or implicit, which presupposes that it is a priori possible to determine what the public interest consists of. To respect this point of equilibrium, it is necessary to internalize this normative dimension within the collective action by means of which members of social groups construct their public interest, and consequently to integrate the hypothesis of a gap between the requirements of the public interest and the way in which members of a group produce a collective action. It is for this reason that we propose to define the problem of the conditions for satisfaction of the requirements of the public interest or of the common good as conditions that must be respected in order for a (collective) action *to maximize, to the extent possible, the satisfaction of the normative expectations of its members*. Such a definition internalizes the possible gap between the general expectation of rationalization and the way in which the actors themselves conceive of the interests to be satisfied. This internalization yields the benefit of avoiding the presumption of a possible a priori definition of such expectations.

A definition along these lines also yields what R. Mayntz perceives as the *second methodological gain* of the common goods approach to the public welfare or the public interest. This second methodological gain consists, as R. Mayntz discerns, of the fact that this current approach broaches the question of the public interest in terms of *a theory of action*. "It is in fact a distinct characteristic of the common goods approach to public welfare to be action oriented" (Mayntz 2002: 21). As posed within the social sciences nowadays, the question consists of inquiring into the form of governance that should govern collective action in order to ensure that the best possible of all intentions is fulfilled. "The action orientation of the common goods perspective quite naturally directs attention to the actor constellations and action orientations conducive to their achievement. In this way governance becomes a focal factor, and the form of governance which is most conducive to their achievement plays a major role in the discussion about common goods" (Mayntz 2002: 21).

Inquiry into governance is thus nowadays directly dependent on a theory of action, that is, on a grasp of the operations by which an intentional action is implemented. Indeed, this approach to the question of the public interest, which frames the question in terms of a theory of action, also accounts for the recent use being made of the term "governance" to designate what has traditionally been called "regulation" or "government".[4] Use of the term "governance" quite simply reflects the surmounting of the dual attitude mentioned above: one branch of this attitude inquires into the question of the public interest in terms of the spontaneous harmonization of various private interests while the other supposes that the requirements of the public interest are satisfied by virtue of the fact that action has been imposed or produced by an authority (the state or its agents) believed to represent or incarnate this interest. In the process of surmounting this dual attitude, the question of sole recourse to the market or forms of governance by hierarchical control becomes problematic. As R. Mayntz (2002: 21) points out, "[T]oday the term governance is most often used to indicate a mode of governing that is distinct from the hierarchical control model characterizing the interventionist state." "Governance", she goes on, adopting a formulation characteristic of neo-institutionalist economists, "is the type of regulation typical of the cooperative state, where state and non-state actors participate in mixed public/private policy networks". Undoubtedly this formulation indicates very clearly that what is sought nowadays in the way of a form of governance for collective action cannot be reduced either to market self-regulation alone, or to traditional command-and-control forms of regulation. However, it should be handled with care, because it could imply the resolution of many questions that are in fact still unresolved, as is made clear by the current state of discussion on the theory of governance.

This explains the procedure followed in the present part of this book and what is thereby placed at issue. Our intention is to adopt a progressive procedure. We will not directly address the question of the conditions for governance in the public interest in the comparatively abstract terms of theory of action. Rather, the procedure we mean to follow will take the internal dynamics of current discussion on theory of governance as its point of departure and show how the encounter between the opposing positions makes it possible to expose the "blind spot" that affects them all. What is at stake in this procedure is thus not a critique of existing approaches, but a test of the hypothesis that existing approaches are affected by a limitation consisting of a weakness in how they deal with the theory of collective action.

In conducting this critique, we will not be so much concerned to describe the content of concrete propositions developed under these approaches. The concern will rather be, above all, to examine how these approaches conceive of the factors on which depends the possibility for the operation of selection that determines that any collective action will satisfy, to the extent possible, the normative expectations of its participants. In other words, what we are addressing is the theoretical framework necessarily (and very often implicitly) presupposed by the various approaches to governance when it comes to the "normative nature" they ascribe to the governance mechanisms they put forward. By "normative nature" is understood the capacity of such mechanisms to best satisfy the collective (or public) interest of the actors involved. In effect, if we reconstruct the internal dynamic of contemporary research into governance theory, we observe an increasing

4 Regarding this change in terminology, see Chapter 4, note 3 below.

will to extend and strengthen institutional mechanisms (that is, incentives). This strengthening is itself no more than the consequence of an ever-expanding attention to the conditions needed for the success of the learning operation required for the selection performed by a collective action to "maximize", to the extent possible, the satisfaction of the normative expectations of its participants.

Our own hypothesis is that, in spite of the gains represented by the various categories of incentives suggested by the different successive stages of contemporary research on governance theory, these stages still require a furthering of the analysis of the conditions for success of the learning operation. If we adopt, as our guiding thread through present-day research, researchers' willingness to delve deeper and deeper into the black box of the learning operation that influences a governance system's capability for maximizing satisfaction of "the public interest", our project will consist of reconstructing this dynamic and attempting to shed light on the persisting opacity in researchers' implicit approach to collective action and to the learning operation it depends on. In other words, we will be shining a light into researchers' own persisting black box.

From this perspective, it appears to us necessary for three successive stages to be differentiated in governance theory. To understand these three stages, it must first be shown to what extent the dynamic that underlies them emerges from a shared base, namely what is commonly called the "neo-institutionalist turn" in the social sciences.

As W. Powell and P. Dimaggio (1991: 1) have shown, the expression "new institutionalist" is ambiguous. (A word here about our use of the words "neo-institutional" and "neo-institutionalist" to qualify things and people associated with the movement of new institutionalism. "New institutional" and "new institutionalist" can also be so used and are synonymous with our terms. We have mainly preferred "neo-institutional" and "neo-institutionalist" for reasons of syntactic simplicity). It covers various trends that have recently emerged in economics,[5] political science, sociology, organization theory, and theory of law.[6] Clearly, it is in relation to the renewed role of institutions in the theory of collective action that the transformed approach (exemplified, as we have seen, by R. Mayntz) to the question of the conditions for satisfying the public interest has been most salient. Recall that this transformation entailed the questioning of the fallacious assumption that there exists harmonious self-regulation among the elements rationally required to satisfy the public interest, whether the foundation for this self-regulation consists of market mechanisms or a given public authority assumed to transmit and impose the requirements for the successful functioning

---

5 On the differences between the "old" and the "new" institutionalism in economics, see (Rutherford 1994).

6 As found in some of the trends of research on law and economics, as well as the development of the law and society movement in the 1960s, in particular (as we will show below, at Chapter 2) through the renewal of the contract approach put forward in the field of socio-legal studies.

of the social system. What has led to this transformation are twin features present, whether in whole or in part, in all neo-institutionalist undertakings. W. Powell and P. Dimaggio provide a good account of these twin features. One feature derives from an emphasis on the limitations on all individuals' capacity for rational calculation. The other defines a still more significant breach with the form of methodological individualism endorsed by the approach to governance so dear to economists. It emphasizes the role of shared common meanings in all social interactions and thus imposes the obligation to analyse collective actions in terms of interaction mediated by language, and not solely as a simple juxtaposition of calculations for the optimization of individual preferences.

The first of these two features has received its most prominent expression in the new institutional economics. But even though other disciplines have not necessarily endorsed the technical framework or the specific consequences yielded by cost transaction economics, the basic principle has turned up everywhere. This principle embodies a willed self-distancing from the usual approaches of rational choice theory. As W. Powell and P. Dimaggio write, "[T]he New Institutional Economics adds a healthy dose of realism to the standard assumptions of microeconomic theory. Individuals attempt to maximize their behaviour over stable and consistent preference orderings, but they do so, institutional economists argue, in the face of cognitive limits, incomplete information, and difficulties in monitoring and enforcing agreements".[7] The second characteristic is not so commonly encountered in the work of economists; but it is highly visible in certain approaches from within political science, as well as in sociological and organization-theory approaches. It is closely linked to H. Garfinkel's development of the discipline of ethnomethodology and also to the cognitivist turn that has left its imprint on psychology; and it holds a privileged position in the work of the Carnegie School on organization theory. This characteristic consists of emphasizing the role of routine in individual and collective behaviour. Neither individual nor collective behaviour can be analysed as the simple product of a calculation to optimize individual preferences; they are necessarily a function of a system of shared rules embodied within institutions. It follows that within these institutions, henceforward, "the new institutionalism … locates irrationality in the formal structure itself, attributing the diffusion of certain … operating procedures to interorganizational influences, conformity, and the persuasiveness of cultural accounts, rather than to the functions they are intended to perform" (Powell and Dimaggio 1991: 13). An approach that is forcefully and explicitly advanced in H. Simon's theory of procedural reason (and embraced by R. Cyert, J. March, and J. Olsen) can be discerned here. Support for this approach has come in the form of the work of A. Tversky and D. Kahneman on stereotypes and biases.

7 The same authors make the familiar point that, according to transaction cost economics, "institutions arise and persist when they confer benefits greater than the transaction costs (that is, the costs of negotiation, execution, and enforcement) incurred in creating and sustaining them" (Powell and Dimaggio 1991: 3–4).

These two characteristics describe the framework within which has emerged, in spite of internal divergences, the "neo-institutionalist" dynamic that governs contemporary research on governance theory. The various approaches to which this dynamic gives rise must be understood within the context of this frame of reference. Our own choice of the theoretical positions we consider to be most representative among the current achievements of neo-institutionalist research was made with the aim of doing justice to each of the two traditions that have progressively developed by taking an emphasis on one or the other characteristic as a departure point.

We have chosen to emphasize three theoretical approaches in Part II of this book. The first is represented by the efforts of neo-institutionalists, following R. Coase and O. Williamson, to nuance the rational choice theory approach advanced by so-called neoclassical economics (Chapter 3). The second is especially clearly represented in the recent work of certain jurists and political scientists, and it is based on the wish to make possible a "relational and collaborative approach to governance through dialogue" (Chapter 4). The third is based on a wish to develop a "pragmatist" approach to collective action (Chapter 5).

As has already been indicated, and as will be more fully demonstrated below, these approaches amount to stages within a single research dynamic. The dynamic in question plays out an increasing will to further our understanding of the learning operation that influences the capacity for a collective action to choose behaviours that will maximize fulfilment of the normative expectations of its participants. As will be seen, this furthering in turn takes the form of a decreasing tendency to assume that the ability of actors to carry out necessary adjustments and learning are a given. Correlative to this, the furthering in question implies a progressive expansion of the institutional devices that must be set up to make possible the learning necessary to the success of the operations of choice that will determine collective action.

Beyond their differences and their progressive gains, however, these three approaches also feature a shared trait, which constitutes a symptom of their shared weakness. The process we are about to undertake will thus also consist of a demonstration of the recurring difficulties these various approaches encounter and the ways in which these difficulties relate to shared unexamined presuppositions. We will show how these presuppositions manifest as a common allegiance to what we might call an institutionalist approach to governance in the public interest. It is true that this approach aims to surmount the traditional dual belief that either market-mechanism-based self-regulation alone or imposition of rule by a public authority, established by this or that mechanism for public representation, suffices to ensure maximum fulfilment of the normative expectations of the members of the group. Yet, even though the conditions for such governance in the public interest now oblige us to complicate the institutional design of the mechanism of governance, the assumption persists that the issue of the conditions for such satisfaction of the requirements of normative expectations amounts to defining the good institutional design of a governance mechanism. It is assumed that, whatever the revised manner of reflecting on the form of this institutional design (distribution of property rights through reduction of transactional costs; stakeholding approach or institutional incentives to ensure learning by trial and error), this *form* represents conditions for such governance.

As will be seen, the difficulties faced by the various approaches that exist at present within the neo-institutionalist current of thought cannot be met and surmounted unless a shift is achieved away from this institutionalist belief and attention is granted to what will determine the use made of these institutional mechanisms. The reason is that, contrary to the institutionalist belief, no mechanism, whatever form it takes, has the power to define or entail its own conditions for application. In this perspective, no mechanism can produce its intended effects except as a function of the way its use is oriented. Its use, in turn, depends on how the actors become aware of the necessary shift mentioned above and on how they intend to involve themselves in the way the teleological orientation that affects this use is determined. Once the "black box" of the neo-institutionalist and pragmatist turn has been explored and reconstructed, we will specify the contribution made by a genetic construction of the "reflexivity"[8] of the collective action that is wiped out by any neo-institutionalist or institutionalist approach to governance (Chapter 6).

8 We should note at this point that the term "reflexivity" here acquires a different meaning than that given it by several current "neo-institutionalist" approaches to governance, whether (for example and as we mentioned earlier) relational and collaborative approaches or experimentalist ones. We will return below to this difference in meaning, one that must be kept clearly in mind if ambiguity and confusion are to be avoided.

Chapter 3
The First Neo-institutionalist Approach: The New Institutional Economics

What we propose is obviously not to provide an exhaustive account of the richness of the approaches that constitute then neo-institutionalist trend that emerged from the work of R. Coase and O. Williamson. Nor is it a question of critiquing their significant contribution. Their transaction cost approach allowed for supplementing the approaches that had emerged from the theory of agency and property rights[1] and for better accommodating the complexity of the institutional arrangements through which economic agents now strive to deal with the "uncertain" contexts which have weakened their capacity for "rational anticipation". Moreover, the neo-institutionalists' commitment to paying increasing attention to hybrid forms of governance and public-private partnerships in order to compensate for the failings of previous forms of governance, including the decentralized forms suggested by neoclassical economic approaches, have significantly enriched debate on the reform of public policy.

Our approach will be different. We wish to highlight two characteristic aspects of the approach to governance suggested by the neo-institutionalist economists. The first aspect relates to the paradox that the neo-institutionalist economists' approach appears unable to surmount. Despite the fact that the point of departure for this approach consists of wishing to become free of the neoclassical economists' fallacious belief in the "perfect" rationality of economic agents, the neo-institutionalists' recent approaches have reflected repeated errors in regard of this requirement. The second aspect follows from the first and relates more directly to the question of governance of the public interest: the first aspect has led neo-institutionalist economists to resort in the end, in a

1 These theories are well known. As D. Weimar (1995: 10) writes, "Agency theory sees organizations as bundles of explicit and implicit contracts defining the relationship between principals and agents who take actions on their behalf ... Agency theory is primarily concerned with the situations of asymmetrical information between principals and agents. Typically, agents have information, or can take actions, that are hidden from principals ... The theory assumes that principals and agents design the most efficient contracts that are compatible with their individual incentives. It also assumes that contracts are complete and enforceable with respect to mutually observable actions and outcomes ... [;] transaction cost theory ... shares with agency theory a focus on contracts. Unlike agency theory, however, it allows for the possibility that contracts may be incomplete, because all contingencies cannot be anticipated, and imperfectly enforceable, because detecting and punishing noncompliance is costly".

truly behaviourist fashion, to the classic "public" mechanisms as a way to make up for the deficiencies of decentralized forms of governance. It is at this level that the critiques that will open the way (as will be seen in Chapters 4 and 5) to the deliberative (or relational and collaborative) and pragmatist approaches to governance will be formulated.

Recent neo-institutional research has clearly perceived the internal ambiguity in the undertaking of O. Williamson, the movement's founding father. It is not that the transactionalist analysis he puts forward remains "rooted in the an-evolutionary nature of the economy of equilibrium, as some overhasty critiques would lead us to believe" (Brousseau 2000a: 1203). While somewhat late in the day (essentially in his 1996 publication), O. Williamson does take into account, in his analysis of the role of institutions as conditions for the efficiency of forms of governance, the evolutionary processes and the importance of inquiring into the structures of governance from the point of view of their capacity to adapt. But as E. Brousseau (2000a: 1203) points out, O. Williamson assigns a highly problematic role to competitive selection, and this in fact enables him to "reconcile, as does Alchian, a hypothesis of bounded rationality with the idea that agents are led to behave in compliance with the canons of individualist and calculative rationality". This way of conceiving evolutionary processes leads O. Williamson to restore a kind of "perfect rationality". According to O. Williamson, E. Brousseau (2000a: 1203) notes:

> Competitive selection disciplines economic agents. In fact, they possess a rationality that is calculative (although not of L. Savage's kind) that allows them to learn and anticipate, albeit imperfectly. Thus they foresee that will need to adapt post facto, even though they cannot foresee the necessary adaptations in advance. This leads them to conceive flexible coordination structures (hybrid and hierarchical ones). Moreover, with the experience acquired, they supplement and enhance these governance structures, which had begun by being incomplete and imperfect. Thus O. Williamson puts forward two strong hypotheses about the nature of the process of competitive selection: it chooses the efficient forms—those that minimize transaction costs—and it is (at least partly) predictable.[2]

2 Note, however, that O. Williamson anticipates to some extent the critical response that is now addressed to the solution offered by the economists of the Chicago School. O. Williamson (1987), in contrast to the property rights and agency cost theorists (such as H. Demsetz, M. Jensen, and W. Meckling; see on this J. Vromen 1995: 60), critiques the idea that evolution necessarily produces the solution that is most efficient "in itself": what emerges is only the most efficient solution among those actually tested. The reason for this, of course, is his partial borrowing of H. Simon's idea of bounded rationality. This also explains why, when he refers explicitly to H. Simon, O. Williamson emphasizes that only a "weak form of selectionism" is acceptable (see, for a definition of this expression, Williamson (1996: 379)). This restriction, however, does not prevent the ultimate reinstatement of a form of perfect rationality which he set out to surmount.

An approach of this kind to the processes of selection thus restores, not just the hypothesis of bounded rationality, but what economists call a kind of perfect rationality. The approach taken to the learning processes assumes that the processes for rationalizing the world (that is, the establishment of a kind of coordination that is as efficient as possible with respect to agents' normative expectations) are the product solely of the "natural" competencies that economic agents enjoy. No doubt, in contrast to classical economists, this current of thought emphasizes that the solutions through "equilibrium" depend on the establishment of institutional mechanisms. Moreover, these, on one hand, cannot be reduced to the mere play of the market nor even to the incentive contract mechanisms that contractualist theorists have recently identified; and, on the other hand, they are subject to readjustments and improvements that emerge from collective learning. But the conditions needed to ensure the efficiency of these mechanisms and to ensure that they will effect the "hoped for rationalization" of the world are assumed to be always-already given as capacities inscribed in individual minds. E. Brousseau, like many neo-institutionalists, does see that this Williamsonian approach to the learning process—and in consequence, to governance mechanisms—ends in a failure to respect the original project, which was to break with the epistemological assumptions of a marginalist analysis made in terms of equilibrium.[3]

True, this "epistemological inconsistency" has not prevented neo-institutionalist research from furthering—as R. Coase indeed suggested in his Nobel Prize acceptance speech—its descriptive analyses of the complexity and variety of the hybrid forms of governance within which current efforts at setting up public-private partnerships are taking place. But various authors have nevertheless paid attention to the theoretical issue and have tried to further the way O. Williamson conceived the operation of "selection" of the kind of coordination of the collective action, and constructed the limits of rationality/institutional dynamic/institutional design. Moreover, we can add that this "epistemological difficulty in thinking the limits of rationality" does not just relate to theoretical speculation. So long as this difficulty is not resolved, we will be led, at the level of governance theory, to the "practical difficulty" consisting of how to avoid the assumption that the conditions are always-already given for emergence of the "public" mechanisms that must be associated with private decentralization mechanisms in order for a collective action to be as efficient as possible (that is, in order for it to maximize to the extent possible the normative expectations of the social group). And the hypothesis we would like to put forward is that the attempts made to deal with the "epistemological difficulty" raised by the Williamsonian approach prove decidedly deficient and indeed reproduce, in spite of themselves, the very epistemological ambiguity they so successfully identified in the work of the founding father of neo-institutionalist economics.

3 "Thus, even though the Williamsonian analysis makes a clear break, through its premises, with a marginalist analysis in terms of equilibrium, it is nevertheless true that it does not infer all the conclusions implicit in this position" (Brousseau 2000a: 1203).

We believe there have been two main attempts to surmount O. Williamson's epistemological weakness. The first is that made by the evolutionary thinkers and the second was given its most representative expression by D. North. We will proceed from our inquiry into D. North's position to an inquiry into E. Brousseau's, whose aim has been to develop a position that synthesizes the gains made by both the evolutionary thinkers and D. North. Examining E. Brousseau's position will have the benefit of allowing us to explicate still better the problematic presuppositions we will reveal to be implicit in D. North's attempt, presuppositions that are made at both the epistemological level and that of theory of governance.

An initial clarification is required. From a terminological perspective, it is obviously inadequate to present evolutionary theory (developed essentially, as is well known, on the basis of R. Nelson's and S. Winter's work (Nelson and Winter 1982)) as an attempt at a neo-institutionalist surmounting of the problems posed by the Williamsonian approach of bounded rationality and competitive selection. It is not the aim of the evolutionary approach to broach the question of the dynamics of economic processes in transaction cost terms, as adherents of new institutional economics would have us do. Thus, it is only in a broad sense that this attempt at surmounting the Williamsonian epistemological ambiguities may be classified among neo-institutionalist approaches. The point is that, beyond the obvious differences between these two trends in current economic thought, together they represent the most important expression of the recent attempts by economic theory to broach the question of the most efficient possible kinds of collective coordination by exposing the psychologically and epistemologically unrealistic nature of rational choice theory and by a commitment to taking into account, in a radical manner, the consequences of the boundedness of economic agents' rationality.[4] This accounts

4 Here we are in agreement with the position defended by E. Brousseau. He too privileges, in recent economic research, analysis conducted within the transaction cost economics approach (represented mainly by the work of O. Williamson and D. North following the trend begun by R. Coase's insights) and the evolutionary economics approach (represented mainly by the work of R. Nelson and S. Winter, G. Dosi, L. Marengo, and C. Freeman; and to these may be added the work of P. David and B. Arthur on path-dependency): "One of the reasons why I privilege the analyses conducted within these two theoretical approaches over that of other approaches such as dynamic games (Schotter), property rights (Demsetz), economy of law (Posner), constitutionalism (Vanberg), neo-Austrian (Hayek), and so on, is that these two schools stand out from the others for their capacity, over the past few years, to go beyond the level of a mere programme. Without claiming these other approaches have remained wholly unverified, I would nevertheless argue that neo-institutional theory on one hand and evolutionary theory on the other stand out from those other currents of thought, by virtue of a number of essential contributions ... that have generated theoretical and empirical work that has allowed for specifying and unifying the conceptual bases of the two schools; stating and testing conjectures; and validating the explanation for some schematized facts. This work has both generated many analytic developments and allowed for the precise identification of certain limitations of these theories" (Brousseau 1999: 192).

for their common interest in supplementing the approaches of incentive contract theory by expanding the focus to more complex forms of governance (hybrid and hierarchical governance mechanisms associated to varying degrees with the fields of intra- and inter-firm relations). But this also, and above all, accounts for the current commitment by economists working in the two trends to go beyond recourse to the hypothesis of natural selection that economists, including A. Alchian, M. Friedman, F. Machlup, and indeed O. Williamson, have advanced as a way of dealing with the anti-marginalist critique of neoclassical theory of the firm developed in the 1930s and 1940s in the United Kingdom by the Oxford Research Group and in the USA, mainly by R. Lester.[5]

How then do the evolutionary thinkers modify the approach to competitive selection deployed by O. Williamson? And in what way does their evolutionary reinterpretation remain epistemologically problematic and ambiguous?

The evolutionary approach's contribution to Williamsonian theory does not consist of the idea of learning. O. Williamson, working with H. Simon's bounded rationality hypothesis, was already pondering the question of economic

5 As J. Vromen (1995: 14) points out: "The main target of the criticism of the anti-marginalists was the neoclassical theory of the firm … [. I]n this theory it is assumed that entrepreneurs, who are supposed to determine the behaviour of firms single-handedly, are profit maximizers. Profit is maximized if marginal revenue and marginal cost are equal …[;] the assumption of profit maximization implies that the price and output policy of entrepreneurs is that they expand production up to the point where marginal revenue and marginal cost are equal …[;] the antimarginalist criticism is inspired by empirical findings that are taken to show that entrepreneurs do not adopt such a price and output policy based on marginalist deliberations". The response of A. Alchian and others in terms of natural selection is well known. A. Alchian proposed that the theorems of the neo-classical theory of the firm remained true even if it turned out to be inaccurate that entrepreneurs are "profit maximizers". Perhaps, in fact, the behaviour of entrepreneurs did not result from deliberations involving an optimizing calculation. No doubt, noted A. Alchian, in a context of uncertainty, rational actors do not have at their disposal all the elements necessary to calculate the balancing of costs and benefits "at the margin". But this consideration is irrelevant. It does not invalidate the laws established by the neoclassical theory of the firm concerning the evolution of the industrial market. The logic of the "impersonal forces of the market" effectively operates such that in the end only those firms survive which develop strategies identical to those that would permit a definition of the optimizing calculation: "those who realize profits are survivors; those who suffer losses disappear" (Alchian 1950). The logic of current results is therefore sufficient. It is of little importance to presuppose the ways in which the behaviour of entrepreneurs would ensure the realization of these results. M. Friedman, and later G. Becker, proposed the same thesis. The market functions "as if" the actors were "profit maximizers". Only those survive who, by chance, by rational calculation, or by some other way, have adopted strategies corresponding to the most efficient strategy, which is the only one that is able to ensure success. "The process of 'natural selection' thus helps to validate the hypothesis or, rather, given natural selection, acceptance of the hypothesis can be based largely on the judgment that it summarizes appropriately the conditions for survival" (Friedman 1953: 22).

agents' choice of governance mechanisms on the basis of the idea of learning. E. Brousseau points out:

> [I]nferring a portion of the consequences of the bounded rationality hypothesis, O. Williamson acknowledges that agents' choices as regards governance structures may be erroneous or at least not optimal. Economic agents improve existing governance structures in light of what they learn about their coordination difficulties and the efficient features of the solutions they use (Brousseau 1999: 199).

Possibly, O. Williamson may have been influenced by the work of those who initiated the evolutionary movement, R. Nelson and S. Winter. And, in fact, it is above all O. Williamson's work subsequent to the 1982 publication of R. Nelson and S. Winter's "An evolutionary theory of economic change" that reflects endorsement by the founder of transaction cost economics of the idea of learning (Williamson 1985, 1991, 1993, 1996). Moreover, R. Nelson and S. Winter are themselves victims of the same ambiguity—not to say inconsistency—as that already identified in the work of O. Williamson. As we saw, despite the hypothesis of agents' bounded rationality, O. Williamson would maintain the idea that agents nevertheless proceed to choose "efficient" forms of governance, that is, those that minimize transaction costs. To arrive at this conclusion, he assumes the existence of a process of "natural" selection of agents' cognitive operations. But he provides no explanation as to the way this selection mechanism operates and combines with the learning process. R. Nelson and S. Winter maintain, in a manner as problematic as O. Williamson's, the duality of the process: it is a learning process and it is a process of natural selection. But in contrast to O. Williamson, they are not satisfied merely to postulate this combination. On the contrary, they do try to open up the "black box" it represents. And in opening the black box, simultaneously, they indirectly reveal how epistemologically problematic is this perspective that combines efficient equilibrium constrained by a process of natural selection with agents' adaptive learning. And in so doing, they force evolutionary theory to transform its hypotheses about the conditions that must be respected so that agents "select" the forms of governance that "maximize" their normative expectations. Before going on to examine this transformation, let us take a quick look at how R. Nelson and S. Winter attempted to open up the black box this operation represents if the twofold notion of learning/natural selection is maintained.

R. Nelson and S. Winter attempt to unify the approach to firms' individual behaviour in terms of a "satisficing" routine and the approach to industry's collective equilibrium in terms of natural selection. They postulate that the routines that define firms' behaviours[6] correspond to genes in the biological theory of natural

6 R. Nelson and S. Winter pursue their inquiry as part of the theory of the firm, which also constituted the context for the discussion on the anti-marginalist critique conducted by

selection. Selection is carried out on routines, or more precisely on the rules actors adopt to fix their behaviours, and thus on the rules actors apply when they carry out their learning activities. R. Nelson and S. Winter thus seek, in a subtle and innovative manner, to establish an analogy between "routines" and "genes" such that they invoke a plausible mechanism of "genetic" transmission, or what they call a "replication mechanism", just as any technically sound theory of natural selection would entail. Indeed, it is in this context that they argue that they embrace a "Lamarckian" theory of natural selection. The routines transmitted (in the sense of being reproduced by numerous firms) are argued to be themselves the product of learning activities undertaken by firms faced with unsatisfactory profits.

The problem arises when it comes to articulating this approach to individual behaviour with the idea that changes at the collective level are the product of a natural selection mechanism.[7] In R. Nelson and S. Winter, this problem is all the more salient because they seek to describe the whole process in formalized language. The problem results from the difference between the operating method of the "adaptive learning" mechanism and that of natural selection, even though both take place reflexively, that is, by way of a feedback loop. This difficulty has been well explained by J. Vromen (1995: 119):

> The first difference is that adaptive learning typically implies changes within individuals. Learning individuals typically improve their behaviour in the sense they learn to behave in ways that lead to satisfactory results ... The results that are brought about by adaptive learning pertain to another level of analysis than the results that are produced by natural selection. Whereas natural selection produces changes at a *populational* level, adaptive learning generates changes in *individual* organisms ... Natural selection as an explanatory concept presupposes individual stasis. It presupposes that there are stable, inheritable traits in a population of individual organisms.

The articulation of the two mechanisms in one unified process therefore poses a problem. How to maintain that the process of change at the level of firms will operate prior to that of natural selection? Without being able to do that, the process of "search" integral to learning will not have allowed the reconstitution of a sufficiently stable population of routines, allowing change by means of natural selection, to operate. In their formal models:

A. Alchian and M. Friedman. F. Hayek, on the other hand, pursued his inquiry as part of a theory of cultural evolution based on a theory of individual learning.

7 In the terms of the theory of natural selection, this change, constitutive of a new equilibrium, signifies a change in the frequency of "genes" within the "gene pool"—that is to say, within the framework of a theory of the firm, a change in the population of rules of behaviour adopted by firms.

> natural selection and adaptive learning are assumed to have different time scales. Natural selection typically is assumed to work slower than adaptive learning. It is assumed that natural selection comes in only after learning processes have come to an end.

But, as J. Vromen (1995: 125–6) further notes:

> [I]t is also clear that this assumption is questionable, to say the least. There is no reason to assume *a priori* that the process of selection is slower than the process of search, let alone that the selection forces are waiting patiently in the wings for all firms to terminate their search.[8]

This difficulty, which R. Nelson and S. Winter fail to deal with except at the cost of an artificial and unrealistic postulate, is obviously connected to another difference between the two mechanisms, which concerns the processes through which these mechanisms may generate collective equilibrium.[9] By leaving the explanation for this equilibrium to the mechanism of natural selection, the question of how to "think" this equilibrium solely on the basis of the resources provided by a theory of learning is circumvented.

As we said, it is this difficulty, which is the stumbling-block encountered by R. Nelson and S. Winter's attempt to better construct the articulation merely

8 It is symptomatic that in their informal comments, R. Nelson and S. Winter (1982: 169), themselves acknowledge that it is nevertheless more realistic to recognize that the two processes work simultaneously. But their project is to construct a formal evolutionary model integrating and unifying both the theory of learning and the theory of natural selection. Interestingly J. Vromen also notes that R. Nelson and S. Winter, in their informal comments, sometimes adopt another strategy in order to cope with this difficulty. They suggest, in agreement with the notion of organizational learning developed by H. Simon, R. Cyert, and their successors, that learning is itself regulated by second-order rules and that there is thus a hierarchy of "routines". Natural selection does not work on the first-order routines but on the second-order learning rules. The question is, however, only deferred. It is important to know if this change concerning the rules relating to learning procedures itself generates stability and, on the other hand, if it makes it possible to predict, at the level of individual firms, sufficiently stable (and therefore repetitive and predictable) "first-degree" behaviours. With surprising lucidity as regards the success of his own theoretical approach, S. Winter (1986) observes, as J. Vromen (1995: 124) notes, that "this condition for predictability is not likely to be met in reality".

9 "The criterion for reproductive success in natural selection is the same for all individuals in the population. The criterion can hence be said to be objective. In the economic domain, this means that having positive material means is a sine qua non for persistence; whether firms are profit seeking or not, in order to stay in business they have to acquire material means. Adaptively learning individuals, on the other hand, may all have different aspiration levels. They may have different motives and targets. Hence, there may be a multitude of subjective criteria here" (J. Vromen 1995: 120).

postulated by O. Williamson between learning and natural selection, that has led neo-institutionalist economic inquiry (in the broad sense, that is, inquiry by evolutionary economists and transaction cost economists)[10] to try to better trace the dynamics of economic phenomena and consequently better understand the conditions that must be in place for these dynamics to result in forms of governance of collective action that are as efficient as possible. The transformation of both O. Williamson's model and R. Nelson and S. Winter's consists precisely in contemplating the dynamic of collective action solely on the basis of the idea of learning and no longer having recourse to the idea that social processes are guided by a process of natural selection, as processes in the natural world are.

But making a process of "selection by learning" independent of any process of natural selection entails rethinking the question of whether the learning process automatically leads to the most efficient possible form of governance (whether by coordination or by cooperation)—that is, to one that maximizes, to the extent possible, fulfilment of the normative expectations of the social group's members. And this accounts for the very special attention given to the learning process itself. This attention is to be credited mainly to evolutionary authors; but their lessons have been learned by transaction cost economists, foremost among them D. North. To unpack the changed approach that has resulted from this development and show the difficulties that continue to hamper that approach, we will focus on the position presented in a recent article by L. Marengo and G. Dosi (2005) as an exemplification of the views of evolutionary economists and on D. North's position (and its use by E. Brousseau) as an exemplification of the views of transaction cost economists.

However, before analysing these two positions, we will make a preliminary observation that draws attention to one clear sign of the problematic nature of the attempts made by both evolutionary thinkers and, in their recent work, transaction cost economists to resolve the epistemological ambiguity in the positions held by O. Williamson on one hand and R. Nelson and S. Winter on the other.

The fact is, the abandonment of any reference to the biological theory of natural selection and the consequent commitment to rely solely on a theory of learning to grasp the dynamics of organizing collective action have not taken place without an intermediate step. This step was given one of its most significant expressions in evolutionary game theory, developed by evolutionary theorists during the 1980s and 1990s. It consists of an acknowledgement that the social world cannot be reduced to the biological world.[11] For this reason, the dynamics of collective action and the selection of the most efficient possible kinds of coordination cannot be contemplated in terms of "natural selection". This also explains the fact that, at the social level, it is not possible to found the optimality (even in O. Williamson's "weak" sense) of equilibrium strategies solely on the

10 As O. Williamson himself (1996: 40) explicitly says, following K. Arrow, "transaction costs economics [is only] a part [of] the New Institutional Economics movement".

11 See especially (Maynard Smith 1982).

play of the evolutionary mechanism of natural selection. But at the same time, it is assumed that operations "analogous" to the process of natural selection guide the selection of equilibriums specific to collective action. These are the operations of individual and collective learning and of cultural imitation. This analogousness is assumed to make possible the generation, when it comes to collective action, of the conditions for an optimal dynamic of equilibrium.[12] Of course, the recent evolutionary and transaction-cost-economists (like D. North) do not endorse such an assumption and are thus, so to speak, aware of the failure of evolutionary game theory to validate it.[13] But it is interesting to note that, despite their commitment to go beyond this intermediate step, they propose approaches to the dynamics of collective action (and the conditions required for those dynamics to maximize, to the extent possible, the fulfilment of normative expectations) that unquestionably reproduce the theoretical framework implicitly adopted by the most representative of the evolutionary game theorists. It is all the more important to emphasize this point because the same analytic framework is without any doubt being applied by current authors in the law and economics trend. It would appear that current economic research, even in cases where awareness has been attained about the limitations of any theory of collective action in governance based on the idea of natural selection (including theories indirectly so based and theories that use natural selection as an analogy, like evolutionary game theory), is nevertheless incapable of surmounting those limitations. Let us see, then, what analytic framework evolutionary game theory leads to. We will then touch on the way it is reproduced by one of the most representative theorists of social norm theory as currently being developed within the law and economics school and finally on the way it underlies both the evolutionary approach of G. Dosi and L. Marengo and D. North's neo-institutionalist approach.

In the perspective we have adopted, two lessons can be drawn from the work of the evolutionary game theorists.

---

12 As J. Vromen (1995: 136) says, "In a sense evolutionary game theory can be regarded as a generalization of 'optimization theory' in biology. Optimization theory in biology studies what features of individuals optimize their fitness. Optimization theory is suited to deal with frequency-independent selection: selection processes in which the fitness of individuals depends only on the *natural* environment. Evolutionary game theory is devised to analyse *frequency-dependent* selection. In frequency-dependent selection, the fitness of individuals depends not only on their natural, but also on their *social* environment. That is to say, the fitness of particular phenotypes in a population depends on their frequencies in the population".

13 As U. Witt (1997), a contemporary evolutionary theorist, somewhat radically puts it, "... evolutionary game theory—whose sole relevant application to economics is the proof that preferences are heritable—cannot on its own account for the meaning of the term 'evolution' in economics. Economic behaviours adapt much more rapidly than would be possible in genetic evolution, which stretches over generations. Consequently, other forms of variation and adaptation must play a decisive role".

The first is that the most important authors working in this current of thought have themselves been obliged to acknowledge the comparative failure of their initial project, which was to show that the "internal" dynamics of a collective game result in establishing the most efficient strategies. But what do we mean by comparative failure? We mean that these authors have been obliged to acknowledge that adoption by a group's member of an optimal strategy unquestionably depends on conditions external to the dynamics alone (those of learning) of the collective game itself. Without going into the reasoning followed by these authors,[14] we will merely mention two main attempts and their outcomes.

The first of these attempts is that made by E. Ullmann-Margalit (1977) and A. Schotter (1981), who have sought to further the efforts of F. Hayek. As we know, F. Hayek, like R. Nelson and S. Winter, proposes that actors (whether individuals or firms) do not in effect behave like the "profit maximizers" of neoclassical theory, which had already been challenged by the antimarginalists. On the contrary, an economic actor displays routine behaviour. Such an actor is satisfied to apply the rules of behaviour that have usually provided satisfactory guidance in the past. However, when this routine yields unsatisfactory results, a "search" activity for new rules takes place. A process of learning by trial and error thus drives forward the way an individual or a firm makes decisions and entrenches her, his or its behaviour. But F. Hayek considers that the adaptive resources of the individuals who are members of a social group are such that they will adopt the rules of behaviour likely to create the conditions for optimal global coordination. The collective action is guaranteed to generate optimal coordination by the organicist presupposition according to which individual actors automatically take account of the constraints associated with their organic relationship with the social whole. The competitive mechanism of coordination thus ensures optimal equilibrium, by means of the internalization of the norms necessary for coordinating individual behaviours. The organicist presupposition allows F. Hayek to guarantee that all the individuals share an interest in coordinating their plans in an optimal manner. Thus from the outset, the hypothesis of a conflict of interest that generates divergent meanings assigned to the ends being pursued is rendered inoperative. The presupposition that operates in orthodox economic theory of general equilibrium[15] is thus restored. According to F. Hayek, the transmission of efficient rules of behaviour to all the individual actors is assumed to operate by means of an imitation mechanism, which thus

14 On this point, see our *The Action of Norms* (Lenoble and Maesschalck 2003: 58–ff) and see especially (Vromen 1995: 174–89).

15 Note that the kind of social coordination theorized by F. Hayek on the market model does not exclude necessary support by rules. In fact, rules are put forward as the very condition for optimal coordination. The difference is that these rules are assumed to emerge solely from social interaction and not from the authoritarian mechanisms of a hierarchical, centralized organization. Hence, indeed, F. Hayek's well-known valuation of customary law and precedent at the expense of written rules issued by a legislator.

plays the role of a replication mechanism. The critique of this position is fairly obvious and has often been made: The thesis can only be tenable if inter-individual relationships prove able to be contemplated on the model of the pure coordination game, in which no conflict of interest is likely to result in a deficit in optimal equilibrium. The development of cooperative games, and in particular the typical hypothesis of the prisoner's dilemma, has shown that the competition game alone can lead to sub-optimal dominance strategies.

This is precisely what E. Ullmann-Margalit and A. Schotter have grasped. They have sought to take up F. Hayek's project and develop it further, not in the framework of coordination games but rather that of cooperative games (one-shot cooperative games and recurrent cooperative games). In contrast to F. Hayek, however, E. Ullmann-Margalit and A. Schotter ultimately recognize that neutralizing the non-cooperative strategy and establishing the respect owing to the agreement that ensures cooperation can only result in prescriptive intervention by a third party, as in the thinking of T. Hobbes.[16] Clearly, we are far from the cooperative equilibrium established by the mere play of evolutionary self-regulation. But there is a second lesson to add to this first one. That is that these authors are obliged to acknowledge not just the need for a condition "external" to the game itself to generate cooperative equilibrium and the form of governance that maximizes the fulfilment of collective expectations. They must further acknowledge, as J. Vromen (1995: 180) points out, "that the external authority can only enforce an already existing tacit agreement among the individuals". It should be noted, though, that these authors do not define the conditions needed to make possible the emergence of such a tacit agreement—they indisputably assume them to be "given".[17]

The second attempt—well represented by the work of R. Axelrod and R. Sugden—results in the same two lessons, though at the outset they construct divergent strategies. Although both of these authors wish to demonstrate that the establishment of an efficient strategy does not require an external authority, they too end by having to acknowledge, whether implicitly or explicitly, that the cooperative strategy emerges from a learning process that would itself be impossible but for

16 As A. Schotter (1981: 11) says, "It is common knowledge that the famous prisoner's dilemma game can be solved through the use of a binding contract that is enforceable by an external authority".

17 As J. Vromen (1995: 180) points out, "Ullmann-Margalit explicitly announces that she is not going into this question. She does not analyse the mechanisms and processes that are responsible for the generation of the tacit agreement. Likewise, Schotter states that the most that a game-theoretic account can do is to show that some institution is stable. Schotter does suggest, however, that the mechanism that produces the emergence of institutions is learning. Individuals are assumed to learn not only to restrict themselves, but also so that they can rely on the self-restriction of the others". J. Vromen immediately raises the obvious objection such an assumption gives rise to: "[T]he problem is that long before the new rule of self-restriction establishes itself as the rule that is followed by all individuals, the first pioneers or innovators must have found their way in a hostile environment".

certain conditions external to those that define the rules of the initial game. This external condition is especially well explicated by R. Sugden, who sees that the establishment of such a strategy requires the group members to assign the same, univocal meaning to the basic rule of the strategy, which consists of playing the "hawk" (that is, being "aggressive") in situation U and playing the "dove" (that is, being "pacific") in situation V, deemed to be asymmetrical (or contrary) to U. If some players interpret the lack of symmetry (that is, the meaning of the opposition between U and V and what is meant by the corresponding "aggressive" and "pacific" behaviours), maintenance of the efficient cooperative strategy in an equilibrium state will not be established. R. Sugden, however, assumes that the framework that will ensure the fixing of this single meaning will be a given provided by the social group's cultural tradition. Thus, we are dealing simultaneously with the idea of a necessary external condition, the cultural tradition, and the idea of this cultural tradition's capacity, assumed to be given, to fix a single interpretive framework for the social group's expectations. To better understand the nature of the presupposition deployed by R. Sugden, it is helpful to briefly describe the reasoning recently carried out by one of the most representative of the law and economics authors in connection with this question of the "emergent social norms" on which the establishment of an efficient cooperative strategy (that is, in our terminology, of a form of governance "in the public interest") depends. Pausing to consider this example will allow us to highlight effectively the presuppositions involved in the evolutionary thinkers' arguments and, as will be seen below, in the arguments taken up by G. Dosi and L. Marengo as well as by D. North.

R. Cooter (1994, 1996a, 1996b, 1997) has sought to inquire into the impact of the internalization of social norms on cooperative strategies. One of this author's theses is that the internalization of the norms produced within a self-regulated group increases the supply of "local public goods" and modifies equilibrium to the benefit of those individuals who adopt a cooperative strategy as part of the "mixed equilibrium" found among evolutionary equilibriums. We need not pause over the problems created by this thesis, which relies on a kind of reasoning directly inspired by R. Axelrod and R. Sugden's efforts, which we have just seen to be problematic. What concerns us here is that R. Cooter nevertheless names the conditions for efficiency that the social norm must satisfy if it is not to result in "evolutionary traps", that is, in "inefficient equilibriums". Stating these conditions leads R. Cooter to what he calls "weak utilitarianism",[18] which takes the form of this theorem: "Strategies that evolve into social norms in a free business community will be efficient in the absence of non-convexities or spillovers to other communities". Far be it from us to contest these two conditions. But it is impossible not to notice that R. Cooter's formulation takes away with one hand what was given with the other. Specifically, the two conditions are these. First, the norm's non-convexity

18 To the contrary, R. Cooter (1994: 226) notes, "'Strong utilitarianism' would hold that every efficient equilibrium in a game will evolve into a social norm".

means that there cannot be multiple equilibriums in a community.[19] Second, it is considered that there is "spillover" when the norm of the community in question harms another community. R. Cooter's thesis is that a judge (or a public authority) must not uphold a norm that has emerged "spontaneously", that is, solely from the self-regulating play of evolutionary dynamics, unless it corresponds to the two specified conditions for efficiency. But how are the required non-convexity and non-harmfulness to another community to be defined? The illustration of the mountain with more than one peak would suggest that such a definition could be devised from a perspective external to the community itself. We are far from wishing to slide into the facile game of interpretive and postmodern relativism. But it is just as problematic to adopt the "objectivist" presupposition of an external point of view in whose name one could measure the gap between the global optimum and the local maximum,[20] or the sum of the "externalities" that reflect harm inflicted on another community. In other words, what R. Cooter omits is the question of the conditions that make it possible to pass judgement on the conditions for efficiency. Once again, it would appear that the capabilities for formal reasoning that all the individual actors would necessarily share suffice to determine the meaning of these conditions.

One way of understanding R. Cooter's assumption is to say he adopts an externalist realist epistemology. He assumes the existence of an external standard of measurement that makes it possible to determine the meaning of a judgement by which members of a social group can determine matters as controversial as those concerning the definition of what is harmful to another group. As we know from the simple sociological facts of present-day society, this assumption is highly problematic and debatable. It is an assumption that reflects an epistemological operation we already detected in other authors. This operation consists of assuming as given, by means of a formal mechanism integral to the very dynamics of either collective history or the individual mind of every economic agent, the capacity to produce the conditions necessary for the establishment of collective governance that maximizes fulfilment of the group members' normative expectations. As we will now see, this same operation is replicated in the thinking of G. Dosi and L. Marengo on one hand and D. North on the other, despite their commitment to surmounting the epistemological ambiguities harboured by neoclassical economics, by O. Williamson's thinking, and by the thinking of all who, directly

19 "One kind of evolutionary trap occurs when local progress is global regress. To illustrate, suppose that some climbers try to ascend a mountain in a fog by following the rule, 'Always go up'; if the mountain has a single peak, this rule will get them to the summit. If the mountain has several false peaks, this rule will get the climbers to a local peak, but not necessarily to the summit. In technical terms, local improvements lead to a global maximum on a convex surface, whereas local improvements lead to a local maximum on a non-convex surface" (Cooter 1994: 225).

20 Recall this expression of R. Cooter's, cited above, to describe non-convexity: an "evolutionary trap occurs when local progress is global regress".

or indirectly, retain a reference to the idea of natural selection in order to reflect on the theory of learning and the conditions needed for collective learning to generate "governance in the public interest".

Let us first focus on the recent attempt by the evolutionary thinkers to reflect on the theory of learning outside the framework of natural selection. After that, we will examine D. North's neo-institutionalist attempt.

As mentioned above, the evolutionary economists' effort to grasp the dynamics of collective action on the basis of a theory of learning released from the fallacious effects of an analogy with the biological concept of natural selection is given a highly illuminating form in L. Marengo and G. Dosi's recent article, Division of Labor, Organizational Coordination and Market Mechanisms in Collective Problem-Solving (Marengo and Dosi 2005).

We will not dwell here on the well-known critique made by the evolutionary thinkers, which L. Marengo and G. Dosi (2005: 306) review, regarding the inadequate attention paid by both mainstream economics and transaction cost economics to the relationship between "the efficiency properties of different organizational forms" and "the learning opportunities which they entail", "independently of any issue of incentive compatibility and transaction governance". It is well known that according to the evolutionary thinkers, this weakness accounts for the failure of both mainstream and transaction cost economists to take into account the role played by technological development in the organization of intra- and inter-firm relations, as well as those economists' inadequate attention to the conditions that foster the development of the innovative capabilities of production units in the economic market. This critique clearly accounts for the particular attention the evolutionary thinkers wish to grant to the "learning process" and consequently to the conditions that must be respected if it is hoped to foster collective problem-solving capabilities and thus the most desirable forms of collective governance. It is this particular aspect of L. Marengo and G. Dosi's argument we wish to focus on here.

The authors' main thesis is easy to understand. As they write:

> [T]he main argument can be stated as follows: the division of problem-solving labor into decentralized decision units coordinated by markets determines which solutions (that is technological and organizational designs) can be generated and tested by the selection process. On one hand, this division is necessary for boundedly rational organizations in order to reduce the dimensions of the search space, but on the other hand, it might well happen that the division of physical and cognitive labor is such that the best designs will never be generated and therefore never selected by any selection mechanism whatsoever. In particular, we show that everything being equal, the higher the degree of decentralization, the smaller the portion of the search space that is explored and therefore the lower probability that the optimal solutions are included in such a portion of space. Finally one can easily prove that computing the optimal division of problem-solving activities is more difficult than solving the problem itself; thus

> we cannot assume that boundedly rational agents in search of solutions to a given problem do possess the right decomposition of the problem itself (Marengo and Dosi 2005: 308).

Of course, as H. Simon has observed, "[R]ational agents must necessarily proceed by decomposing any large, complex and intractable problem into smaller sub-problems that can be solved independently". But "at the same time, the extent of the division of problem-solving labor is limited by the existence of interdependencies. If sub-problem decomposition separates interdependent elements, then solving each sub-problem independently does not allow optimisation". Thus:

> [I]t is important to remark that the introduction of any decentralized interaction mechanism, such as competitive markets for each component, does not solve the problem … Thus, interdependencies undermine the effectiveness of the selection process as a device for adaptive optimization and they introduce forms of path-dependency with lock-in into sub-optimal states that do not originate from the frictions and costs connected to the selection mechanism, but from the internal structure of the entities undergoing selection (Marengo and Dosi 2005: 309–10).[21]

After trying to formalize these properties and to confirm experimentally the necessary trade-off between "decomposability" and integrated coordination in the organization of the division of learning labour, the authors arrive at the following observation. Of course, the "speed of adaptation" is greater among locally decentralized entities. But the question remains: "[C]an optimal organizational structures (or optimal technological designs) emerge out of decentralized local interactions?" The authors observe at the end of their labours:

> [T]his is only possible under some special and rather implausible conditions and …, on the contrary, the advantages of decentralization usually bear a cost in terms of sub-optimality … Our model also highlights the subtle trade-offs between decomposition levels, degrees of suboptimality of the achievable outcomes, and

21 The authors note that this property of learning processes is not without ties to this other property: "[T]hat, in general, the search space of a problem is not given exogenously, but is constructed by individuals and organizations as a subjective representation of the problem itself. If the division of problem-solving labor is limited by interdependencies, the structure of interdependencies itself depends on how the problem is framed by problem-solvers … As shown by many case studies, major innovations often appear when various elements that were well known are re-combined and put together under a different perspective. Indeed, one can go as far as to say that it is the representation of a problem that undermines its purported difficulty and that one of the fundamental functions of organizations is precisely to implement collective representations of the problems face" (Marengo and Dosi 2005: 310–11).

> adaptation speed. Together, it casts strong doubts on the general validity of an "optimality-through-selection" argument in the sphere of organizational and technological designs and, more in general, of any "optimistic" view of market selection processes that can be found, for instance, in Alchian and Friedman, as forces that substitute individual optimization with evolutionary optimization (Marengo and Dosi 2005: 323).

It is this that accounts for the necessity for highly integrated organizations to compensate for or counterbalance the kind of coordination specific to "decomposed tasks (possibly coordinated via market-like mechanisms but also via mechanisms based on the interaction of quasi-independent units within simple organizations)" (Marengo and Dosi 2005: 323). These findings, the authors conclude, "are fully consistent with vast empirical evidence suggesting that new technologies develop in highly integrated organizations because of the need to control the strong interdependencies that characterize difficult problems". From this perspective, it could be suggested that:

> [O]rganizations could actually play the even more fundamental role of building collective representations of the problem to be solved, and that such representations could act as frames within which the division of labor takes place inside and across organizations (Marengo and Dosi 2005: 324).

This position, which is representative of current evolutionary theory, elicits three observations that will reveal the theory's intrinsic limitations.

(1) First, L. Marengo and G. Dosi's position makes it possible to grasp their implicit conception of the learning operation, a conception that has two features. First, from a perspective developed by H. Simon in economic theory, the learning operation is conceived of as an operation of selection by trial and error, making it possible to select the kinds of coordination deemed by the group members to be most efficient. The second feature is that, in contrast to biologically based approaches referring to "natural selection", this selection operation is conceived of as directly dependent on its initial "restriction". This point was already emphasized, as was seen above, by evolutionary game theorists, and in particular J. Maynard-Smith.[22] The selection operation can select only according to something that is a given at the outset, which is not assumed to be subject to transformation by the learning operation itself. This second feature leads to what might be called an "externalist" conception of learning. We will see below that the contribution made by the pragmatist and experimentalist approach to governance, currently

22 As was quoted above (note 12): "Evolutionary game theory is devised to analyse *frequency-dependent* selection. In frequency-dependent selection, the fitness of individuals depends not only on their natural, but also on their *social* environment. That is to say, the fitness of particular phenotypes in a population depends on their frequencies in the population".

being advanced by C. Sabel in particular, is distinguished from the evolutionary approach precisely by this point and that it seeks, just as a pragmatist perspective requires, to develop an "internalist" approach to learning and to the governance of collective action. For the evolutionary thinkers, the only way to modify what may prove to be the overly restricted nature of the initial given consists of deploying an external factor in view of "expanding" all the initial hypotheses (or, as H. Simon might say, all the initial routines) that are to be tested by the learning operation with a view to selecting the one that is most efficient at solving the problem that has triggered the collective action. The innovation—that is, the expansion of the initial representation by expanding the possibilities present at the outset—cannot result from the learning operation itself. That is why L. Marengo and G. Dosi (2005: 306) consider that "a selection mechanism can indeed, under certain conditions, select for the fittest structures, but only if the latter exist in the first place. Selection can account for the convergence of a population toward some given form, not for the emergence of such a form".

(2) This "externalist" approach to learning simultaneously accounts for the approach taken to governance, that is, that of the institutional mechanisms that must accompany the learning operation if the latter is to result in "optimality" or at the very least in the kind of organization of collective action that satisfies, to the extent possible, the normative expectations of its participants (governance in the public interest). As the authors say, representation of the local actors must be "expanded" by means of an external mechanism that, as might be said, hierarchically "imposes" a collective representation. E. Brousseau[23] justly remarks that the evolutionary thinkers provide little definition to the kind of organization that is required to impose this "expansion" of decentralized actors' local representations from outside and ensure that learning results not in what L. Marengo and G. Dosi call a local maximum but in a global optimum. But even if the form taken by this organization thus continues to be a black box, it reproduces in many respects the institutional form of the solution arrived at by the evolutionary game theorists and by R. Cooter writing in the law and economics current. On one hand, it is assumed that a point exists, external to local actors, where "the" collective representation can be defined that will ensure adequate bases[24] for the most suitable possible kind of collective action to be selected on a trial-and-error basis. On the other hand, this "integrated" representation will be imposed on the actors as they conduct their local learning operations. Self-regulation does not "naturally" lead to an "optimal" form of governance. It only results in such governance to the

23 As E. Brousseau (1999: 194) says, "[T]he organization remains the 'black box' of evolutionary theory". Similarly, a little farther on and still more explicitly, he (1999: 196) writes, "[A]t bottom, the evolutionary firm, and indeed all forms of organization, are no more than a black box comparable to the firm of traditional neoclassical theory, about which we do not know how resources are combined inside it".

24 In the language of R. Cooter, this representation will allow for the selection of the kinds of regulation that avoid evolutionary traps (see above, note 19).

extent that it is "guided" from the outside by a representation of the problem to be solved and the constraints to be respected, a representation that "integrates" all the individual points of view and thus guarantees a global collective representation of the problem. What we are seeing here is a process that was already present in the thinking of A. Schotter, who made the production of an optimal strategy dependent on a hierarchical mechanism—and therefore one external to the agents—and to its necessarily being underpinned by a "tacit agreement" by all group members. The same process was also present in the thinking of R. Sugden, who made this optimal strategy dependent on the need for all of the social group's members to share a single collective representation, which he assumed to be guaranteed by the external mechanism of the dynamics of cultural tradition. Incidentally, it should be noted that, in adopting this process, these various recent trends in economic inquiry are adopting a model of thinking that is well known in political philosophy. This is the approach to inquiry into the question of collective action adopted during the first stage of modern political philosophy, more precisely during the period bounded by T. Hobbes at one end and J. Rousseau at the other. But to take this approach to inquiring into the question of collective action is to disregard the fact that subsequent political philosophers—in particular I. Kant and J. Fichte at the start of the nineteenth century—clearly discerned its difficulties, indeed dead ends. One indication of these difficulties can be found in some of the presuppositions endorsed and left unexamined by the approach to learning taken by the evolutionary thinkers. Let us review some of these presuppositions.

(3) The way of conceiving of the hybridization of decentralized kinds of coordination[25] with their necessary external and hierarchical complements rests on three presuppositions. Each of these presuppositions relates to "capabilities" that the evolutionary thinkers assume to be given and whose conditions for possibility they therefore do not inquire into. If we analyse L. Marengo and G. Dosi's way of conceiving of the hybridizing mechanism that is needed to optimize the learning operation, we find that there are three operations for which, as regards economic agents, the needed capabilities are in each case assumed to be given.

The first operation is obviously one of generalization. This operation is deployed to construct the social group's collective representation. At this first level, two "capabilities" are assumed to be given. First, it is assumed that the operation for generalizing (or "integrating", as L. Marengo and G. Dosi say in less technical language) points of view happens naturally. It is assumed that the actors have a "natural" capacity to decentre their individual point of view, that is, to put themselves in the other person's place, to see the other person as another similar to oneself and consequently to adapt their own perceptions with a view to constructing a representation of the problem to be solved that incorporates this needed generalization. Next, it is assumed that *the* suitable frame for this

25 That is, as L. Marengo and G. Dosi (2005: 323) say, forms of coordination "via market-like mechanisms but also via mechanisms based on the interaction of quasi independent units within simple organizations".

generalizing operation is automatically given. In effect, it is assumed that it is possible to inquire into the problem from an "Archimedean point" that would allow for identifying the individual points of view that must be taken into consideration and then generalized (integrated). The evolutionary thinkers argue that it is necessary to "expand" the local representation mobilized by decentralized agents. This "expansion" must make it possible to go from a restricted local representation to a broader (collective) global representation. But whence comes it that we can assume the capabilities necessary for the operation of determining what is the right *collectivity* to take into consideration in order to arrive at an adequate representation of the problem to be solved?

The second operation is one that the "general" performs on the "local". The "institutional" hybridization suggested by the evolutionary thinkers assumes that the collective representation is "grafted" onto the local representations deployed by the decentralized agents. How does this "application" of the general to the local, that is, of the central to the local, take place? Here again, in neglecting to analyse the conditions for possibility of such an operation, the assumption is made that there "naturally" exists a certain capability. This may be the capability of the institutions that represent the collective group to efficiently impose the necessary adaptation of local representations; or it may be the capability of local agents to automatically transform their "local" representations and adapt them to "global" representations.

The third operation relates to "local" learning. Of course, current evolutionary thinkers acknowledge that self-regulation on its own does not necessarily result in selection of the best possible collective action. They believe that decentralized coordination only leads to selection, through the effect of local learning, to a "local maximum" and not a global optimum. But even with the mere assumption of this local "success" of the learning operation, there is a highly problematic assumption of "local competency for learning". With this assumption, capabilities are once again being assumed to be "naturally given" and accordingly, no attention is given to what would be indispensable to ensuring their production. In effect, it is assumed that all the actors in this local interaction are prepared to make all the behavioural changes that adaptation to this local maximum would entail. They are not only assumed to be disposed to accept the constraints and limits that the best possible coordination with other people from the perspective of the local context and everyone's representations would entail. They are also assumed to be naturally capable of perceiving and agreeing to all the adaptations necessary in their own representations, such that the latter can achieve the best possible fulfilment in the local context.

These three features of the way the evolutionary thinkers envisage the learning operation and the *hybrid nature* of the mechanism of governance that will permit the collective action to fulfil participants' normative expectations to the extent possible explain why the evolutionary thinkers, despite their project to surmount the limitations of previous stages in economic theory of collective action, reproduce those stages' epistemological framework and basic model. This is also the reason for the two recent attempts by research in the social sciences to resume that process of surmounting and to examine more deeply the question of the conditions for possibility of collective learning and of the institutional building of public-private partnerships. Before analysing this new stage of current research in theory of governance, one last aspect of recent attempts by neo-institutionalist economic theory remains to be addressed. As was said above, transaction cost economists have also attempted to surmount what we called O. Williamson's "epistemological ambiguity" and, more generally, that of the usual economic approaches to the process of economic change; in making this attempt, transaction cost economists have relied on the evolutionary thinkers' focus on the learning operation. At this juncture, we must consider the recent attempt made by D. North.

Clearly, it is not merely for the sake of historical completeness that we wish to make a rapid detour via D. North's attempt. And in fact, we will not here describe D. North's undertaking itself. Rather, we will restrict ourselves to a single aspect of his thought that will enable us to highlight even more clearly what remains "unthought" or "assumed as given" in neo-institutionalist economic approaches to governance and that also accounts for the need felt by many today to go beyond the limits of those approaches or at any rate to extend the gains made by them.

D. North, of course, wished to supplement the Williamsonian approach by showing that the economic dynamics of a social group must be analysed not just at the level of what O. Williamson calls "mechanisms of governance" but also at the level of the institutional environment, which consists of formal and informal norms on which social interactions depend and by which social interactions are framed. That is not the issue that concerns us here, even though it is a key aspect of transaction cost economics. What is important from our present perspective is the way D. North seeks to inquire into the historical learning dynamic at the level of this same institutional framework. The question D. North asks on this score is how to account for the evolution of each socio-economic system and for the fact that socioeconomic systems do not appear to produce the same economic results on completion of their internal dynamics. His answer to this question received its main expression in an article he co-authored with J. Knight (1997). It was subsequently further developed in his most recent work (North 2005).

This answer, however, is not always easy to pinpoint. D. North clearly endorses the commitment expressed by L. Marengo and G. Dosi to get clear of any "biological" approach to the selection operation[26] and to rely exclusively on the resources of a

26 "[I]t is important to emphasize two significant distinctions between biological and economic evolution. In the former variation occurs through mutation and sexual recombination along Mendelian lines. There is no close analogy in economic evolution. And … the selection mechanisms in evolutionary theory are not informed by beliefs about the eventual consequences as they are in economic evolution. And indeed, in the latter, it is the intentionality of the players as expressed through the institutions they create which shapes performance" (North 2005: 66) and also, "Cultural traits do not possess attributes parallel to those of genes and indeed the growing literature of the new institutional economics makes abundantly clear that institutions

theory of learning.[27] But unlike L. Marengo and G. Dosi, he does not develop an in-depth, rigorous analysis of learning; perhaps in consequence of this, he also does not offer a clear presentation of the solutions he would advance in order to avoid the inefficiency effects that the "path-dependency" linked to every learning operation risks triggering. Furthermore, even though D. North aims, in a nuanced way, to open up his approach to action to a theory of "human intentionality" and thereby to an epistemological approach, the latter remains very underdeveloped. D. North is satisfied to refer more or less allusively to the connectionist approach and to certain discussions in anthropology and cognitive psychology; he does not engage with recent work in analytic philosophy that represents the epistemological extension of these discussions and that would undoubtedly require him to revise some of his implicit presuppositions. An approach of this kind calls for caution in the effort to produce a more theoretically based reconstruction of it. Caution is all the more appropriate given that D. North is the first to emphasize the current limits of our scientific understanding of the operation of the social transformation of modes of governance and, a fortiori, of the conditions that would render such a transformation "efficient". What we wish to highlight, however—even at the risk of obscuring some of the subtlety of D. North's approach—is that that approach remains imprisoned in what we called above an externalist conception of learning. Although this externalism is less "radical" than that of the evolutionary thinkers L. Marengo and G. Dosi, it still does not allow for the question of the conditions for an "efficient" transformation of social governance *to be constructed* in terms that would make it possible to avoid the problematic presuppositions of the evolutionary position (see (2) below). And this, it seems to us, is what accounts as well for the fact that the transaction cost economists who have taken on board D. North's advances over O. Williamson resort to an "externalist" position and its implications in dealing with how to understand the hybrid nature of public-private partnerships, that is, in dealing with how to compensate for the deficiencies of *pure* decentralized coordination—even though D. North himself has not expressed his views on these issues. To demonstrate this, we will refer to the illustrative position adopted by E. Brousseau with respect to the regulation of the Internet marketplace (see (3) below). Just before proceeding to examine the problematic aspects of D. North's approach—and they do not overshadow his very real advances—we will briefly describe the key features of his argument (see (1) below).

(1) D. North's position on the issue that concerns us here can be viewed as consisting of three main components.

The first relates to D. North's emphasis on what he calls a theory of human intentionality and its consequences for his cognitive perspective on culture

must be explained in terms of intentionality of humans. Informal norms develop that blend the moral inference of genetic origin with the intentional aims of humans, which together provide the backbone of what we should mean by the term culture" (North 2005: 42).

27 D. North (2005: 25) refers explicitly, in fact, to G. Dosi regarding what he calls a theory of the "building blocks" of an "evolutionary theory of learning".

and economic evolution. D. North's basic idea is that, in the social world, the fundamental process is that economic change is a function of a collective learning dynamic. This process is, in fact, a function of an uninterrupted search by which all individuals strive to solve each new problem they are faced with.[28] This search by trial and error is always a function of the beliefs that guide them and that are incorporated into their social institutions. Economic dynamics are thus the expression of an intentional aim by human society in general, which takes effect through a search for learning that tests its belief systems again and again and adapts those belief systems to new contexts. The emphasis here is thus on the role of culture. The idea is that the evolution of the social system is the expression of an ongoing intentional learning process influenced by the collective beliefs embodied in each society's institutional contexts:

> There is an intimate relationship between belief systems and the institutional framework. Belief systems embody the internal representation of the human landscape. Institutions are the structure that humans impose on the landscape in order to produce the desired outcome (North 2005: 49).

D. North relies here on the theory of culture developed by E. Hutchins:

> [C]ulture is not any collection of things, whether tangible or abstract … It is a human cognitive process that takes place both inside and outside the minds of people … Culture is an adaptive process that accumulates partial solutions to frequently encountered problems (Knight and North 1997: 221).

28 "If uncertainty is a constant in explaining institutional change, what difference does it make when the uncertainty changes from that associated with the physical environment to that associated with the human environment? All three of the sources of economic change—demography, stock of knowledge, and institutions—have been fundamentally altered … The growth of population has led to a world of ubiquitous externalities as humans were forced into ever closer proximity to each other, but in the additional context of the revolutionary changes in technology it has produced new social problems to be solved. The driving force in the development of the human environment has been the growth in the stock of knowledge which has revolutionized production technologies and provided the potential of a world of plenty. Equally it has created weapons of mass destruction capable of destroying us. The resultant institutional development has created more and more complex structures designed to deal with the consequent novel problems facing societies. Institutions as the incentive structure of societies have produced diverse inducements to invest in, expand, and apply this growing knowledge to solve problems of human scarcity. The implications for consciousness have been that such inducements have expanded the human creative potential and in combination with diverse cultures produced widely varied responses to the novel problems confronting human as a result of these changes. But the responses have not always been creative and productive" (North 2005: 43–4).

Through the construction, then, of the "artifactual structures" that belief systems and institutions constitute, societies engage in ongoing learning, that is, in ongoing "adaptive reorganization in a complex system" (Knight and North 1997: 220). Thus, D. North (2005: 47) stresses, "the learning process appears to be a function of (1) the way in which a given belief system filters the information derived from experiences, and (2) the different experiences confronting individuals and societies at different times".

The second component explicates the idea that this process of collective learning by which human intentionality is produced does not always lead to results that D. North considers efficient:

> [T]he responses [of such learning processes] have not always been creative and productive. Sometimes, the way experiences have interacted with consciousness has led to institutions that resulted in stagnation with resultant human frustration in the context of more dynamic societies (North 2005: 44).

Writing in the vein of B. Arthur's widely known work (Arthur 1994), D. North highlights the phenomenon of path dependence, which affects every learning operation:

> Path dependence is a fact of history and one of the most enduring and significant lessons to be derived from studying the past. The difficulty of fundamentally altering paths is evident and suggests that the learning process by which we arrive at today's institutions constrains future choices.[29]

How can we ensure such a change will take effect and that the learning operation will be *efficient*, that is, that it will lead to the transformation of existing institutions that is required to satisfy the *intention* (the normative expectation) that justifies the operation?

D. North's answer to this question—which constitutes the third component—has two aspects.

---

29 (Arthur 1994: 77) and also this helpful passage: "The interaction of beliefs, institutions, and organizations in the total artifactual structure makes path dependence a fundamental factor in the continuity of a society. Path dependence is not 'inertia', rather it is the constraints on the choice set in the present that are derived from historical experiences of the past. Understanding the process of change entails confronting directly the nature of path dependence in order to determine the nature of the limits to change that it imposes in various settings" (Arthur 1994: 52). Elsewhere, J. Knight and D. North (1997: 224) write, "[B]elief systems exhibit path-dependence such that history matters, and this can significantly affect the trajectory of growth in economy. Our analysis has the following methodological implication: explanations of economic performance should place primary emphasis on social context as opposed to failures of individual cognition or rationality".

First, the key to "economic success"—and thus of success in learning—is the presence, within the institutional framework specific to a society, of institutions that make learning possible and provide incentives to learn. "Put simply the richer the artifactual structure the more likely are we to confront novel problems successfully. That is what is meant by adaptive efficiency; creating the necessary artifactual structure is an essential goal of economic policy."[30] Here D. North provides examples drawn from history to illustrate his hypothesis. Thus he explains that the appropriate artifactual structure is what accounts for the difference in economic success between Genoese traders and the traders of other, contemporary Mediterranean societies. The Genoese cultural norms made possible the development of institutions suited to a vast and complex market.[31] Societies' capacity to adapt and adopt the institutional framework suited to a new environment thus depends on existing institutions—not only the formal rules, but also, above all, the informal norms specific to the cultural belief system. The more the institutional framework develops cognitive competencies, that is, capacities for learning, the more efficient adaptation will be.

We could even go further. D. North discerns to some extent the "reflexive advance" proper to modernity. That is, what is also constitutive of the modern Western world's specific economic success is its adoption of institutions characterized by being organized as institutions intended to foster learning. Here, D. North turns to F. Hayek, saying:

---

30 (North 2005: 70). Also: "Successful economic development will occur when the belief system that has evolved has created a 'favorable' artifactual structure that can confront the novel experiences that the individual and society face and resolve positively the novel dilemmas. Failures will occur when the novel experiences that the individual and society face are so far removed from the artifactual structure of the evolved belief system that individual and society do not have the building blocks of the mind and artifactual structure to resolve the novel problems" (North 2005: 69). Further: "What I have termed adaptive efficiency is an ongoing condition in which the society continues to modify or create new institutions as problems evolve. A concomitant requirement is a polity and economy that provides for continuous trials in the face of ubiquitous uncertainty and eliminates institutional adaptations that fail to resolve new problems" (North 2005: 169).

31 "Avner Greif has done the most systematic study of the effect of cultural values upon economic performance in comparing Genoese traders with traders who adopted the cultural and social attributes of Islamic society in the Mediterranean trade of the eleventh and twelfth centuries. The traders from the Islamic world developed in-group social communication networks to enforce collective action. While effective in relatively small homogeneous ethnic groups, such networks did not lend themselves to the impersonal exchange that arises with the growing size of markets and diverse ethnic traders. In contrast, the Genoese developed bilateral enforcement mechanisms which entailed the creation of formal legal and political organizations for monitoring and enforcing agreements—an institutional/organizational path that permitted and led to more complex trade and exchange" (North 2005: 75).

> [T]he best recipe for confronting such novel situations is the one that Hayek put forth many years ago and that has been the source of US material success, which is maintenance of institutions that permit trial and error experiments to occur. Such a structure entails not only a variety of institutions and organizations so that alternative policies can be tried but also effective means of eliminating unsuccessful solutions. Adaptive efficiency evolves only after a relatively long period of evolving informal norms and we know of no shortcut to this process (North 2005: 163).

But at the same time—and this is the second aspect of his solution—D. North wishes to be prudent about the perspectives opened up by this point of view. Prudent not just with respect to guaranteeing the future success of the institutions that have characterized the "United States' societal development";[32] prudent also, and indeed especially, because, as D. North emphasizes, we do not yet have a full account of the operation by which it would be possible to "manipulate" cultural norms. The process by which this transformation may be managed remains incompletely understood: "[W]hile formal institutions can be changed by fiat, informal institutions[33] evolve in ways that are still far from completely understood and therefore are not typically amenable to deliberate human manipulation" (North 2005: 50). It is because knowledge of this process is still inadequate that, today, we still face difficulties in successfully grafting onto other, less economically successful societies[34] the institutional conditions that ensure the current success of rich economies:

> [W]e still do not know how to create polities that will put in place economic rules with the correct incentives. We still have an incomplete understanding of the complex institutional and technologically interdependent structure of

32 "[T]here is no guarantee that [this] flexible, adaptively efficient institutional structure will persist in the ever more complex novel world that we are creating. The ubiquity of economic decline of civilizations in the past suggests that adaptive efficiency may have its limits" (North 2005: 169).

33 "The intimate interrelationship of beliefs and institutions, while evident in the formal rules of a society, is most clearly articulated in the informal institutions—norms, conventions, and internally held codes of conduct. These informal institutions not only embody the moral codes of the belief system, which tend to have common characteristics across cultures, but also embody the norms particular to individual societies, which are very diverse across cultures" (North 2005: 50).

34 "In a country without a heritage of formal and informal consensual political institutions, the road to an effective political system requires either an authoritarian ruler with an understanding, desire, and ability to put in place the necessary economic rules and enforce them, or the much more lengthy process of piecemeal development through non-governmental organizations (NGOs) and effective foreign aid in which educational, health, judicial, or other assistance is effectively designed and delivered with the objective of transferring the essential knowledge and skills to the resident population" (North 2005: 164).

political economies which is necessary to improving their performance (North 2005: 168).

(2) From our perspective, this position of D. North's calls for two comments that will enable us to see how he remains a prisoner of what we called, in our commentary on the conception of learning developed by L. Marengo and G. Dosi, an "externalist" approach to learning.

The first comment relates to D. North's methodological procedure. While this topic may seem to have little connection to the specific issues of learning and the conditions for social change, it will enable us to clarify the "externalist presupposition" D. North *unconsciously* adopts in analysing those issues. Indeed, let us pause a moment over what may appear obvious to many but is unquestionably more problematic than it appears. We can invoke two factors here. One directly concerns the theory of science. We have already quoted the passage from D. North which presents the view that, in the sphere of human actions, any naturalistic (or biological) approach to selection fails to grasp the constructivist dimension of intentionality. Decisions by human beings are necessarily constructs of meaning that are constantly subject to reinterpretation in the light of interactions with the environment. But if it is the case that, in the human sphere, we are always dealing with a "belief" system, how are we to view the process by which D. North wishes to deploy an instrument external to the belief system in order to measure and evaluate the success of the learning processes that constitute the economic history of various cultures? In effect, D. North is evaluating cultures' capacity to adapt efficiently to the requirements of "economic success". But why should we assume that this "standard of measurement" can be defined in a manner external to the cultural system—which D. North himself recognizes as the determinant of all collective action. Does this not amount to assuming the "meaning" of the intentional aim is *not* itself defined by the belief system of the social group that undertakes the learning process? Does it not amount to assuming this "meaning" can be defined independently by a certain science—the science of economics—unattached to any belief system? The presupposition operating here goes even further. Isn't it common sense to see that any aim by a social group to increase wealth is an aim that is accompanied by a set of value judgements tending to integrate other, concomitant objectives into this aspiration? And it is the set of all these integrated objectives that defines the complex—inexplicit—objective the social group strives to fulfil. To pinpoint an objective and define it according to the measurement instruments provided by present-day economic science is obviously an acceptable undertaking. But to measure, as D. North does, the success of collective learning operations that are assumed to underlie any collective action is altogether another matter. To do so is to assume that it is possible to define from outside a social group the *meaning* of the objectives the groups adopts. Thus, it is to assume that there exists an "objective" measure for the meaning of a statement (that is, of an intentional action) that is external to the practice by which the statement is produced. This epistemological option adopted by D. North does not just appear incompatible with the cultural constructivism he embraces to explain his approach to collective action. It also rests on a kind of externalist realism that today, following the work of W. Quine and H. Putnam, is highly problematic.[35]

A similar process underlies D. North's approach to the theory of learning. This constitutes the substance of our second comment. The process in question consists of assuming that the conditions for the "success" of the learning operation are ultimately guaranteed by a mechanism external to the learning operation, a mechanism whose conditions for possibility are assumed to be given and therefore not the focus of specific attention. This is what we have termed an external conception of learning. What then is D. North's model? If we make an effort to reconstruct this model, it would appear to contain two basic ideas. The first emerges if an effort is made to understand the conditions for possibility, according to D. North, of the collective learning process that defines all collective action. Recall that D. North believes that any social group is always in process of adapting. But since he rejects the reductive hypothesis of natural selection, he acknowledges that operations of selection through learning may not result in the most "efficient" forms of governance.[36] As we saw, it all depends on whether institutions (consisting of formal and informal norms) are in place in the social belief system that will make possible the learning required by the nature of the new problems the social group is faced with. The more cognitive experiences a social group accumulates that make it open to trying new solutions suited to the nature of the new problems to be solved, the more chances it will have to carry out efficient learning. The notion of chance is appropriate at this stage. D. North himself (2005: 169) uses it expressly in relation to the success of the learning process that led the USA to select an efficient institutional system. This development, he observes, "was more good fortune than intent". Note that, in holding this view, he is not acting inconsistently with his commitment to account for collective action and the process of social change in terms of the intentionality of human action. The intentional dynamics means that human history, through the effects of culture, is mobilized like an ongoing intentional learning activity. Humanity is assumed to be in the grip of an ongoing process of reinterpretation—and thus of increase in its store of knowledge—regarding its symbolic systems, such that it constantly adapts better and thus becomes more efficient in its fulfilment of its objectives. Of

35 W. Quine and H. Putnam have worked, in contrast, to develop an "internalist" approach, also known as "semantic holism", and accordingly to condemn all epistemological "mentalism". Semantic holism and the rejection of mentalism consist precisely of viewing meanings (that is, the intentional aims of operations of judgement) as far from being physical or computational entities stored in the mind but rather as always dependent on the meanings of other elements. These other elements' own meanings cannot be assumed to be fixed and determinable by applying formal rules. On this, see especially (Putnam 1988: 1–18: Chapter 1 "Meaning and Mentalism").

36 That is, in D. North's objectivist language, forms that are economically productive, and in our more internalist language, forms that maximize to the extent possible the satisfaction of the group members' normative expectations (that is, governance in the public interest).

course, individual human beings are the actors in this collective process. But the agents' intentionality is itself predetermined by the intrinsic potential (the path-dependence) of the kind of social knowledge that constitutes the "cultural web" they are rooted in. The "good fortune" in question is thus one of the properties of this web. At bottom, D. North is here reprising the classical argument of economic approaches to selection that we noted in L. Marengo and G. Dosi: the "efficiency" of what is selected through learning is a function of what was available at the outset: one can only select what already exists. D. North emphasizes that what must exist is a cognitive practice likely to solve the problem adequately. Thus if Genoese traders were able to be economically more efficient than their "Islamicized" peers, this was because they were no longer subject to communitarian kinds of responsibility.

A second idea complicates D. North's system, however. D. North is himself indisputably dissatisfied with the mere idea of a collective intentionality subject to the play of chance. His presupposition of a historical intentionality in process of "learning" leads him to envisage a second operation to define the conditions for productivity of collective learning processes. In contrast to L. Marengo and G. Dosi, he does not resort to the idea of a hierarchical social mechanism to "expand" the strategies available from the outset. Instead, adopting the classic "technological and formalist" posture of modern science,[37] he claims that scientific research must be pursued to identify the internal mechanisms that will allow for the "manipulation" of the informal norms that constitute culture and thus the better mastery of the intentional learning operation that constitutes any collective action. This, after all, is the meaning of the statements cited above (see Chapter 3, notes 32 and 33). Modern Western society has been able, thanks to the proliferation of its cognitive practices, to benefit from a kind of advance in reflexivity. This society, more than any other, has been able to equip itself with institutions that mark it as a society consciously organized with learning in view. But, as D. North sees it, this advance in reflexivity does not guarantee its own perpetuation. It is possible this success will come to an end. These institutions do not guarantee that future novel problems will be soluble using the same cognitive practices. Thus, we are still faced with the "frequency-dependent" selection mechanism.

On the other hand, D. North's implicit position is that this still-uncompleted reflexive advance could possibly be extended by the developments of science—that is, through a better understanding of the operation of "human manipulation" of informal norms.[38] A supplementary "reflexive" advance—potentially a definitive one—could be achieved: it would allow for attaining mastery of the operation that guarantees the success of the learning operation; it would thus allow society to learn how to learn. Once having developed a scientific understanding of the formal mechanisms of the operation of intentionality, we would be able to "manipulate" social nature *technologically* in the same way that physics or biology permits us

37 This is clearly not unrelated to his highly classical external realist epistemology.

38 D. North (2005: 70) also speaks explicitly of a better elucidation of what he calls the "sources of human decision-making".

to "manipulate" nature. A position of this kind appears to us to be implicitly tied to those other of D. North's positions we identified above and is coherent with the conception of the intentional collective subject he invokes in setting out his theory. Culture conceived of as the ongoing learning process of human beings dealing with an ever-new environment is indisputably related to the idea of a subject endowed with a capacity and commitment to learn that leads, by the very logic of cognitive increase, to wanting, and being ultimately able, to acquire knowledge of its own intentional operations.

Here again, as with L. Marengo and G. Dosi, though in a less radical manner, recourse emerges to an externality that ensures the conditions for success of the learning operation. The externality is here provided by the historical dynamics of the collective subject, that is, by the hermeneutic dynamics of culture. D. North's position is less radical than the other authors' because he conceives of these dynamics, not only as incomplete, but also in the classical manner of modern reflexivity: it is by the intentional subject's turning back over the laws of its own intentionality (by its learning to learn) that the conquest of the conditions for a self-regulation that has at last been mastered will take place. This approach recalls the kind of reflexive modernity U. Beck and A. Giddens write about. It also prefigures the pragmatist experimentalist undertaking we will examine below. But in contrast to pragmatist experimentalist authors, D. North does not perceive the need to try to internalize the conditions needed for such a reflexive advance. The advance is assumed to be acquired through the dynamics of science, that is, through the internal dynamic of the requirements of the intentionality specific to history.

Such an approach is not without institutional consequences at the level of the theory of governance. Of course, D. North has not really expressed a point of view on this issue.[39] His discourse is either more theoretical or more that of the historian of economics. But the externalism of his theory of learning may account for a feature of the thinking of transaction cost economists who justly wish to take on board the real advances D. North has brought to the theoretical framework of neo-institutionalist economists. This feature is that they end by inquiring into the compensatory mechanisms for the inadequacies of pure decentralized coordination by using the hierarchical model of recourse to the public authorities. The public authorities are assumed to employ a rule of governance that favours the redefinition of the cognitive framework for the common interest. Thus, the public authorities are understood to possess the function of reflexive legitimacy they were already credited with by classical democratic political theories. An

39 Recall, however, the quotation at n. 80: the position expressed there is typical of policies currently in vogue in the field of international institutions, which, in assuming the efficacy of NGOs' activities, skirt an important question: Why could the effects of NGOs' activities in countries where efforts are being made at transformation not also be a function of the use that will be made of those effects by the people of the host country? And thus why would "the essential knowledge and skills [transferred] to the resident population" not be reinterpreted according to the perceptions of the "belief system" of that population?

especially representative example may be found in the work of E. Brousseau on the regulation of the Internet.

(3) The idea, of which E. Brousseau is a notable exponent (Brousseau 2001a, Brousseau and Currien 2001) of a hierarchical governance framework for the development of the digital economy features the principal characteristics of a model of governance based on D. North's theories and designed to ensure mastery of the operation that guarantees success of the process of social learning. We will use the digital economy to illustrate how this model can be applied.

On one hand, there are opportunities for growth concentrated in the emerging technological bubble of the digital society. These opportunities are essentially the product of a set of socio-historical factors of a nature similar to those that fostered the emergence of financial capitalism among Genoese in the time of Machiavelli. It could be said that in the same way as "the Genoese developed … mechanisms which entailed the creation of … organizations for monitoring and enforcing agreements—an institutional/organizational path that permitted and led to more complex trade and exchange" (North 2005: 75), the digital society has created a set of new behaviours that have allowed for the emergence of a new context of cooperation and exchange exemplified by the development of the open source society.

On the other hand, it is necessary to stabilize this kind of process in order to guarantee the perpetuation of what is learned and to prevent what has been learned from being appropriated by special interests to the detriment of social development as a whole. In the realm of the Internet, these risks are felt all the more keenly for the speed with which new problems of both a technical and a political nature arise.[40] Even on the level of the coordination of the technical operations that underpin the system's development, the question soon arose of the optimal method of supervision and control that would allow for protection of the interests of an increasing number of users, in the face of the formation of de facto monopolies likely to divert the system's development towards their own purposes and simultaneously reduce its potential for diversification and innovation.[41] To

40 "The essence of the debate over (Internet Corporation for Assigned Names and Numbers) ICANN's Mission lies in the nexus between ICANN's technical coordination role, its operational role, and its policy role. There are some who see ICANN as merely an agent to carry out technical, operational instructions. The ERC does not support this view because it leaves unanswered the question of responsibility for the policy-development work necessary to provide answers to precisely what instructions should be followed, that is, answering the question: 'if not ICANN, then who?' We have not found any credible answers to that question offered by those who favor a purely technical operational ICANN, other than transferring such responsibilities to some international treaty organization, a direction that is viewed with disfavor throughout most of the community (as judged by the comments we received), or to a constellation of organizations that would again beg the question of who will coordinate these organizations" (Committee on ICANN Evolution and Reform-ICANN 2002).

41 M. Mueller (2002: 157) writes that in 1997, the president of the USA adopted a directive on electronic commerce with a recommendation "to make the governance

avert this risk, it was thought that it was necessary to "frame" norms that had been established in a decentralized way and thus "compensate for" their incompleteness, that is, watch out to ensure the chances for opportunistic behaviour were suitably reduced and future access to new opportunities for growth be kept open. At this point, it seemed a "third mechanism" (in the sense of a mechanism standing outside the parties) was needed to ensure the hierarchical organization of the rules. This hierarchical organization must guarantee *extrapolation* to the broadest possible interests of a community of the system's users and thus reinforce the system's development. This is the kind of mechanism that E. Brousseau puts forward. He (2001a: 370) proposes the creation of a hierarchy among, on one hand, various private and specific institutional settings that can develop "collective coordination solutions" "that apply to families of more specific but related cases" and, on the other hand, an ultimate regulatory authority that would settle conflicts between the rules and the private norms. It is in fostering the development of this mesosocial level that an operational cognitive framework for settling rule-based disputes is to be redefined.

The role of this authority would not consist of directly controlling the contents of the solutions that actors would be called upon to contemplate. It would act from the outside, leading parties to employ dispute resolution procedures and thus keeping open the possibility[42] of valuing the new goods produced and the new behaviours developed from the perspective of their potential for expansion. Under this proposal for a hierarchical governance framework, the *third mechanism* for conflict resolution does aim to "take into account the interests of the widest possible community" (Brousseau 2001a: 370), but only while limiting the role of the governance mechanism to favouring negotiation between actors who are *already involved.* This mechanism is thus intended to complement the network's capacity for openness in order to prevent self-regulatory processes from being appropriated to serve the interests of special-interest groups. The internal capacity for openness is thus assumed to be given. In a context of this kind, it is assumed that individual "virtual" communities are already displaying a principle of openness in their way of functioning. The idea here is that these communities' *culture of use* implies generating externalities that have implications that go beyond their own interests, such as allowing for the dissemination of public-interest information related to teaching or to not-for-profit organizations, allowing citizens to provide certain services, and so on.[43] Furthermore,

---

of the domain name system private and competitive and to create a contractually based self-regulatory regime that deals with potential conflicts between domain name usage and trademark laws on a global basis." Mueller is referring here to President Clinton and Vice President Gore's directive, "A Framework for Global Electronic Commerce" (The President's Information Infrastructure Task Force, 1 July 1997).

42 Formally by state guarantee and concretely by coordinated rejection of monopolistic strategies and de facto monopolies.

43 See also, for an analysis of positive externalities specific to internet public goods, the work of A. Héritier (for example, A. Héritier 1998) and the Max Planck project on

the opportunistic appropriation of these "public goods" by some users may already be subject to penalty in comparatively large communities through the management of directories and the means of accessing the network (Brousseau and Curien 2001: 12). But this mechanism for openness may prove to be insufficient when it comes to dealing with previously untested ethical problems (for instance, how to bar access to racist sites) or with certain monopolistic tendencies inherent in managing scarce addresses and a scarce capacity for transport. That is why a *third mechanism* for dispute resolution and "monitoring" to prevent monopolistic behaviours is necessary: to reinforce and maintain the network's capacity for openness, which is already manifest in the various user communities' self-regulation. The issue at stake in hierarchicalization is thus the capacity to "supervise self-regulatory processes" so that "the dynamics of the competitive process may be guaranteed for the long term" (Brousseau 2002: 132).

Thus the formula used by E. Brousseau (2000b: 42) can be summed up in a proposal for action at two levels: on one hand, fostering the proliferation of mechanisms for self-regulation based on the actors' aggregated competencies (the famous "culture of use") in such a way as to complement contractual mechanisms; on the other hand, to build as well, on the model of negotiated decision-making (of the kind found in the sphere of alternative dispute resolution), a third mechanism for regulating the common good that would be endowed with powers of control. This role could be filled by specialized intermediate institutions: ones that would be closer to given spheres of activity (and would thus share meaning with them), better suited to circulating information in order to reduce opportunistic behaviours, and more efficient at resolving disputes specific to the sphere in question. And in fact, during its brief existence so far, it is in this role that the Internet Corporation for Assigned Names and Numbers (ICANN) has won the greatest recognition and reinforced interest in a kind of hierarchical governance for this sector by which trade disputes could be resolved amicably (Froomkin 2002). The third mechanism of hierarchical governance has thus relied essentially on a procedural mode of governance that makes alternative dispute resolution (ADR) processes possible.[44]

Thus, the line of reasoning that has prevailed in the neo-institutionalist tradition in economics has consisted of taking into account the specific nature of a culture of technical innovation associated with the free flow of information in the technical community to try to establish governance of this "Genoese" process of self-development and avoid limiting its chances for survival to the

Internet public goods directed by A. Héritier and C. Engel (presentation available at http://www.mpp-rdg.mpg.de/netgood.html).

44 However, by using control over Internet addresses as the lever of a global public policy on information, ICANN may have provided the regulatory model for a new social order that tries to combine technological neutrality with the weak legitimacy of governance mechanisms based on the self-regulation of the majority actors (Klein 2002). But at the same time, it has fostered cognizance of these mechanisms' inefficiency from the perspective of the protection of the interests of the widest possible user community (Froomkin 2003a, 2003b).

mere reproduction of the contractual mechanisms that organize marketplace competition. This hybrid mechanism consists of building a coordinating mechanism (a dispute resolution mechanism) that allows the innovating culture to choose, from among offers of contractual relationships, a set of measures that guarantee against the appropriation of common resources by holders of exclusive property rights. As for the public authorities, they play a support role *vis-à-vis* the intermediate coordination mechanisms and a monitoring role to mitigate the risks of collusion (Brousseau 2000b: 43) and thus protect the interests of all potential users of future developments.

An analysis of the process followed by E. Brousseau reveals that it rests on two characteristics that show, in turn, how it is based on what we have called the first stage of the current dynamics in theory of governance, that is, the economists' neo-institutionalist approach. The first of these two characteristics can be aligned with the "Northian" orientation of E. Brousseau's line of reasoning, that is, the very strong and highly problematic assumption of a capacity, in the community of Internet users, for self-reflexive development that is, as in the case of D. North's Genoese traders, simply given. This assumption unquestionably accounts for the notably *economic* approach to negotiation taken by E. Brousseau, that is, an approach that remains inspired by the theory of rational choice and that views joint action as consisting of coordination by means of the negotiation of compromises. To assume as given a culture of use that guarantees the existence of the capacities needed for the best possible fulfilment of the normative expectations of the group's members has its consequences. It results in failing to pay attention to the conditions necessary for social interaction to produce learning and development effects. In fact, these conditions are understood to be able to be laid down only from outside, in a "procedurally formal" manner, by an authority whose role is precisely to guarantee the collective quest for legitimacy. This is the locus of the essential difference between the neo-institutionalist economic approach to governance and the second, third, and fourth present-day approaches, which we will explore in Chapters 4, 5, and 6.

Of course, self-regulation is assumed to be incomplete by itself. But the first, framing, assumption accounts for the way this incompleteness of self-regulation is understood and the externalist dimension of the way the solution for it is conceived. The incompleteness remains conceived within the traditional terms of opportunistic behaviours and the need to "impose" a frame of reference of joint action or negotiation. Even though the intention is to escape from the traditional model of hierarchical intervention via the commandment to good behaviour, and we are thus at the mercy of the actors' being disposed to negotiate with each other, the process remains deeply externalist. On one hand, it is difficult to see the difference between a "controlling and monitoring" activity of this kind and E. Ullmann-Margalit's and A. Schotter's recourse to T. Hobbes' *Leviathan* as a way of guaranteeing a cooperative solution and watching over respect for the right to engage in competition by eliminating monopolistic behaviours. But on the other hand, even if we assume that this intervention is not reducible to the traditional "power to sanction" of the hierarchical state, this results in a comparatively "weak" approach to the mechanism for negotiated dispute resolution that must be imposed on actors involved in litigation. The mere existence of a formal framework for the settlement of litigation, of the kind we are familiar with today in the World Trade Organization, for example, is assumed to be able to assure the cooperative solutions required for the appropriate self-development of web-based communities. This is what makes it possible to assume that the mere fact of this governance system's being imposed by an external authority suffices to ensure respect for the conditions of "good governance". The concept of "negotiated joint action" gains no depth as regards what underlying conditions would be required in connection with the expansion of the number of necessary participants in such negotiations, the conditions that would allow for guaranteeing the emergence of a common culture of trust, the conditions for empowerment, and the conditions likely to promote development of a common culture of learning. As will be seen below (Chapter 4, 148–63), like O. Williamson, E. Brousseau makes "restricted" use of I. Macneil's relational theory of contracts, (even if without explicitly referencing I. Macneil). In so doing, he prevents himself from developing a more expansive approach to the conditions required for a wider understanding of the relational nature of contracts such as is developed, for example, by P. Vincent-Jones in the context of a relational and collaborative approach to governance.

We can go further in detailing the problematic impact of the "externalist" approach to learning that inheres in the transaction-cost-based analysis, going beyond what is revealed by attention to the role of the intermediate mechanisms associated with the dispute resolution mechanisms of E. Brousseau's model. These intermediate mechanisms are limited to making possible the working out of "collective coordination solutions" (Brousseau 2001a: 370). It is the third mechanism of organizational governance that is assumed to allow, on its own and from outside, a redefinition of roles and codes in the collective search for solutions. Hybridizing, like recourse to negotiation processes or fora, makes it possible to protect, during a first round, against vulnerability to opportunistic inputs and, during a second round, against undermining cognitive motivation with excessively high institutional governance costs. Thus the coordination problem is assumed to be resolvable at the individual and collective levels simultaneously (Brousseau 2000b: 40).[45] The solution consists of hierarchicalizing the two functions, one of which inheres in organizational experience and the other in actors' cognitive capacities, and the first of which is assumed to lead to the second. The process of organizational governance that allows for selecting the most efficient solutions is assumed to bring with it a logic of anticipation in the actors involved, and this allows them to foresee "the outcome of the selection process and integrate this forecast into their choices" (Brousseau 1999: 201). The extrinsic reference to hierarchical objectives is assumed to complement the innovative effect of initiatives based

45 The mechanism is considered to be "capable not only of channelling individual behaviours, but also of accumulating experience and allowing experimentation" (Brousseau and Rallet 1998: 1609).

on decentralized participation and intrinsic motivation.[46] But at the same time, it has the effect of rendering incomplete the political culture of centralized control over the collective processes for "imagining public regulatory bodies capable of understanding the uniqueness of the issues and practices" specific to the actors' inventiveness (Brousseau 2000b: 43).

While E. Brousseau often refers to D. North, we should nevertheless be clear that what subsists of D. North's "Genoese" process, which we have applied by analogy to actors in the information technology sphere, is "the increased capacity for play" (Brousseau 2000a: 1206: note 3) of some of the actors concerned by the traditional economic regulations of this marketplace. In the face of this situation, for E. Brousseau, the issue consists mainly of avoiding "locking" this dynamic and innovative population into orbit around under-efficient equilibriums. In this context, the benefits of recourse to an externalized third mechanism consist of the fact that, to foster the implementation of flexible arrangements between the actors and thus enhance their chances of thickening their networks and of networking while running fewer risks, action is being taken on the institutional design rather than interventions being made directly on practices.

The benefit of the external mechanism is that it keeps open the principle of institutions' *amendability* in line with the imperatives of the social context. Public action can thus be organized at two levels: that of attention to fostering the adaptation of institutional designs and that of attention to avoiding the hijacking cooptation of these opportunities for flexibility via collusion among actors.

Thus the external mechanism is assumed to mitigate the effects of a kind of "endemic ignorance" by actors regarding optimal institutions: since it is impossible to rely on the convergence of optimal institutional choices, we must act on the governance arrangements that orient those choices by limiting the possibilities that

46 In contrast, the freeware sector (Foray and Zimmerman 2001) provides an example of a proposal for governance that suggests avoiding such an "extrinsic" reference to hierarchical objectives. D. Foray and J. Zimmerman do not suggest mechanisms that would foster external regulation on the model of a new public good that is to be protected. Rather, they suggest another approach that consists of exploring mixed mechanisms that would allow private operators and restricted innovating communities to become involved in hierarchical governance of shared issues (the intermediate mechanism). Under this second approach, the state would no longer be responsible for intervening as a referee to protect a new kind of collective good from being appropriated by opportunistic interests. Instead, the state would propose a frame of reference for resolving disputes that directly threaten the widest possible diversity of development and accessibility of resources in the information society. In this scenario, the third mechanism shifts towards guaranteeing the exchange of knowledge between licensers and freeware developers. (Post 2000). What is presupposed is that the third mechanism will be sufficient to enable the adjustment of practices and to work out reciprocal expectations. A proposed approach to governance of this kind is closer than E. Brousseau's to the model we identify as the second stage in the dynamics of current research on governance, which we call a "relational and collaborative approach to governance" (see Chapter 4).

can be contemplated. This selective property of governance arrangements derives from their processes of formation or social emergence. This is the process that ultimately determines the possibilities for choice by increasing or reducing the capacity for adaptation or self-amendment of a given governance arrangement. The slippage that takes place *vis-à-vis* D. North's reasoning consists precisely of the way action on the process of governance arrangement formation is understood. In E. Brousseau, it is reduced to transformations in institutional design based on the presupposition that, in order to prefer institutional systems that make flexibility of arrangements possible, it is sufficient to pay attention to the requirement for this flexibility. In D. North, the requirement for progressive mastery of innovative processes by means of the transformation of institutional systems is based on the quest for a meta-stabilization of social reflexivity, which is not assumed to be given. But on the other hand, what is assumed to be given is the capacity to construct it on the basis of the development of a social culture of innovation and adaptation. According to D. North, this is how the conquest of the conditions for a self-regulation that has at last been mastered is to take place. In contrast to E. Brousseau, D. North thus sees the need for a better account of the operation that guarantees the adaptability of institutional arrangements, even though, as was seen above, he also believes that this operation can be achieved and can construct itself through the evolution of scientific culture alone.

Chapter 4

The Second Neo-institutionalist Approach: Towards a Relational and Collaborative Governance Through Dialogue

Background

If we work to reconstruct the current process being conducted by those who inquire into the question of governance (or regulation),[1] we can identify two recent efforts to further and indeed go beyond the neo-institutionalist approaches developed by economists. While not ignoring the economists' debate, these efforts nevertheless rarely rely directly on them.[2] In fact, the theoretical instruments used to build approaches to governance are largely borrowed from other disciplines than those made use of by evolutionary and transaction cost economists. The three-stage reconstruction of the internal dynamic of current research is therefore not immediately apparent solely from a reading of the relevant literature. This reconstruction and a comparative evaluation will only emerge from our adoption of an external perspective on the three processes. This perspective consists of examining the various current approaches to governance (or regulation) from the

---

1 As we know, the term "governance" is currently often used in preference over "regulation", or, in other contexts, "government". As M. Hajer and H. Wagenaar point out in their introduction to the excellent recent collection they edited on the subject of governance "in a network society", "[T]he emerging vocabulary of governance speaks to a widely acknowledged change in the nature of politics and policymaking. The prominence of the new vocabulary also illustrates a widespread dissatisfaction with the limited reach of 'set solutions' to thorny political issues imposed through top-down government intervention" (Hajer and Wagenaar 2003); these same authors appropriately refer readers to a collection edited by J. Pierre for an analytical overview of this terminological change within the scholarly community: *Debating Governance*, Oxford: Oxford University Press, 2000. This does not, however, prevent certain authors whose works are at the heart of the current inquiry into decentred forms of governance from continuing to use the word "regulation" For example, see the work of J. Black (2001b).

2 We must, however, point out a notable exception. C. Sabel has developed his own pragmatist experimentalist undertaking (see Chapter 5), making direct reference in particular to weaknesses he perceives in the neo-institutionalist economic approaches. Two of his texts especially testify to this purpose: Neither Modularity nor Relational Contracting: Inter-firm Collaboration in the New Economy (Sabel and Zeitlin 2004); A Real Time Revolution in Routines (Sabel 2006).

point of view of the theory of collective action that they explicitly or implicitly make use of. As we have seen, the first stage includes responses by evolutionary and transaction cost economists as a way to complement approaches from neoclassical economics and agency theory that are deemed reductive or incomplete. Two other responses that embody a progressive furtherance of this first stage emerge mainly from the work of jurists and political scientists.

A convenient way of presenting the main features of these latter two responses is to situate them in relation to the discussion raised in the legal and political science literature by the movement to proceduralize law and politics, which sprang up in the USA during the 1950s and subsequently spread to the world's social democracies. This movement brought about a significant transformation in the ways public action is exercised, in order to ensure increased participation by citizens and interest groups and thereby develop a more *responsive* legal system[3] and a more participatory model of political life. We have written elsewhere (Lenoble and Maesschalck 2003) about the dynamics opened up by that development and we will not revert to the topic here. In any case, it is now generally familiar. We will only recall that, beginning in the 1970s, the first way of restructuring public action that was proposed—interest group politics[4]—was subjected by economists to a significant critique. The idea behind this critique was simple: it was a matter of questioning the presuppositions of the procedural approach advocated by interest group politics.[5] Not only, economic critics said, did interest groups act on the public stage solely from a strategic perspective, so that public action was often monopolized by the most powerful groups. But as well, nothing guaranteed that the compromises resulting from such a public decision-making process would satisfy

3 This is the expression that has been used since 1978 by two authors (Nonet and Selznick 1978) who were among the first to attempt to inquire into this development from a sociological perspective.

4 Inherited from the pluralist political theory of the 1950s that was also known as "interest group politics", this later movement of interest group politics was based on the idea of making the rationality of public policy developed by the administration depend on the possibility provided to all the concerned interest groups to provide the authorities with their input, and thereby enabling the authorities to devise regulatory compromises. This led judges to subordinate the legality of administrative actions to respect for the procedural conditions guaranteeing this form of participation. In a parallel development, judges themselves, in the context of litigation on fundamental rights (principally litigation on respect for racial equality), were enabled to carry out new kinds of intervention (public law litigation). The goal, in the context of certain public policies (those relating to the management of prisons, public-sector housing, hospitals for the mentally ill, etc.), was to create negotiating spaces, under judges' ultimate guardianship, in which to develop the substantive conditions which public policy had to satisfy to ensure the effective implementation of the rights to equality and human dignity. Thus, whether at the level of judges or of administrative authorities, the conditions for rationality of public policy (legitimacy and efficiency) were presumed met by the opportunity provided to concerned interest groups to communicate their views.

5 See especially (Elhauge 1991, Stewart 1985, 1990).

the requirements of an optimizing rationality. Finally, such a model for collective organization remained unalterably dependent on the command-and-control regulatory model and consequently reproduced its unintended consequences. Although this critique evolved and gained strength using the theoretical tools provided by agency and transaction cost theory, a third perspective evolved alongside it. This last perspective sought to integrate and synthesize the dual dynamics opened up by interest group politics and its economic critique.

Since the 1990s, numerous authors have stressed, like J. Braithwaite and I. Ayres (1992), that:

> the regulation-deregulation dichotomy has long outlived whatever usefulness it may have had: it is no longer very useful to speak in terms of governmental versus private institutions. Instruments of public policy appear increasingly to involve a blend of public and private resources (Grabovsky 1995).

We believe that in relation to the research opened up by this third perspective, it is possible to identify two new approaches to governance that have worked to further neo-institutionalist economists' understanding of the conditions needed for collective action to maximally satisfy the normative expectations of its members. Three factors define the process that underlies these approaches.

(1) The first factor consists of an endorsement of the critique, initiated by economists, of the unintended consequences of what is customarily referred to nowadays as command-and-control regulation. Whatever the theoretical way of constructing the argument, the basic idea is that this traditional form of regulation suffers from a fundamental weakness: it cannot anticipate the effects of its application. The operation of applying a rule is in fact autonomous and cannot be anticipated by the author of the norm. For this reason, if it is desired to adapt regulatory procedures by incorporating factors on which the way of applying the regulation will depend, forms of decentring regulation must be organized.[6]

6 As J. Black (2001b: 105–6) summarizes: "As many have noted, 'command-and-control' is more a caricature than an accurate description of the operation of any particular regulatory system, though some are closer to the caricature than others. Essentially the term is used to denote all that can be bad about regulation: poorly targeted rules, rigidity, ossification, under- and over-enforcement, unintended consequences. The extent to which command-and-control does or does not live up to its caricature is an empirical question which has been debated elsewhere (see Baldwin 1997, Cunningham and Grabovsky 1998: 38–ff). Relevant for our purposes, command-and-control regulation posits a particular role for the state against which 'decentring' analysis is counterposed. It is 'centred' in that it assumes the state to have the capacity to command and control, to be the only commander and controller, and to be potentially effective in commanding and controlling. It is assumed to be unilateral in its approach … based on simple cause-effect relations, and envisaging a linear progression from policy formation through to implementation. Its failings are variously identified as being, inter alia, that the instruments used (laws backed by sanctions) are inappropriate and unsophisticated (instrument failure), that government has insufficient

(2) However, decentralization is conceived from a different perspective than that from which economists usually address it. Viewing private actors as simple maximizing agents, even with bounded rationality, as conceived by H. Simon, is here deemed too reductive. Instead, emphasis is placed on the communicative resources that the various actors possess, which, if deployed and set in motion, make it possible to ensure the adjustments required to solve the problems a social group is continuously faced with. The form of governance here sought as a replacement for classical hierarchical forms (consisting of unilateral decisions made by the public authorities) is thus conceived on the model of an aggregation of the various actors' communicative competencies. What is needed is to set up negotiated forms of decision-making. The various actors' participation thus takes the form of a collaboration and dialogue organized among the actors involved. As R. Stewart (2003: 448) has written, "[V]arious forms of flexible agency-stakeholder networks for innovative regulatory problem-solving have developed in order to avoid the limitations of top-down command regulation and formal administrative procedures".[7]

Thus, a shift takes place; granted, it is not a matter of giving up either the participatory dynamics specific to interest group politics or the usefulness of economic incentives. Rather, the emphasis will now be on planned organization of the collaboration among the actors involved. J. Freeman (1997: 6) thus quite rightly points out:

> [W]hile it is undoubtedly possible to show there are elements of interest representation in collaborative governance, I distinguish them to underscore that collaboration requires us to focus on adaptive problem solving whereas interest representation seems riveted on controlling agency discretion.

In the same vein, she notes as well that the formal administrative procedure used in the framework of interest group politics:

> also undermines the implementation of rules by failing to encourage dialogue and deliberation among the parties most affected by them. This is one of the key criticisms that motivated proposals for stakeholder negotiation of rules. Reformers

---

knowledge to be able to identify the causes of problems, to design solutions that are appropriate, and to identify non-compliance (information failure), that implementation of the regulation is inadequate (implementation failure), and that those being regulated are insufficiently inclined to comply (motivation failure)".

7 R. Stewart (2003: 448–9) provides a few examples of these new forms of regulatory device: "agency-supervised regulatory negotiation among representatives from industry, public interest, and state and local government to reach consensus on new agency regulations outside the formal administrative law rulemaking processes; cooperative arrangements involving governmental and nongovernmental entities in delivering family services or administering Medicare, and negotiation, in the draconian shadow of the Endangered Species Act, of regional habitat conservation plans by federal natural resource management agencies, private landowners, developers, and state and local governments".

> believed that if parties had no "ownership" over the rule-making process, they would be less likely to view rules as legitimate (Freeman 1997: 12).[8]

True, this results in an emphasis on the need to privatize certain forms of governance, as the economists suggest. This privatization, however, is conceived from a different perspective than that of economic theory.[9] Although, as will be seen below, the theoretical frameworks developed by various authors who subscribe to this approach to governance vary—ranging from systemic functionalism through communitarian republicanism, J. Habermas' formal pragmatics, and pragmatism—J. Braithwaite and I. Ayres effectively pinpoint their shared divergence from economic theory. In this new perspective, they write, governance

8 Moreover, "[T]he nature of the participation sought in collaboration differs from that contemplated by interest representation. Meaningful participation enables the contributions of the most affected parties to be institutionalized and gives them some responsibility for the regulatory regime. By 'institutionalized' I mean that participation should be an ongoing feature of the decision-making process. Instead of inviting responses to the agency's proposed solutions, which are themselves offered to fix preconceived problems, institutionalized participation involves opportunities to formulate questions as well as potential answers: it requires a blurring of lines between those inside and outside of institutions responsible for governance" (Freeman 1997: 27).

9 As indicated earlier, economic inquiry into governance has largely focused on what O. Williamson calls private ordering, which mainly concerns private relations. Within this perspective, what he calls hierarchical relations are mainly reflected upon on the basis of the theory of the firm. To the contrary, inquiry by the authors associated with the second stage of current research in the theory of governance generally deal with governance devices that bear on broader social relations than these private ones. This is the reason why the same terms have acquired different extension fields. Thus we saw that, for L. Marengo and G. Dosi, decentralized forms of coordination refer to coordination "via market-like mechanisms" or "via mechanisms based on the interaction of quasi-independent units within simple organizations" (cf. above, Chapter 3, note 25). Those authors who have studied what J. Black calls "decentring regulation", in the context of what we are referring to as the second stage of governance scholarship, use the term "self-regulation" with a broader meaning. In this perspective, "[S]elf-regulation encompasses a wide range of arrangements, from private ordering without resort to legal rules to state-enforced systems of delegated rules ... When used in a legal context, ... it connotes some degree of collective constraint, other than that directly emanating from government, to engender outcomes which would not be reached by individual market behavior alone" (Ogus 2000), for the expression "co-regulation" see also F. Cafaggi, cited below at note 21. It should, however, be noted that, within transaction cost economic research, it would appear that attention is being increasingly paid to those intermediate forms of self-regulation that fall between mechanisms for private ordering and society's general institutions, which interest D. North (on this, see E. Brousseau and E. Raynaud, The Economics of Private Institutions, 2005, working paper, on file with the authors). These differences in terminology are not, however, significant for the purposes of our inquiry. The question we are concerned with relates to the theoretical framework presupposed by (and very often implicit in) theories of governance.

rests on "republican institutions that are oriented to persuading actors to deliberate in a socially responsible way". They continue:

> Under such institutions, the public interest is fostered as a result of such public-regarding modes of deliberation. These republican institutions are contrasted with market institutions that seek to foster the public interest by aggregating the endeavours of actors who all pursue their private interests (Freeman 1997: 47).[10]

It is thus possible to speak of a "public-regarding privatization".[11] It is true that the "republican" or "communitarian" language used here by J. Braithwaite and I. Ayres in discussing P. Petit represents just one possible theoretical approach. As was observed above, it is far from being the only one or even being widely shared.

---

10 The building of governance institutions intended to organize a form of dialogue sets up what the authors call a "regulatory culture" or "regulatory communitarianism". It is helpful to cite J. Braithwaite and I. Ayres's account of what they mean by this. The passage in question displays very clearly their assumption that merely establishing a form of ongoing dialogue and laying out the "communicative ethic" it requires will suffice to ensure the performance of the adjustment and learning operation that the "efficiency" of governance depends on, such that governance will optimally satisfy the normative expectations of group members (see below). They write: "It is the notion of regulatory communitarianism that brings the empowerment theory within the republican tradition of normative theory. Liberal theory finds special attraction in market institutions that assume that individuals will behave in a self-interested way; institutions are designed so that such self-interested actions will aggregate to produce the public benefit … While market institutions purport to leave the psychology of individuals untouched, socializing institutions are designed to affect citizens in such a way that they behave as if they were primarily concerned with the public benefit. Although liberal theory finds special appeal in market institutions, republican theory finds special appeal in socializing institutions. Socializing institutions seek civic virtue by changing the deliberative habits of citizens … The regulatory culture advocated seeks to modify the deliberative habits and behavioral dispositions of actors, not just to tinker with payoffs of actors whose psychology is untouched. Through mobilizing social disapproval against those who sell out to cheaters and those who are unreasonable with cooperators, the regulatory culture seeks to foster an internalization of a concern for the other player that is in the public interest" (Freeman 1997: 93). True, the authors discern that deliberative organization does not suffice on its own. But in failing to construct the institutional conditions specific to the deployment of "civic virtue", they rely exclusively on "social disapproval", that is, on the mobilization of natural, "pregiven" cooperative capacities found within every social group. As will be seen below, they thus fall short of what the pragmatists have sought to develop.

11 See J. Freeman (2000b, 2003). Other relevant work by political scientists includes J. Kooiman (1993) and R. Rhodes (1997, 2000: Chapter 4), who concentrates mainly on a decentred theory of governance, itself linked to an understanding of governance as network. See also G. Peters (1995, 1998).

What it is important to emphasize, however, is how it diverges from the methodological individualism of rational choice theory, as specific to economists. It is this divergence that the concept of governance by what we call the aggregation of communicative competencies is intended to identify. This mode of structuring deliberative dialogue makes it clear that what is at stake is no longer rational anticipation through the maximization of individual preferences. We find here a dimension consisting of the transformation of individual preferences by taking into account a requirement specific to the whole that the individuals are a part of. It matters little whether the requirement is conceived of in terms of civic virtue in the republican manner, a moral principle of universalization in the Habermasian and Rawlsian manner, or even as systemic codes in the systemic functionalist manner. This is also the reason why the mechanisms of governance are viewed as incapable of optimally satisfying the expectations of the group members unless they are built on other resources than those associated with exclusive calculation of the maximization of individual preferences, and thus of market mechanisms only. Individual actors are viewed as the repositories of other resources and capacities than those they deploy when "seeking to maximize their individual preferences". But in order to activate the potential for satisfying the collective requirements entailed by these other capacities of the individual actors, a specific mechanism is required, which is precisely that of planned organization designed to aggregate these deliberative and communicative competencies. Such a form of negotiated pooling of resources is assumed to ensure the activation of the capacities for determining collective requirements. This also explains why the whole question of cooperation is no longer analysed solely in terms of game theory. It is assumed that it is possible to cast issues in a deliberative form, and that doing so produces the expected adaptive effects, because it rests on cooperative resources that an economic analysis made exclusively in terms of individual preferences cannot take into account.

It now becomes clear to what extent this approach to governance results in extending the inquiry beyond the stage reached by the economists. The weaknesses in cooperative capacities of pure decentralized coordination, which the most clear-thinking economists encountered when they recognized the aporias produced by employing analogies with the theory of natural selection, are now compensated for, not only by recourse to hierarchical mechanisms, but by recourse chiefly to an expanded range of participants in the negotiating mechanism and by attending to the organization of the conditions for deliberation such that these stakeholders' empowerment can be assured. This does not at all rule out recourse to contracts and economic incentives nor the granting of a continuing major role to public authority; but the contractual mechanism is now situated in a broader context, which compels reflection on the requirements of an approach framed in terms of communicative collaboration.

From this perspective, this new approach to governance marks an effort to attend to the *internalization* of the conditions for adjustment required by the learning that the success of the governance operation depends on. It remains the case, however, that, while this commitment to attend to the internalization of the conditions for satisfying the learning operation explains why present-day research on governance theory has experienced the need to continue within the dynamics initiated by neo-institutionalist economists, it also accounts for the internal dynamics of this second governance trend. The fact is that, as will be seen, this commitment has expressed itself in stages. What is more—and this thesis is at the heart of the present inquiry—even in the "pragmatist" version that is the most highly developed and most recent version of this trend, this commitment to internalize the conditions for learning remains imperfect and unquestionably insufficiently fulfilled. Before demonstrating this last point, however, it will first be necessary to show how the second approach displays an internal progression that proves this approach is itself not reducible to the mere model of an aggregation of communicative competencies.

(3) The element of the mobilization and organization of the actors' deliberative and communicative competencies, even though it operates within all the positions currently working to further the new institutionalist process inspired by rational choice theory, is not sufficient as a way of characterizing those positions. A third element must be adduced, which in turn requires the differentiation of two distinct perspectives among these positions. That is why we pointed out above that there were two successive stages in the current effort to further the gains made by neo-institutionalist economic approaches to governance.

As was indicated above in the references to J. Freeman, it is correct to say that the emphasis placed on the need for the planned organization of a collaboration, in order "to encourage dialogue and deliberation among the parties most affected", is conceived from a perspective focusing "on adaptive problem solving". But this relationship is not conceived of by all authors in the same way. On one hand, some consider that organization of the collaboration alone—that is, the aggregation of communicative competencies alone—suffices to generate the adaptive capability needed to solve problems in the most satisfactory way possible from the point of view of group members' normative expectations. On the other hand, some authors reason that such an aggregation does not suffice on its own, and that it is necessary to grant, besides, *specific attention* to the conditions required to generate this learning capability. On the first view, these learning capacities are believed to be provided and activated simply by placing the various actors in dialogue. In contrast, the second view considers that assuming the learning capacity to be conferred by communicative aggregation on its own is theoretically problematic, and that, on the contrary, specific supplementary conditions are needed. It is true that this theoretical issue is rarely explained for its own sake in the work of the jurists and political scientists interested in this approach to governance. The very great majority of authors who have sought to inquire into this question of governance are little concerned to flesh out the theoretical underpinnings they implicitly rely on. Nevertheless, if careful attention is paid to the theoretical models explicitly or implicitly relied on by these authors, a dynamic emerges that is internal to all present-day approaches to governance that are in the process of furthering the gains made by economists' neo-institutionalist research. To explain this dynamic, we will identify texts that lay out the two approaches referred to above.

The first approach—the one according to which learning capacities are conferred by the aggregation of communicative competencies alone, which we have named the approach of relational and collaborative governance—is itself found in two versions. One of these succeeded the other, as if, from within this approach to governance, many people perceived the difficulties produced by its epistemological presuppositions. In order to present the first of these two successive versions, we will rely on I. Macneil's relational theory, and, to expose its limitations, on systemic and functionalist theory (such as G. Teubner's), which it sometimes relies on (mainly in British scholarship). The second version, which succeeded the first, in itself constitutes an intermediate stage in the progress towards the second approach, because it emerges from the commitment to inquire into specific conditions superadded to the aggregation of communicative competencies alone. An expression of this intermediate position found in the recent legal literature is an article by S. Burris, P. Drahos, and C. Shearing (2005) entitled Nodal Governance.

The second approach—which we propose to call hereafter the pragmatist approach to governance—furthers the inquiry into learning conditions. Contrary to the first, it considers that the deliberative cast alone, even when so managed as to respect the conditions for stakeholders' empowerment or to ensure respect for the conditions for rational argumentation, does not suffice to guarantee the learning operation required for the best possible problem-solving. This second approach thus aims to better inquire into the conditions internal to the learning operation, and to inquire into the institutional conditions necessary to prompt the actors to acquire the adaptive capacities needed for the deliberative mechanism to be a "problem-solving" one and thus meet, to the extent possible, the requirements of the collective interest. As we shall see in Chapters 5 and 6, however, this second approach to governance, the pragmatist one, cannot be properly understood unless we differentiate between two profoundly different versions within it: an experimentalist version and a more reflexive one—mainly defended by D. Schön and C. Argyris—which attempts to deepen and expand the conditions needed to ensure the success of the collective action. For now, we will limit ourselves to providing a preliminary exposition of the move effected by the experimentalist version, which we call the experimentalist pragmatist approach and which represents the first step in the attempt to extend the conditions for the learning operation beyond those envisaged under the relational and deliberative approach.

Numerous authors are currently working with the experimentalist pragmatist approach.[12] Two current trends of research in particular, however, exemplify it more

12 See, besides E. Ostrom's, V. Ostrom's and C. Sabel's works mentioned below, J. Forester (1989, 1993, 1999), D. Farber (1994, 1999).

specifically and in a more fully developed manner. E. Ostrom and V. Ostrom have spearheaded the first of these trends.[13] The second was initiated by C. Sabel and is being developed by several authors writing in his wake.[14] Both were developed in

13 Although we will not be examining these authors' approach to the conditions that must be respected for a self-organized system to best satisfy the requirements of adequate regulation, we should like to note here that those conditions are far from being reducible to the interpretation that R. Mayntz and A. Héritier appear to give to Ostroms' theory, in particular in the work cited above at note 2. In reducing this to an incentive theory based essentially on a principal-agent approach to collective action, they appear to forget the other essential element of E. Ostrom's work, which consists of her accurate perception that such an approach is inadequate to define the necessary conditions for the adaptation and learning operations required by any diachronic analysis of the conditions for efficiency of a collective action. Besides discussing the incentives that determine the economic theory of agency, E. Ostrom, relying on the background provided by V. Ostrom's theoretical political philosophy (see V. Ostrom 1973, 1991, 1997), has developed the idea that a system of governance should be "a polycentric governance system" (see E. Ostrom 1999 and R. Wagner 2005). In a system of this kind, the actors are assumed to behave like players in a series of games that are both simultaneous and sequential, in which each action can be construed as a move made in several simultaneous games. To produce the appropriate meta-player behaviour, these actors must use "time outs" to resolve disputes by organizing themselves deliberatively and collectively learning from their failures and reinforcing their shared rules (V. Ostrom 1997: 227–8). These rules must, as a matter of priority, turn *critical attention* to the equal positioning of all the players and prevent opportunistic behaviour (V. Ostrom 1997: 242).

14 The underlying idea is easy to understand. It's a matter of restructuring the "institutional design" of our liberal democracies, so that a true ability to learn by trial and error is ensured. This transformation of our democratic institutional models would result in a form of democracy that J. Cohen and C. Sabel sometimes call "directly deliberative polyarchy": "In directly deliberative polyarchy, collective decisions are made through public deliberation in arenas open to citizens who use public services, or who are otherwise regulated by public decisions. But in deciding, those citizens must examine their own choices in the light of the relevant deliberations and experiences of others facing similar problems in comparable jurisdictions or subdivisions of government. Ideally, then, directly deliberative polyarchy combines the advantages of local learning and self-government with the advantages (and discipline) of wider social learning and heightened political accountability that result when the outcomes of many concurrent experiments are pooled to permit public scrutiny of the effectiveness of strategies and leaders" (Cohen and Sabel 1997: 313). The idea, then, is to see to the empowerment of the actors involved, which would guarantee that their collaboration would generate an effective problem-solving capacity, that is, the learning capacity required by the necessary adjustment to the desired transformations of context. The main institutional mechanisms suggested are those that would establish "iterated co-design", "benchmarking", and a mechanism for "error-detecting" (see the highly illuminating text by C. Sabel (2006) cited above at note 2). We will deal with this experimentalist and pragmatist governance approach in greater detail in Chapter 5, mainly to identify its theoretical presuppositions and the justifications for the changes it proposes to the neo-institutionalist approaches (both the economists' and the relational-deliberative approaches) presented above. We wish to note

direct relationship with economic governance approaches[15] and seek to extend and go beyond them by relying on more philosophical instruments.

In the case of V. Ostrom, the theoretical framework is mainly that of political philosophy. He bases his position on an interpretation of the potential inherent in the American federalist model supported by Montesquieu, J. Rousseau, the Scottish Enlightenment, and A. de Tocqueville. From this perspective, the idea of a polycentric democracy can be viewed as consisting of an intellectual and cultural break making possible a passage from "power over" to "power with"—a formula adopted from T. Jefferson (V. Ostrom 1997: 274). "Polycentric orders are open systems that manifest enough spontaneity to be self-organizing and self-governing. But the maintenance of such orders depends on intelligent deliberation to correct errors and reform themselves" (V. Ostrom 1991: 243). The passage to power-with is believed to open up on its own new horizons in political sciences featuring an art of associations and self-governance (V. Ostrom 1997: 276–7) designed to enhance the capacity for error correction (V. Ostrom 1997: 271). It is through the systematic organization of "deliberative vigilance"[16] and ongoing self-evaluation by means of public governance structures (V. Ostrom 1991: 227) that the guarantee of an enhanced capacity for self-correction (V. Ostrom 1997: 293) and a broadened ethos of self-governance is to be sought.[17] But this way of incorporating the fallibility of human intelligence into the procedures of experimentation within democratic self-governance (V. Ostrom 1997: 271) tends to obscure the limitations of the mechanisms for self-governance within polycentrism that are revealed by V. Ostrom.

On this score, C. Sabel has rightly observed that the institutionalization of cooperative solutions continues to obey internal imperatives other than those that would guarantee the reflexivity of a polycentric system. Thus the fact that mechanisms for cooperation make it possible to enhance the capacity for self-correction does indeed satisfy an important polycentric requirement. But this does

here merely that this experimentalist and pragmatist approach to governance is currently being developed and promoted by numerous jurists and political scientists. Besides, of course, C. Sabel, these include M. Dorf (who has applied the model to the question of the judge's role), W. Simon (who has applied it to the issue of fundamental rights), J. Liebman and A. Fung (who apply it to the issues of labour law and school reform), and B. Karkkainen (who applies it to the issue of environmental protection). See A. Fung and E. Wright (2003), A. Fung (2003), A. Fung (2001), A. Fung, D. O'Rourke, and C. Sabel (2001), J. Liebman and C. Sabel (2003), B. Garrett and J. Liebman (2004), C. Sabel, A. Fung, and B. Karkkainen (2000), B. Karkkainen (2000), B. Karkkainen (2003), C. Sabel and W. Simon (2004), W. Simon (2004), M. Dorf and C. Sabel (1998), M. Dorf (2003), M. Dorf and C. Sabel (2000).

15 On C. Sabel, see above, note 2.

16 This is our term for a standing mechanism of intelligent deliberation designed to effect self-correction.

17 "The future of democracy, then, turns upon one another's experience in constituting and reconstituting systems of self-governance that can be adaptive to time-and-space exigencies and that can achieve complementarities with others" (V. Ostrom 1991: 270).

not meet a different requirement of the institutionalization of cooperative solutions, namely to provide a guarantee of the effective and enduring, or sustainable, transformation of behaviours, beyond the provisional alignment of certain instances and circumstances. "Alignment by itself does not secure continuing cooperation" (Sabel 1994: 159). In some cases, for instance those of common pool resources (Sabel 1994: 158–9), it may even be supposed that the specific social context of a problem also places constraints and limitations upon possibilities so that the decision to cooperate has already been largely brought about. In such a case, an appropriate context is enough to activate it as the optimal choice. For C. Sabel, the real test of a cooperative mechanism is rather its capacity to lead to effective changes in behaviours by developing mechanisms that, in incorporating discussion of the new possibilities produced by cooperation, strengthen the process of cooperation under way and thus reduce uncertainty as to its continuation. As he points out:

> [People who are cooperating] can never know the outcome of their efforts at cooperation in advance. But the success of learning by monitoring at all levels of economic development shows that in speaking of their possibilities they are exercising the very faculties needed for realizing them (Sabel 1994: 159).

In response to this challenge, C. Sabel derives support directly from the more epistemological tradition of J. Dewey's and C. Peirce's American pragmatism,[18] and, in the same vein, from recent work in the theory of language and the theory of meaning.[19] Although this epistemological opening is not explored for its own sake, it certainly accounts for C. Sabel's insight into the epistemological inadequacies of both the economists' neo-institutionalist efforts and the early versions of the deliberative shift in the stakeholding approaches, and accordingly of the need to better construct an internalist approach to the learning operation on which all public interest governance depends. It is for the same reason that we will take the experimentalist pragmatist approach developed by C. Sabel as an exemplification of this last stage of current research in the theory of governance. The explicit invocation of a "theory of judgment" in C. Sabel's approach via its referencing of J. Dewey and C. Peirce will make it easier to see how this approach, despite its significant gains, does not itself adequately respect its stipulation of an internalist approach to the learning operation and how it thereby lays the basis for an extension of the institutional conditions for public interest governance. But we anticipate. The inquiry into this experimentalist approach, the weaknesses with which it continues to be beset, and the nature of the extensions it calls for will be conducted in Chapter 5. We must first briefly explain the two versions of the first approach taken by the deliberative turn towards furthering the economists' neo-institutionalist theory of governance. As seen above, these two versions of what we labelled the relational

18 For an explicit reference to these two thinkers, see (Dorf and Sabel 1998: 284–5).

19 More specifically, see C. Sabel's 2006 text cited at note 2 above.

and collaborative governance approach will be explained by recourse to an examination of three trends of thought that in our view clearly display its spirit and presuppositions: the recent trend of thought based on I. Macneil's relational theory; the trend of thought sometimes encountered that refers to N. Luhmann's systemic approach; and the trend of thought called the nodal governance approach, recently developed by S. Burris, P. Drahos, and C. Shearing.

Before proceeding to our overview of these trends of thought, a final observation is necessary. It has already been remarked that all the approaches to governance addressed here, which seek to further the gains made by the neo-institutionalist economic approaches, affirm a form of "self-regulation" based on a deliberative collaboration by all the parties concerned. It is worth noting that this affirmation implies abandoning neither the belief in a role for the public authorities nor the belief in recourse to hierarchical mechanisms. Certainly, the relational and collaborative approach ends, as we have seen, by modifying exclusive recourse to hierarchical mechanisms, envisaged by some economists as compensatory for inadequacies in cooperative capacities once they recognize that there is no recourse to a mechanism analogous to that of natural selection in biology. Here, recourse to a hierarchical mechanism is theorized in relation to the general context of the relational and deliberative approach. Obviously, public authority itself often becomes part of the negotiating mechanism.[20] Besides this, however, account is clearly taken of the fact that the activity of self-regulation itself necessitates a form of regulation designed to define and guarantee respect for the conditions required by the self-regulatory mechanism. The nature of this form of "regulation of self-regulation" varies according to which of the versions presented above of the collaborative and deliberative activity is argued to govern self-regulation.[21] It is in relation to this specific role of law that many authors have progressively arrived at the proposal that the expression "reflexive law" be used. This is an ambiguous expression, covering as it does approaches to reflexivity that are diverse and often insufficiently developed. The expression "reflexive law" was initially proposed in connection with the most reductive version of what we have termed the relational and collaborative approach to governance, that is, the functionalist and systemic one, in particular as advanced by G. Teubner. Subsequently, a second use was put forward for the most fully developed version of the theory of governance that the deliberative turn has lately arrived at. This is the use advanced by adherents of the experimentalist and pragmatist approach in connection with the theory of the learning operation that they deploy. We wish to state as of now that our own use of the expression "reflexive

20 See P. Vincent-Jones (2006) and J. Freeman (2000).

21 It is in this perspective that, in our view, the increasing recourse to a form of co-regulation, at the expense of sole recourse to "self-regulation", can be understood. On this topic, see F. Cafaggi, (2005). For a definition of the concepts of self regulation and co-regulation, see F. Cafaggi, "Gouvernance et Responsabilité des Régulateurs Privés", EUI LAW 2005/06 available at http://cadmus.iue.it/dspace/handle/1814/3//browse-date?top=1814%2F3328.

governance" (or "reflexive law)" is linked to the proposal we will make to extend this latter approach by expanding its way of developing the reflexivity internal to every operation of judgment (see Chapter 6, especially 202–12, for more observations concerning the expressions "reflexive law" or "reflexive governance").

The Theoretical Underpinnings of the Approach of Relational and Collaborative Governance Through Dialogue

In this section, we intend to show certain presuppositions underlying the theoretical framework relied upon by authors who espouse the approach of relational and collaborative governance through dialogue. These presuppositions explain why, under this approach (in contrast to the experimentalist pragmatist one), the relational mechanism or mechanism for dialogue is supposed to suffice on its own to ensure the accomplishment of the learning operation required for collective action to succeed. We have seen that this approach to governance developed essentially during the 1990s, as a direct extension of the economic critique of the command and control and interest-group politics regulatory models deployed in early efforts to reform welfare states. Indeed, the most prolific source of publications dedicated to this approach has been the work of jurists and political scientists who have endeavoured to describe and comment on the institutional reforms initiated during the nineties in the USA,[22] Australia,[23] and the United Kingdom.[24] Among the British and Australian publications in this vein are found, in our view, some of the best efforts to build this new approach to governance. Of these, we will deal principally with two. The first is that of P. Vincent-Jones, who has sought specifically to describe and assess some of the distinctive features of the new governance regime implemented, in the name of the new contractualism, in the United Kingdom during the 1990s and since. The other is one presented in a recent article associated with the Australian inquiry into this matter, which is being pursued at the institute run by J. Braithwaite at the University of Canberra.[25] As mentioned, we will also look briefly at the way many Australian and British authors writing on the subject support their position by invoking N. Luhmann's systemic theory, since his work

---

22 See A. Gore and National Performance Review Staff, *From Red Tape to Results: Creating a Government that Works Better and Costs Less* (1993).

23 In this connection, see B. Morgan (1999: 51), who writes of "the inception in Australia in 1995 of a particularly wide-ranging and comprehensive meta-regulatory regime".

24 See in particular the Welfare Reform Green Paper, *New Ambitions for Our Country: A New Contract for Welfare* (Cm 3805) (1998), issued by the government of Prime Minister Blair in the United Kingdom; and the link made by New Labour between development and the new contractualism: (Vincent-Jones 2006: 10–11) and references cited there.

25 The Regulatory Institutions Network (RegNet) of the Research School of the Social Sciences at the Australian National University in Canberra.

is especially revealing of the internal limitations of the theoretical framework of the relational and collaborative governance approach.

(1) We begin, then, with the highly suggestive and productive work done by P. Vincent-Jones on the new public contracting, with its references to I. Macneil's theory as a means of reflecting upon the conditions that must be respected by this new contractual mode of regulating the management of public services if it is to be responsive.

As P. Vincent-Jones indicates, there has been:

> an increasing use of contract as a regulatory mechanism across a broad spectrum of economic and social relationships in Britain over the last 25 years. Since New Labour came to power in 1997 the trend has accelerated. Contractual governance has spread rapidly beyond the spheres of economics and public administration into social policy. The experience of contractualization, however, has proved highly problematic (Vincent-Jones 2006: 347).

The new public contracting is "a subset of government by contract characterized by the delegation of powers to public agencies in contractual arrangements preserving central government controls and powers of intervention" (Vincent-Jones 2006: 3).[26] In the health, education, and social-care sectors in which this new regulatory approach is being so applied, quasi-markets are therefore organized. They are distinguished by a:

> double regulatory structure, entailing regulation by contract within hierarchical frameworks. The purchasing agency's use of contract as an instrument of

26 "The three main forms of this novel type of regulation are identified as administrative contracts, economic contracts, and social control contracts" (Vincent-Jones 2006: 3). "Economic contracts"—to which we limit our own discussion here—"are contractual arrangements directed at improving public services through competition and/or the devolution of management powers to public purchasing or commissioning agencies in a variety of hybrid forms beyond simple market or bureaucratic organisation. The focus on competition and marketization reflects a part of the New Public Contracting reform agenda which is distinct from managerialism. In addition to efficiency, the regulatory frameworks within which such contracts operate also embody values of social justice, equity and redistribution. Policy initiatives here are about the better use and coordination of resources that lead ultimately to the production of public services … [T]he economic organizational role of the New Public Contracting is evident in the operation of quasi-markets for education, health, and social care resulting from the major structural reorganizations of these public services since the 1980s, but it features in public service provision more generally" (Vincent-Jones 2006: 22). In such "quasi-markets", then, we find a "double regulatory structure, entailing regulation by contract within hierarchical frameworks. The purchasing agency's use of contract as an instrument of regulation is dependent on the conditions that have been specified (extra-contractually) in the regulatory regime (Vincent-Jones 2006: 22).

> regulation is dependent on the conditions that have been specified (extra-contractually) in the regulatory regime.

Of course, besides this articulation of a horizontal relationship (between the public purchasing agency and the service provider) with a vertical relationship (between this public purchaser and the central authority),[27] there is the relationship among all these actors and the individual citizen—who is also the service provider's customer—to take into account. And in fact, it is essentially as regards the role assigned to the citizen within the regulatory mechanism as a whole that P. Vincent-Jones sees the need for the present regime to bring greater institutional depth. The question asked is in effect about the institutional conditions that must be satisfied for this new, contractual, form of governance to become more responsive. The key theoretical instrument P. Vincent-Jones[28] uses to answer this question is I. Macneil's relational contracting theory. However, the use he makes of I. Macneil's work differs from that made of it by O. Williamson in his theory of transaction costs. As is well known, what interested O. Williamson was I. Macneil's diversification of the modes of contract-based governance and his denunciation of the reductionism of neo-classical economists, who believed that contractual relationships could all be reduced to the "spot contract" model.[29]

---

27 "The advantage of quasi-markets compared with the market as a mechanism for delivering public services concerns the greater level of public control exercised through the hierarchical element in the regulatory structure. The values at stake in the operation of economic contracts therefore include distributive justice and the public interest, in addition to more familiar economic values of economy and efficiency" (Vincent-Jones 2006: 28).

28 It should be noted, however, that P. Vincent-Jones wishes nevertheless to take other theoretical instruments into account in defining the conditions for "responsiveness" of this new form of governance. To this end, he dedicates a whole chapter of his book to presenting various current approaches to governance. More important, on the basis of this chapter, he suggests that the institutional reforms that will have to take place to improve the deliberative participation by all the actors involved in this new form of governance of public services be structured to allow a "capacity for innovation, learning and adaptation" (Vincent-Jones 2006: 88, 91, 353). Reference is thus explicitly made to the work of C. Sabel. It can thus be said that P. Vincent-Jones discerns the need (which we explain in Chapter 5) to open up the relational and collaborative approach to being furthered by the experimentalist and pragmatist approach.

29 I. Macneil, says O. Williamson, "argued that it was naive to proceed as if there were only one, single, all purpose law of contract" (Williamson 1996: 370). Alongside the kind of contract that serves as the specific instrument of governance by the market, there exists long-term contracting (alternately, the distinction is often made between discrete and relational contracts), in which, because of the uncertainty that marks their relations over time, the parties must put in place specific institutions to manage the adjustments their relationship will have to make to changing conditions. O. Williamson observes that this second kind of contract constitutes a type of governance mechanism intermediate between the two other institutional forms of "private ordering": the market and hierarchical organization.

As noted by P. Vincent-Jones in agreement with D. Campbell (2001), this interpretation of I. Macneil's thinking, while accurate, overlooks a more essential dimension of the meaning of contract relationality. Relationality is not characteristic only of contracts that cannot be reduced to spot contracts. In reality, it is a characteristic of any contract, to the extent that it defines what underlies the conditions for possibility specific to every contractual relationship. These underpinnings constitute the "normative context of parties' behaviour" (Vincent-Jones 2001: 73). This context is manifested in every contract. At the same time, however, it reflects a normative context. We will come back to its dual factual and normative nature. I. Macneil extracts from it what he calls "common contract norms", which to some extent constitute a form of positive natural law, in the sense that these norms do not necessarily imply their own shaping into formal positive law and can be expressed in the form of informal norms that structure the social space and should be acknowledged as obligatory if one wants to ensure an adequate context for all forms of contractual relations.[30] I. Macneil has framed this normative context in the form of "ten contract norms". It is mainly on this basis that P. Vincent-Jones has defined institutional improvements in the new public contracting regime. He stresses that these improvements should make it possible to find "solutions to problems identified with the operation of contract norms" and they "lie as much in responsive institutional and organisational design as in the reform of legal structures" (Vincent-Jones 2006: 32). These improvements are of two kinds. The first relates to what P. Vincent-Jones calls relational conditions. They are of lesser concern to us here.[31] In our view, they relate to the relationality specific to the contractual relation itself.

But P. Vincent-Jones himself lucidly and subtly recognizes that this relationality to some extent requires that it be inquired into regarding its own conditions for possibility. The relationality specific to contract engages deeper requirements, as a second-order relationality:

30 "The contract norms have overlapping internal and external dimensions. External norms include custom, morality, conventions, and a wide range of institutional constraints in addition to those provided by the legal system. Contracting behaviour itself generates and reinforces norms internally within particular relationships; the more long-term the relationship, the more ongoing relation becomes a source of obligation … In this conception, any adequate description of how the law governs, or prescription of how the law ought to govern, must be founded on an understanding of the ways in which social exchange behaviour both gives rise to and is supported by the common contract norms" (Vincent-Jones 2006: 5–6).

31 These conditions consist of "(1) sensitivity on the part of regulators to the circumstances in which regulation occurs, (2) the presence in contractual relationships of norms of planning and consent necessary to support discreteness and presentiation; (3) the bindingness of obligations in those relationships, combined with norms of fairness and reciprocity; and finally (4) trust and cooperation in the performance of contracts" (Vincent-Jones 2006: 348).

> [T]hese relational elements are necessary, but not sufficient, conditions of responsive regulation. Stable and cooperative relationships that benefit regulators and regulatees might be a mask for inefficiency, ineffectiveness, or fraud or corruption. The result in such a case would be to defeat the overall purpose of the regulatory regime. Again, the efficiency gains of relational contracting might be outweighed by disproportionate damage to other values such as equity or social justice, or harm to the interests of other stakeholders, such as consumers (Vincent-Jones 2006: 348).

It is in order to take this second-order requirement into account that it is necessary to enhance the quality of institutional and organizational design by organizing a better deliberative model for the various actors involved in the complex regulatory mechanism, that is, at the level of determination of the "standard settings" that will define the general requirements of the regulatory framework. The improved transparency and deliberation that will entail better involvement by the citizens who are the "consumers" of these contractual regimes is thus intended to better organize collaboration among all the actors involved in this new form of complex governance.[32] This requirement for the strengthening of the "public deliberation in policy and decision making on public service issues" (Vincent-Jones 2006: 347) thus obviously implies greater transparency and public accountability. But it is enabled, above all, by what P. Vincent-Jones (2006: 349) calls "the securing of

32 It should be noted that, while P. Vincent-Jones' line of argument is based on I. Macneil, it brings out in a highly productive way matters that remain implicit in the latter's work. The question of whether P. Vincent-Jones' interpretation is or is not consistent with I. Macneil's explicit position is immaterial. As we know, I. Macneil has been interpreted in numerous ways. Further, as we have observed, P. Vincent-Jones, like D. Campbell, embraces an expansive interpretation of his views, whose well-foundedness we believe emerges if the effort is made to discern the deep insight of I. Macneil's project. Indeed, the link made here between contract norms, relationality, and the improvement of the deliberative structure bears a family relation to I. Macneil's 10th contract norm, which he defines as requiring "harmonization with the social matrix" (Macneil 1980: 57). The link, under the new public contracting, between the requirement for harmonization and the requirement for better deliberative organization among the actors involved (that is, among the public authorities, service providers, and citizen/consumers of public services) only serves to show that the kinds of actors involved in this new public service regime entail a return to I. Macneil's social matrix. As P. Vincent-Jones perceives, "[T]his responsive regulation/relational contract approach stresses the need to take into account all the constituencies involved in contractual processes, beyond the interests of 'the parties' individually or dyadically conceived" (Vincent-Jones 2006: 136). If, like P. Vincent-Jones, we consider that "the quality of regulatory linkages and relationships, analysed in terms of the relationality of 'contract' norms, is a vital factor contributing to the effectiveness (and hence ultimately responsiveness) of the New Public Contracting" (Vincent-Jones 2006: 134), we come to see that the conditions for effectiveness both trigger and entail conditions for legitimacy, that is, conditions relative to the quality of the public deliberation that must govern the adoption of the contract provisions.

citizen empowerment through appropriate forms of public participation, coupled with effective mechanisms for the redress of grievances".[33]

True, as already indicated, P. Vincent-Jones acknowledges that this deliberative method should also guarantee true collective learning,[34] while considering whether this requirement can be deduced from a relational approach to governance or whether it requires its own distinct theoretical model.[35] We believe that the answer to this question is "no". This is all the clearer if, as P. Vincent-Jones himself states, one accepts that "the reflexive conditions for the successful operation of collective learning … cannot be taken for granted".[36] This is indeed what we hope to reveal lying within the relational approach of the new public contracting. Our aim is to show that, if one reflects on the requirements of contractual governance using the theoretical instruments of relational theory, one observes that the model for the empowerment of the actors engaged in deliberative cooperation supposes the adaptive capacities for optimal governance as regards the actors' expectations to be a given, solely by virtue of the actors being placed in relation with each other. This characteristic is

33 In a recent article, P. Vincent-Jones (2005) has developed this idea very clearly. He notes that this requirement is addressed by the implementation of "hybrid governance structures" (for example, the implementation of a mechanism that enables the citizen/consumer to obtain reparation in the event of a service provider's failure to satisfactorily deliver the appropriate service. Such reparation would be obtained through an ombudsman working with an "industry specific tribunal", and the citizen/consumer would not be under obligation to prove a "contractual nexus". On this, see (Vincent-Jones 2005: 918–19). Above all, however, the requirement is addressed by strengthening "citizen involvement in contracting regimes". "Of crucial importance to responsiveness is the manner of determination of service standards … [R]egulation cannot be responsive where standards do not reflect the needs of service recipients … The service standards in particular sectors might be collectively established through tripartite consultation between public purchasers and consumers and representatives of provider organisations. The ultimate aim would be to render explicit for all interested parties the quality of services that consumers could reasonably expect, and the terms on which services would be provided. The standards thus established, including procedures for complaints handling and dispute resolution, might govern relationships between contractors and consumers regardless of the public, private, or voluntary sector identity of the service provider" (Vincent-Jones 2005: 922).

34 P. Vincent-Jones acknowledges that "the value of contractual exchanges may be enhanced through the capacity of regulatory schemes to facilitate collective learning among the various public, private, and voluntary bodies engaged in public service networks" (Vincent-Jones 2006: 353).

35 "Both regulating and regulated entities need to adapt within and learn from their environments, taking account of new information and adjusting their activities to core values and purposes. A hypothesis that might be tested in further research is that relationality … and collective learning are closely related features of responsiveness, and that the latter is dependent on the former" (Vincent-Jones 2006: 353).

36 (Vincent-Jones 2006: 92) continues: "Rather the task for institutional designers is both to identify these conditions and to determine the role of the state in their affirmative creation".

linked to the (epistemological) presuppositions of relational theory itself. That is why this approach ends by conceiving of the conditions for a collective action that optimally satisfies its members' collective interests[37] as what we have called a simple aggregate of the communicative competencies of the actors involved.

It is therefore not sufficient to interpret the relationality of contract in a broader manner than O. Williamson's. Certainly, the restricted interpretation he offers is a sign of the insufficient consideration given to the underlying relational conditions that constrain the possibility for "implementing" the normative expectations inherent in a contractual relationship. The expansive interpretation P. Vincent-Jones advances enables a furthering of the transaction cost approach by opening it up to the deliberative approach associated with what some have called the stakeholding approach to governance.[38] This concept of relationality does not, however, get us any further ahead in opening up the black box this deliberative collaboration constitutes. In fact, quite the contrary: it is assumed that the operation of communicative aggregation suffices on its own to effect the adjustment and learning required for cooperation to maximize fulfilment of the world-rationalizing expectations that every regulation is designed to implement.

The thought of I. Macneil itself reflects this assumption. His concept of contract norms itself implies it. These contract norms, I. Macneil notes, are "norms in a positivist sense," that is, "a pattern or trait taken to be typical in the behaviour of a social group". In that case, he continues:

> [T]he norms about to be described would be simply extensions of the basic elements of contract we have already discussed. But I wish to be more expansive and to include in the concept of norm not just the way people *do* behave, but the way they ought to behave as well … [T]hus, the term is used … to connote both actual behaviour and principles of right action (Macneil 1980: 37–8).[39]

In relation to the norm regarding solidarity between contractants, he observes that this solidarity corresponds to the organic solidarity brought about by the increased division of labour that technological developments in modern societies lead to:

37 That is, what is customarily called the public interest under a regime such as that of the new public contracting.

38 On this point, see (Deakin and Michie 1997).

39 As is well known, I. Macneil believes that these norms are present across all modern societies. "These norms, while basic, are only intermediate, intermediate between behaviour in particular contractual relations, and the great flow of modern history. True, they often have immense and fundamental consequences for the shape and direction of societies in which they occur. Moreover, given the premises of basic contractual behaviour, I believe those consequences are inescapable" (Macneil 1980: 37–8).

> The greater the division of labor in a society, the more evident [these contract norms] are in the lives of everyone. And all of [these contract norms], particularly in combination, have integrative effects. These norms become part of the common conscience (Macneil 1980: 99).[40]

The positive nature of this normative feature of contractual behaviour is not just attested, according to him, by empirical observation; it is also logically deducible: "[I]t is also based on a process of reasoning along lines proposed by David Lewis and Edna Ullman-Margalit, who demonstrate how behaviour leads logically to convention and convention leads logically to norms" (Macneil 1980: 38). We will not pause to dwell on the error of identifying D. Lewis' position with E. Ullman-Margalit's. We have already seen above that this is incorrect, and that E. Ullman-Margalit's project consists rather of seeking to overcome the aporias found in D. Lewis. What is more revealing to note is that, in relying on D. Lewis, I. Macneil makes clearly manifest what could already be inferred from our previous observations: he considers that the relational constraints that define the spirit of every true contractual engagement are inevitably internalized by any social group that is acquainted with the phenomenon of contractualism. These constraints are in effect the product of a collective game of the pure coordination type, as described by game theory.[41] In assuming that any society in which the fact of contractualism is to be found can be reduced to a simple coordination game where the interpretation of the meaning of the contractual requirements is concerned, I. Macneil assumes that a shared culture of cooperation is a given within any society.[42] He thus assumes that all the social actors will spontaneously

40 I. Macneil writes as follows, in a highly Weberian vein: "To recognize how strong these norms can become as an element of the common conscience in the presence of great division of labor, we need look no further back in history than to the not yet entirely deceased Protestant Ethic. It was a conglomeration of the common contract norms: strong beliefs in the integrity of roles—mandated by God indeed—in the mutuality achieved by hard work and consensual exchange, in the creation of power through private property, and in restraint of power in favor of a kind of individual liberty" (Macneil 1980: 99).

41 Recall that D. Lewis (1969: 58) understands a convention as follows: "A regularity R in the behavior of members of population P in a recurring situation S is a convention if and only if, in any instance of S:

1. everyone conforms to R,
2. everyone expects everyone else to conform to R;

Everyone prefers to conform to R on condition that the others do, since S is a coordination problem and uniform conformity to R is a coordination equilibrium in S".

42 Thus I. Macneil supposes that the meaning of the solidarity requirements related to a contractual commitment results from the spontaneous search for coordination among the actors, as if the possible conflicts of interpretation of such meaning lead inevitably and automatically to the choice of a common conventional solution representing a Nash

arrive at the same meaning. A corollary assumption is that the capacities needed to ensure the application of the rationality requirements needed for the shared fulfilment of the expectations of every partner to the contract are imprinted in the minds of social actors. Of course, I. Macneil does not believe that all individual actors always spontaneously comply with these constraints. In this respect, contract norms are indeed norms. But he takes as a given the social culture that makes possible the application of these norms by means of the collective instruments established for this purpose. Moreover, and this is what concerns us here, he assumes that the game of setting all the actors concerned by the contractual situation (all the stakeholders) in deliberative motion will result on its own in the mobilization of pre-existing capacities on which the fulfilment of the normative expectations harboured by the contractual context depend.[43] It is quite specifically this assumption, with its implied reference to D. Lewis' model for the origins of the building of a common culture of the adaptation requirements inherent in the cooperative ideal of deliberative action, that justifies an experimentalist pragmatist process of theoretical furtherance.

Before we explain, by means of one more example from recent research on the theory of governance, how this research has sought to further the first version of the relational and collaborative approach, it will be useful to make a rapid tour of a second theoretical instrument found in the European legal literature on regulation. As we shall see, several European (mainly British) and Australian authors believe that their approach is supported by N. Luhmann's systemic functionalism, as interpreted by the sociologist and jurist G. Teubner.

(2) There is no need to describe in depth here the approach to law as an autopoietic system developed by G. Teubner on the basis of N. Luhmann's theory of social systems.[44] The idea is very easy to grasp. The social system is understood to be composed of subsystems said to be "autopoietic", that is, cognitively open to the environment but normatively closed. Each subsystem is regulated by its own internal logic and unceasingly reproduces itself while adapting itself to transformations in its environment such that it is always in a state of equilibrium. From a regulatory point of view, it is this autonomy that explains why:

> no system can act directly upon another, and attempts to do so will result in Teubner's regulatory trilemma: the indifference of the 'target' system to the intervention, the destruction of the 'target' system itself, or the destruction of the intervening system (Black 2001b: 109).

---

equilibrium (on the best possible solution, or on one of the best possible solutions if, as J. Nash does, one considers that there are several possible).

43 For a similar critique of H. Hart's use of D. Lewis' model for understanding the concept of law, see Part I, and also J. Coleman (2001b: 94).

44 See (Teubner 1989, 1993; Teubner and Febbrajo 1992).

According to G. Teubner, this explains that clear awareness of the limits of the capacity of any system, including the legal system, to regulate another system must lead to the law's evolution towards reflexive law.[45] Its function must not be understood to be instrumental;[46] it should be limited to promoting the self-regulating capability of every social subsystem.

The relevance of invoking this systemic and functionalist theory resides not so much in its having been extensively used by numerous British and Australian authors as a theoretical justification for the initial version of the decentring approach to regulation[47] that we call relational and collaborative. Rather, the pertinence of exploring it here resides in the fact that the aporias and epistemological weaknesses of this "reflexive" theory of law are especially helpful in illuminating the reasons to go beyond and further that initial version. It is true that, in contrast to the work of other authors (such as J. Braithwaite, C. Parker, T. Prosser, C. Scott, and P. Vincent-Jones) who have recently especially well developed and helped build this version of the theory of governance, the systemic approach to law offers the advantage of opening up inquiry into the theory of governance to a more directly epistemological phase. On this score, it anticipates one of the major attractive features of the experimentalist pragmatist approach developed by C. Sabel. At the same time, however, it reveals all the more clearly through its own weaknesses the epistemological weaknesses of this theory of governance. It thus enables us to throw into even clearer relief the lesson we sought to draw from I. Macneil's relational contract theory. This is so even though several authors, including P. Vincent-Jones, C. Parker, C. Scott, N. Lacey, and J. Braithwaite,[48] explicitly state that their own approaches to governance do not

45 (Teubner 1994). As P. Vincent-Jones (2006: 96) quite rightly comments, in this perspective, the term reflexivity "refers to an organization's 'relationship with itself' or, more simply, to self-regulation". We will see below the other meaning acquired by the term "reflexivity" under a pragmatist and experimentalist approach to governance and, lastly, under the deepened version of the pragmatist approach that we propose.

46 G. Teubner, After Legal Instrumentalism: Strategic Models of Post-Regulatory Law, in *Dilemmas of Law in the Welfare State*, 1985, 299–325.

47 Recall the evocative title of J. Black's article (2001b) cited above: Decentring Regulation: Understanding the Role of Regulation and Self-regulation in a "Post-regulatory" World.

48 "Teubner's passing reference to Macneil in his analysis of the threat to modern democracy posed by privatisation and the decline of the nation state has created an opportunity for exploring the relevance of the relational theory to the macro-phenomenon of 'globalisation'. In one view, the reduction in the 'conscious coordination' of the world economy and the growth of private governance regimes may indicate a need radically to re-think our notions of contract and the role of the state, but this task may be addressed within relational theory, and nothing but confusion is added by the language of autopoiesis" (Vincent-Jones 2001: 84). See, in the same vein, C. Parker, C. Scott, N. Lacey, and J. Braithwaite (2004): "One need not adopt systems theory, as Teubner does, to see [questions about effectiveness, responsiveness and coherence] as a useful heuristic for the types of questions that lawyers and regulationists might ask about regulating law".

depend on the deployment of G. Teubner's systemic approach as a basis for their validity. The fact is that the epistemological weaknesses of G. Teubner's reflexive law approach manifest in an illustrative and more fundamental way the weaknesses of the form of functionalism implied by any assumption that the deliberative mechanism suffices on its own to ensure the success of collective learning.

What is the reason for these weaknesses? Quite simply, that systemic functionalism itself contradicts the epistemological principle on which it purports to base itself. The notion of the autonomy or autopoiesis of every system merely expresses in more epistemological terms what H. Putnam quite rightly called the principle of semantic internalism or holism, to which we referred above (Chapter 3, note 35). Any critique of command and control regulation is implicitly based on an intuitive grasp of this epistemological principle, even though this principle is rarely formalized and expressed as such. What is always present is the idea that the conditions for applying a rule (that is, the factors on which its effects depend) are internal to its implementation and not susceptible of formalization—that is, the idea that these conditions cannot be reduced to the conditions that formally justified adoption of the rule. Operation of the application is thus autonomous from the operation of formal justification.[49] Now, if one wishes to respect the requirements of a holistic or internalist grasp of the operation of judgment, we cannot, as H. Putnam has so clearly shown,[50] but draw attention to the incompatibility with this principle of any functionalist (and therefore any systemic) approach. To assume, as N. Luhmann and G. Teubner do, that every subsystem is "regulated" by a formal (binary) code which predetermines the development of this subsystem and guarantees its ongoing adaptation to the transformation of its environment, contradicts the principle of autonomy and normative closure with which adherents of this approach counter

49 This same insight underlies what is called, in the theory of law, the "interpretive turn", which also underlies many jurists' tendency (misplaced, in our view) to see in judges a regulatory instrument for rationalizing the social.

50 See H. Putnam's two crucial pages in *Representation and Reality* (1988: 103–5). As he writes: "[F]unctionalism started out by rejecting the naive idea that propositional-attitude descriptions (e.g., 'believes that there are a lot of cats in the neighbourhood') correspond one by one to brain states, species-independently. Yet—and this is its Achilles heel—it did assume that they correspond to brain states in this way in each individual organism" (1988:105). A postulate of this kind is indeed contradictory. The problem it poses relates to the internalism of the explanation aimed at by functionalism. To remain internal to the use of operative reason, functionalism "cannot postulate an explanatory mode that transcends conditions of usage by trying to fix those very conditions of usage by means of a 'meta-discursive' process of ascribing mental states to intentional states. As a theory, computationalist functionalism requires transcendence of the computational usage of reason and the stating of meta-computational conditions which computationalism is expected to validate at the same time as the conditions themselves are understood to justify it" (Maesschalck 2001: 243).

traditional theories of intentionality (and therefore of regulation).[51] Thus systemic functionalism fails to fully grasp the very insight that drives it.

This internal contradiction in functionalism also explains another internal inconsistency within this project, at least in the form that G. Teubner gave it. Since it relates to law, G. Teubner's project to promote the attainment of a new stage of development in the legal system, a stage of a reflexive nature, clearly contradicts the functionalist project itself. On this score, N. Luhmann is immeasurably more rigorous, calling attention to the implicit revival in G. Teubner's work of an instrumentalist approach to law.[52] N. Luhmann's critique of G. Teubner is defensible not only because G. Teubner's project ends by indirectly rehabilitating the agenda to use law as, in effect, an instrument of social engineering (to use N. Luhmann's terms).[53] It also merits endorsement above all because it reflects the misconception of functionalism itself. Functionalism can only be descriptive, since it entails taking as given the conditions necessary for the operation of collective learning, that is, the adaptation necessary for a system to be as well "balanced" as possible (that is, using our own terminology, the adaptation necessary for the success of governance that maximizes fulfilment of the normative expectations of the actors involved). In contrast, G. Teubner's second inconsistency reflects his valid insight that the consequences of Luhmannian functionalism are inadequate. His "normative" commitment to suggest the promotion of a more reflexive legal system reflects his insight that self-regulation on its own does not necessarily result in such an *equilibrium* and that it requires rather a specific institutional incentive. And yet, given his functionalist epistemological assumptions, he cannot adequately construct this normative requirement.[54] These assumptions prevent him from adequately

51 As evidenced, for example, in the case of law, by critiques of any "instrumentalist" approach to law, that is, any agenda to effectively make law an instrument of social engineering.

52 On this topic, see D. Patterson's excellent recent analysis (Paterson 2006).

53 (Luhmann 1992).

54 An analogous problem underlies a recent analysis of the term "regulation" by J. Black, who suggests that the term necessarily invokes an element of intentionality and can therefore not be used in reference to the operations of the market. ("Or are we, or should we be, concerned with intentional attempts to control or order people or states of affairs (albeit mindful of the unintended consequences of those intentions)? I would argue we should be so concerned: 'regulation' is otherwise indistinguishable from all other questions of social control and ordering. To reflect this, regulation could be defined as 'the intentional activity of attempting to control, order or influence the behaviour of others'. Such a definition uncouples the activity of intentionally attempting to control etc from the actor of government, so enabling a decentred understanding of regulation. However, by retaining an element of intentionality it excludes the categories of market forces, social forces and technologies" (Black 2002). J. Black is right to want to link the theory of regulation with the theory of intentionality. Nevertheless, it is a mistake to believe that market mechanisms do not entail an element of intentionality. Her project to maintain a dimension of "transcendence" in the theory of regulation is thus wholly appropriate, not only for the methodological

developing an internalist analysis of the learning operation. It is also for this reason that he is unable to perceive that the aggregation of communicative competencies within a social system does not suffice on its own to enable a collective learning operation.

That, in fact, is the explicit project of the pragmatist and experimentalist movement in the theory of governance, which we will be examining to see if it fully respects the requirements of an internalist approach to the learning operation. But a final observation is necessary before we proceed to this examination. Several present-day authors have already recognized the weaknesses of a simple version of the relational and collaborative approach through dialogue, even though they have not reached the point of entering the stage of the experimentalist approach. We can thus speak of the emergence in recent research of a second version of this latter approach, and therefore of an intermediate effort to further the dynamic to which the relational and collaborative approach to governance has given rise. To illustrate this, a brief presentation of an article recently published in Australia will be helpful.

(3) Reconstruction of the dynamic internal to current research in the theory of governance brings to light a commitment within the relational and collaborative approach to governance to throw off the belief that the aggregation of communicative competencies suffices on its own to guarantee respect for the conditions necessary to governance that will maximally satisfy the collective interest. This commitment is currently being pursued from various perspectives. At present, it is shared by the majority of jurists and political scientists who wish to analyse the various governance techniques developed within the post-regulatory state (to use J. Black's and C. Scott's terminology).[55] This indeed is the essential reason offered for promoting the development of diverse forms of co-regulation

reasons she puts forward, but also, and above all, for epistemological reasons (every theory of collective action necessitates reference to an element of intentionality). But because J. Black makes use of a very classical concept of intentionality, she wrongly concludes that reference to market mechanisms, as defended, for instance, by neo-classical economists, does not also assume a theory of intentionality. This is manifestly an interpretive error about market theory. Every economic market theory is obviously associated with a certain theory of intentionality, as rational choice theory illustrates. Whatever the criticism that could be made of the theory of intentionality deployed by rational choice theory, it cannot be denied that market theory relies on a certain theory of intentionality. Such a denial could only arise out of a classical and highly problematic conception of intentionality. As with G. Teubner (whose thinking J. Black's seems, indeed, to be quite close to), the difficulty of building an internalist approach to the role played by intentionality (and thus by transcendence) in action accounts for this misinterpretation of rational choice theory and market theory.

55 As already indicated, even P. Vincent-Jones, despite his reliance on I. Macneil's more theoretical tool, defends the usefulness of techniques that might be called "meta-regulatory", for example, techniques designed to promote the collective learning ability (see above).

and meta-regulation at the expense of techniques of self-regulation. C. Scott (2006) writes that, as is suggested by the term itself:

> [M]eta-regulation is the process of regulating regulatory regimes and it is what governments are doing when they attempt to stimulate or steer self-regulatory regimes towards public ends (as with co-regulation) or when they seek to develop general instruments of control over public regulation (as with regulatory impact analysis and other processes of regulatory review).[56]

The line of research initiated by J. Braithwaite on the phenomenon of meta-regulation provides us with a typical instance of increased attention to the conditions for capacitating actors. The text we wish to look at is a recent article by S. Burris, P. Drahos, and C. Shearing called Nodal Governance (Burris, Drahos, and Shearing 2005: 30–58):

> Nodal governance is an elaboration of contemporary network theory that explains how a variety of actors operating within social systems interact along networks to govern the systems they inhabit ... Our theory posits that governance in such systems is substantially constituted in nodes—institutions with a set of technologies, mentalities and resources—that mobilize the knowledge and capacity of members to manage the course of events (Burris, Drahos, and Shearing 2005: 33).

However, the authors realize that this form of self-regulation through simple interaction among all the actors does not suffice on its own to guarantee the full effectiveness of the action:

> [N]odes have different capacities to interact with, and influence other nodes and the course of events. The capacity of a node to influence or regulate depends in large part upon its resources—broadly defined to include a wide range of forms of capital in the Bourdieuian sense (Burris, Drahos, and Shearing 2005: 39)

In this respect, the authors continue, the organicist vision of F. Hayek (or, we would wish to add, of D. Lewis as used by I. Macneil—see above) is inaccurate. "Nodal conceptions of governance ... focus attention on the way in which resources and knowledge are brought to bear through nodes" (Burris, Drahos, and Shearing 2005: 40). They go on to provide examples of the influence on the effectiveness of governance of the ways that capacities for empowerment are organized, that is, the way that actors' participation in these nodes is organized. The first example

56 As noted by B. Morgan, "[T]he notion of meta-regulation is simple at heart: it captures a desire to think reflexively about regulation, such that rather than regulating social and individual action directly, the process of regulation itself becomes regulated" (Morgan 2003 as quoted by P. Vincent-Jones 2006: Chapter 4, note 80).

they provide, an empirical reconstruction of the discussions that took place when the TRIPS was passed,[57] and specifically of the dominant role played by the alliance between the USA and the multinational pharmaceutical company lobby, "demonstrates why nodal governance is not necessarily democratic governance or governance that secures more 'goods' than 'bads' for the population as a whole; in order for nodal governance to be democratic the relevant nodes and networks must satisfy tests of representativeness, accessibility and deliberation that were devised in light of some set of democratic ideals" (Burris, Drahos, and Shearing 2005: 47). This conclusion is in line with that reached by P. Vincent-Jones using his expansive interpretation of relational theory. The second example will make it possible to explain, to some extent, the way the authors deepen the concept of empowerment and thus make possible increased attention to the conditions for *capacitation.* The example they analyse is that of a "South African initiative to create institutions of 'local capacity governance' to govern security and justice" (Burris, Drahos, and Shearing 2005: 33); it illustrates how the local institution's capacity was strongly enhanced by the attention paid by the central authorities to the resources necessary for organizing meetings and ensuring the possibility for effective participation by the population, as well as their attention to the resources necessary for information and expertise to be applied.[58]

In devoting attention to the conditions for the capacitation of the actors involved in the interaction, these authors are merely opening up a perspective that has already been more fully developed in recent inquiry into political theory. Indeed, they remain within what is effectively a classical perspective not far removed from the incentive approach of economists who long ago directed their attention to information asymmetries. Current inquiry into collaborative governance through dialogue[59] has expanded the concept of attention in an effort to further inquiry into the conditions that structure the capacity for such collaborative governance in a network society to maximally satisfy its members' normative expectations. It could be said that this inquiry, in a manner of speaking, continues the investigation of this question long ago begun by J. Habermas. As is well known, J. Habermas defined such conditions in the context of his formal pragmatics.[60] With authors such as J. Innes and D. Booher, for example,

57 The World Trade Organization's Agreement on Trade-Related Aspects of Intellectual Property Rights.

58 "One critical nodal relationship is with a unit of a school of Government at a South African university that provides administrative, regulatory supervision and research support as the implementing agency for" these local community institutions. Moreover, "[T]his nodal link provides a place through which international funding to support these functions has been channelled. At one point links were established with a Swedish university that provided a link to Swedish Government aid funding" (Burris, Drahos, and Shearing 2005: 51).

59 This expression is drawn from J. Innes and D. Booher (2003).

60 For a reflection on the impact of J. Habermas on the field of governance theory, see (Black 2000, 2001a). For a defence of a position inspired by J. Habermas in the literature on the regulation of public services, see (Prosser 2005a, 2005b).

the emphasis goes beyond J. Habermas' formal approach and directs attention to the devices needed to generate shared confidence among participating actors and ensure the emergence of "shared identities, shared meanings, new heuristics and innovation" (Innes and Booher 2003: 39). In thus expanding the attention granted to the conditions for empowerment, this inquiry poses a new question: "how collaborative planning can result in system adaptations" (Innes and Booher 2003: 47). In posing this question, the inquiry mandates the opening up of what had remained a black box in the relational and collaborative approach to governance. It opens up the road to a fresh stage in the dynamics of research in the theory of governance, that is, the pragmatist approach to governance.

Chapter 5
Political Pragmatism and Social Attention

The experimentalist and pragmatist approach developed mainly by C. Sabel[1] constitutes, in our view, the most fully worked-out effort to conceive of the internal conditions of the learning operation and of how to translate these internal conditions into institutional mechanisms that foster the actors' acquisition of the adaptive capacities required for participation in a deliberative problem-solving process. This approach firmly distances itself from all theorizing involving mechanisms based on the reinforcement of external mechanisms for coordination or hierarchical governance. Rather, it explores, in a more concrete manner, the internal transformations of collective action that are likely to foster the learning of new behaviours. In diametrical opposition to evolutionary economists, pragmatists work from the hypothesis that innovation, that is, the transformation or displacement of the representations provided by expanding the possibilities in existence at the outset, can only result from the learning operation itself.

The *internalist* solution that constitutes the contribution of pragmatist experimentalism is to be found in the way collaboration internal to the process of collective action is conceived. According to this conception, such collaboration shapes an internal teleology that guides the selection of new possibilities. For C. Sabel, this teleology results from the inter-group relationships constructed by the pragmatic mechanisms that themselves lead to the setting in motion of a logic of inquiry that ultimately allows not just for choice, but for *choice as to how to choose*. The more specific contents of this process of shared inquiry remain, however, as we will see, essentially a black box in C. Sabel's work.[2] Yet this constitutes the key element that enables an understanding of how social attention can be transformed from an operation of selection *vis-à-vis* a given set of possibilities (selective attention) into an operation of broadening of the set of available possibilities by means of a change in the perception of the problems to be solved (genetic attention). Moreover, this element has a direct relationship

1 See Chapter 4, notes 2 and 14. In the next chapter, we will take further the distinction, which is internal to the pragmatist approach itself, between C. Sabel's more experimentalist approach and D. Schön's and C. Argyris's more reflexive approach.

2 That is why we suggest a fourth stage—which we call the "genetic approach" (see Chapter 5, 189–99, and Chapter 6)—in the development of theories of governance. This genetic approach relies on the elucidation of new conditions associated with exploration of this black box, insofar as D. Schön's attempt to open up it, as presented in this section, will prove to be insufficient.

with J. Dewey's pragmatist perspective. For J. Dewey (1986b: 108), inquiry is an operation of "the controlled or directed transformation of an indeterminate situation".

In seeking to open up this black box, we must resort to D. Schön's explanation of the process of reframing. According to D. Schön, the internal process, which C. Sabel assumes to be a given, rests on a displacement of concepts. But how does this displacement occur? If we grant that it is made possible by pragmatic problem-solving deliberation (Helper, MacDuffie, and Sabel 2000: 473), it nevertheless poses a problem in connection with its dependence on a source of internal guidance (that of the inquirer and that of the reflective practitioner) that can direct the attention of the interacting groups so that a transition occurs from *selective attention* to *genetic attention* and the end result is a reframing of problematic situations. We thus arrive at the limitations of D. Schön's effort to conceive of how innovation occurs within the learning processes specific to collective action: something is still missing. The lack in the pragmatist undertaking is the elucidation of the specific internal mechanism that would make *capacitation* for displacing behaviour operational; that is, that would enable the transition to another kind of attention (genetic attention) and another kind of relationship with the possibilities by the actors involved in the process.

It thus appears important to differentiate between two aspects of the solution proposed by pragmatism to the question of the learning operation. On one hand, the acknowledgement of a teleology internal to the learning process relies on recourse to a collaborative model of inter-group relations that replicates the presuppositions of the linguistic turn and concentrates on the conversational process available to discussion groups, as well as the process of justification that is assumed to guarantee trust among members of these groups. On the other hand, acknowledgement of the capacities for innovation of the actors involved in collaborative processes leads the pragmatist proposal to explore the black box of the conditions for transforming behaviours. Under this second aspect, it goes beyond the conversational model and seeks to better understand how the redefinition of behaviours during a search for solutions that follows a logic of inquiry takes place. However, the pragmatist proposal does not, in our view, manage to satisfactorily combine these two aspects of its solution. It continues to presuppose that action taken on institutional design could somehow stimulate a rule for action that already exists in the minds of the actors involved in the problem-solving.

In order to understand these more epistemological issues associated with democratic experimentalism, we must resituate them in the context of the broader theoretical discussion surrounding developments in political pragmatism. This exercise will make it possible to better grasp the tension between the conversational model on one hand and the metaphorical learning model on the other. The highlighting of this tension first requires that we differentiate between two contributions made by recourse to pragmatism in current theoretical discussion in the social sciences and political philosophy. Pragmatism's first contribution consists, specifically within political philosophy, of *an effort to go beyond* deliberative theories of democracy. Its second contribution consists, specifically within the social sciences, of *an epistemological break*, in the theory of action, with comprehensive and ideal-typical approaches to the normativity of norms. The reason it is necessary to highlight the distinction between these two contributions is that the first often ends by obscuring the potential impact of the second. As has been observed by authors such as H. Joas, the discussion in political philosophy that constitutes an engagement with deliberativism has played the role of a kind of screen as regards the epistemological resources of the American founders of pragmatism. This discussion, focused on the figure of R. Rorty, is the one that tends to be spontaneously cited as an approach to grasping the issues raised by the pragmatist turn in the social sciences. And yet this turn has been driven by a more radical dynamic, epistemologically speaking, than that of the discussion emerging from political philosophy.

Nevertheless, this first discussion of R. Rorty and deliberativism has been significant, in that it has made it possible to open up perspectives for going beyond the deliberative orientation, even though the epistemological resources were lacking to make that orientation operative at the level of a new theory of collective action. Thus in this first discussion is found an opening up to the role of the imaginative world and to metaphorization, linked, however, to a linguistic philosophy of social deliberation/conversation that is attentive to the public role of the descriptions and vocabularies constructed by social actors. On the other hand, what is not found therein is any specific attention to the conditions for the conceptual displacement necessary to assign an effective role to this function of metaphorization within the process of collective action and instituting of shared norms. Thus, whereas the first discussion tends to obscure the implications of the second as regards the philosophical reception and potential impact of political pragmatism, its epistemological issues actually entail that it be illuminated by means of the second discussion, as well as entailing a demonstration of how the second accomplishes the purposes of the first but in a more radical way. This second discussion accomplishes these purposes while shifting the centre of attention to the building of collective capacities for action and away from the strengthening of the communicative competencies of the individuals involved. It is only thus that we are able to understand how, while it goes beyond the Rortyan model of pragmatism through its conception of organizational learning, democratic experimentalism nevertheless remains dependent on the black box associated with the first aspect of linguistic deliberative pragmatism, namely the notion of conversational mechanisms available within the minds of the actors involved.

The Contribution of the Linguistic Turn to Political Pragmatism

In the first stage of our inquiry, we will briefly revisit certain aspects of R. Rorty's political thought in order to show that his conception of the transformation of social meanings in the public sphere remains obscure: on one hand, this conception does incorporate J. Dewey's requirement that social intelligence about the conditions for collective action be displaced (pragmatic virtue); but on the other hand, it continues to refer to a conversational-type model that assumes that the identity of action emerges spontaneously through the praxis of discussion. R. Rorty thus recognizes the internal teleology of the conversational dynamic without referring to standard norms of discussion; but at the same time, he refers to the actors' practical disposition to arrive at shared reference points within this process without addressing the need to acquire or build this disposition, that is, to act on it.

A fundamental aspect of J. Dewey's thought that has been highlighted by the Rortyan critique of deliberativism resides in its handling of the distinction between public and private (Dewey 1986a: 244–5). This handling requires that two aspects of the public-private distinction be taken into account: on one hand, the need for a consequentialist approach to the two concepts (private and public); and, on the other hand, the need to keep the individual and groups of individuals on the same level as constitutive entities within social interactions. The result is a conception of the public that is defined by *specific attention* to "the scope and impact of the consequences of acts" (Dewey 1986a: 245) that are capable of affecting other individuals than those directly involved in a transaction. But this consequentialist conception of the consideration of interest as regards a broader community assumes, in a more radical manner, that this communitarian potential is taken into account, both in relation to isolated individuals and in relation to individuals as members of various groups in society. The issue, then, is to establish a link between the fulfilment of potentialities within joint activities and the need for a shared order to guarantee interaction among these different activities. The link thus established concerns the fulfilment and expression of collective identities on one hand, and, on the other hand, the principles required by these collective identities' enrichment and mutual interchange in a shared space. Thus we have, on one side, the question of the creation of multiple "we's" whose consequences are manifested beyond a private agreement between parties and, on the other side, the requirement that confirms or disconfirms these experiments in identity expression, namely the requirement that they be able to be part of a process of interchange and strengthening of shared values.

To do justice to these two dimensions of J. Dewey's thought about the public, R. Rorty adopts an anti-representationalist position concerning the requirements for individual fulfilment and an anti-foundationalist position concerning the requirements for justification of a shared order. The problem consists of conceiving of the public sphere as framed by the question "Who are we?" (in a consequentialist perspective: commitments to a potential "we") and as framed by the question "Who could be affected by our promises?" (what future goals, what openings are made within the contingent order of the existing vocabularies).[3] These two questions make it possible to discern a process of differentiation of social identities within a given conventional space and the process of opening up (non-closure,

3 See, for example, (Rorty 1996).

detotalization) of this space itself to new expressions that challenge its fitness to express human potentiality. Thus a tension is set up between the capacities already given for fulfilling fertile identities and the exclusion of other capacities assumed to negatively affect those first capacities. In other words, the criterion of differentiation of identities (the anti-representationalist thesis) is insufficient on its own to guarantee a public space if the beliefs in a foundation that guarantees this differentiation cannot themselves be challenged (the anti-foundationalist thesis). A space is public, then, when it guarantees revision of the beliefs in its self-preservation, that is, when it organizes the *experimentalist* relationship between exclusion and inclusion. The question is thus not to know whether a breach is acceptable or not, since no breach in the space of differentiation can be evaluated from a foundationalist point a view. The question is rather to determine what is assumed by a revision of beliefs; how a breach can open up and come to be an acceptable expression; how it can find a niche for itself within the shared space and progressively manage to *displace* the acknowledged foundational beliefs.

In R. Rorty, the mediation in question remains essentially *linguistic*. It takes as given that the conversational practice (the capacity) that animates public space is a totality in process of self-expression or as an experimental process. Capacities for differentiation and inclusion stand out from this conversational habitus of the public space. With this conversational background as a foundation, metaphors clearly appear as the alternative to the formal pragmatics of argumentation. "Ways of speaking" have their own inferential resources: they educate the feelings, that is, the ability to attend to new expressions of suffering and expectations for the fulfilment of human potential. By destabilizing beliefs, metaphors—or "ways of speaking"—*enlarge* beliefs' linguistic receptiveness and *make possible the enrichment of* the vocabulary and the continuation of its process of differentiation.

For R. Rorty, the pragmatic (and not the logical) process that metaphor makes possible is adequately accounted for by the breach that, at the prompting of metaphor, feelings become capable of realizing within a given vocabulary. According to this approach, this process thus shares with the deliberation that R. Rorty aims to critique a dual presupposition: that of a conversational habitus that is already a given within any democratic public space, and that of linguistic mediation as being necessary to guarantee the self-preservation of this public space. In a word, it presupposes identity and virtue.

In the field of political philosophy, this dual presupposition has opened up two movements in the pragmatist effort to go beyond deliberativism. There is on one hand a movement to show the need to take into account the usual process of identity formation as a condition of the use of deliberative procedures (thereafter operating as only one function among others in the social differentiation entailed by involvement in decision-making processes). On the other hand, there is a movement to reveal the need to reinforce the role of pragmatic virtues in guaranteeing a concern for minority opinions and values within public decision-making procedures.

From the perspective of the first movement, pragmatists have defended the idea that adequate kinds of participation cannot be determined in advance, that is, independently of social *experimentation* and the usual actor identity formation made possible by this experimentation. Thus, according to C. Misak (2000: 108), "[T]he kind of deliberation that is appropriate is something that will come out only through thought and deliberation". The question is thus not what are the conditions for setting in motion individual argumentative competencies in an interaction space that guarantees "a cooperative search for the truth, within which the force of the better argument alone can influence the outcome" (Habermas 1993: 154–5, 1993: 50). Rather, and more radically, the question is that of a method of social experimentation capable of guaranteeing new forms of collective action. "Indeed the self will only be formed through thinking and decision-making. It is only in the midst of inquiry that we discover who and what we are, what we want, and what fits best with the evidence and argument" (Misak 2000: 108).

From the perspective of the second movement, authors like M. Festenstein (1997: 168–9) aim to defend the need to go beyond the internal constraints of adherence to the most universal point of view or the most acceptable behaviour. In this last context, the only behaviour assumed to guarantee all participants' adherence is the one that affirms the rational acceptability of majority rules for deliberation. And yet other pragmatic virtues can be deployed to guarantee the fulfilment of shared interest, in particular that which validates *attention* to minority preferences. Minority preferences are not only the source of capacities for experimentation that allow for the creation of actors' identities and their collective motivation. They also safeguard pluralism of motivation as regards respect for the results of the deliberative process of justifying public decisions. Further, they thereby avoid restricting the deliberative process of justifying public decisions to a mechanism that is coercive and demotivating to groups placed in the minority (Festenstein 1997: 168–9).

Certainly, the thinking of these two movements is more attentive to the processes of collective decision-making than are R. Rorty's reflections. But this attentiveness is only designed to free our understanding of these processes from subjection to the deliberative perspective. And thus in effect, it confirms the appropriateness of the way R. Rorty revisits J. Dewey. In this perspective, it is the tension "differentiation of identities—reinforcement of virtues" that must frame the attention to capacities for participation in the public space, and engagement in the decision-making process is to be viewed in this frame.[4]

4 In contrast, as we will see, experimentalists such as C. Sabel take a different approach to overcoming deliberativism (and to revisiting J. Dewey). For them, it is the experiments in participation that are themselves to be viewed as the frame for the differentiation of identities and the reinforcement of virtues.

The Contribution of the Pragmatist Turn to the Social Sciences

The ambiguity we have identified within the Rortyan position makes it possible to illuminate the specific contribution made by the turn towards pragmatism in the social sciences. On one hand, the pragmatist turn in the social sciences does not take for granted an internal teleology supported solely by the pragmatic merit of conversational mechanisms or structures of deliberative framing. It seeks to determine the conditions for a mechanism likely to prompt the deroutinization of practices through the cooperative incentives it provides. Thus it seeks to provoke, within practice as already standardized, a shock or a state of disequilibrium through cooperative participation in problem-solving processes. On the other hand, the pragmatist turn in the social sciences seeks to extend this initial action taken in relation to the organizational conditions for learning towards a second action that directly concerns the transformation of practices themselves and the reframing of the conditions for collective action. This second action has to do with the logic of inquiry insofar as it alters the relation of collective action to the range of its possibilities. But even though the need for this second action has been clearly perceived, we will see that it remains essentially a black box that D. Schön attempts to open up.[5] This black box consists, as we will see, of an assumed self-reflexive property of collective action.

In the field of the social sciences, the pragmatist turn relies on a more complete epistemological break with the presuppositions of deliberativism. Deliberativism is understood more radically as a kind of subsystem that embodies a typical model of regulation as intervening directly in the public space. But public space constitutes a much broader system formed from the set of all collective decisions made and aiming at the best possible fulfilment of the potentialities of all the individual and collective entities involved. Thus it is the search for shared solutions and involvement in decision-making that, *prima facie*, constitutes the public space as J. Dewey was able to define it, viewing it as a communitarian process based on cooperative collective action:

> Wherever there is conjoint activity whose consequences are appreciated as good by all singular persons who take part in it, and where the realization of the good is such as to effect an energetic desire and effort to sustain it in being just because it is a good shared by all, there is in so far a community (Dewey 1986a: 328).

J. Dewey distinguishes two foundational moments in the development of this cooperative collective action. First, he identifies the moment of association that allows for the accumulation of goods from which all can derive benefit and "which gives a direction to the conduct of each one" (Dewey 1986a: 329). In this

5 The initial approach to D. Schön's pragmatism just made in this chapter will be rounded out in Chapter 6, as we seek to better pinpoint what distinguishes his generative approach to collective action from the genetic approach that we will advance.

first moment, cooperation with others is a condition for the liberation and "the fulfilment of personal potentialities" (Dewey 1986a: 329). The second moment is that of the "flow of social intelligence" (Dewey 1986a: 371) that results from the various local groups' mutual emulation as a result of the exchange of experiences and discussion about them (Dewey 1986a: 370). This flow of social intelligence constitutes the moment that corresponds to the liberation of collective potentialities properly so called. It is the result of a process of inter-group learning.[6] As H. Putnam (1992: 199) writes:

> For Dewey the democracy that we have is not something to be spurned, but also not something to be satisfied with. The democracy that we have is an emblem of what could be. What could be is a society which develops the capacities of all its men and women to think for themselves, to participate in the design and testing of social policies, and to judge results.

The pragmatist turn in the social sciences may be viewed in this light: for the pragmatist, it is necessary to *experiment*, that is, to take into account the training of individuals' capacity for self-destination, a capacity for involvement and cooperation in problem-solving processes. The pragmatist establishes a tension between the moral "we" that is given and implicit and the explicit potential "we", the "we" of the community that must be built and that calls for a force for social creation in order to make the transition from a centralized social process aiming at the division of labour to a decentralized social process aiming at the involvement of all the various groups in a process of innovation.

This kind of approach shows that it is possible to identify stages in the transformation of actors' competencies in relation to their involvement in a process of collective action. The vector of learning then becomes the building of those processes of collective action likely to fulfil the requirements of participatory mechanisms directed towards problem solving.

To organize a "joint activity" between the actors involved and initiate learning processes, certain conditions must be fulfilled such that intermediate cultures of collective action are constituted. These conditions are usually omitted when they are simply confused with the mechanisms assumed to motivate participation. In order to make it possible to take ownership of a process of collective action, it is necessary for members of the subgroups involved to experience confidence in a project conceived of as a *joint activity*,[7] involvement in mutual support in the

6 "From the standpoint of the groups, it demands liberation of the potentialities of members of a group in harmony with the interests and goods which are common. Since every individual is a member of many groups, this specification cannot be fulfilled except when different groups interact flexibly and fully in connection with other groups" (Dewey 1986a: 328). See also (Dewey 1982: 186).

7 We think in particular of M. Bratman's model of "shared cooperative activity" (Bratman 1992), used by J. Coleman (2001b) in the context of the analysis of the concept

implementation of the project, and ultimately the emergence of new spokespersons to intervene in the decision-making process and make the joint action ever more susceptible of ownership. And this must first take place at the local level, in order to find solutions through collective organization and management of shared problems.

Democratic experimentalism, especially as it is understood by C. Sabel, without any doubt constitutes one of the most characteristic expressions of this pragmatist turn in the social sciences, in that it goes radically beyond solutions (discussed in the first two sections of this chapter) that neglect the conditions in which learning mechanisms can be owned. For authors writing from the perspective of the pragmatist turn, "democratic experimentalism"[8] designates "the overall system of public problem solving that combines federal learning with the protection of the interests of the federated jurisdictions and the rights of individuals" (Dorf and Sabel 1998: 288). The advantage of such a system of collaboration, in which individuals learn from each others' successes and failures, is that it has the capability to reduce the vulnerability created by the decentralized search for solutions (Dorf and Sabel 1998: 284–8). A second advantage of this kind of system resides in the attention it pays to the specific function of groups in the process of internalizing learning mechanisms. This system is based mainly on the "self-reflexive sociability" (Sabel 1994: 159) of the groups of actors that have been constituted as "publics" capable of learning by evaluating their collective actions (Sabel 1994: 158).

Under the deliberative models, an underlying psychology of moral development remained tied to a mentalist conception of the development of social norms. The issue was clearly the development of individual competencies for judgement, as for example in L. Kohlberg's model.[9] The idea was that the process of acquiring individual competencies for argumentation depended on the setting in motion of argumentation within settings organized to promote deliberation on a participatory model. Thus the group constituted a kind of *intermediate cultural setting*, with its own references and codes whose function was to strengthen participants' mental capacities by acting on the expected practical effects of the behaviour of a member who tries to be loyal and honest with regard to the group.

In democratic experimentalism, it is clearly the competencies for collective action of groups themselves that are at issue. This kind of approach relies simultaneously on the capacity for self-regulation of the actors involved at the local level and the capacity of the regulatory power to guarantee an exchange of knowledge and practices based on the prevalence of equality of standing and freedom, both within each experiment and among the experiments themselves. What is sought is twofold social learning: the social learning that results directly

of law (on this, see Part I).

8 On the more theoretical issues related to this approach, see J. Lenoble and M. Maesschalck (2003), *Towards a Theory of Governance*.

9 See (Power, Higgins, Kohlberg, and Reimer 1989). L. Kohlberg's thought represents a significant bridge between that of J. Rawls and J. Habermas as regards the presuppositions of deliberativist proceduralism (see Lenoble and Maesschalck 2003: 156–ff).

from participating in the cooperative search for solutions within a local process of experimentation; and the learning that results from evaluating and comparing different local solutions at the level of the governance mechanisms. At each of these levels, *inter-group relations* are at issue. That is why, in the view of authors such as M. Dorf and C. Sabel, the contribution of pragmatism lies in its model of learning by monitoring, in which practical incentives such as comparative assessment, co-design, and error detection are implemented to promote the exchange of knowledge and experiences during the testing of workable solutions (Dorf and Sabel 1998: 286–7). Under such a model of governance, at the national level the goals and content of public policies must be minimally defined, vague, and general, in order to allow for experimenting with solutions at the level of the local federated entities.

The major features of pragmatism retained by C. Sabel assume an epistemological break with the presuppositions of deliberativism. This break radically differentiates his thinking from the Rortyan perspective. It relies, on one hand, on a conception of inference that is not limited to the pragmatic matter of the revisability of beliefs, but also deals with the rules of engagement in collective action. According to this conception, what matters in a learning process is the conditions under which the methods selected manage to transform themselves internally into their own implementation.[10] On the other hand, it also rests on a conception of the relation to new social goals or possibilities that calls for a more complex theory of the contribution to action made by inquiry. On this score, C. Sabel emphasizes the metaphorical nature of the learning associated with the pragmatist mechanisms of benchmarking.[11] In social terms, the pragmatic function of inquiry consists of placing the identification of problematic situations on the same level as the theoretical explanation of their consequences, since these two actions result from the same practical operation of discriminative attention to the interactions elicited by normative choices.[12]

On this score, C. Sabel's theory of the "non-standard firm" is highly characteristic. It constitutes a typical example of the institutionalization of cooperative solutions in a non-constraining situation, that is, in a situation where other valid choices of solution could have been made. The issue of

10 According to H. Putnam (1990: 219), "Dewey and James extended Peirce's observations by making explicit the idea that methodology itself is something that evolves in the course of inquiry".

11 See (Sabel 2006: 130). See as well page 135: "The process of re-evaluating goals parallels the process of searching out and assessing narrower design choices. Thus the 'center' of the encompassing pragmatist institution—acting on behalf and with the help of representatives of the individual subunits—metaphorically or openly benchmarks its overall objectives, looking for goals like the current ones, but arguably better on some dimension".

12 J. Dewey (1986b: 502) writes of making use of discriminative or selective observation to determine, for example, whether or not a given legislative measure works, relying on a comparative method that situates it within a system of well thought-out alternatives.

the choice of this kind of solution is thus unequivocally central, because the organizational process relates to zones of ambiguity where reference to the interests, values, and standards of organization remain unclear. In these zones of ambiguity, what the actors *will* or *will not* do "depends on the particulars of the situation, including, of course, the actors' changing understandings of their possibilities" (Sabel 1994: 158). How these situations are made to yield benefits is what makes it possible to differentiate two kinds of organizational culture of the firm, only one of which is based on a pragmatist option. According to C. Sabel, the non-standard firm can be considered to be a *process of collective action*. Contrary to the standard model of the firm based on the *routinization* of tasks and their incorporation into a hierarchical structure (Sabel 2006: 111), non-standard theory favours the systematic revisiting of routines and the exploration of the ambiguities within a decentralized (polycentric or federalist) structure. The non-standard firm thus has a relationship to more dynamic and open learning: whereas the standard firm combats the ignorance endemic among its human resources by simplifying tasks, the non-standard firm promotes cooperative behaviours as the means to find new solutions *vis-à-vis* complex tasks. The strategy of the non-standard firm thus proves fruitful not just in the short term, that is, during the time needed for a problem-solving process to yield the solution to the problem identified. It is also fruitful in the medium term, because it enables the learning not only of how to choose solutions but also of *how to choose how to choose solutions* (Helper, MacDuffie and Sabel 2000: 478).

C. Sabel emphasizes the pragmatic mechanisms that make possible the setting in motion of a *pragmatic collaboration*. In the context of the non-standard firm, all these mechanisms—benchmarking, simultaneous engineering, and the error detection method—are incorporated into a "just in time" problem-solving procedure and based on a process of inter-group exchange that assumes *rules of engagement* that require mutual monitoring of each participant's contribution (detection of performance failures), information sharing for a mutual understanding of the situation to be explored, and the mutual assessment of each participant's reliability in relation to the joint activity. These rules of engagement constitute the frame of reference for *learning by monitoring* via the pragmatic mechanisms established.

Beyond these pragmatic mechanisms governed by rules of engagement, however, a further dimension of the process of collective action remains to be determined. This is the joint activity properly so called, namely the *inquiry*. The role of the mechanisms and their procedural context is only to create a *path* that will lead the actors to seek solutions within a "circumscribed space of possibilities" (Helper, MacDuffie, and Sabel 2000: 468, Sabel 2006: 124) whose contours and contents are not known to them ahead of time. This path confirms the actors in their disposition to an "urgent suspicion that habitual beliefs are poor guides to current problems" (Helper, MacDuffie, and Sabel

2000: 469): it imparts the force of *quasi-routine*[13] to the critique of the "suitability of current routines" (Helper, MacDuffie, and Sabel 2000: 468). As C. Sabel writes, "[W]here hierarchy produces the information asymmetries of mutual ignorance, learning by monitoring in effect creates an information symmetricizing machine" (Helper, MacDuffie, and Sabel 2000: 472). A force of this kind is necessary because at the moment when it is set in motion, action (properly so called) on routines, acquired habits, and beliefs intensifies uncertainty and the awareness of difficulties. But it is always just a preliminary to the action of inquiry.

The question of *shared inquiry* is fundamental: it is a question of managing to free problematic situations of ambiguity by means of the process of inter-group cooperation put into place. C. Sabel writes of the "collaborative investigation of ambiguity" (Helper, MacDuffie, and Sabel 2000: 470) and "problem solving deliberation" (Helper, MacDuffie, and Sabel 2000: 473). Clearly these expressions emphasize the organization of inter-group exchanges in discussion spaces (Helper, MacDuffie, and Sabel 2000: 469, Sabel 1994: 145). But they also reveal a particular dimension of the rules of engagement that is designed to protect the shared process from opportunistic behaviours, or "free-riding effects", that could hijack the benefits produced in common. The pooling of information thus plays a twofold role: it protects against opportunism and it symmetricizes information, thus making possible an increase in shared knowledge. But this increase depends, above all, on another practice that is more directly connected to the activity of inquiry properly so called. Beyond the sharing of information about each participant's intentions and capacities, what is at issue in this process is also mutual teaching designed to make the relations between the technical competencies and the strategies of research and development understandable. It is only in this way that it becomes possible to open up existing routines and undertake the joint redeployment of the resources invested in the process of inquiry.

In this perspective, the *alignment of interests* by means of the process of collective action becomes a practical effect that cannot be dissociated from the reconfiguring of solutions through the joint activity of inquiry. Indeed, the inquiry incorporates this construction of a shared view of the problems and goals to be

---

13 Formulations such as "routinely questioning the suitability of current routines" (Helper, MacDuffie, and Sabel 2000: 468) and "the routines they use for interrogating and altering their routines" (Helper, MacDuffie, and Sabel 2000: 468–9) are cast paradoxically for rhetorical effect. Standard "routinization" has a wholly different meaning than that of collective action. It results from options for the division and simplification of labour in order to produce a chain of limited operations that are externally related to each other (Helper, MacDuffie, and Sabel 2000: 461). That is why the formulations just mentioned seek to convey the need to engage with existing routines by adopting an analogous force that is at least as powerful as they are in order to destabilize them. Pragmatic mechanisms and the rules of engagement can thus be viewed as playing the role of *quasi-routines* in order to "systematically provoke doubt" (Helper, MacDuffie, and Sabel 2000: 469, Sabel 2006: 121).

pursued in solving the problems, because it broadens all the actors' attention to include the context of their action and thus the interest-based factors specific to the ways the various groups operate in solving a problem.

Nevertheless, C. Sabel is silent on how the construction process that is supposed to lead to the transformation of the perceptions and logic of action takes effect. The *logic of inquiry* that is at the heart of pragmatism remains a black box. The only indication we are given is the example of inquiry by the method of the "five whys" (Helper, MacDuffie, and Sabel 2000: 468, Sabel 2006: 121). This example names two properties needed by the joint activity of inquiry in a pragmatic context: the mechanism of the sharing of experiences among collaborators and the reconstruction of long causal chains (without being detained by immediate causes or causes assumed to be obvious). In other texts, C. Sabel uses other formulations for these two properties but still does not open up the black box of the logic of inquiry. In Learning by Monitoring, for example, he describes the mechanism for sharing experiences as a "process of continuous discussion of the possibilities and of joint goals".[14] This mechanism is understood to allow for an exploratory use of communication in such a way as to investigate the limitations of each participant's underlying positions. The second property takes shape through the reconstruction of identities and of representations of the world, that is, as a revision of beliefs based on the reciprocal identification of the limitations of each position in the perspective of shared action (in other words, it takes shape through a cooperative game (Sabel 1994: 146). In this kind of mechanism, attention is shifted to create an informative *disequilibrium* (Sabel 1994: 148) that allows for the envisaging of new forms of cooperation. We thus see how the actors *learn how to learn* (Sabel 1994: 158).

To learn how to learn, then, a *shift* is necessary and this implies specific *attention* within the collaborative process. "The notion of rule governed learning by monitoring can ... accommodate evidence of diversification and disruption of relations by shifting attention from the extent to the character of collaboration" (Sabel 1994: 146). It is not just a question of paying attention to what one is learning: one must also pay attention to how one is learning. C. Sabel focuses on the mechanism of *disequilibrium* (Sabel 1994: 148–9) produced by the exploration of other points of view and interpretations of a situation. In going beyond the limits of their own position, a group of actors will be brought to redefine the parameters that led them to adopt that position and build new positioning. They thus derive a benefit from the very *vulnerability* of their initial position (that is, from its limitations) by being willing to explore other positions that are caught up in the same disequilibrium that is driven discursively by the mechanism of joint inquiry. But this mechanism itself remains under-explained. One enters into it following an induced disequilibrium and one emerges from it with a new understanding of one's role in solving a problem and more broadly in taking part in a joint activity. All this happens because of a shift in attention.

14 "A continuous discussion of joint possibilities and goals" (Sabel 1994: 145).

A group can thus learn to organize and define itself *vis-à-vis* other groups. In fact, it is desirable that this paradigm be applied to public-private partnership situations (Sabel 1994: 150): learning by monitoring helps in "creating a common framework of understanding that allows [groups] to assess the shortcomings of their joint activities" (Sabel 1994: 155).

What of the conditions for this awareness: in what conditions, and how, does it manage these transformations? On this point, C. Sabel offers no more than a comparatively weak social notion of reflexivity, conceived on the deliberative model and thus far removed from pragmatist requirements for a concept of "joint" learning:

> [R]einterpretations proceed through argumentative encounters in which the individual attempts to establish an equilibrium between his or her views and social standards by recasting both. It is this reflexive capacity to embrace different forms of self-expression that defines persons as individuals and creates new interpretative possibilities for society (Sabel 1994: 156).

This concept of reflexivity is supplemented by a concept of inter-group learning that assumes it is possible to determine what rules—beyond individual reflexive competencies—guarantee a redefinition of roles (Sabel 1994: 158).

Thus, if the model deployed by C. Sabel calls for a second-order attention as a key aspect of the logic of inquiry, the process of producing such second-order attention remains a black box. Informative disequilibrium, the exploration of ambiguities, the revision of beliefs: these are all mechanisms that can result in increased *first-order* attention, that is, direct attention to a new solution for a problematic situation. What is at play here are the conditions for "disentrenching inquiry" (Sabel 2006: 124)[15] in order to turn one's attention away from the usual information about advantages and disadvantages. The result is *choosing better* rather than *choosing differently.* Choosing better means shifting attention to the choice of how one chooses. It requires a change in the overall approach, the approach that operates in the selection of projects at the company level and that governs the selection of reform plans at the state level. It is when choosing how to choose is in question that the issues of errors on a major scale and with long-term effects come into play.

Now in the experimentalist model, all this happens as if merely making the shift beyond accustomed habits and forms of evidence must not just result in an immediate impact on the choice of solutions, but also produce, in some spontaneous fashion, an indirect effect on how solutions are chosen. But the specific properties of the inquiry that are expected to make this form of self-*capacitation* of second-

15 This concept of self-reflexivity used by C. Sabel (2006) in A Real Time Revolution in Routines is already to be found in D. Schön (1963: 197): "Our technology and our institutions affect thought not only directly, by the changes in behaviour they force upon us, but indirectly—by presenting themselves as projective models for our theories".

order attention possible are not specified. All we know is that what is involved in these properties resides in a *shift* inherent in the inquiry itself, by virtue of its being an unaccustomed project. Thus it is by adopting the pragmatist method itself as a method of social experimentation, that is, by linking the idea one can form of a state of affairs to the imaginative capacity one has for changing that state of affairs, that the self-reflexive property of collective action is manifested (Sabel 1994: 159). Reason achieves attention to a possible shift *and* attention to how one pays such attention *simultaneously* (Helper, MacDuffie, and Sabel 2000: 478).

On this score, the concept of *metaphoric learning* is hardly of any help to our progress, because it reproduces the juxtaposition of the two orders of attention by once again reducing the second order to the first. Metaphor does not teach (in the strict sense) how to learn nor how to choose how to choose. It teaches how to identify the limits of the representations and descriptions conveyed by the various groups involved in a conversational exchange and how to opt for a *revision of categories* that will make it possible to clear away ambiguity, that is, for the *reciprocal clarification of meanings* through a creative compromise similar to that of translation (Sabel 2006: 126). The indirect result is a process of social construction of meanings through cooperative meaning-making and recourse to metaphorical comparisons (Sabel 2006: 127). These two mechanisms do not, however, explain on their own how it is possible on one hand to learn to give priority attention to this kind of social construction or on the other hand to learn to use it collectively.

The Contribution to Political Pragmatism of the Theory of Learning: D. Schön's Contribution

It remains, then, to elucidate this twofold move which the pragmatist turn in the social sciences has identified as necessary but which it has not managed to fully construct: one move that requires the specific reframing of the conditions for learning in collective action and another move that requires determination of the conditions for learning how to do this learning, or more simply for the reflexive property of the society that enables it to have recourse to "reflection-in-action" (Schön 1996: 163).

We can find this more radical explanation of the *logic of inquiry* in D. Schön's theory of metaphorical learning. The departure point for this explanation, which was developed during the 1960s, is obviously "mentalist". Metaphor is conceived as work done by the individual imagination, and acts of individual creativity are the sources of paradigm shifts (Schön 1963).[16] But this emphasis

16 D. Schön (1971: 130): "Freud, for example, during the time he was working on *The Interpretation of Dreams* existed, in the medical and the larger social worlds of Vienna, as a marginal man. Norman Thomas occupied a marginal position in American life for decades until his ideas (not his person) found their way into the mainstreams of public policy".

on the metaphorical power of language offers the benefit of identifying its central displacement mechanism and its specific role in learning. The theory of metaphor thus points towards the pragmatic question of the production of new behaviours capable of changing the initial givens of a situation and acting on actors' capacities:

> As [the child] learns to ride a bicycle after he has learned to ride a little one; as he learns for the first time to run, or to eat with a fork; in virtually all learning, the child can be seen shifting old patterns to new situations, using the old as projective model for the new, just as he treats his first encounter with school through the metaphor of his family (Schön 1963: 108).

While avoiding over-estimating the imaginative and individual nature of these examples, we can retain the underlying definition of the metaphoric process as such: it is understood to reside in *seeing as*, that is, more precisely, in the *projective displacement* (Schön 1963: 88) of past models onto new situations, which allows for a *framing* of the production of new behaviours.

This concept of framing, though implicit in D. Schön's early work, is a key factor in his transition to a theory of the role of metaphor in collective action. At the collective level, it is the way groups of actors equip themselves with interpretive frames for their interests that makes their positions incommensurable with those of other groups of actors. These frames are what conduce to groups' *selective attention*. Group members become more attentive to some aspects of a given situation and in consequence also become capable of reinterpreting the facts in light of the selected aspects. In this kind of situation:

> The adversaries do not disagree about the facts, they simply turn their attention to *different* facts. Further, when one is committed to a problem frame, it is almost always possible to reject facts, to question data (usually fuzzy, in any case), or to patch up one's story so as to take account of data without fundamental alteration of the story (Schön 1993: 151).

The force of such positions resides in the *normative function* fulfilled by their frames. This normativity derives from the metaphoric power of language. The frame functions at the collective level as does metaphor at the individual level. It elicits a kind of "policy-analytic literary criticism" (Schön 1993: 149). A group of actors' shared frame of reference is based on an interpretive rule that consists of relating all the features of a situation and the events that can arise within it to the internal coherence of a foundational metaphor. It is in this sense that D. Schön talks of "generative metaphor", as N. Chomsky talks of "generative grammar".[17] He writes as follows of generative metaphor:

17 See the reference to T. Kuhn in (Schön 1996: 183–4).

> The metaphor which accounts for centrally important features of the story—which makes it understandable that certain elements of the situation are included in the story while others are omitted; that certain assumptions are taken as true although there is evidence that would appear to disconfirm them; and, especially, that the normative conclusions are found to follow so obviously from the facts (Schön 1993: 149).

This generative metaphor is the principle of selective attention within the collective frame that justifies the actors' positions. It is also its principle of reproduction and thus its implicit principle of learning.

To elicit a logic of inquiry, it is necessary to become attentive to the role played by this framing, that is, to pay attention to the generative metaphor in which it originates and that produces the rule for interpreting and incorporating the facts. In so doing, one focuses one's attention on the *projective mechanism*, which consists of transposing habit (or the familiar) onto the unaccustomed (or the unfamiliar) or of associating neutral subject matter with familiar images (Schön 1963: 89). What the attention retains from the operation of this projective mechanism is the *connection* established between two levels of consciousness: one that is spontaneous and undirected and another that is reactive and seeks to compensate for the undirectedness of the first level by means of an idea or form capable of conferring meaning. "We are asked not merely 'What do you see in X?', but 'Find Y in X'" (Schön 1963: 88). The moment one tries to grasp this meaning-generative process specifically, one passes from *selective attention* (first-order attention) to *genetic attention* (second-order attention). And from the moment such attention is established, inquiry is possible. In situations of conflict of interest between different groups, the advantage of such attention is that it allows for the opening up of the black boxes that the various groups are relying on to justify their positions. If the diverse processes for specific trait selection and for guided rereading of the facts are revealed through "shared inquiry" (Schön 1993: 151), a different structuring of the frames that the various actors relate to becomes possible. Such a restructuring of frames is valuable not just because it eases conflict by providing a fresh perspective on the situation. Reframing a situation means, above all, making new roles possible, opening oneself up to the possibility for new behaviours.[18] Thus a connection is established between the *cognitive work* of restructuring frames, based on the features of the concrete situation, and the *redescription* of the participants themselves as they grasp the issues involved in their relationships with the other participants (Schön 1993: 158).

D. Schön is thus surely the thinker who, to this point, presents the fullest account of the black box of *joint inquiry*, which constitutes the central point of the pragmatist turn in the theory of collective action. It is the transition to second-

18 "The new question leads to a reframing of the roles of the various parties" (Schön 1993: 155).

order attention, that is, to genetic attention, that makes it possible to grasp the projective mechanism that can broaden the field of agonistic behaviours.

A major difficulty does, however, persist in this fuller version of the pragmatist turn: this difficulty resides in the mechanism for *intelligent learning* (Schön 1936: 89). Conflict situations require intervention by an invisible hand, that of the *inquirer* who is capable of *directing attention*. The stimulus provided by the inter-group relationship is not sufficient: outside guidance, the gaze of a third party, is needed to launch the process of redescription.

In his later work, D. Schön envisaged two solutions to this problem of the guiding of attention. On one hand, he sought to indicate what conditions make it possible to incorporate a kind of such guidance on the part of the professional practitioner (182–6); on the other hand, he refined his conception of inter-group relations so as to better specify the particular conditions of the process of inquiry that make it possible to reframe action (184–6). After presenting these two solutions, we will show the limitations of this learning model (186–9).

Building the Attention of the Reflective Practitioner

All the significant developments in D. Schön's theory in the area of professional practice have considerably enriched his theory of the role of attention in organizational learning. This process of evolution in his research also resulted in his focusing on the assumed capacities of actors facing problematic situations. In one context, actors appear to be the prisoners of sterile mechanisms that lead them to harden the deadlocks within problematic situations by intensifying the conflicts among viewpoints. In another context, they appear to be explorers supported by mechanisms that stimulate their reflexive potential and lead them to interact constructively with other points of view by making an effort to understand them from inside and to revisit their own points of view in light of what they have learned.

Recalling the question he was asked by the director of security in a chemicals company, D. Schön (1996: 352) again delineates two kinds of behaviour:

> In one division of his company, people had learned a way of working with federal regulators that they had found extraordinarily effective. As they developed new chemical products and gathered data on their environmental effects, they made full and immediate disclosures to the federal regulators. They had discovered that when regulators had early access to data and were able to participate in its interpretation, they were inclined to work cooperatively with the industry's representatives … But in other divisions of the firm … regulators were considered as adversaries who should be fed tailored information packaged in carefully prepared cases submitted for approval.

D. Schön thus pinpoints two possible types of behaviour. One is to develop an oppositional strategy towards a group identified as harbouring opposing interests to one's own. In this case, that group consisted of federal civil servants with the power to block or delay, for reasons of health or environmental safety, the granting of consent for the use of a substance in production processes. The other type of behaviour is to develop a strategy of collaboration with that same group. In the example before us, this collaborative strategy included early information sharing. The strategy banked on transparency and included involvement in the interpretation of the regulations in force. Thus, in this strategy, the risk of early refusal was accommodated as a trade-off for the indirect benefits generated by an ethos of cooperation. And indeed, the strategy did succeed in reducing procedural delay, because mistrust related to the withholding or distortion of information was removed.

One can see how, with strategies of the second kind, the correlation is made between the removal of unclarity and the enrichment of previously opposed stories (or just stories that previously had the potential to harbour conflicting interests). The innovative employees discovered a factor that undermined their existing strategy for preparing their dossiers: federal representatives were led to suspect bias in the presentation of results. What could be viewed by one side as preparation time made longer by the intent to transmit results that were full and impervious to challenge could be viewed by the other side as the withholding of information in order to better cover up deficiencies and questionable results. The logic of contradiction of these two causal stories could have been extended. But instead, the innovative strategy took off from a different approach to the problem: it experimented with collaboration in order to remove doubt about the interpretation of results. It therefore experimented with a different way of managing the reciprocal flow of information and interpreting the regulations in force.

For the professional, then, the question becomes knowing how to direct and validate reflection-in-action so as to decide whether to follow a new path. Since what is in question is the validation of the signs that professional actors notice by making use of their reflexive skills, D. Schön (1991: 348) proposes recourse to an approach based on K. Popper's theory of inquiry. This consists of devising a test of validity by means of a process that makes possible the trial, the falsifiability, and the proposal/revision of the pre-given frames. How should a practitioner proceed in order to test her or his reflexive observations in action? Under what conditions can the practitioner succeed in testing the validity of her or his observations? The answer is to view these observations as hypotheses that are subject to invalidation. To succeed in doing this, the practitioner has no choice but to confront these observations with other, invalidating, hypotheses, while progressively developing the frame for a new story that unites her or his reflexive requirements to the fresh observations that emerge from the mechanism of inquiry. This process assumes that three conditions are satisfied:

- the elicitation, identification, and multiplication of stories capable of providing causal representations of reality that invalidate each other;
- verification of the robustness of these hypothetical stories;
- choosing among these stories according to the practitioner's basic categories and her or his approach to the setting in which action is taking

place, in order to build a potential frame for a new story (the story that will be produced by the change in practice).

D. Schön clearly specifies under what conditions a practitioner succeeds in transforming defensive behaviour into collaborative and creative behaviour within the process of inquiry. The practitioner must begin from the destabilization of acquired positions (a shock) and then aim at comprehensive displacement supported by critical attentiveness to the boundaries crossed. The role played by the *underlying story* of the inquiry itself, however, remains vague. It is inter-group relations that will make possible its specification.

The Role of Inter-group Relations in the Guiding of Attention

The Popperian test plays a role in guiding the practitioner's reflexive skill, just as it can play a role in guiding a researcher faced with the different stories associated with a problematic situation. Its application, however, supposes the exercise of this skill to have been prompted by the idea that a cooperative story may open up new possibilities for solutions by changing the positions currently held by the various actors involved. D. Schön even believes that, in order to surmount blockages, it is necessary to elicit a kind of direct transplantation of elements from one group to another, so that a shock is provoked and displacement is achieved by the coming into contact of mutually invalidating perceptions.[19] We must therefore specify the role played by inter-group relations in D. Schön's theory, since this role sheds light on the significance of the underlying story for the process of inquiry, which will open up onto a new framework for action for a new collective history.

In the examples he chooses, D. Schön always succeeds in distinguishing different subgroups within a given population according to their ability to collaborate with their adversary. This he does by adhering to two principles. First, he relies on the way the various subgroups report on their relationship with another group that is identified (by virtue of its divergent interests) as an adversary. Second, based on these narratives, he compares the subgroups with each other, and in so doing he reveals an independent variable, such as age group or geographic location. The usefulness of the second principle lies in the fact that it confirms the exo-group nature of the differentiation D. Schön is focusing on. The stories reflect the cultures of subgroups that perceive themselves as distinct. The sources of the

19 "In order to achieve such outcomes as these, professionals engaged in the political contention of the policy-making process would have to be capable of inquiry within an adversarial setting. They would have to be capable of advocating and acting on their own views of reality while at the same time subjecting them to reflection, of taking an adversarial stance toward their opponent's views while at the same time striving to understand them. Professionals in conflict with one another would also have to be capable of reciprocal reflection-in-action" (Schön 1996: 350).

differences between subgroups that are part of a single population that is in an adversarial situation depend on the specifics of each situation.

Telling of one of his encounters with activists working for a consumers' association, D. Schön (1996: 351) recounts as follows the reactions he drew by suggesting "a new strategy which combined adversarial process with cooperative inquiry":

> The oldest participants found the suggestion unthinkable: how could they cooperate with their traditional enemy? The middle-aged participants were intrigued but skeptical. The youngest asserted that the idea was a familiar one, which some of them were already pursuing. They were helping consumer product manufacturers to develop programs of product safety, reliability, and quality assurance in order to comply with the regulations which the consumer movement had helped to put in place (Schön 1996: 351).

But why define exo-group relations within a population so sharply if the distribution of group membership can be assumed to be random when different situations are placed side by side? For instance, if this last example is placed beside the previous one from the chemicals industry, age and class variables become irrelevant. In fact, the interpretive hypothesis related to the variables comes into play in order to reinforce the building of the underlying story the inquirer is telling himself and, at a more basic level, to aid in the specific search for a suitable path to a solution. In applying these two principles, the inquirer can confirm and enrich his own generative story, which seeks to reveal the comparative benefits of strategies for behavioural transformation that will enable a form of cooperative attitude to the adversary within a process of shared search for solutions.

Two kinds of exo-group relation are thus necessary to the inquirer's story: the relation between groups that share a common adversarial attitude towards another group, and the relation between a group and one or more groups identified as its adversaries. It is in the various narratives about the second type of exo-group relation that mutually invalidating elements will be encountered; and the existence of these invalidating elements is itself explained by reference to the first type of exo-group relation. The question then becomes whether or not to cooperate, in what state of mind, and with what goals (within what process). Next, it becomes possible to differentiate overt opposition, marked by a complete refusal to collaborate, from latent opposition, which consists of engaging in biased or curtailed collaboration by concealing information and maintaining suspicion towards information received. A final strategy invalidates these two: it consists of overt, early, and constructive collaboration that effectively creates the conditions for a true third culture produced by a change of attitude regarding divergent interests and regarding the possibility for setting common goals.

By crossing the two kinds of exo-group relations with each other, D. Schön succeeds in constructing his own underlying story and presenting adversarialism as a variable datum that is capable of broadening the range of possible behaviours as previously identified. For this broadening to take place, two conditions are required: it must apply to the divergent stories of the groups involved and thus enable collaborative ownership of the stories; and it must be confirmed by other situations in which this broadening process made it possible to develop better solutions.

This approach to inter-group relations reveals two requirements to supplement the Popperian test. To falsification (trial-error-elimination) must be added a test of reciprocity of the underlying story proposed by the practitioner to the groups concerned and a generalization test allowing for reference to be made to other processes of collaborative enrichment.[20] Thus we can distinguish among three test requirements. Together, they produce the conditions for building a new framework for action:

- the requirement for a falsifying test, consisting of envisaging all the experiments it is possible, in practical terms, to carry out in order to refute all the assumed constructions of reality (or causal stories), including the researcher's;
- the requirement for a reciprocity test, consisting of creating a behavioural world open to shared-collaborative reflection-in-action (possible uses of the categories deployed by the collaborative story);
- the requirement for a generalizing test, consisting of relating story enrichments in a specific frame to other experiences of the same kind (this assumes there is a tie-in with a more general research program).

This reframing action represents an advance over the pragmatist mechanisms of co-design, benchmarking, and error detection. In this case, what was at issue was to envisage the surmounting of selective attitudes that made it impossible to transform the relational structures and thus the perception of the various roles that are accessible. With this advance, learning is not understood to be oriented solely towards the inference of new behaviours stimulated by a practical environment of exchange and experimentation. Learning is also understood to involve retrospective decoding while taking account of the repetitive power of selective frames. D. Schön thus seeks to destabilize the pre-given relational positioning of the actors involved. His aim is to decentre practitioners and lead them to revisit the conditions of the framing of their roles. Table 5.1 provides an overview of this advance over pragmatist approaches:

The Limitations of this Learning Model

In the reframing operation, the relationship between the two types of story and the possibility for a new framework for action complicate and enrich the link

20 It is thus that, for example, in various contexts, D. Schön can note the role played by the norms that are assumed to regulate opposing interests. Here, the conflict appears tied to dissatisfaction with the consequences of this kind of regulation. The shared search for a solution consists of making a different application of the normative frame possible through the collaborative process.

Table 5.1 Pragmatist Approaches to Collective Action

	Central Operation	Anticipated Impact
Experimentalism: C. Sabel M. Dorf J. Cohen H. Simon J. Zeitlin	Pragmatization of mechanism for collective action	Enabling new collective capacities for problem-solving by choosing how to choose
Reflexive learning: C. Argyris D. Schön	Reframing the representation of collective action and increasing practitioners' reflexivity	Enlarging the possibility of new roles by producing "new meanings, new heuristics, and new stakeholder identities"

previously established between the two types of attention. This relationship also shows how much importance D. Schön attaches to pinpointing the conditions that will guarantee the transition to innovative reframing within a process of inquiry. Nevertheless, two factors always seem to be presupposed for the learning process to be implemented: first, the actors' mental capacity to generate possibilities thanks to their ability to develop "reflection-in-action";[21] second, the institution's capacity to identify problems and seek mechanisms likely to overcome them. The inquiry banks on the potential for congruence between these two presupposed conditions by assuming that it is possible to formulate a rule for institutional action that reflects these capacities, on the condition that this rule is, in turn, underpinned by an internal rule of operation. In this way, it would be possible for an institutional mechanism for inter-group relations to exist and be coupled with an inquiry-based rule for learning.

In organization management terms, we can hypothesize that a strategic choice of selective attention (a single loop) might suffice to set in motion the *genetic attention* with which the actors could revise routines (a double loop). As for how to learn how to learn, that question would be relegated beyond the field of action and become the concern of more specialized work to highlight general rules that account for the success of this kind of choice. Thus an existing expanded skill at reflection-in-action would need to be updated by a new kind of action-science (Schön 1996: 353–4). This solution is close to D. North's hypothesis about the progress of scientific rationality and fits well with J. Dewey's conception of the emergence of a new science of practice.

There exists a scenario less burdensome, however, than that which relies on waiting for science to take the measure of human actors' assumed practical

21 In practical terms, it is a question of participating while "holding back" in order to pay attention to a broadening of the possibilities emerging from the various reconstructions of a given problematic situation. See (Schön 1991: 356).

capacities. D. Schön himself notes that there is a limit to the applicability of a rule for objectivizing inquiry (Schön 1991: 358), because the objective knowledge that it works to produce remains dependent on how the rule is applied and used in problem-solving and thus on the link it establishes between its procedures and its objectives, according to the specific features of its pragmatic frame. Reference to the building up of a science of practice assumes wholly different verification methods than those used for practical experimentation. And it is not so much this kind of reflexive closure that is in question when reference is made to the rule for inquiry on which the whole process of innovation in collective action rests.

Rather, the question is, more simply, whether at the end of the day the only action capable of setting this process in motion consists of using an appropriate mechanism to stimulate the use of a rule that already exists in the actors' minds. The issues are entirely different if we cease to assume that, one way or another, pre-given rules and always-already available capacities exist, as though what we wished to do were to explain innovation a posteriori. It is the underlying story that snags this implicit conception of collective action, specifically the belief in "the existence of a widespread capacity for reciprocal reflection-in-action" (Schön 1996: 353), when in fact this belief invalidates itself by simultaneously exposing a society in which "each contending party sees a piece of the reality and embodies his perception in a view which he treats as a battle-cry" (Schön 1996: 350). This story, which underlies the pragmatist ontology, over-estimates capacities for redescription while emphasizing the precariousness of their implementation by means of appropriate conversational mechanisms. It conceives of the production of the social imaginary world as resulting from an imbalance produced by the perspectivism of viewpoints in relation to the limited resources of social coding. Such an underlying story could wipe out the advances made by the pragmatist turn. In our view, there are three such advances and they constitute the epistemological framework needed in order to arrive at what was called, in Chapter 3, an internalist approach to learning:

(1) Collective action is not defined by the fact of coming to terms with an external shock that forces a turn towards the resolution of a disequilibrium alien to the collective action. Collective action is structurally a problem-solving process. Its openness to the problematic situation and its relation to the shock are constitutive of it. Without this relationship to the shock, it fades into routine.

(2) Collective action is exclusively defined neither by a selective relationship with the existing set of possibilities nor by a creative relationship with new possibilities; that is, its identity is not determined exclusively by the kinds of relationship that could be triggered from the outside (to the extent that they are optional). Rather, collective action is defined from within, by a kind of relationship with the possibilities that results from a reflexive balance between the selection and the generation of possibilities.

(3) Collective action does not develop according to pre-defined rules and capacities. Rather, collective action builds its rules and capacity to evolve in accordance with the coupling of its reflexivity to its process of social

experimentation. Even if the mere notion of a "reflexive skill" does not constitute an adequately developed construction of the condition for reflexivity, it still allows for better delineation of the significance of an internalist approach to learning. Under this approach, collective action evolves in accordance with the yoking together of an internal teleology and a form of self-capacitation. It broadens its range of possibilities by its inquiry and it applies those possibilities to a reframing of its fulfilment.[22]

The question posed by such a conception of inquiry brings us back once again to J. Dewey's fundamental concern with integrating *new ways of acting* on prior experiences by means of a definite plan for observing the transformations that these new ways have thus produced (Dewey 1986b: 107). According to this conception, the achievement of the just social order is not a guiding ideal, but rather a moment to be experienced as a form of fulfilment of the internal potential of a system of rules in process of self-development. This more strictly inferential and internal teleology devises the destination of a system of rules as a function of an internal "vector" for setting capacity in motion, to self-capacitation,[23] and to experimentation capable of broadening the range of problem-solving possibilities and envisaging new roles in the light of the reframing of shared stories.

From a Pragmatist to a Genetic Approach to Governance

The argument presented in the three first chapters consisted of demonstrating how what we call the neo-institutionalist dynamic has driven current approaches in governance theory. The most significant aspect of this dynamic consists of how it conceives the collective learning operation necessary for the transformation and expansion of actors' representations required for any collective action.[24] Every approach to the institutional design required for governance of a collective action to ensure, to the extent possible, satisfaction of its members' normative expectations (that is, to ensure it constitutes "governance in the public interest" or "democratic governance") is a function of the way the conditions for success of this learning operation are conceived. We have differentiated three approaches found at the heart of the institutionalist dynamic. The first led neo-institutionalist economists to resort, in a highly behaviourist fashion, to public mechanisms to compensate for the deficiencies of decentralized forms of governance. The second and the third constitute efforts to react to that first venture. They lead either to the approach we

22 Recoding is thus always a function of new possibilities, is directly generative, and does not constitute a return to the selective.

23 As will be presented in fuller form below, in this chapter (189–99) and in Chapter 6, this requirement for self-capacitation remains insufficiently theorized by pragmatists (such as D. Schön) because of what we have called above the underlying story of pragmatist ontology.

24 That is, required if the collective action is to fulfill the intentionality that drives it.

have termed relational and collaborative or to the pragmatist approach developed as part of the pragmatist turn. These three approaches embody three very different ways of envisaging the coupling of the expansion of representations with collective learning. Yet they can also be interpreted as three stages of a process in constant progress, a process leading to an ever furthered understanding of the conditions necessary for the success of this learning operation, and to growing recognition of the necessity for the internalization of these conditions. This progression implies a simultaneous expansion of these conditions, because the requirement for internalization entails displacing the question of conditions. That is, the question of the conditions for learning becomes, as well, the question of the conditions required for the actors to be capable of learning; and it must ultimately arrive at the requirement for actors' self-capacitation, that is, the requirement that actors organize themselves to learn how to learn. It is true that this ultimate condition has not yet emerged from the three current stages of the neo-institutionalist dynamic. Indeed, it points to their internal limitation. However, as we will see, at the same time it constitutes the further step they require and thus, in a sense, their logical fulfilment. It is to meet this requirement that we speak of the necessity of a "genetic approach" to governance, which we will do no more than introduce in this section and which we will present more fully in Chapter 6.

What, then, is the dynamic internal to the three successive approaches we have differentiated in discussing the coupling of representation and learning? The first stage consists of producing this coupling from the outside, as the consequence of the shock triggered by an external factor. The second stage consists of internalizing the coupling by acting on the conditions for bringing together the actors involved (expansion of the interaction to include all the stakeholders, empowerment of the actors, or respect for the conditions of rational argument) in such a manner as to give rise to a kind of internal expansion of what is possible. The third stage furthers this process of internalization by asking the question of what conditions are required in order to acquire *the capacity to learn*. It seeks, in effect, to internalize the shock that should provoke the actors involved to acquire the adaptive capacities needed to transform their representations.

The difficulty encountered by the two first efforts to explicate the need for an internalist approach to the learning operation (a difficulty discerned by the pragmatist approach) relates specifically to a restrictive conception of learning. If the first two stages are compared to the third, one sees that the first two share a restrictive conception of learning according to which something that is a given at the outset cannot be understood to be subject to transformation by the learning operation itself. Given this, the expansion of the representations cannot be conceived except in terms that remain external to the learning operation itself. The consequences of such a theoretical approach are significant. A restricted approach to learning results in not "expanding" attention to the learning conditions necessary to make possible the adjustment of actors' representations that is required for the intended effects of the external mechanisms to be produced.

> Thus, according to L. Marengo's and G. Dosi's evolutionary schema, a collective representation can be imposed in an external manner, hierarchically, that is, by a "grafting" operation. The success of this graft is understood to result from a competency, assumed to be a given, of the actors involved in a decentralized interaction to integrate this more "general" point of view—that is, the competency to adjust their local point of view according to the desired grafting on of the more general representation imposed from outside.[25] The learning operation plays out only at a second stage, enabling a circling back *from* this embrace of a more general point of view *towards* local situations, in such a manner as to take account of the constraints and limitations demanded by the best possible coordination with other people from a local-context point of view.

Similarly, according to the relational and collaborative schema, the question of adjusting representations is reduced solely to organizing collaboration by meta-regulations, as in the case of nodal governance. We now have a full juxtaposition between the learning process and the aggregation of deliberative competencies. The deliberative process that regulates the regulation is assumed to engender, by itself, the adaptive capacity necessary to resolve problems in the most satisfactory way possible from the point of view of group members' normative expectations. In both perspectives, it is impossible to conceive under what conditions the expansion of the possibilities existing at the outset could result from the learning operation and consequently *be itself dependent on the learning operation*: the learning operation is understood to take place after the expansion in question; or else to act directly only on the expansion of the set of actors involved, on the assumption that they possess a capacity for self-revision which the expansion is therefore not required to construct but rather to stimulate (or, to use an economists' expression, "to incent" (Scott 2006: 20)). There exists, then, a close relationship between a restrictive conception of learning and an expansive conception of the capacities required for the operation of the adjustment and expansion of the representations of the actors involved in a collective action.

It is here that what we have called "the operation of reflexivity" arises.[26] The concept of reflexivity refers to "the operation" by which a social group seeks to respond to its perception of the need to adjust its capacities for action in light of the experiences gained and of the projection of its identity of action. Restrictive conceptions of learning lead to "incomplete" approaches to reflexivity. In opening up the question of learning to a consideration of the conditions required for learning

25 On this point, see above, 167–70. Note that it was also observed that, even with this grafting operation, the evolutionary approach still assumes that two other operations can be carried out solely on the basis of actors' natural competencies: the "generalized" operation necessary for determining this more general point of view and the operation of integration required by the evolutionary assumption of a "natural" capacity to construct the "local maximum".

26 See Introduction to Part II.

how to learn, adherents of the "experimentalist pragmatist" approach to learning call for a broadening of the field of the learning operation, and, by corollary, a broadening of the field of the conditions required for its success. This pragmatist "turn" in governance theory thus opens up towards a more "complete" approach to the reflexivity of collective action, even though it is its own internal dynamic that makes possible the recognition of the supplementary stage that it requires.

To make clear the nature of the various approaches to the reflexivity of collective action that lie behind the successive stages of current research on governance theory, we can revert to a consideration of one of the most prominent writers on neo-institutionalism today, D. North. An examination of D. North's thought makes it possible to clearly reveal the limitations of the conceptions of reflexivity implicitly deployed by the first two stages of governance theory research, while pointing to the contribution, as well as the persisting limitations, of the pragmatist approach. He is, in effect, a hybrid figure. Granted, he continues to work within the framework of the first stage, that of economic neo-institutionalist research. We saw above that he is closely linked to the recent efforts by transaction cost economists to synthesize the contributions of R. Coase and O. Williamson, as well as those of evolutionary economists. Nevertheless, at the same time, D. North has laid down the foundations for surmounting the limitations he is working within. We have already indicated that his theoretical perspective cannot be reduced to either that of the evolutionary thinkers or that of the transaction cost economists, including E. Brousseau, who have sought to apply it in governance research. That is why we can speak of the hybrid nature of D. North's theoretical position. As a neo-institutionalist economist, he remains dependent on a conception of learning theorized within the frame of reference of an external factor. But in his undertaking to deploy a form of reflexivity external to its construction of learning, whose function would be to guarantee the internal development of the culture of learning, he opens the way to a form of reflexivity that exposes the limitations of the forms of reflexivity deployed in the first two stages. These limitations are more fully addressed by the pragmatist approach, and in particular by D. Schön.

Thus D. North's thinking allows, first of all, for highlighting the incompleteness of the forms of reflexivity implicitly deployed by the first two stages of the coupling between representation and learning. The first kind of incomplete reflexivity corresponds to the idea of the equilibrium of subsystems in a decentralized model of coordination. Such a concept of equilibrium assumes that the actors involved have the competency for local learning that will enable them to select a "local maximum", that is, the best possible satisfaction within the local context, in light of their perceptions, and their capacity for reflexive adjustment of their local representations to the collective representation being imposed upon them. It is a question of seeking to adjust individual positions in light of an external reflection on the part of "the public interest", projected from outside. The second form of incomplete reflexivity invokes the idea of expandability and the incorporation of different possible positions within the framework of a rule of argumentation. In this instance, reflexivity operates according to a predetermined institutional frame of reference, which relies on the ideal requirement for a rule of collaboration. The issue here is to act at the level of the standard settings that define the general requirements of the regulatory framework in such a manner as to strengthen the quality of the institutional and organizational design by proposing a better placing in deliberative relationship of the various actors involved in the complex regulatory mechanism. Recourse must be had to a broader rule for cooperation (expansion of the set of actors in the interaction to include the various stakeholders; expansion of the requirements for these stakeholders' empowerment; expansion of the constraints on the organizing of the aggregation of communicative competencies, such as respect for the rules of argumentation and respect of fundamental rights; and so on). As well, the institutional cooperative frame of reference is applied as an internal requirement for an expansion of the set of actors involved, or of the positions to be taken into account. Under this second approach, it is assumed that greater transparency and better public deliberation will entail better involvement by citizens, who are the consumers of contractual regimes, in order to better organize collaboration among all the actors involved in this new form of complex governance.

But D. North also opens up a perspective on a third possible form of reflexivity. This third form requires, on one hand, the adjustment of representations, without relying on actantial competency as a given (as, for example, in the thinking of evolutionary economists); but on the other hand, it also seeks to take into account the conditions for the transformation of the capacities for representation, without relying on a simple institutional rule whereby "the process of regulation itself becomes regulated" (Morgan 2003: 490) (as with the work of adherents of the relational and collaborative approach). That is, D. North is careful, as we indicated above, to identify the internal mechanisms that would make it possible to act on the constituent norms of the learning culture specific to the rationality of any collective action, while internalizing this action to a shared culture of collective action. The question would be how to guarantee mastery of the operations by which society comes to learn how to learn, through this culture's reflexivity on itself. Like W. Dilthey and J. Dewey in their own times, D. North discerns in this question the issue of a new social science capable of technologically manipulating social nature by progressively acquiring knowledge of the laws governing its own intentional operations.

True, D. North's solution is limited to conceiving of this synthesis, once again, in an external manner, as being determined by the development of collective rationality itself. The reflexive advance internal to the culture of collective action is supposed to be necessarily acquired by means of the dynamic of science, that is, the dynamic specific to the intentionality of history. But this solution points to still another perspective (appearing as if in recess) by giving access to the question of the acquisition of adaptive capacities by the actors themselves; and it envisages a solution that, in its own way, takes account of conditions internal to a collective learning process without erasing reference to the shock that provokes the reflexive advance.

The advantage of pragmatism is that it seeks to internalize the necessary conditions for such a reflexive advance by adopting a new solution in relation to reflexivity. This solution consists of internalizing the process of meta-stabilization of the reflexive shocks that D. North discerned; in this instance, the process is internalized by being made to apply to a test internal to practice. This test is an operation of inquiry into the frameworks for practice, designed to produce a shock in those frameworks and result in displacement of the framing capacity itself in favour of innovation. This model for reflexive practice (*reflexivity 3*) offers the benefit of combining use of an external constraint that imposes limits on interaction (*reflexivity 1*) with internal constraints (expansion of the range of stakeholders, empowerment, deliberative rules, and so on) imposed on the way interaction is organized (*reflexivity 2*) within a process internal to the collective action itself. This process is based on the capacity of the practices themselves to make a reassessment of their frameworks by trying out new forms of cooperation.

What the reference to D. Schön brings to this trajectory consists of a furthering of C. Sabel's experimentalist approach and a better grasp of the meaning of this third form of reflexivity, which is internal to the process of collective action. D. Schön makes it possible, first of all, to show that the issue of such a reflexivity cannot be reduced to a shift in the focus of selective attention, as if, in order to act reflexively, it were sufficient to shift the usual attention that guides one's selection from among possible choices of behaviour towards meta-regulations enabling the regulation of the regulations themselves. While it is true, as already indicated in the Introduction to this part of our book, that all the institutional incentives revealed by the three neo-institutionalist approaches (economic, deliberative, and pragmatist) are necessary to guide the selection operation, they remain inadequate and need to be supplemented with attention to conditions of another kind. A shift in the manner of asking the question of the conditions for learning proves necessary as an opening onto second-level conditions, in relation to the three categories of condition brought to light by the three first stages in current governance research. It is this shift that D. Schön intuits and, in falling short of sketching it out in full, he does no more than disclose it. For him, the issue does not reside in a shift in selective attention but rather in changing the attention *itself* in line with the construction of a reflexive action that makes it possible to learn how to learn. To make a change in the attention, it is necessary to set in operation pragmatic conditions for experimentation and, depending on the nature of the shock they produce, seek to give rise to a generative advance by questioning routines and reframing practices. This is the attention to openness that is made possible by experimentation itself, and that ought, on its own, to constitute learning how to learn and guarantee a constant program of "deroutinizing vigilance" or "reflexive shock". This attitude of genetic attention characterizes the work of the reflective practitioner whose professional practice is unceasingly subjected to second-level examination in order to identify new representations of the causal processes capable of invalidating the previous ones and enrich the operation of selection from among all possible choices by expanding the available possible choices. It is thus that such a practitioner acquires what D. Schön calls double vision. She or he adheres firmly to her or his framework for action but is always ready to change it and cause it to evolve.

But the attention thus brought to bear on the problem of the capacities needed to organize such that one can learn to learn itself leads to the necessity to extend D. Schön's work, and, as we have just said, supplement the three categories of conditions for public-interest governance already identified through the three stages of present-day discussion on theory of governance. That is, the limitation of this more complete conception of reflexivity proposed by D. Schön resides in the mentalism that underlies it. Internalization of the process of learning is carried out at the cost of postulating a rule, already a given within the minds of the actors involved in the pragmatic process, which, in keeping them attentive "in one corner of their minds", ensures they do not remain the prisoners of their own routines. And, indeed, D. Schön considers that this rule for behaviour, once integrated, could even become a kind of ethics of research. But if once again, in order to learn how to learn, the question consists of deploying an already-given rule for guaranteeing the start-up of this specific learning operation, we cannot strictly speak of the self-capacitation of learning, even at a second level. Rather, the reflexivity in question does not fully play its own operative role but is reduced to separating out possible levels for the application of existing competencies; it is, in fact, conceived in the same way as in the approach seeking to shift selective attention from regulations towards meta-regulations. In experimentalist pragmatism, we do indeed find attention of a specific kind, but it does not constitute the possible result of adaptive learning. It, too, is an existing resource that requires appropriate stimulation. The pragmatic mechanisms revealed by C. Sabel play this role of stimulant or of incentive. And as for the innovative process of inquiry, it assumes the incentive provided by the collaborative shock as a basis for focusing on the experience of the shock itself and transforming it into a reflexive/deroutinizing shock, thanks to the rule for the metaphorical broadening of the frameworks for action. Learning is thus the process that results from application of this rule of metaphorical broadening, in the context of a shock that has been reflected upon and focused upon for the sake of its deroutinizing effect.

The idea that there could exist a more radical version of such an internal process remains beyond reach, because of the mentalist nature of the rule for learning it relies on. If no rule of this kind were assumed at the outset, but were rather considered as something that needed to be acquired directly through the pragmatic process, then the action would incorporate *in itself* an effective transformation of the capacities for cognitive framing of the action. It is, indeed, the manner of producing such a cognitive framework within a given setting that should be transformed by this action. We would then have *reflexivity in a fourth sense*, not hitherto explored and yet unceasingly sought: the reflexivity of the self-transformation of the capacities for the cognitive framing of action by means of a process internal to collective action itself and supported by internal conditions for its fulfilment. In D. Schön, in contrast, the conception of the process of transforming capacities unquestionably rests on semantic presuppositions, more specifically on the presupposition of the ability to redescribe shared stories and consequently to produce new frames of meaning to apply to social interaction.

To understand the *condition for reflexivity* that we suggest be taken into account, it is necessary to place it in the perspective of the gains made during the three preceding stages that we have differentiated in our reconstruction of the neo-institutionalist dynamic. These gains already make it possible to better grasp the conditions for recourse to learning within governance mechanisms. Recourse to learning requires elicitation of those reflexive capacities of social groups that enable them to respond to their perceived need to adjust their practices.

Neo-institutionalist economists have highlighted the need, in order to achieve this objective associated with the ways of using learning mechanisms, to diversify existing incentive frameworks and multiply them, specifically by taking action on property law, incomplete contracts, rules for interaction, and so on (stage 1 of the neo-institutionalist dynamic).

For their part, jurists and political scientists have stressed the need to expand the range of ways of participating, with a view to taking into account the interests of the maximum number of actors involved (expanding the range of actors in the interaction to all the various stakeholders). At the same time, they have joined to this expansion of the range of those involved, empowerment mechanisms such as constraints on argumentation, cognitive resources, financing conditions, and so on (stage 2 of the neo-institutionalist dynamic).

Last, the experimentalist path that has emerged from the pragmatist turn in the social sciences has shown the value of recourse to specific pragmatic mechanisms to elicit a collective problem-solving dynamic that allows for the internalization of the shock of interaction within the learning process. This is a matter essentially of benchmarking, simultaneous engineering or co-design, error detection methods, and so on. Further, this problem-solving dynamic is articulated with the taking into account of the inquiry conditions within a *collective action process.* Such a taking into account endows the problem-solving with a kind of internal teleology that leads to going beyond the sole immediate goal of learning and simultaneous acquisition of the capacity to learn how to learn. In this pragmatist vein, D. Schön proposes a way of incorporating these two dimensions into the attitude of the reflective practitioner that brings to the fore the conditions for vigilance "in the course of action on action" by means of a shift of attention or a principle of "double action" (stage 3 of the neo-institutionalist dynamic). All these institutional incentives are designed to produce effects at two distinct levels of intervention. On one hand, they are intended to act on the actors' capacity for adjustment by serving as pragmatic devices assumed to bring to life the potentialities of the collective action (we refer to them in this guise as "action"). On the other hand, as if the authors in question wished to ensure that these mechanisms will harbour a teleology that the inciting of the actors would not guarantee on its own, they are also designed to strengthen the effects of the initial devices and ensure the attainment of the desired results (we refer to them in this guise as "action on action"). We are thus faced with a "principle of double action" that merely reinforces the external nature of the learning mechanisms being contemplated. On one hand, the devices put in place work to mobilize actors involved through participatory mechanisms incorporated into the deliberative process. On the other hand, these very mechanisms are themselves subject to a specific design intended to predetermine their role in the search for a regulatory optimum, as if there existed a rule for networked cooperative action which served to direct the actors towards cognitive frames that are better suited to the identification of their common interests.

Nevertheless, even if we ascribe to these two levels of action a kind of self-correcting virtue owing to the effect of action on action, that still does not address the weakness inherent in the fact that the account of the construction of these institutional mechanisms has not paid due attention to the internal learning conditions that must accompany such construction. The proposed "institutional incentives"—whether they are intended to stimulate the actors' capacity for adjustment or to better guarantee that the first deployment of incentives results in the desired effect—feature the same weakness: they presuppose a rule capable of producing self-reflection within collective action. Reason is expected to attain simultaneous attention to a possible shift and attention to this way of paying attention, and it is expected to attain this while complying with the principle of double action. Thus attention is lacking to those conditions internal to collective action that are needed in order to "learn how to learn". Even the double action principle does not account on its own for how it is possible on one hand to learn to privilege attention to this kind of action and on the other hand to learn how to make collective use of it. It is just this that our hypothesis about reflexivity is intended to develop. This new approach to learning will allow for ceasing to presuppose that there somehow exist pre-given rules and capacities that are always-already available and propose a conception of learning as an inferential teleological process that constructs its rules and capacities for transformation according to its reflexivity and the broadening of the range of its possibilities.

From our own genetic perspective, the lack of attention just identified reflects two problems that call for specific recognition and clarifies how our proposition will lead to the complementing and completion of neo-institutionalist incentives on two levels. One level is that of the attention needed so that the effective transformation of practice can be organized in light of the identification of those of the actors' resistances that are elicited by currently operative behavioural blockages. The other level is that of the attention needed so that collective use may be made of new conditions for positioning, in order to prevent the re-occurrence of these blockages within the functioning of the very learning mechanisms that are assumed to be leading to the surmounting of the blockages.

On these two levels, it is necessary first to take account of the fact that any "institutional intervention" takes on meaning only according to the practice it seeks to engender and cannot be established without provision being made from the outset for a mechanism to evaluate the adjustments of practice that it elicits (the transformation of existing perceptions and efforts at adjustment). Thus we believe it is necessary to be able to determine on an intervention device that will act at the institutional level and enable the actors involved to take ownership of the learning processes and adapt them according to identified existing blockages.

Next, it is also necessary to be able to evaluate whether the choice of this "institutional solution" allows the actors to effect the transformation of behaviours and of the representations associated with the problems identified. To make possible this shared learning about how to construct a specific position concerning the choice of solutions, it is necessary to pay specific attention to the actors' internalization of the conditions for transforming practice that are made possible by the learning process.

In contrast to D. Schön, who views this internalization as depending on two kinds of attention, one selective and the other generative, that make possible new frames for the semantic production of action (see 179–89), we propose a new shift that will allow for *desemanticizing* D. Schön's proposal for an effective accounting of the pragmatic conditions for learning how to learn. Our aim is to ensure, through this shift, that our account of the learning processes to be put in place will not rely on the assumed effects of rules of behaviour that guide people towards good cooperative practices and towards the role adjustments that would necessarily flow from that. By idealizing the rule of experimentation that allows for radical change resulting in a cooperative optimum, D. Schön semanticizes his conception of learning. This makes it impossible to grasp under what conditions the transformation of positions within a new frame for interaction truly allows for avoiding the recurrence of blockages and failures that have already been identified. Nor does it allow for identifying the difficulties that may arise in the necessary reconstruction and restructuring of the positions that contributed to this blockage.

What is at stake in our shift is the evaluation of the limits of the new frames being tested from two perspectives internal to the learning processes themselves, that is, from two perspectives held by the actors involved in the processes. From the first of these perspectives, it is a question of evaluating the risks of the possible recreation of blockages already identified as being produced by the positioning of other actors on whom, for the purposes of the interaction, one remains dependent. From the second of these perspectives, it is a question of evaluating the difficulties specific to a particular actor's positioning in order to change the kinds of position that the actor identifies as needing to be surmounted.

The result of this twofold shift should be a change in the conditions for intervening with the actors undertaking a learning process. And this change should, in turn, result in pragmatically extending the actors' involvement in the process, that is, in enabling them to themselves become actors in their learning process by evaluating the internal limitations of its experimental frame and thus undertaking its necessary decompletion as a process of collective action.

Thus our proposal for the radical pragmatization of learning processes consists of a twofold shift in the intervention process under way: one shift at the level of institutional action and one at the level of the actors' involvement. The first shift consists of setting up an intervention mechanism designed to identify blockages associated with the identities of action already in operation among the actors involved. The second consists of a requirement that the actors involved then take ownership of the intervention mechanism in such a way as to present their perspective on the difficulties encountered in reconstructing and restructuring the positions that contributed to these blockages. This twofold shift should result in the actors transforming their own involvement in the experimental context, in line with their specific commitment regarding the management of the learning process and the direction that it should take.

Table 5.2 below provides an overview of the advance offered by the genetic approach over the experimentalist pragmatist and reflexive pragmatist approaches.

Table 5.2 From Pragmatist to Genetic Approaches to Collective Action

	Central Operation	Anticipated Impact
Experimentalism: C. Sabel M. Dorf J. Cohen W. Simon J. Zeitlin	Pragmatization of mechanism for collective action	Enabling new collective capacities for problem-solving by choosing how to choose
Reflexive learning: C. Argyris/ D. Schön	Reframing the representation of collective action and increasing practitioners' reflexivity	Enlarging possibility of new roles by producing new meanings, new heuristics, and new stakeholder identities
Genetic approach: J. Lenoble/ M. Maesschalck	Shifting the conditions of collective action in relation to identity making*	Transforming collective identities of action by identifying former blockages and going beyond correlative behavioural repetitions

* See Chapter 6 on the expression "identity making".

Chapter 6

Towards a Genetic Approach to Governance

This chapter will present the approach to "reflexive governance" that we advocate in this book as representing both the extension of the pragmatist turn in the social sciences and a more radical and complete fulfilment of the requirements for reflexivity presupposed by the pragmatist turn. So far this approach, which we call "genetic", has been no more than announced and briefly sketched out in previous chapters. The concern was essentially to differentiate it from the advances achieved by the pragmatist approaches[1] by emphasizing the reinforcement of the "condition for reflexivity" that it implies and that justifies the twofold shift—institutional and actantial—proposed at the end of the last chapter. While D. Schön's pragmatist proposal already broadly emphasized a kind of semantic increase in practitioners' reflexivity, based on the ability to redescribe roles in the context of interaction, our proposal takes over the term "reflexivity" and assigns it a more strictly pragmatic meaning: that of an operation of self-transformation by which a social group seeks to respond to its perception of the need to adjust its capacity for action according to its acquired experience (reflectibility) and the projection of its identity of action (destinability). Under this meaning, reflexivity consists of a process that is internal to collective action and rests on internal conditions to its fulfilment.

Given the different uses of the term "reflexivity" that underlie the various theoretical spaces we have traversed and the need nevertheless to grasp the precise pragmatic use we can give it in the context of a genetic approach, it will be necessary first (and by way of a prerequisite) to clarify the scope of the expression, in light of the reconstruction emerging from the trajectory traced through the first three chapters of this part of the book. We will then be in a position to resume and take further the final stage of the reasoning that was presented in those chapters, which led to the outline of our approach to governance. This approach as we said, consists of furthering the pragmatist approach to governance to include an expanded account of the conditions for success of the learning operation. As already said, we call the approach to governance that we are advancing "genetic". Lastly, to illustrate the contribution that a genetic approach can make and the institutional consequences that flow from its application, we apply this approach to a concrete case: Finally, using the genetic approach, we analyse the transformations of ways of acting that Belgian unions today must implement in order to deal with the liberalization of public services in the energy field (that is, the reduction of state involvement) and increase in the application of free market principles.

1 See the overview in Table 5.1, Chapter 5.

Clarifications about the Use of the Concept of Reflexivity

The three first chapters advanced the terms "reflexivity" and "learning" as constituting a way to characterize a system of governance capable of maximizing fulfilment of the normative expectations held by participants in a collective action. In so doing, they differentiated four approaches to governance to be found within current inquiry into governance. The implications of both the terms and the differentiation call for clarification.

C. Scott recently stated that "reflexive governance involves the establishment of institutions and processes which facilitate the actors within a domain for learning not only about policy options, but also about their own interests and preferences" (Scott 2007). While this definition is not inaccurate, it poses the risk of generating more indeterminacy than precision. For this reason, certain observations are called for.

First, in itself this definition defines the reflexive dimension of a governance mechanism by referring to the idea of learning. To put it another way, a form of governance would qualify as reflexive if it favoured the success of the learning operation required to satisfy the normative expectations of participants in a collective action. By limiting itself to this consideration alone, this definition of reflexive governance covers all four approaches to governance identified in the first three chapters. That is, not only the collaborative-relational, pragmatist, and genetic, but also the neo-institutionalist approaches share the characteristic of reasoning about the conditions for "efficient" or legitimate governance in terms of a learning operation. The approach of neo-institutionalist economics has drawn attention to the weakness of neo-classical economics approaches, which resided in their interpretation of economic evolution in terms of natural selection. Thus, even if the neo-institutionalist economics approach does not explicitly call its inquiry into the theory of governance "reflexive" and rarely deploys a theory of learning, it can indisputably be termed "reflexive", or referred to as an approach that aims, in contrast to approaches of neo-classical economics, to promote the learning operation of actors involved in a collective action. Clearly the same goes for the three approaches identified in the first three chapters as working to take further the neo-institutionalist economics approach. These, too, rely explicitly on the commitment to better understand the conditions needed for the success of the learning operation. The idea of reflexivity thus understood means simply that the transformation/adaptation of a given context effected by a given collectivity will not satisfy in the best possible way the actors' expectations solely on the basis of this spontaneous display of their "natural" competencies. An adaptation of this kind would require the actor to conduct a "return" over her or his "accustomed competencies and behaviours" with the aim of acquiring new competencies. This operation of "reflexive return" would require specific institutional mechanisms. Thus if we define the idea of reflexivity through the idea of learning, all the various approaches identified above could be termed reflexive, regardless of the significant differences among them.

Significant inconveniences are associated with this option, however. In particular, it prevents seeing what distinguishes these four approaches to governance from each other, once we go beyond their common commitment to avoid the fallacious assumption of a process of natural selection guaranteeing the constant adaptation of our collective actions towards a "social optimum". What distinguishes them is precisely their different ways of conceiving of the learning operation (and thus, the reflexive operation that any learning operation entails).[2] True, as has already been mentioned, many of these approaches do not undertake to develop an explicit theory of this learning operation. Indeed, this is the reason why several of these four approaches are developed without an awareness of each other. Scholarly discussion of the question of governance is being conducted today within various disciplines, and often these various disciplinary discussions are conducted without attention to research being done in neighbouring disciplines. Consequently, the proponents of the four approaches identified above are often unaware, not just of what the approaches have in common (namely, that they take an approach to governance in terms of how actors' learning is facilitated), but, a fortiori, of what differentiates them when it comes to their conception of the conditions for success of the learning operation. Moreover, in turning our attention to the differences in the way they conceive the conditions for success of a learning operation, we gain a further benefit.

This benefit consists of the fact that the potential fruits of this investigation are not purely theoretical or academic. They are also practical and they relate to the construction of the governance mechanism. Comparing the four approaches with respect to their conceptions of the learning operation makes it possible to see that they lie on a continuum, or gradation. What emerges is that these four approaches reflect increasingly "expansive" conceptions of the conditions that must be satisfied to ensure the success of the learning operation. Things unfold as though these four approaches implicitly reflected four successive stages of a single process of inquiry, with each successive stage working to further and expand the understanding of the conditions necessary for the governance mechanism to enable actors to produce the best possible solution to the collective-action problem they are working to solve. It is at this level that the consistency between these four approaches appears. Our concern here will be to show how the idea is expressed of the possible "progressive expansion" of the institutional conditions that could be set up to ensure the success of the learning operation implied by any governance in the public interest.

The issue at stake here is a presentation of the consequences for a theory of governance of a hypothesis that takes seriously the underlying dynamic of present-day research and the more penetrating inquiry into the learning operation that is driving it. On this score, the concern that dominated the first chapters of Part II was

2 This is why, from the outset, we have indicated that our own definition of reflexivity corresponds to a genetic conception of collective action that appears to us necessary if the learning operation is to take on its full pragmatic radicalism.

to lay down the basis for a reconstructive framework allowing for an evaluation of the various bodies of theory according to the degree of attention each one pays to the "reflexive" capacity that a governance mechanism disposes of for the purpose of maximizing the learning operation it implies, as a function of the normative expectations of the actors involved.

This is why it does not seem productive to limit the definition of "reflexive governance" (as C. Scott suggested) to "the establishment of institutions and processes which facilitate [the learning of] the actors". Any form of "reflexive governance" is a function of the explicit or implicit conception of the learning operation that underlies it. Any inquiry into "reflexive governance" must therefore include the question of the differences in conception of the learning operation that can today be observed in the four "reflexive governance" approaches differentiated in the first three chapters. Indeed, C. Scott's contribution reflects this necessity. After having defined reflexive governance as that which "facilitates" the learning operation, he states: "Learning, with open and deliberative processes, might cause participants not only to conceive better techniques or instruments but also, beyond policy solutions, to reorder the way that the policy problems are conceived and prioritised" (Scott 2007). It remains the case that such an approach to the conditions for success of the learning operation, conceived in terms of "open and deliberative processes", is very specific. It is far from being widespread or taken for granted by all theories that address the question of governance in terms of the learning operation. In fact, it is specific[3] to the second approach to governance identified above—the one we referred to there as the "collaborative and relational approach to governance".

Accordingly, it is helpful to recall that the most distinctive features of the four current approaches to governance whose perspective on governance is a "reflexive", learning-theory-based one (see 204–6 below.) In so doing, we will be able (207–13 below) to clearly identify why it is possible to speak of the furthering and the progressive "expansion" of the conception of the conditions for success of the learning operation that a governance mechanism will have to take into account if the best possible fulfilment of the expectation of actors involved in a collective action is to be assured.

Four Approaches to Reflexive Governance

Within the various current disciplinary approaches, we have identified four approaches in theory of governance that, implicitly or explicitly, inquire into the question of the conditions for good governance in terms of collective learning.

3 It would therefore appear difficult to link such a definition of governance, as C. Scott does in his article, to practices that he analyses more specifically, namely "experimentalist" practices developed by the OECD and the EU under the open method of coordination. These efforts at experimentalist practices should rather, be analysed in terms of the reflexivity- and learning-based approach developed within the pragmatist version put forward by C. Sabel et al. under the label "democratic experimentalism".

The first we termed "neo-institutionalist economics". As we explained, this term should be understood in a broad sense, because it is intended to cover both research in transaction-cost economics, as emerging out of the work of O. Williamson and R. Coase, and research conducted within the frame of reference of evolutionary theory.

The second we called the "collaborative-relational approach through dialogue". It could also be called "deliberative", since it is distinguished by the idea that the conditions for success of the learning operation require an aggregative and deliberative shaping of the communicative competencies of the various stakeholders.

The third approach we called "pragmatist". As its name suggests, it is distinguished by its inquiry into the conditions for success of the learning operation on the basis of an explicit reference to pragmatist thinkers, J. Dewey in particular. The pragmatist approach to governance cannot, however, be properly understood unless we differentiate between two profoundly different trends within it. Although both these trends cooperate in furthering and expanding the presentation of the conditions for success of the learning operation developed by neo-institutionalist-economist and deliberative thinkers, they differ from each other in their understanding of this process of furtherance and expansion. The first of these two trends is represented by the experimentalist (or democratic experimentalist) approach of C. Sabel et al. The second, which ended by emphasizing the incompleteness of the experimentalist approach and recommending its furtherance, was developed by D. Schön in collaboration with C. Argyris and M. Rein. It is based essentially on an increase in practitioners' reflexivity in order to make possible the experimental process of reframing and role redefinition. To distinguish between these two currents within the pragmatist approach, we will refer to the first as "experimentalist pragmatism" and the second as "reflexive pragmatism".

The fourth approach is the one espoused by the authors of this book. We have referred to it several times as the "reflexive" approach to governance[4] to emphasize that it extends and radicalizes what is intended to be the most expansive conception of the conditions for "reflexive" return required for the success of the learning operation. However, terming this approach "reflexive" runs the risk of ambiguity for two reasons. First of all, as was seen above, the idea of reflexivity seems often, in present-day work in the social sciences, to be related exclusively to the idea of learning per se, without being extended

---

4 We have also sometimes used the expression "pragmatic and internalist". While accurate, this designation may prove hard to use because it is too closely linked to certain technical philosophical assumptions. That is, this designation is based on the idea that the fourth approach, while it shares with the deliberative and pragmatist approaches the commitment to broach the question of learning as the basis for a "pragmatic" approach to the conditions for success of the intentionality of an action, also aims to emphasize the weakness of the deliberative or pragmatist conceptions associated with the pragmatic turn.

to the scope or the precise nature of the conditions required for the success of learning (cf. above the definitions of "reflexive" proposed by C. Scott and S. Deakin). As well, even if we wished to reserve the term "reflexive" governance for an approach that specifies one particular conception of these conditions, the term would still court ambiguity, since it is already currently applied to several different approaches to governance. For example, G. Teubner's systemic theory, C. Sabel's experimentalist pragmatism, and D. Schön's reflective pragmatism all explicitly view themselves as theories of reflexive governance. That is, the use of the word "reflexive" is affected by the same difficulty as is the word "procedural" in theory of law and democratic theory: They are terms that come to be perceived at a given moment in the progress of scholarly research as reflecting a significant insight, but that are used with such diverse meanings that the very success of the terms risks giving rise to more ambiguity and imprecision than to theoretical or practical advances. For this reason, we suggest the term "reflexive governance" be limited to denoting the overall process guiding current research in theory of governance, which covers all four approaches identified here. On the other hand, to differentiate the understanding of reflexivity specific to the approach to governance presented in this book, which is associated with a commitment to take further and to radicalize the way the pragmatist approach (as expressed in both C. Sabel's democratic experimentalism and D. Schön's reflective pragmatism) defines the conditions for success of the learning operation, we propose referring to a "genetic" approach to governance.[5] The implications of this choice of the term "genetic" will become clearer below, when we pursue further the reasons for going beyond the "reflexive pragmatist" approach to governance advanced in D. Schön's thinking and adopting our "genetic" approach to reflexive governance. As will be seen, the term "genetic" is intended to take two factors into account. On one hand, the set of conditions for production (that is, engenderment) of actors' capacity to carry out the "reflexive" work required for the success of the learning operation; and on the other hand, the setting up of institutional conditions likely to guarantee effective implementation of the actors' commitments. Before we expand on this point, however, we must present a second clarification. It consists of a brief but precise overview of the factors that characterize the four approaches to governance and differentiate them from each other, which have to do with these approaches' varying conceptions of the conditions for success of the learning operation required to ensure maximal fulfilment of the normative expectations of participants in a collective action.

5 It should be noted as well, although this is not the place to examine the question in detail, that the fourth approach allows for specifying the meaning of reflexivity as it operates in any collective action, whether in the context of the term "reflexive governance" to designate an approach to governance that resists the lure of a theory of natural selection or in the context of discussions of Habermasian or systemic "collaborative-relational" and pragmatist approaches.

The Conditions for Success of the Learning Operation

The essential idea underlying this presentation of current discussion in theory of governance is thus twofold. First, the current discussion rests on a shared conviction that any approach to the regulation of a collective action that assumes "natural selection" of the behaviours required to maximize fulfilment of the actors' normative expectations leads to inadequacies that clearly emerge in the arrangement of governance mechanisms. Therefore a "selection" of this kind entails a learning operation. Second, this discussion results in four approaches that form a progression with respect to the scope of the conditions required to ensure the success of the learning operation. Each successive stage, without invalidating the positive gains of prior approaches, nevertheless deems those gains insufficient and considers that supplementary conditions must be taken into account in designing governance mechanisms. What essential trait characterizes each of these stages? That is, what is the "value added" that the "collaborative-relational" approach (approach number 2), the pragmatist approach (approach number 3), and the genetic approach (approach number 4) aim to contribute to the prior stage; or, in other words, what is the weakness or inadequacy that each of these approaches views as having been overlooked by the approach that it seeks to improve or to go beyond? Later on, we will expose in depth the reasons for, and the nature of, the weaknesses that the fourth approach, *the genetic approach to governance*, identifies in the third approach, that is, the pragmatist approach, both in its experimentalist form and in the reflexive form presented by D. Schön, C. Argyris, and M. Rein. Now, we will better explicate the nature of the "going beyond" that the genetic approach is designed to effect, as well as the institutional consequences this has in terms of the building of governance mechanisms. In the present section, we will limit ourselves to showing how the genetic approach is linked to the process of expanding the conditions for learning that made possible the theoretical review presented in the previous three chapters. Thus here, we will briefly and clearly review the passage from the "external conditions" for learning as found in a neo-institutionalist regime to the "internal conditions" for learning in the other three regimes examined. We will thus make a clear review of the specific features of the first stage of the progression that can be observed in present-day research in theory of governance within the *neo-institutionalist economics* approach (see (1) below) and its ongoing furtherance and expansion, first by means of the second, *deliberative* or *collaborative-relational*, approach; then by means of the third, *pragmatist*, approach in its two successive forms (experimentalist and reflexive); and finally by means of the genetic approach (see below).

(1) The conditions for learning in a neo-institutionalist regime The most characteristic feature of the neo-institutionalist economics approach is what we called in Chapter 3 its "externalist" conception of learning and what we could consequently call its "externalist" conception of governance. As was shown in the previous chapter, this externalist conception is observable not just in the work of

both transaction-cost economists and evolutionists, but also in the writings of those who, like D. North and E. Brousseau, have worked to synthesize the gains made by those two schools of economic thought. What does an "externalist conception of learning" mean, and what are its implications for governance mechanisms?

The basic idea is related precisely to the way these economists have sought to "surmount" the weaknesses or inadequacies they detected in the theory of natural selection that underlie neo-classical economic theory, and in consequence in the ascription of excessively great virtues to the market mechanism alone. The reason natural selection cannot operate in human groupings is precisely because it is a function of something that is a given from the outset. As L. Marengo and G. Dosi (2005: 306) put it, "[A] selection mechanism can indeed, under certain conditions, select for the fittest structures, but only if the latter exist in the first place. Selection can account for the convergence of a population toward some given form, not for the emergence of such a form". But the neo-institutionalists' notion is precisely that this datum present at the outset is not assumed to be subject to transformation by the learning operation itself. Any selection operation, unless it is "incited from outside", is constrained by the same limitation. This second characteristic results in what might be called an externalist conception of learning. For the evolutionists and the neo-institutionalists,[6] the only way to alter the nature of the given present at the outset consists of deploying an external factor in order to "expand" the set of initial hypotheses (or, as H. Simon would put it, the set of initial routines) that are to be tested by the learning operation, in view of choosing the one that seems most powerful to solve the problem that set the collective action in motion. Innovation—that is, the expansion of representation by broadening the possibilities present at the outset—cannot emerge from the learning operation itself.

This "externalist" approach to learning also accounts for the approach to governance, that is, the approach to the institutional mechanisms that must accompany the learning operation in order for the latter to result in "optimality", or at least in the form of organization of the collective action that satisfies, to the extent possible, the normative expectations of its members, that is, governance in the public interest. An "expansion" of local actors' representations is needed by means of an external mechanism that "imposes", hierarchically so to speak, a collective representation. E. Brousseau[7] is correct that the evolutionary thinkers insufficiently define the form of organization that must impose this "expansion" of decentralized local actors' representations from outside and must ensure that learning will yield a generally optimal outcome. From this perspective, many current neo-institutionalist studies (such as those of E. Brousseau himself,

6 And in fact, as was seen in Chapter 3, this is the institutional form taken by the solution arrived at by theorists of evolutionary games and by R. Cooter working in the law and economics framework.

7 As E. Brousseau (1999: 194) remarks, the organization continues to be the "black box" of evolutionary theory.

including those that examine Internet governance) work to make explicit the nature of these external mechanisms that, it is argued, must increasingly take the form of hybrid "public-private partnership" mechanisms. What is important from our perspective, however, besides the gains yielded by this identification of the nature of these mechanisms, is the externality that they embody. The idea is present therein that only an external mechanism could "incite" the acquisition of the competencies needed to allow for the most "efficient" possible operation. This expansion of the competencies (that is, the expansion of the set of representations present at the outset, from among which the actors select the solutions deemed the best possible) is assumed to be (and to be capable of being) incited from the outside by a hierarchical supervisory mechanism.

(2) The turn towards the internal conditions for learning It is precisely as regards this "externalist" approach to learning—and in consequence to governance—that the second (deliberative), third (pragmatist), and fourth (genetic) approaches to governance are distinguished from the approach of neo-institutionalist economics. What they have in common is a shared commitment to "internalize" the conditions for success of the learning operation. In contrast to what is the case with the externalist approach, the desired transformation of behaviours/ representations is viewed as resulting from the very organization of the learning operation with respect to decentralized interaction. Of course, the form that the effort at internalization takes varies, depending on whether the approach is collaborative-relational, pragmatist, or genetic. As has already been pointed out, the effort at internalization is made increasingly expansive, in the sense that the "internal organizational constraints" imposed on the manner of organizing the form of cooperative action that is to be henceforward applied to decentralized action are progressively increased. The deliberative or collaborative-relational approach is characterized mainly by the commitment to organize the "aggregated communicative competencies". Concretely, the issue consists essentially of organizing venues for cooperative deliberation by all the parties involved. It is in the increased number of these venues for participation and of the actors involved in deliberation that the conditions for transforming "routines" and "selecting" the best possible solutions for collective problems are expected to be found. Thus a twofold process characterizes this initial effort at deepening the inquiry conducted by neo-institutionalist (in the broad sense) economists.

First, there is the perception that action on its own by an "external" hierarchical mechanism for supervision will prove inadequate to yield the hoped-for results. This first idea is significant. After all, on what basis can we assume that those who will apply this external mechanism will do so "in the same spirit" as that which prevailed when the external system was set up? Is it not the case that the familiar critique of the command-and-control approach is relevant here? The work of S. Deakin (2007) makes it possible to clearly illustrate this first process, which underlies the justification for the proposal that the approach of neo-institutionalist economics be continued in a "more reflexive" direction.

As S. Deakin shows, working on the basis of G. Teubner's systemic theory of "reflexive law", the usual law and economics approach deals too reductively with the complexity of the processes that drive the evolution of social behaviours. The autonomy of legal subsystems—for example, that of company law—makes it clear that a voluntarist introduction of a shareholding approach to corporate governance, at least into legal systems in societies with a European orientation, will not necessarily result in the effects claimed by those who support voluntarism in the name of economic logic. The reason is that the "interpretation" given to it will also depend on the traditional cohesiveness of our legal entities. And these legal entities, at least in Europe, require one to take into account the more "integrative" dimension of the nature of the company. What is in question here is not just the "cultural or ideological" dimension. "Culture" is embedded in the legal constraints that govern the way the legal system nowadays defines what is "legal" and "illegal". Any new legal reform that may be sought will necessarily have to take into account the inevitable effort at the harmonization of laws. If then, we act on the basis of this necessary legal harmonization, or congruence, would it not be more "efficient" to improve conditions favouring such congruence by means of appropriate systems? As F. Carvalho and S. Deakin (2010) have pointed out, this congruence might require setting up mechanisms that favour taking better cognizance, within companies, of all their components (the stakeholding approach) and in so doing, taking better cognizance of what we nowadays call corporate social responsibility.

It is on the basis of this first process that we can come to understand the second distinctive feature of the "deliberative" project. Since any external system is at risk of producing effects solely as a function of the "contexts" specific to its addressees, it is precisely necessary to "act" on the way relations among these decentralized actors are organized. The "aggregate" shaping of "communicative competencies" among all the actors involved must be organized. It is on the basis of this deliberative involvement by all "stakeholders" that, thanks precisely to this communicative and deliberative system, one can look for the "expansion" of routines that the success of a learning operation requires and, in consequence, the selection of a normative solution that will maximize fulfilment of the normative expectations of all the actors. Recent research performed in the context of the Reflexive Governance Network (REFGOV) by H. Adlard and T. Prosser (Prosser et al. 2010) on the evolution of energy governance in the UK and by P. Vincent-Jones and C. Mullen (Vincent-Jones and Mullen 2010) on the evolution of governance in the health field in England illustrate very well the institutional initiatives taken in these two sectors towards supplementing and furthering the neo-institutionalist-economics-based reforms that accompanied the first steps towards market liberalization during the 1980s and 1990s (that is, towards the reduction of state involvement and the increased application of free-market principles in these fields). At the same time, this research also makes clear the problems and negative consequences that these "participatory" and "deliberative" "reflexive" mechanisms appear to give rise to. In fact, both these studies show that the limitations of exclusive recourse to the mechanism of "aggregating communicative competencies" to ensure the success of a learning operation are becoming increasingly clear. Undoubtedly, as is recognized in the collaborative-relational approach to governance through dialogue, it is useful to take specific action on decentralized interaction. Thus this initial furtherance of the externalist approach is needed. But it proves, in turn, to be insufficient. H. Adlard and T. Prosser (Prosser et al. 2010), concerning these new institutional initiatives, said:

> [T]he ... most important problem is that of a lack of trust in relation to these processes ... [This reform] is undermined by the serious failure of trust in relation to the new arrangements and by the failure so far to implement the types of institutional reform to re-create trust.

Similarly, P. Vincent-Jones and C. Mullen points out that the limitations of participatory procedures are becoming increasingly evident and that it is becoming clear that specific mechanisms must be set up to reinforce actors' capacitation and develop a "capacity-building role" (Vincent-Jones and Mullen 2010). However, as was stressed in Chapter 4, this "attention" to the problem of actors' "capacity" needs to be properly understood. That is, it tends to be broached in very different ways depending on whether one takes the deliberative (collaborative-relational through dialogue), pragmatist, or genetic approach. The question of "actors' capacities" as a condition for the success of the learning operation is not articulated in the same way by the three approaches. It is necessary here to recapitulate three points in order to clarify the issues involved in this important question.

The first point is this. We must remember that there has recently appeared, within the deliberative approach,[8] a will to break away from the belief that aggregating communicative competencies will on its own ensure respect for the conditions needed for governance capable of satisfying collective interests to the extent possible. Thus from within this approach there has emerged attention to questions of the empowerment of actors as a condition, besides the sole condition of the shaping of aggregated communicative competencies, that must be imposed[9] in relation to decentralized interaction. The concern here is especially to strengthen capacities for argumentation. This implies, P. Vincent-Jones and C. Mullen continue, "that citizens have, or can acquire, relevant knowledge or understanding. This also implies developing methods of debate which maximize the input of relevant ideas, questions and experience, knowledge and understanding" (Vincent-Jones and Mullen 2010).[10] But whatever the expansion sometimes granted to these conditions

8 On this, see Chapter 4, 148–65.

9 In this regard, see S. Burris, P. Drahos, and C. Shearing (2005: 30–58), although this article conceives of capacity building, in a highly classical manner, in terms of informational asymmetry.

10 Contrary to what is sometimes thought, in this perspective, there is no evolution from the collaborative-relational mode of social learning towards democratic experimentalism. Rather, this kind of attention to the encouragement of social dialogue remains wholly within

for empowerment,[11] the question of actors' capacitation is never framed in the terms chosen by the authors writing in the reflexive version of the pragmatist approach (D. Schön, C. Argyris, and M. Rein), still less in the preferred terms of our genetic approach to governance. This is because what distinguishes these latter two approaches is precisely the specific way they work to radicalize the question of the level at which actors' capacity is to be built.

The second point is this: It must be noted that this question of building actors' capacity is in no way related to the furtherance proposed by the first version of the third approach to governance, the one called "pragmatist". As has been pointed out, this third approach has taken two successive forms, with the second of these working to surmount the weaknesses that continued to hamper the first, that is, the experimentalist pragmatism advanced by C. Sabel and others under the name "democratic experimentalism". The weakness that the reflexive pragmatism of D. Schön, C. Argyris, and M. Rein highlights within democratic experimentalism is precisely that this approach obscures the question of actors' capacitation. The furthering of the deliberative approach brought about by democratic experimentalism in no way relates to the question of the strengthening of actors' capacities. It relates rather to another level. The advance from which theory of governance benefits under this first version of the pragmatist trend is the insight that, besides the deliberative shaping of the communicative competencies of the actors involved, it is also necessary that the "negotiation" be organized in an experimentalist manner. That is, it is necessary that actors be engaged in a process of joint inquiry in order to "allow themselves" to be taught by the results of an experimental encounter between existing solutions and new problems requiring solution. In this sense, the process of "internalizing the conditions for success for the learning operation" is strengthened and a new condition is highlighted, consisting of organizing decentralized interaction in such a way that it is ensured that actors engage in a joint process of inquiry. This "expansion" of the conditions for success of the learning operation is reflected, according to C. Sabel, in the requirement that three new conditions be fulfilled in building systems of governance: co-design (and thus collaboration among those who define policy and those responsible for implementing it), benchmarking, and monitoring.

The third point is this: What distinguishes both reflexive pragmatism (embodied in the work of D. Schön, C. Argyris, and M. Rein) and the genetic approach from experimentalist pragmatism is the commitment to pursue the inquiry already begun within the collaborative-relational approach through dialogue, that is, the

deliberative logic. As will be seen below, democratic experimentalism implies wholly different kinds of shift and attention.

11 In authors such as J. Innes and D. Booher, the emphasis goes beyond J. Habermas' formal approach and involves attending to the systems required to generate common trust among actors and ensure the emergence of "shared identities, shared meanings, new heuristics and innovation" (Innes and Booher 2003: 39).

inquiry into the need to pay attention to strengthening actors' capacities. Certainly, experimentalist pragmatism, with its requirement that a joint process of inquiry be organized, has already allowed for an advance over deliberative approaches. The error of that trend, however, is that it overlooks the "obstacles" that may hinder the success of a learning operation when it is assumed that actors' "spontaneous capabilities" suffice for the success of the "joint experiment". Indeed, no inquiry into these capabilities has been initiated within the experimentalist pragmatist trend. In tandem with this, both reflexive pragmatism and the genetic approach work to further and radicalize the inquiries broached by adherents of the "deliberative" approach into the question of the conditions for actors' capacitation. This furthering has been effected by the reflexive pragmatism by means of the "key" concept of "defensive strategies" that actors may deploy unconsciously and that would lead actors to restrict the field of their "representations" as compared with what is needed for the maximal fulfilment of the normative expectations held by participants in a collective action. As will be seen, the genetic approach continues to deploy this "attention" to the question of "defensive strategies" as it works to better think through the conditions for surmounting them.

We can now turn to a consideration of the meaning of the furthering suggested by the reflexive pragmatist trend, in comparison with both deliberative approaches and experimentalist pragmatism. And on this basis we will then be able to shed light on problems that D. Schön's pragmatist approach is likely to remain faced with and the reasons why we propose extending the pragmatist approach towards a fourth one, which we call the "genetic" approach.

The Genetic Approach to Governance

The contribution of the experimentalist pragmatism proposed by C. Sabel consists of pointing out that communicative aggregation on its own—even when specific attention is paid to the resources needed to compensate for informational asymmetry and ensure equality in capacities for argumentation—is not sufficient to guarantee the desired maximization of fulfilment of the normative expectations held by members of a social group. It is further necessary to ensure that participants in the development of a common norm are organized in such a way that they allow themselves to be taught in common by the results of joint experimentation with solutions viewed as the most rationally acceptable ones for the problem at hand. It is only by establishing this joint inquiry by all who are participating in the choice and implementation of the solutions under consideration that the co-design of a "norm" likely to satisfy all the interests involved to the extent possible will be developed.

The reflexive pragmatism of C. Argyris and D. Schön takes this experimentalist process even further, and this pursuit of the process leads to the replacement of the "experimentalist" version of the pragmatist approach with a more "reflective" one. While it takes over the idea of necessary co-design by all involved in the implementation process, their theory of double loop learning (also known as reflective learning and organizational learning) claims to further open up the "black box" of co-design and shed light on its conditions for possibility. The idea is that the joint inquiry process that co-design implies will only yield the desired results if attention is paid to the actors' stereotyped behaviours, or routines. That is, "attention" to the lessons emerging from the trial by experimentation of the solutions under consideration does not suffice on its own to effect the necessary "adjustments" to pre-existing behavioural models and approaches customarily used to solve problems, and to determine on the strategies deemed to be the most rational. The adjustment of these "contexts of analysis" (frames) does not occur spontaneously as the simple product of the "shock" that results from experimenting with the solutions under consideration in a new context of implementation. The "reframing" operation calls for specific conditions. It requires that particular attention be paid to potential "defensive strategies"[12] that participants in the "joint experimental inquiry" may resort to as a way of ensuring their pre-existing "frames" are reproduced, a process that neutralizes the shifts in behaviour and approaches to problems that the unaccustomed nature of the problems to be solved might impose. This specific attention thus constitutes a condition for the possibility of successfully choosing the norm sought for. This condition reflects the need to organize reflexivity—that is, actors' return over their pre-existing frames of analysis. If "reflective attention" of this kind is not organized, the institutional co-design mechanism will not ensure the "capacities" needed for the success of the operation. D. Schön (Schön and Rein 1994: 206–7) writes, in fact, of "capabilities", thereby emphasizing that, if this necessary attention is not mobilized, the capabilities needed for the success of the operation may be altogether lacking. This "reflective attention", and the "capabilities" that, according to D. Schön, it is responsible for generating, will obviously feature attention to the "frames" that underlie our accustomed approaches to problems. But it will also entail specific attention to the need to create and maintain a "climate of mutual trust among policy inquirers" and develop both the "ability to put yourself in the other party's shoes" and the "ability to act from a frame while cultivating awareness of alternative frames" (also referred to as the "ability of double vision") (Schön and Rein 1994: 207).

As D. Schön and his colleagues point out, this kind of attention is undoubtedly currently little cultivated in the institutions where future policy-makers are trained, be they business schools or public policy schools. In fact, such institutions have a stronger allegiance to the development of cognitive competencies based on "rational choice approaches" than to those associated with "frame-reflective approaches to policy controversies". But it is precisely by orienting training programmes towards this mode of reflective attention that the attitudes and competencies specific to "reflective attention" will be developed. It would appear as if the mere incitement

12 On "defensive routines" and "defensive dynamics", see (C. Argyris and D.A. Schön 1996: 103 and 275).

to paying this kind of attention will automatically generate the attitudes and competencies required for a capacity to transform one's "frames". As the authors in fact write, it is in a way sufficient to "encourage" the actors to adopt such a reflexive approach for the approach itself to develop, seemingly as the potentiation of a competency or capability that is already tacitly present in all the subjects and whose deployment merely requires that attention be paid to it.[13]

It is here that the assumption that operates within the conception of reflexivity deployed by D. Schön, C. Argyris, and M. Rein's reflexive pragmatism makes itself felt. As was pointed out in Chapter 5 (Schön and Rein 1994: 109), the furthering achieved by the pragmatist trend in comparison with the deliberative approaches and experimentalist pragmatism consists of having the success of a collective action[14] depend on the setting up of a process that will stimulate, by means of a suitable mechanism, the use of a rule that already exists in the actors' minds. Thus the assumption is that, in some manner or another, there exist pre-given rules and capacities that are already available. This assumption is based on the belief, clearly voiced by D. Schön (1996: 353), in the "existence of a widespread capacity for reciprocal reflection-in-action".

What are the implications of this assumption? A brief review of D. Schön's reflexive pragmatism will allow us to better highlight what it implies. D. Schön's approach offers the advantage of seeking to articulate the structure of the "reframing" operation that is to emerge from joint inquiry and the specific "attention" this inquiry will elicit when one is faced with a new problem or a conflict to resolve. As was observed above,[15] D. Schön tries to provide an account of this operation in terms of metaphoric learning. However, his analysis of the learning operation in the terms of metaphor reflects certain powerful assumptions. The frame each actor spontaneously deploys must be understood, according to D. Schön, as a "generative metaphor"[16]

13 D. Schön and M. Rein observe that, in contrast to business schools and policy schools, schools of design (mainly architecture schools) tend, in the context of study programmes developed in their design studios, to be more attuned to what is required by co-design that is attentive to the requirements of possible reframing. "The generic conditions of the design studio constitute a practicum that becomes reflective when students are encouraged to reflect on the understandings they bring spontaneously to design projects, as well as on the meanings of their coaches' words and actions, and when their coaches reflect on the theories and processes they bring to their own demonstrations and descriptions, as well [as] on the understandings and puzzlements revealed by their students' attempts at designing" (Schön and Rein 1994: 208).

14 That is, the capacity to satisfy the normative expectations of its members, to the extent possible.

15 See Chapter 5.

16 "The metaphor which accounts for centrally important features of the story—which makes it understandable that certain elements of the situation are included in the story while others are omitted; that certain assumptions are taken as true although there is evidence that would appear to disconfirm them; and, especially, that the normative conclusions are found to follow so obviously from the facts" (Schön 1993: 149).

that, in a sense, constitutes the actor's rule of identity. Every actor has specific interests that define her or his own identity within the social group. But a feature of this rule of identity is that it has a dual function. Its character as a "rule" guarantees the outcome of a twofold operation.

On one hand, it allows the actor to assign to the specific context she or he is faced with the "meaning" that corresponds to her or his "own identity" and adopt a corresponding role. On the other hand and at the same time, it guarantees its own variation, that is, its own ongoing adjustment to the transformations associated with differing contexts. That is why it is called "generative". It produces a rule for the interpretation and integration of the facts. Thus it makes possible the "representations" of specific situations and guarantees the possibility of assigning a "meaning" to each of them. It defines how the facts will be selected that will, in turn, determine the meaning to assign to the situation that must be solved (this is the first operation).

At the same time (and this is the second operation), this rule also guarantees the success of the learning/adjustment entailed by ongoing changes in the specific contexts that have elicited the problems to be solved. This rule of identity—inscribed in actors' minds—ensures that, despite the constant newness of the problems to be solved, the actors will transpose the unaccustomed (the new) onto the known (the familiar). It is this that the idea of the generative metaphor points to: the rule guarantees social actors' capacity to re-read metaphorically, as "analogues" of previous experiences, new situations needing solutions. By means of this inventory of the similar (which allows for perceiving the new as an analogue of the old), the representation that a social actor assigns to a given situation as a function of her or his own identity (or interests) adjusts itself. Variation is made possible by the rule itself. This rule, in the manner of a "plan", or schema, that can be applied to the construction of an image, guarantees the construction of a representation with due respect simultaneously to the specific features of the given context and to the requirements of the identity rule. That is why we use the expression "schematic approach to representation" to designate this approach to solving the question of the conditions for possibility of an identity representation and the variant forms it takes according to the context in which it is applied.

This also helps in understanding why we referred to an "incentive" approach in connection with the theory of "reflective" learning developed by D. Schön, C. Argyris, and M. Rein. According to these pragmatist authors, it is in a sense "sufficient" to pay attention to the problem of reframing for the identity rule inscribed in the frame to be automatically deployed, and for the twofold operation the rule is thought to guarantee to take place—simply because attention has been focused on the necessary "adjustment" to the frames.

It is just this "schematic" assumption of a rule stored in the minds of actors participating in a collective action, along with the incentive approach to governance associated with it, that must be challenged. It is on this score that, in our view, the pragmatist project—not just in the "Deweyan" and "experimentalist" version of which C. Sabel is the exponent, but also in the more "reflective" version developed by C. Argyris, D. Schön, and M. Rein—requires correcting and taking further: correcting, because the underlying assumption must be exposed; taking further because the exposure of this assumption entails, not a challenge to the organization of governance proposed by the pragmatists, but completion through an indication of the complement it calls for.

An examination of four points will make it possible to understand the nature of the shift that must take place *vis-à-vis* this schematic approach to the conditions for possibility of an identity representation, as well as the nature of its variation according to its contexts of application.

(1) First, the operation by which one adopts an identity—that is, by which one represents oneself in a twofold way, through one's objective self-identification with certain interests in a given context of action as well as through one's position as subject (that is, in the present instance, as an actor able to interact with other actors in order to advance [support] one's interests)—is not an operation that occurs automatically or spontaneously. Its "success" requires specific conditions to be present and consequently a specific form of attention. It is indeed to the great credit of D. Schön, C. Argyris, and M. Rein that they intuited the weakness of traditional approaches to governance, in particular deliberative approaches, as regards this matter of actors' capacity to form appropriate representations of the circumstances and of their own interests. They rightly saw that all the usual approaches to governance cancel out the difficulties specific to this operation. As was seen above, they highlighted how often "routines and defensive strategies" prevent actors involved in a collective action from forming appropriate representations of new problems to be solved and from cooperatively taking part in the joint inquiry that the search for an appropriate solution entails. Such defensive strategies are clues to the existence of a "handicap" in one's ability to suitably represent the problem to be solved: The actor remains the prisoner of what might be called a "repetition compulsion" that obstructs the self-adjustment process needed for the operation of representation to succeed. It could be said that this repetition compulsion—or defensive strategy—points to the failure of the "subject formation" capacity, that is, the capacity to form one's identity and be able to represent the interests at stake within a given situation. True, as has been observed, pragmatists like D. Schön do not have at their disposal the epistemological tools to pursue this insight. Since they adopt a schematic, rule-based approach, they assume that it is sufficient to pay attention to the difficulty in order to automatically "activate" the actors' innate competency to form a subject. Thus they do not manage to construct epistemologically what they nevertheless intuit to be an operation whose success cannot be assumed to be the result of automatic competency.

Their insight requires a supplementary epistemological stage to avoid the pitfall of an assumption of actors' innate competency to ensure the automatic success of the operation of constructing an identity representation. To avoid this pitfall, it is necessary to conceive this "capacity for self-representation" as the product of an operation of "terceization"; that is, as the product of an operation that requires, as part of the process of self-construction, the invocation of a third element whose externality makes possible the actor's construction of her or his image—the image that will enable her or him to identify herself or himself (and her or his interests) in a given context of action. What does this mean? An initial metaphor will help in understanding our use of the term "terceization". Reference to a mirror clearly conveys the nature of the operation of representation. To represent oneself is to give oneself an image: it is to "recognize" oneself in an image. But, as the metaphor of the mirror makes clear, it is necessary to "recognize" oneself in the other that an image consists of. Thus it is necessary to first grant existence to this otherness, to this differentiation between oneself and this image that is reflected back from the mirror. Absent this operation of differentiation, the operation of representation cannot achieve success. To put it in still more metaphorical terms, if I am to recognize myself in the mirror, the third factor represented by the mirror must be invoked. The frame of the mirror is the condition for possibility of the existence of the image that the subject recognizes as self and identifies with. Thus the success of the operation of representation entails conditions for possibility closely associated with the process of differentiation or terceization. It is the need for a device that ensures the existence of this operation of terceization that D. Schön's schematic approach ends by cancelling out. On this basis, we can revert to a discussion of the two dimensions implied by the operation of identity representation that pragmatists like D. Schön and C. Argyris appropriately emphasize, all the while believing its success to be guaranteed by the presence of a rule stored in the mind of every actor.

The issue at stake, then, is the capacity to form an identity. Identity-making has two dimensions. On one hand, it consists in the capacity to form an image. On the other hand, it consists in the capacity to transform that image.[17] The second dimension implies that one experiences one's identity as "a form capable of varying", that is, as a form with no determinate content. It is important that we not identify ourselves with a determinate or specific image that would take shape as a single identification. This twofold dimension is what allows a group the conditions for possibility of subjecthood. The subjectivation process implies the capacity to identify oneself, to take on an identity. Correlatively, however, this identification must be accompanied by the perception of one's identity as a simple form whose contents can be determined and transformed through action. It is, in fact, just this twofold dimension of the relationship that a group has with its own identity that makes possible the "capabilities" D. Schön writes about. That is, the capability of "double vision", which allows one to put oneself in another's place, is wholly determined beforehand by the capacity for recognizing an otherness, that is, of not limiting one's self-identification to a single image. Thus it is first

17 These two dimensions complement the twofold nature of identity discussed above (objective identification and positioning as subject). That discussion broached the question of identity from a perspective that at that juncture was still static. Added now to "image making" is the genetic dimension of the self-transformation of the image, through which the establishment of externality and the operation of terceization take effect.

necessary for the identity relationship to inscribe within itself what has been called a logic of terceization that installs an "externality" within the relationship that every actor has with himself or herself. On the construction of this "externality" depends the success of the twofold operation entailed by any "joint inquiry" in search of a solution that will "maximize to the extent possible" the fulfilment of the expectations held by parties in a collective action. Let us now seek to explicate more concretely the need to install an "externality" within the relationship every actor has with himself or herself—or itself.

A more concrete approach will allow us to better conceptualize the kind of institutional mechanism, over and above the mechanisms already highlighted by the neo-institutionalist economics, deliberative, and pragmatist approaches, that the capacity of a system of governance to satisfy to the extent possible the intentionality governing any collective action depends on.

(2) To effect this operation of *terceization*, every collective actor must submit to a twofold operation.

The first operation concerns the actor's relation to the "past". This is a matter of "reconstructing" the actor's relationship with "collective identity-making". With this question as the starting point, the actor must examine itself and reconstruct the form its identity assumes through its past actions. Note the rich semantic ambiguity of the expression "collective identity-making", which implies that a collective actor experiences itself in its organic capacity to be organized as a collective actor "representing and aggregating" the various members it is comprised of. But "collective identity-making" also implies a "modal or functional" dimension, that is, a dimension related to the possibility of operating and representing itself as a collective actor in a context of action. The collective actor must experience itself through its capacity to represent itself, that is, to form an identity whose substantive representation can vary and adapt according to transformations occurring in the contexts of action. Thus what is at issue here is the first dimension of the establishment of the capacity to be an actor (that is, the operation of self-capacitation). This dimension, as we have just observed, concerns the relation to the past and works to construct this capacity to form an "image", to be "reflected" in an image subject to variation. For this reason, we can speak, more precisely and rigorously, of a dimension of reflectibility.

The second operation internal to this construction of "self-capacitation" concerns not the relation to the past but the relation to the future. The question governing this second process is that of "ability-to-do". What transformations must be carried out in the way the actor has given meaning to its identity? What means, what "ability-to-do", must it adopt in order to ensure, in the new context that it is faced with, the realization of this identity form "with no fixed contents", which it defines as its own "collective identity-making"? Under what conditions can it make this form effective in the context of the new constraints on action? Thus the current situation is re-examined in the light of the identity form that underpins it (retrospective relation, associated with reflectibility), but also in the perspective of transformations necessary to ensure the fulfilment of this form in a new context for its application. This, then, is the second dimension of the *establishment of the capacity to be an actor* (that is, the operation of self-capacitation). As we have just seen, it concerns the relation to the future and works to construct the capacity to adapt one's "image" according to what is entailed by the fulfilment of the "identity form" one takes on as one's *destiny*. For this reason, we may speak, precisely and rigorously, of a dimension of "*destinability*".[18]

It is only through this twofold operation that the modification of a representation that is associated with what "pragmatists" call "joint inquiry" can be rescued from the "unconscious repetition" that, through the "defensive strategies" that are its telltale signs, limits the shifts required to solve the problem the actors are faced with. It is because they overlook the need for this twofold operation of "self-capacitation" that D. Schön, C. Argyris, and M. Rein's conception of the reflexivity at play in all learning is too narrow. As we have seen, the reason for this is that the notion of reflexivity developed by the pragmatists remains subordinated to a schematic approach to the construction of the shifts performed by learning. As was seen, the pragmatic shift brought about by joint experimentation is not the mere auxiliary of the transformation of representations, as might be inferred from the notion of reflexive return implicit in the "looping" metaphor. Joint experimentation consists of an inferential relation to experience that has consequences for both an anticipatory relation to the current situation, to the extent that the situation is capable of evolving (destinability), and a retrospective relation to it, to the extent that it is subject to being re-read and re-appropriated in various ways, depending on what the future will bring (reflectibility). This reflexive position, simultaneously open to anticipation and retrospection, also makes it possible epistemologically to determine an inferential relationship with concepts that goes beyond the schematizing logic of representation and contemplates the concepts themselves concretely, as possible guides to action that are open to their own fulfilment, rather than as sets of constituted meanings burdened with the task of fixing meanings and defining identities. The diachronic prevails over the synchronic; a forward-looking posture prevails over a backward-looking one. But note that this idea of "forward looking" includes the renewed take-up of the retrospective dimension that leads to a redefinition of the meaning of the kind of reflexivity in question.

This epistemological clarification was needed in order to be able to go on to the institutional level and address the problem of management of the learning process. That is, it allows us to understand why effectively "inciting" actors to reflexivity requires, besides having recourse to the mechanisms clearly highlighted by experimentalists and pragmatists like D. Schön, C. Argyris, and M. Rein, that we act on actors' capacities. It also makes it possible to understand the operation of self-capacitation as attention paid to two questions reflecting the dimensions

18 Whence the idea of defining the term "reflexivity" as the operation of self-transformation by which a social group seeks to respond to its perception of the need to adapt its capacities for action according to its acquired experience (reflectibility) and the projection of its identity of action (destinability).

of reflectibility (collective identity-making) and destinability (ability-to-do) that together constitute the reflexive operation by which an actor constructs its capacity to build a representation—of itself and of the context.

(3) This reflexive attention to the operation of "self-capacitation" also makes it possible to give a better account of a certain dimension that the language of pragmatist authors tends to pass over in silence. Talk of "framing" and "reframing" leads one to believe that the shift performed by the learning operation implies substituting one representation for another. But to speak of substitution or transformation suggests that the transformations just carried out result in the erasure of former representations and the emergence of a wholly new representation. The reality is more nuanced. Even a pragmatist author like C. Sabel, in fact, acknowledges the necessity for such a nuanced reading in describing the changes at work in the field of companies and companies' organizational forms. In line with what is now an abundant scholarly literature in the theory of the firm, C. Sabel points to the emergence of a "non-standard" kind of company. In contrast to the standard model of the firm based on the routinization and hierarchical integration of tasks (Sabel 2006 : 111), non-standard theory privileges the systematic challenging of routines and exploration of ambiguity within a decentralized structure. The approach of the non-standard firm has a relationship to more dynamic and open learning: Whereas the standard firm confronts endemic ignorance in its workforce by simplifying tasks, the non-standard firm promotes cooperative behaviours as a way to discover new solutions in the face of complex tasks. What is peculiar to the strategy of the non-standard firm is that it allows not just for learning to choose solutions, but for learning *to choose how to choose these solutions* (Helper, MacDuffie, and Sabel 2000: 478). C. Sabel is, however, fully aware that the emergence of the non-standard firm does not imply the elimination of old forms of company organization. The two co-exist and in many fields more hierarchical modes of organization would appear to retain their full effectiveness.

In other words, the operation of "substitution" or displacement overlays a complex operation that consists not of a simple substitution but rather of a "combination". If, nowadays, we wish to find the best possible forms of organization, what is necessary is not just to be open to non-standard forms of organization but to be able to determine when and where to preserve the old forms and when and where to replace them with new ones. The construction of the rule that the learning operation entails in order to "choose" the solution that will satisfy the normative expectations of participants in any collective action to the extent possible is more complex than D. Schön's language of reframing (that is, of substituting one representation for another) would lead one to believe. "Semantic" language of this kind risks cancelling out the complexity of the pragmatic shift that the learning operation entails.

To have grasped this is to recognize a symptom of the "reductionism" in the approach to reflectivity developed by D. Schön. We presented above both the epistemological reason for this reductionism (the schematic rule-based approach) and how to surmount it (by expanding reflective attention to the operation of self-capacitation). But this observation now also makes it possible to understand how, at the close of a learning operation that incorporates attention to the twofold dimension of the operation of self-capacitation, the construction of the rule of judgement must in the end attend to the question of the combination of what is to be maintained of the old representations and what is to be transformed in them. Attention of this kind implies attention to the risks of simplification that are often associated with emphasis on the efficiency of new representations, without consideration for how they are to be combined with existing representations.

(4) If the reasons guiding our effort to take further the approach to learning suggested by the reflexive pragmatism of D. Schön, C. Argyris, and M. Rein are grasped, then the implications of this project as regards, not the actor's relationship with himself or herself, but the actor's relationship with other actors and with the institutional mechanisms intended to structure their interactions and reflect their negotiated agreements, will also have been grasped. And clearly what happens at this second level is very important to a theory of governance.

Our critique of the pragmatist approach has consisted of showing that it reproduces the behaviourist assumptions made by the approaches to governance that it sought to overcome. The setting up of incitement mechanisms (joint inquiry and the provision of devices and mechanisms to induce reflective attention to the need for surmounting defensive strategies cooperatively) is expected to produce the hoped-for effects of shifting and cognitive transformation. The mechanism is understood to produce on its own the behaviour expected. The assumption is that the mechanism to some extent operates from the outside, in the manner of an incitement that activates a pre-existing rule that guarantees the hoped-for behavioural transformation. As we have seen, there exists a pragmatic weakness in this way of understanding the conditions for the possibility of satisfying the intentionality that governs any action by a subject. These conditions for possibility necessitate a self-capacitating operation that no incitement mechanism can assume, in a mentalist fashion, to be taken care of by a given capacity stored in every actor's mind.

If that is the case, it is clear that the same flaw of a mentalist assumption taints the expectation that any institutional mechanism set up in a negotiated manner in order to guarantee a cooperative solution will produce, on its own, behaviours in line with the negotiated cooperative agreement. The same asymmetry as was observed in the context of the subject's relationship with itself must be recognized to exist intersubjectively as well. Assumptions of the creation of symmetry must be exposed as having ties to the schematic assumption that was laid bare above. One way or another, it is necessary to critique the assumption that an institutional mechanism is capable of creating a symmetry-producing situation on its own; that is, the assumption that actors involved in a negotiation situation will all line up with the same allegiance to normative constraints for respecting the cooperative requirements negotiated.

This exposure leads, in governance terms, to the necessity of proposing a twofold shift, institutional and actantial, in the processes of intervention in the course of action.[19] The first, or institutional shift consists of setting up a mechanism for vigilance[20] related to the limitations associated with the implementation of the process in existing cultures in use. These have their own capacities for adjustment and transformation of the learning goals, which may prove not to correspond to those required by the operation of self-capacitation. This shift concerns attention to the genetic conditions for identifying the blockages associated with already operating identities of action. The second, or actantial shift consists of a requirement for the actors involved to take back ownership of the vigilance mechanism. This "reappropriation" must allow them, first, to identify the internal limitations of the cooperative frame being tried out, from the perspective of the surmounting of the blockages engendered by opposing positions. Next, it must allow them to formulate their own point of view on the difficulties of reconstructing and restructuring the specific positionings that contributed to these blockages.

To the extent that these two shifts take into account the twofold requirement for reflectibility (collective identity-making) and destinability (ability-to-do) that constitutes the reflexive operation by which an actor constructs its capacity to produce a representation (of itself and of the context), these shifts produce the relevant and efficient practical conditions for implementing the operation of self-capacitation. Thus they should enable the actors to transform their own involvement in the experimental frame into the frame's own self-testing of its limits, from the perspectives both of identifying blockages and of the effective implementation of the requirements associated with surmounting those blockages.

A Case Study in Applying the Genetic Approach: The Transformation of Collective Modes of Action by Labour Organizations in the Context of Liberalization in the Belgian Electricity Sector

We believe that, in grasping the impact of this twofold test, a helpful case study is provided by an analysis of the ways that Belgian labour unions will have to adapt in the face of liberalization in the energy field and more specifically in the electricity sector. To present this example, it will be necessary to make a brief overview of specific conditions in Belgium, from the perspective of this sector's circumstances as well as of the positions adopted by the sector's labour-movement actors and developments in labour relations. Next, we will show how the transformation in modes of action occurs in different ways and results in different strategies, depending on whether the actors deploy an "experimentalist" analysis, a Schön-

19 See our notification about this twofold shift at the end of Chapter 5.

20 The mechanism for institutional evaluation constitutes the traces left in governance mechanisms of the fact that the actors' capacity to make a normative commitment—their rule following capacity—cannot, as is widely assumed, be assumed to be given. For a clear exemplification of this assumption in the pragmatic philosophy of J. Habermas and the pragmatist philosophy of R.B. Brandom, see J. Habermas (2000: 328).

Argyris-type reflexive pragmatist analysis, or a "genetic" approach. We will conclude with a recapitulation of the advances yielded by the genetic approach.

Thus the objective of presenting this illustration is twofold.

On one hand, we will demonstrate the value of a shift at the level of the analysis of the institutional issues. This is the level of "reflectibility" and "collective identity-making", consisting of the identification of blockages and of the capacity to act collectively in order to surmount them. Depending on the perspective taken in conducting the retrospective analysis, the relation and reaction of the actors to the blockages encountered can take very different forms and can even lead to affirming the value of repeating those blockages. As we shall see, only a genetic analysis leads to a re-examination of the possible role of taking into account transformations in identity as the process of governance of the sector in question unfolds. On the other hand—and this is the second objective—we will demonstrate the value of the shift effected at the level of the actors' "destinability" and their "ability-to-do". At this level, the actors' mode of participation in the process of governance can be re-examined prospectively, according to the blockages that must be surmounted and the possibilities opened up by transformations in identity.

Collective Bargaining and the Evolution of the Belgian Electricity Sector's Regulatory Context: Some Facts

In Belgium, the implementation of European directives dating from 1996 and 1998 and respecting the adoption of common regulations for domestic electricity and gas markets took the shape of a reform of the electricity-market authorities and the whole sector's restructuring in line with the principle of the uncoupling of production from distribution as well as transport from sales. The federal government has authority over matters of rate regulation and the planning of electrical production, while regional governments have authority over matters of distribution and local-network management. The new regulatory authorities were set up in 2001. As of March 2003 in the Flemish part of the country and January 2007 in the Walloon part, individuals were able to choose their supply contracts. As of 2001, Electrabel, the traditional operator, restructured its activities into four distinct entities responsible for production, trading, network management, and sales, respectively. These changes did not, however, alter Electrabel's monopolistic hold over each of these four subsectors. Thus it is possible to clearly observe the market-concentration and vertical-integration phenomena identified by the European Commissioner for Competition, Nellie Kroes.[21] Moreover, a report

21 As the Commissioner wrote, "The European Commission has decided to launch two sets of formal proceedings against the agreements for suspected infringement of regulations under the EC treaty on abuse of dominant position. The first is against Electrabel, the traditional operator in Belgium's electricity sector, which is a part of the French SUEZ group; the second is against the traditional French operator EDF" (July 2007).

commissioned by the new regulatory authority (known as the CREG, see below) from the London Economics consulting firm in 2004 observed that:

> [I]deally Electrabel should be broken up so that there were seven or eight generators. However, it was acknowledged this was not feasible under Belgian expropriation laws and Electrabel stated they would not voluntarily break themselves up. London Economics recommended further auctions of existing capacity to encourage new entrants.[22]

Nevertheless, consumers today are definitely dealing with a liberalized market that offers various opportunities for choice from among several electricity providers, while various trades have gone their separate ways, resulting in the restructuring of labour relations in this sector.

In the course of this trend to liberalization, the Belgian legislature and its social partners (the state, unions, and management) have sought to preserve the context of collective bargaining that had regulated this sector. "Since 1955, under the *Comité de Contrôle de l'Électricité et du Gaz* [Committee for the Monitoring of Electricity and Gas] (CCEG), Belgium has enjoyed a regime of co-ordinated action and control that was unique in Europe" (Declercq and Vincent 2000: 17). Its role consisted mainly of "submitting advice and recommendations on rate setting … and on proposed electrical equipment (and natural-gas supply) plans" (Declercq and Vincent 2000: 18). On 21 February 2001, the board of directors of the *Commission de Régulation de l'Électricité et du Gaz* (Electricity and Gas Regulatory Commission, or the CREG) was set up in compliance with a statute passed on 29 April 1999. In line with the spirit that informed the structures that had existed since 1955, the various social partners participated in a process of reflection on moving towards a free-market economy. They all continued as members of this new energy-sector regulatory authority.[23] Their seats on the CREG are distributed as follows:

- seven for labour organizations and organizations that represent small energy consumers;
- seven for employers' organizations and organizations representing large energy consumers;
- nine for public authorities;
- four for other organizations (environmental groups, consumer protection groups, etc.).

22 *Power in Europe*, 25 October 2004: 3, quoted by S. Thomas (2005: 70); this report may be found at the CREG's website under the title *Structure and Functioning of the Electricity Market in Belgium in a European Perspective*, London Economics, October 2004 (http://www.creg.info/pdf/Etudes/ARCG-LE102004.pdf). On pages 17 and 280 is found the more modest recommendation that Electrabel be broken up into three or four operators.

23 Website: http://www.creg.be/fr/.

Thus the energy sector was in a position to count on the effects of a regulatory mechanism external to labour relations, which would be able to present a picture of the transformations under way from a codetermination perspective.

Furthermore, this mechanism was rooted in a system of collective bargaining based on the negotiation of collective agreements that situated the current transformations in a deliberative climate of respect for the interests of all parties. Electrabel, having prepared itself beginning in 1990 for the possible effects of liberalization by ensuring its control of production and of the electricity grid through agreements with its sole competitor, the SPE (*Société coopérative de production d'électricité*),[24] had been able, as part of a sectoral *commission paritaire*, or joint committee (known as CP),[25] to ensure collective bargaining focused on job security and wage-related benefits that had been set up by statute of 5 December 1968. In this climate of cooperation, the Belgian experience of the European job losses in the electricity sector during the 1990s was linked to collective bargaining, which kept recourse to redundancies to a minimum.[26] This unusual social context contributed to the development of the idea that such social stability was integral to sound development by a key sector of the economy that was responsive to public interest.

(1) The Belgian labour-movement actors. What are the specific features of Belgian labour organizations operating in this deliberative context? Generally speaking, Belgian unions have constituted a significant majority voice in social relations since the end of World War II. In many employment sectors, the rate of unionization continues to exceed 90 per cent. Labour organizations are grouped on both an activity-sector and a geographic basis. The *centrales professionnelles* are the activity-based trade unions. On the national level, they are brought together under two broad cross-professional confederations, one that has a Christian-democrat orientation[27] (the CSC, which accounts for 53 per cent of unionized workers) and the other a socialist one[28] (the FGTB, with 40 per cent).[29] These two major actors are both represented in the electricity sector. They are recognized by

24 Together they account for 96 per cent of Belgium's electricity production.

25 This CP, established by statute on 5 December 1968, is known as *Commission paritaire* 326, or CP 326. According to the most recent changes (Royal Decree of 26 March 2004), CP 326 has authority over workers in general and their employers, that is, businesses whose activities consist of electrical and gas energy production, transport, metering, and trade, and laboratories related to these activities.

26 This was so despite a workforce reduction by some 2,400 jobs during this period. The number of job losses in this sector across Europe during this period is estimated at 250,000.

27 Confédération des Syndicats Chrétiens (ACV in Dutch). Website: http://www.csc-en-ligne.be/default.asp.

28 Fédération Générale du Travail de Belgique (ABVV in Dutch). Website: http://www.fgtb.be/CODE/fr/home.htm.

29 A third confederation, with a distinctly minority membership share (9 per cent), is politically liberal in outlook. This is the *Centrale générale des syndicats libéraux de Belgique*, or CGSLB (ACLVB in Dutch).

law as representing workers[30] and enjoy the privileges associated with this status, including that of negotiating collective agreements at both the level of individual companies and the sector level. These agreements take the specific form known as *conventions collectives de travail* (collective labour agreements, or CCTs). These are the only organizations empowered to represent workers on the collective bargaining bodies (that is, the *commissions paritaires*, or CPs, mentioned above).[31] "Social elections" are conducted every four years in each company to fill the union seats on the works councils (known as CE) and workplace safety boards (known as CPPT).

In the electricity sector, the rate of unionization approaches 95 per cent and reflects the national distribution and balance of forces of union membership, with the CSC accounting for 50 per cent of workers and the FGTB for 40 per cent (Vincent and Declercq 2000: 35, Arcq and Aussems 2002: 9). The specific union that accounts for FGTB representation in the electricity sector is GAZELCO,[32] the gas and electricity blue-collar workers', office workers', technicians' and management union, which is a member of the FGTB-affiliated trade union federation called *Centrale Générale des Services Publics* (or General Public Service Federation, though it represents private-sector workers, too). On the CSC side, two trade union federations are present: the *Centrale Nationale des Employés*,[33] or CNE, and the *CSC Electricité et Gaz*, affiliated with the *Centrale de l'Énergie et de la Chimie*.[34]

(2) Two labour-movement cultures. It is worth examining the case of the CSC in order to grasp the changes experienced by labour unions in the sector even before the period of liberalization, whose effects began to be directly felt as of 2001, when the Plan Transform 2003 was announced by Electrabel. From 1954 to 1976, Elcogaz, a branch of *CSC Énergie Chimie*, was responsible for this industrial sector. As of 1976, only one employee status was recognized for the whole sector, covering both blue-collar and white-collar workers. On the French-speaking side, the CNE acquired responsibility for this sector's workers, excluding workers associated with transport-network management, who continued to be represented by Elcogaz. But on the Dutch speaking side, the two federations already present continued to work side by side and were joined

30 Statute of 5 December 1968.

31 These organizations also take part in the management of social security agencies, have the right to set up organizations for the payment of unemployment benefits, and field candidates for the position of "social judges", who preside over labour tribunals.

32 Website: http://www.cgsp.be/code/fr/frameea8c.html; the Dutch-speaking branch is the ACOD-GAZELCO, whose website is at: http://www.acodonline.be/ACOD/Sectoren.aspx?SectorID=5.

33 Website: http://www.cne-gnc.be/.

34 Website: http://csc-energie-chimie.csc-en-ligne.be/secteurs/electricite_gaz/info/info.asp. The Dutch-speaking branch is called ACV Elektriciteit & Gas. Note that before the implementation of the 2001 reforms, activity sectors were reflected in the affiliates in these proportions: 27 per cent in production, 6 per cent in transport, and 61 per cent in distribution.

by representatives of Elcogaz. These three partners came together in 1992 under the *Fédération des électriciens et des gaziers* (the FEG, which, in 2004, became *CSC Electricité et Gaz*).[35]

This internal situation of the CSC significantly altered the order of things in the sector's labour representation and emphasized the divide between two very different cultures of collective action. Thus the CNE felt closer, in terms of its culture of intervention, to the socialist GAZELCO, with which it shared an approach more sensitive to questions relating to the sector's general interests (such as impact on jobs)[36] and consumer interests (Vincent and Declercq 2000: 36). In contrast, *CSC Electricité et Gaz* was concerned, above all, maintaining the ethos of codetermination that had prevailed in the sector's industry-labourer approach, which was more sensitive to the benefits derived from a thriving sector (such as wage-related benefits and tax-free fringe benefits, or benefits in kind).[37]

Thus prior to 2001, two labour-union cultures stood openly opposed to each other in the Belgian electricity sector. The first, industry and labourer based, found itself in a defensive dynamic and remained governed by the "responsible codetermination" strategy that ensured a form of private-sector profit-sharing (with an impact on wages). The other, which bore the stamp of the service industry, maintained the more classic public-service approach conceived in terms of the number of jobs available[38] and an approach framed in terms of service to society and concern with the objective of guaranteeing the quality of service delivered to customers

---

35 Thus this common labour grouping covers *CSC-Énergie*, *ACV-Énergie*, and LBC-NVK (the last representing Dutch-speaking employees) and does not include the natural French-speaking ally of the LBC-NVK, the CNE-GNC.

36 "In 1997, two of the four unions representing workers in the sector campaigned strongly for a reduction in working time to 32 hours in order to safeguard and assist in the creation of jobs. They asked for this reduction to 32 hours to be carried out over a period of six years without loss of pay and to recruit 1,700 people in open-ended contracts. They asked the company that the BEF 30.4 billion profit should be used to create more jobs" (ECOTEC 2001: 24).

37 With the evolution of employment in the sector, *CSC Electricité et Gaz* lost many of its affiliates, and even the trade federations it is affiliated with must now contemplate operating on a larger scale, that is, a merger between *CSC-Bâtiment et Industrie* and *CSC Énergie Chimie*. *CSC Bâtiment et Industrie* itself recently emerged as the end result of several mergers that had occurred with a chain effect in activity sectors such as quarrying, glass, and cement. On the other hand, the outsourcing trend in the economy of the 1980s fostered an increase in the number of affiliates of the CNE, which is now the most powerful federation in its confederation.

38 "A collective agreement was signed between the sector and the two minority unions in May, which provided for the recruitment of 1,000 workers with open-ended contracts and 3,000 temporary workers to make up for 2,500 workers leaving the company through natural wastage over a period of 6 years. The two majority unions eventually also signed the collective agreement on 28 January 1998. On this date the management also promised 'to examine positively' the reduction of working time to 35 hours a week over the course of 1999–2002 under certain conditions, including the preclusion of wage increases,

(and therefore with the quality/price ratio). Thus two possible paths existed and an impasse arose between two opposing visions of the kind of collaboration that should be sought with other actors in the electricity sector: whether to preserve benefits that had increasingly become the prerogative of a minority, or re-situate action in line with the new rules of the game, that is, learn a new role. This impasse, which had already developed before the sector's liberalization, continued to influence labour's strategies in the context of that process.

(3) Evolution in collective bargaining from 2001 to 2007. As for Electrabel, on 30 January 2001, management presented to the group's 35 works councils its Transform 2003 plan to "enhance its competitiveness and offer attractive working conditions" in order to prepare the electricity sector for full liberalization. These goals were summarized in a press release called *Electrabel entame un nouveau dialogue social*, or "Electrabel initiates a new collective bargaining approach". According to management, the group's priorities were three in number and were designed to address increasingly rapid liberalization:

- Restructuring of activities around the four basic headings of production, trading, network management, and sales.
- Research and development for skills to match the market's new challenges.
- Enhancement of the organization's competitiveness through effective and targeted mobilization of all partners involved.

In connection with the requirement for new skills, the press release clearly stated that "certain positions that were useful in a regulated marketplace lose their usefulness in a liberalized marketplace. Conversely, new positions must be created which require new skills (trading, e-commerce, and so on)". Thus 1,700 positions that "were no longer useful in the performance of the four basic activities" were to disappear from the organization's chart in 2003.[39]

This announcement of fresh job losses occurred in a climate that was still favourable to the social-welfare-based negotiation of career termination. It is important to note that in 2000, the average age of Electrabel workers was 45. Thus there was leeway for scaling down the workforce by using such social-welfare-

agreements on increased flexibility, etc. During the discussions on the collective agreement of 1999–2000, these conditions were not accepted by the unions" (ECOTEC 2001: 24).

39 Source: http://www.eurofound.europa.eu/eiro/2001/03/word/be0103343ffr.doc. This estimate was based on the following figures: a workforce of 15,235 as of 1 January 2001, the hiring of 350 new workers to do the new jobs (in compliance with existing collective agreements), retirements, deaths, and voluntary departures, placement measures for finding an employee another position within the same company (including provision for training activities). There remained 800 people whom "it would not be possible to re-direct or reassign within the company". Management announced that a socially acceptable "co-ordinated solution" would be found for these people outside Electrabel.

based mechanisms as early retirement[40] and voluntary departure. It thus appeared that collective bargaining was being channelled in a pre-determined direction associated with job retention and security.[41] This plan was very badly received by workers and their unions, especially the two organizations that now undertook to develop union strategies intended to take account of new imperatives associated with the obligations regarding services of general interest and requirements for universal service. The result was an impasse in collective bargaining that lasted until 2003. It was not until 2004 that a social-planning agreement (*accord de programmation sociale*) on early retirement was signed.

The first consequence of this situation was the disruption of what had been called the "pax electrica", which had enabled Electrabel to maintain the advantages of being a monopoly. In particular, in 2003, the new climate led the CREG, an institution that stood as a symbol of social peace in the sector, to challenge the production agreements reached with the *intercommunales* (public companies with mandates to more than one municipality) grouped together under the SPE.[42] These agreements had confirmed Electrabel's dominant position in the field. The second consequence was that, since GAZELCO and the CNE had stood firm in opposing the 2001 CCTs until September 2003, they received strong support during the social elections of 2004.

Between 2004 and 2007, the social-welfare situation hardly improved in this sector, essentially for two reasons. On one hand, Electrabel continued to pursue its production-sector restructuring strategy; on the other hand, new companies on the scene made sure that they circumvented employment conditions set out by the sector's CPs and worked to obtain recognition under other CPs more favourable to themselves, for instance under CP 218.[43]

In the climate of increasingly rapid liberalization of the years 2001 and 2003, it appeared that the various labour organizations had no choice but to take a

40 Departures in the form of early retirement at ages 52–54 under Transform's CCT and 57–59 under the collective social planning agreement (*CCT de programmation sociale)* for 2003–2004; then departures at age 58 based on interruption or departure with benefits for continuing education under the 2005–2006 CCT.

41 "The possibility exists of taking early retirement over the age of age 57. In addition, there are options for career breaks and reduction in working time. The latter have to be agreed 'upon' at (local) company level" (ECOTEC 2001: 25).

42 Electrabel referred to this initiative as "posturing" and wondered why the CREG had waited so long before denouncing a situation that had been created with the blessing of the public authorities (*L'Écho*, 21 November 2002). In 2003, a widely reported conflict occurred between the local public companies for distribution associated with the City of Liège and Electrabel, with the latter accusing the former of having broken the "pax electrica" of 1991.

43 CP 218 is called *Commission Paritaire Nationale Auxiliaire pour Employés* (Auxiliary National CP for Non-manual Workers). By Royal Decree of 5 January 1957, this CP has "authority over workers whose occupation is of a mainly intellectual nature and who are not covered by any specific national *commission paritaire*". It covers all businesses that are not members of a specific CP.

defensive posture *vis-à-vis* what could only be perceived as a will to deregulate the sector. The mergers that took place in this sector in 2005 (Suez-Electrabel) and 2006 (Suez-Gaz de France) only served to intensify labour organizations' sense of uncertainty about their future ability to preserve their sector's acquired rights.[44]

The Implications of a Genetic Approach and its Value Enhancement

In considering these changes in collective bargaining, the question we are asking is not how transformations in the regulatory model at work in this sector should be analysed, but rather how to analyse the various possible approaches on which participants in this collective action have been able to base, and will be able to base their redefinitions of strategies for action, in the climate of new constraints on collective action that changes in the regulatory context present them with. The hypothesis we put forward relates to the value enhancement that the genetic approach can contribute on this score.

Since the implementation in 2001 of the European directives, collective bargaining has, as was explained above, undergone pronounced change. In this context, the actors' modes of learning were not limited to existing deliberative paradigms. They also took a more experimental turn, in order to generate the capacity to deal with the new order. The splitting apart of trades in different activity sectors (production and distribution) and the weakening of the public service led unions to work out a repositioning of their strategies and representations. To grasp what is at stake, it seems to us that deployment of a pragmatist experimentalist paradigm alone—or even the deployment of a paradigm that is reflective (that is, attentive to actors' conditions for capacitation), like the one presented by D. Schön and C. Argyris—is inadequate. It is necessary rather to implement, in a more precise fashion, a genetic approach to learning, in order to determine the factors that reflexive governance of this sector should take greater advantage of.

Strategy 1. The pragmatist experimentalist analysis If we insist on an experimentalist analysis of the evolution described above, the nature of what has been learned will appear to be essentially defensive.[45] Given the successive sector-

44 The agreements signed in Belgium between the government and Suez were extensively challenged both on the national political scene and by the European Commission. The recent incorporation into SPE's resources of the British firm Centrica does not fundamentally change things. It is still a matter of assigning market shares lower than 15 per cent.

45 Here, benchmarking, co-design, and monitoring mechanisms, mentioned earlier in the context of the discussion of experimentalist pragmatism, were implemented by the actors and made it possible to improve the capacity for engagement with the deliberative mechanism, which, however, was limited to wage and status issues. These mechanisms could however, prove useful for a broader set of issues. But the question remains why a labour player should expand its strategy to include the definition of such issues by resorting systematically to this kind of mechanism.

restructuring plans (as proposed in the production sector) and the opportunism of new entrants hoping to break out of the framework of existing collective agreements (a practice called "social shopping" engaged in mainly in the distribution-company subsector), labour organizations had no choice but to adopt a job-protection and wage-maintenance strategy. Thus the two labour organizations (GAZLECO and the CNE) that stood apart in 2001 from the three that shared a codetermination culture (grouped together within FEG) ended by making wage-related issues their negotiating priority and were accordingly led, in 2004, to sign a collective social-planning agreement (*accord de programmation sociale*) that relied on organizing career termination within the sector's codetermination philosophy.[46]

In that instance, the adjustment was made in favour of a strategy perceived as *unavoidably constrained by the context*, without its interpretive frames being subjected to re-examination. This defensive adjustment was based on the idea that there was no choice but for adjustment to be implemented without reconsidering the interpretive frames supplied by the prior situation, in which what was essential was to take action aimed at the fair redistribution of the sector's profits among workers.

Strategy 2: A Schön-Argyris type reflective pragmatist analysis An analysis that takes into account capacitation for reframing in D. Schön's sense makes it possible to show that the labour actors did not act exclusively from a defensive learning perspective. The principal source of conflict, whose perceptible consequences have to do with wages, relates to another type of issue that shifts the wage issue and removes it from the codetermination paradigm for negotiating wage scales. What GAZELCO and the CNE categorically rejected was a transition to a new management mode focused on the monitoring of skills, whose consequence was the implementation of a system of bonuses linked to merit, that is, a merit-rating system, which was to be applied to employees hired after 1 January 2002. According to GAZELCO and the CNE, this new provision could have resulted in wage disparities of up to 30 per cent between old and new statuses. The new measures risked undermining social solidarity in the sector and rendering it more fragile in view of its ability to restructure so as to take on the new obligations related to services of general interest and requirements for universal service. Similarly, conflict over CPs and CCTs was not limited to the status issues associated with CP 218. GAZELCO and the CNE also denounced Electrabel's misapplication of the legal framework set by CCT N. 72 (which concerned workplace stress), because concepts unrelated to workplace well-being, such as anti-social behaviour, mobility, assessment by one's co-workers, etc., were being

46 They were also led to denounce, in particular, Electrabel's outsourcing strategy, which was designed to offload employees in some of the company's departments from CP 326—the CP specific to electricity and gas companies—to CP 218, the *Commission Paritaire Nationale Auxiliaire pour Employés.*

made subject to assessment.[47] In this instance, there was the question as well of redefining the frame of better cooperation at the sector level on quality-of-life and workplace-safety issues.

It would thus appear that the hard-line positions that formed a part of the line taken by labour between 2001 and 2007 were directed more towards the conditions for redefining the cooperative framework on the basis of the new rules of the game. These organizations also acted through CREG to support measures against price-fixing and against the sector's lack of transparency in dealing with consumers. In the same vein, labour organizations took strict positions on sustainable-development issues in the energy sector. Involvement in negotiations on how to implement obligations related to services of general interest and requirements for universal service, price controls, and energy-policy security was thus reinterpreted in the broad frame of a commitment to the sector's sustainable development.[48]

Strategy 3: A genetic analysis The limitation of these first two analytic strategies is their omission of a fundamental identity transformation underlying the collective-action process that they highlight. If the impasse between the two labour cultures has persisted, as the social elections of 2004 made clear, and if the rejection of the 2001 personnel-management guidelines is found to be as forcefully present as ever in the terms of the 2007 collective agreement, the reason is that an identity repositioning of crucial importance to the actors involved is at play, and those actors are working to incorporate it into their negotiation methods.[49] Thus in the conflicts

47 *Tribune GAZELCO* (GAZELCO newsletter), 23 February 2004.

48 According to the *Fédération syndicale européenne des services publics* (FSESP), the Commission's approach to energy-market liberalization "does not meet the needs of an energy policy that would strengthen independence and focus on sustainable development". FSESP's Secretary General Jan Willem Goudriaan stated that "grave problems such as job losses (300,000 over the last ten years), lack of qualified personnel, and the impact of competition on vulnerable users are not being addressed. Increasing the degree of competition will not make it possible to increase investment in a sector that needs a highly stable framework, rather than a policy with a yo-yo effect. Instead, they will result in price hikes and have serious repercussions for all users". As presented at http://www.euractiv.fr/print-version/dossier/liberalisation-marches-gaz-electricite, Libéralisation des marchés du gaz et de l'électricité, posted on 1 May 2007.

49 This impasse related to collective-action identity was in evidence when the *Commission Paritaire Plénière du Gaz et Electricité* (CP 326) met on 18 October 2007 (CP 326), Marc Desmet presiding. These are the voting results reported by the labour organizations:

GAZELCO: FGTB: 68 per cent against
- CNE: CSC: Over 67 per cent against
- CGSLB. against
- CSC Énergie: 55 per cent in favour

that have occurred since 2001 between unions and Electrabel's management, the unions voluntarily refrained from disrupting service continuity in the sector. That is, they took users' interests into account in framing their actions. More broadly, the positions adopted by the unions show direct references to consumers' interests, in the form of references to matters such as supply guarantees for every vendor, green electricity, the implementation of universal service, the most vulnerable customers, and so on.

These are just some of the signs of the occurrence of a more fundamental change in labour action's identity position *vis-à-vis* the new order. In the past, users' interests were clearly subordinated to those of workers in the sector. This constitutes, in fact, the heart of the impasse between the two labour cultures identified above: the place assigned to users' interests in relation to workers' sectoral and status interests. The impasse between labour organizations is itself entwined with a more fundamental impasse related to the potential for solidarity between workers' and users' interests. It is this more fundamental impasse that has resurfaced in discussions of limiting the right to strike by legislating in favour of a minimum level of service.

A new identity for action In the labour-movement logic that defends state monopolies, better quality of work should result in better service quality for the citizen-user. In the case under consideration, indeed, what was expected to result from actions meant to improve working conditions was a progressive indirect impact on general well-being. C. Offe (2003: 444) has identified this phenomenon in the position adopted by German federations of industrial unions (unions that he describes as "more readily 'other regarding' than company unions"): he argues that this position is more attentive to the consequences that their demands and strategies have on employment forecasts in general as well as on the rate of inflation and their companies' competitiveness. As he continues:

> If there is anything distinctive about the "European" model of capitalism, it is the insight, congealed in a myriad of economic institutions and regulatory arrangements, that the interest of "all of us" will be served if the pursuit of the interest of "each of us" is to some extent constrained by categorical status rights (Offe 2003: 444).

In this perspective, the fragmentation of sectors and the proliferation of regulatory regimes results in the weakening of collective actors, who had been accustomed to act on the basis of traditional mechanisms for collective bargaining (Offe 2003: 463).

Currently, labour organizations are inclined to take account of conditions for collective action using precisely the contrary logic: better regulation of services to the citizen-consumer will result in better working conditions. This mode of action completely alters the received image of collective labour action in the context of a social-capitalist system. Rather than looking for the indirect effects on overall well-being of action taken to improve working conditions, an alternative approach consists of searching for actions with direct effects on the quality of service supply in order to achieve indirect effects on working conditions. This change in strategic orientation represents a blind spot for analyses conducted in terms of the automatic adjustment of practices and the spontaneous revision of beliefs, as assumed by an experimentalist analysis.

Surmounting the impasse between labour organizations In the case of the impasse between opposing labour-movement strategies, it appeared necessary to oppose collective bargaining strategies as deployed by the codetermination option to strategies that prioritized protection of service of general interest and consumer interests. This opposition even influenced collective agreements, taking the form of a tension between merit-based wage provisions and employment provisions that protected career-termination plans.

In shifting towards a new logic for action, organizations that had been stuck in an adversarial stance[50] can now wield a collaborative logic in this sector without abandoning the key element underlying their positions, namely protection of the general interest in the form of the obligation to provide services of general interest. This enables them to adjust their position by linking their service- and employment-based logic to the logic of sustainable development adopted by the other organizations. For them, the sector's sustainable development is just one aspect of a broader commitment to society that includes sustainable development but also takes in cost control, access to green electricity, and universal service standards that can protect all citizens.

A new strategy In the past, users' interests were clearly subordinated to those of the sector's workers. The new positioning must go beyond this impasse. Clearly it's not a question of a simple logical reversal, since the terms involved are no longer the same. A different correlation subsists among different terms. Whereas the citizen-user's interests were *subordinate* to action by the traditional public-service union, what is now in question is *linking* the protection of the interests of the citizen-consumers of these services with the interests of workers in the liberalized market service sectors. Thus the challenge consists in *translating* key issues of energy policy, universal service, and free choice in the marketplace into work-organization issues that transform the labour organization into an obligatory conduit through which the decision-making process must pass.

Increased guarantees of universal service and freedom of choice under fair competition conditions and the defence of an energy policy that is consistent with sustainable-development concerns and environmental constraints: these things can only be advanced if the public interest is placed before workers' interests, even if, for example, keeping nuclear power plants in operation represents a significant component of the interests of workers in this sector. However, implementing this position (the ability-to-do of the new collective identity-making) requires forming

50 That is, those concerned that the labour strategy take account of obligations related to services of general interest and requirements for universal service.

new alliances and being able to go beyond the polarizations created by history as well as by the reforms.

As well, in our view, it is possible to discern the same trend in labour organizations' efforts to form a collective purchasing cooperative with an explicit commitment to the environment[51] and the intention to make energy prices accessible.[52] In this undertaking, labour organizations sought to work within the logic of distribution and find their place within the sector's new state of affairs.[53]

Beware of the Recurrence of the Impasse between Users and Collective Action

Taking this new strategic basis into account, it is possible to identify hot buttons that could trigger recurrences of the old impasses, not just impasses between labour organizations with opposing conceptions of their collective-action identities, but also the impasse we have called more fundamental, between workers' and users' interests. This is especially true as regards the issue of the transition out of the

51 This is the Power4You (www.power4you.be) service. On its website, one finds the following: "The objective of this undertaking is to provide electricity and gas to all under the best conditions. That is, conditions of optimum pricing, contract length, contract-extension and withdrawal terms, consumer protection, and the energy's green quality". According to the weekly *La Libre Belgique*, "Power4You is a cooperative corporation set up on the initiative of the *Centre de recherche et d'information des organisations de consommateurs* (CRIOC [Consumer Groups' Research and Information Centre]). The partners in the co-operative are some 15 organizations and associations, including unions (such as CSC, FGTB, and CGSLB), the *Ligue des familles* [the League of Families], *Vie féminine* [Women's Lives], and others. It is not necessary to be a member of any of these organizations in order to benefit from Power4You's offer. It's possible to sign on by choosing any one of these organizations at random as one's 'intermediary', without having to belong to it. The goal of Power4You is simple: to negotiate a gas or electricity energy-supply contract with an operator with a view to getting the best price. Power4You put several suppliers in competition with each other, and Lampiris won: the specifications in its bid got the best score. In just a few days, Power4You had over 170,000 hits at its Website". Available at http://www.lalibre.be/article.phtml?id=904&subid=1087&art_id=370742. See also *Le Monde*, 8 September 2007.

52 The European Trade Union Confederation had in fact, stated that, in their view, priority concerns about energy policy were the elimination of social inequality linked to unequal access to energy services and the combating of global warming resulting from intensive fossil-fuel use. ETUC believes one way to pursue these priorities is to enhance public and democratic control over energy.

53 True, potentially it thereby lands on a new fault line where a clash of interests could develop. But opting for a position linked to sustainable development could also represent an interesting opportunity for institutional learning as to how to better identify potential conflicts of interest in order to overcome them, perhaps by more radically broadening the cooperative approach that underlies the initiative and that is currently under-publicized. If this were to take place, users would be clearly identified as partners. This position could point to more appropriate conditions for regulating the sustainable development option in reforming the sector.

nuclear field, which could prompt labour to act exclusively from the perspective of job protection. It is also true of the issue of minimum service levels, which always entails the risk of placing workers' interests, in the form of the right to strike, in stark opposition to those of users, in the form of access to service.

However, other behaviours would appear to confirm there is a will to avoid reverting to impasses, given a new collective-action identity. An especially eloquent example is labour's opposition to SPE-Luminus' restructuring plan.[54] Rather than basing their arguments on job loss, labour organizations are addressing the role of the new infrastructure *vis-à-vis* access to green energy.[55] According to their stated position:

> [T]he employees of SPE-Luminus are not interested in exclusively financial logic. They wish to fully carry out the mission they are entrusted with and that they have carried out with professionalism for many decades. This mission is fully in line with the objectives of the Kyoto Protocol.[56]

In this instance, labour action is clearly aligned with the interests of users and citizens in general. Another example is provided by the actions taken to expose the risks that sub-contracting and temporary jobs pose to the sector's continuity of service and service reliability. For example, the following remarks appear in a critique of the SPE call centre's recruitment policy: "500,000 customers are surely entitled to count on a certain number of jobs of indefinite duration. This staffing structure constitutes SPE's brand image and represents the customer's first contact with the supplier, the key component of SPE's sales force!".[57]

A genetic analysis of these elements allows us to view them as more than mere strategic changes in discourse. The examples we have chosen are drawn from the labour organization's *internal* communications and not from communications intended to present the public face of collective action. This really is a case of the creating, within the organization, of a collective identity that is consistent

54 "SPE-Luminus produces green electricity with:

- hydroelectric power plants on the Meuse River;
- wind farms; and
- dual-energy units.

This production of renewable energy makes it possible to prevent the production of at least 110,000 tonnes of atmospheric CO_2 per year" (statement of 15 March 2007).

55 "This restructuring project, if it is carried out, will result in a reduction in the availability of the hydroelectric power stations and thus in a reduction by at least 20 per cent of green electricity production. This production deficit will inevitably have to be compensated by the use of thermal plants and will thus cause the production of 20,000 tonnes of thermal CO_2" (15 March 2007).

56 Source: http://www.spebel.be/oldindex.php?offset=40.

57 21 May 2007. (Source: http://www.spebel.be/oldindex.php?offset=40.)

with public-service and user-interests goals forming the condition for the labour organization's ability-to-do in its new context for action. These positions are guiding action and determining the negotiating positions adopted in the development of current collective agreements. In this context, relations with the CREG are also evolving; and in particular, questions of investment in view of future energy production are taking shape as key talking points in relation to sustainable development, as the case of SPE Luminus makes clear.

What guidelines can be derived from an approach of this kind?

The most important issue to emerge from the genetic approach as regards "ability-to-do" is the change in positioning made in consideration of an outside actor, the "citizen-consumer", and the effort made to redefine a collective identity of action in light of the role of this relationship with the outsider. The power of genetic analysis is that it allows for discerning whether and how a terceization mechanism is operating and how it is acting upon the process of identity-making. Within the labour organizations in question, this effort at identity shift and teleological shift in view of bringing users' interests on board is signalled by the incorporation, first in internal communications (in particular in the form of information campaigns that adopt the user's perspective on liberalization) and then in the internal building of collective bargaining positions, of priorities related to users' interests into the reasons for mobilizing and into the content of activist interventions. Finally, identity shift is also taking shape through public actions that build direct ties with citizens' activist platforms regarding the sector's service requirements. At this point, it becomes possible to identify a set of shared priorities that unite workers in the sector with consumers. These include, among others:

- the need for price controls and for the fair redistribution, through general rate reductions, of profits from increased productivity;
- the need for continuity of service and for a policy for equal treatment in terms of supply;
- the need for adequate and attractive access to green electricity;
- the need for regulations for an open market to be respected and for consumer access to information and consumer freedom to be guaranteed; and
- the need for measures to favour the most vulnerable consumers.

Using the genetic approach, it is possible to better define the issue at stake in this "terceization" process from the perspective both of labour organizations and of the sector's regulation as a whole. For labour organizations, the issue is not in the first instance one of entrenching a new ability-to-do, as if, for example, it were necessary for labour organizations' research departments to adopt the performance indicators of universal service and develop proposals for policy recommendations to labour leaders. Rather, the issue, as the genetic approach makes clear, is the restructuring of these organizations' collective identity, that is, their ability-to-do, in line with the learning made possible by the terceization of their social positioning. See Table 6.1 for a presentation of some

Table 6.1 Restructuring of Labour Organizations' Collective Identity

From	To
"Other-regarding unions" (C. Offe)	"Outsider-regarding unions" (genetic approach)
"Consequentialist commitment" to the general interest	"Incorporative commitment" on plural interests
"The interest of each of us is better served by the constraints of status rights"	where different interests must be translated into new collective-action identities and expressed in new forms of common positioning (going beyond previous impasses)

of the concrete issues related to the restructuring of these labour organizations' collective identity.

One aspect of this issue consists of the self-capacitation that has been produced and that must be produced in order to be able to redefine unions' collective identity-making by means of critical tests that make it possible to identify and go beyond previous strategic impasses. But a second aspect consists of the capacity for transferring this repositioning to demands that relate to the sector's regulation in conjunction with other actors.

By adopting this approach to actors' transformation, the genetic approach also reappraises the capacities for evaluation of the regulatory mechanisms themselves, that is, the way these institutional mechanisms will themselves be able to handle and manage the critical tests and transfers that are necessary to the transformation of the sector's regulation in line with the actors' repositioning as participants in a true joint inquiry. A question essential to the public governance of the sector then arises: how and under what conditions can one organize new ways of negotiating within the sector in order to incorporate the normative potential of this repositioning of collective action.[58]

In the case under examination, it is illuminating to revisit, in light of the genetic approach, the analyses of the sector put forward by the International Labour Organization in 1999 (ILO 1999: 95–97) following the first experiments in liberalization. The ILO's most important finding was its identification of the main defensive kinds of learning, namely the adaptation to new wage strategies and more specifically, in the sector of the new distribution companies, adaptation to a significant requirement for flexibility regarding working conditions. In the second place, the ILO also identified the collaborative kinds of learning that would result from the need to create a new context of cooperation between labour organizations and companies in the sector, in order to ensure workers' protection

58 In the same vein, the CSC's recent positions reflect a will to renew the discussion on the role of the CREG in relation to price regulation and better monitoring of the sector's development (Source: Info CSC, 16 November 2007).

as new areas of autonomous activity were developed, and to manage to take back the collective-bargaining initiative as part of a process in which management would have asserted its position as "principal" (as defined by the principal-agent theory in economics) *vis-à-vis* the public authorities. But it is in connection with a different aspect of collective bargaining that the ILO (1999: 97–8) noted that it will be necessary in the future to take account of a third important issue. This third important element could be constituted by the coming on the scene of a new actor, namely consumers, who are the bearers of specific normative expectations regarding obligations related to services of general interest and requirements for universal service. No explicit articulation was made of this third element with the first two, although it appeared to have the potential to alter the order of things with regard to collective bargaining and regulation of the sector.

In such a context, defensive learning and collaborative learning remain divorced from each other and closed off from a possible experiment in "terceization". Thus one can see how even collaborative learning intended to redefine the context for cooperation in the sector in terms of sustainable development and businesses' social responsibility remains disconnected from potential interaction with the interests of other actors; and indeed entails the risk, in practice, of eventually being partly opposed to other approaches framed in terms of services of general interest and universal service. Since the impasses would not have been identified, they would be capable of neutralizing efforts at repositioning and cut off actors whom it would be beneficial to include.

In fact, impasses persist within the sector's developments that labour organizations have contributed to identifying more explicitly, even though they are not connected only to labour organizations. Thus the idea of the culture of codetermination, according to which users' interests were subordinated to those of the sector's economic development, persists within the present order of things, in the form of the belief that the sector's evolution towards greater profitability and international competitiveness within a liberalized marketplace will ultimately benefit the individual consumer. In the same way, the idea that the impact of the segmentation of the sector (and the issues of labour-relations restructuring that it brings in its wake) can be separated from the public's stakes (such as green energy and reliability of supply) in these activities also constitutes a way of obstructing open discussion of businesses' social responsibility in a context of the obligation to provide services of general interest and requirements for universal service. Scattering labour's forces along this fault line amounts to a failure of normative potential prejudicial to the discovery of new solutions.

To negotiate truly and effectively new regulatory methods in this sector will require, first, that the actors affected by these impasses evolve in a context of joint inquiry suited to their continued transformation. Second, it will require that the process of transformation be equipped with an appropriate system of evaluating the surmounting of identified impasses.

What a Genetic Approach Can Contribute to Collective Learning

What can we retain from this case study? The genetic approach is not defined by opposition to the contribution made by experimentalist and pragmatist approaches of the Schön-Argyris type. Rather, it supplements them and provides them with a better constructed frame for collective actors' self-transformation. The experimentalist approach highlights a process of adaptation in response to constraint, which defines itself at the outset reactively, according to changes in the context, and is thereby led to develop *defensive* positions such as repositioning within wage negotiations (in response to merit-rating) and in relation to career-termination provisions. The Schönian approach shows that these defensive reactions are, however, accompanied by a type of re-examination of the beliefs that make them possible. It thus allows for reverting to the stimulus-response model, but in the teleological perspective of a practical goal, which consists of ensuring the reproduction of an existing ability-to-do in a new social setting. In this analysis, what predominates is the incorporation of new beliefs about the capacity for collective action, such as the sector's sustainable development. The genetic approach supplements the Schönian model by showing that this projection of a new collective identity-making assumes something other than the identification of a rule of reproduction. It assumes a task of identity reconstruction focused in the first instance on a critical examination of the past and, by this means, the identification of impasses that have imperilled the success of actions already undertaken. Thus the collective-identity-making capacity is re-examined and progressively rebuilt, so that new positionings, such as the requirement for better pricing regulations, better employment policies to ensure the accessibility and reliability of green energy, better guarantees of universal service, and so on, can be made possible. Thus it is how the repositioning is guided that will ultimately determine the interpretive frame—the "operators for translation"[59]—to assign to the new power relations, rather than the reverse. The issue consists of allying interests rather than subordinating them to each other. See Table 6.2 for a comparative presentation of the three main approaches to learning that labour unions can adopt in the case study of the electricity sector.

The genetic approach thus makes it possible to reveal the actors' critical operations with respect to the impasses of the past and the operations of "translation" required to overcome them and arrive at a new positioning. This paradigm of self-capacitation is thus directly predicated on the identification of impasses that undermined similar strategies in the past, as in the case of missed opportunities for alliances between public-service workers and those services' users. The value of taking a self-capacitation perspective is that it makes one attentive to initiatives taken to recreate the ties between the actors involved. For example, in the case under examination, what would be needed are translation operations

59 That is, the identification of the new practical issues around which to negotiate the new cooperative relations between participants in the collective action.

Table 6.2 Approaches to Learning and Labour Organizations' Positioning in the Case Study of the Electricity Sector

	Central operation	Anticipated impact	Labour-movement analysis in the electricity sector
Experimentalism	Pragmatization	New collective capacities	New strategic orientations: Defensive behaviour in response to "social shopping" and merit-rated wages
Reflexive learning	Reframing	New roles	Renewing cooperative mechanisms by redesigning representations of social issues such as corporate social responsibility and sustainable development of the sector
Genetic approach	Terceization	New identities of collective action	Transforming the nature of unions' civil society leadership regarding issues such as the obligation to provide public services and standards of universal service

to link users' interests to the negotiation process and thus seek to redefine the operating framework for the negotiations. In this way, a concrete mechanism for the terceization of positioning is identified as a condition for learning.

To produce this repositioning, labour organizations are resorting to critical operations that concern not just their future role but also their past role. The determination of new possibilities opened up by the new context emerges not only from the simple analysis of this changed context. It emerges as well from the attention granted to the limitations of a prior role and the impasses that result from the collective identity creation associated with it. Such "attention" leads to expanded representations of the new context. The diversity and multiplicity of possibilities may be said to gain in "expansiveness".

In tandem, the new positioning attained through this attention to the blockages/impasses associated with the "collective identity creation" previously adopted by participants in the collective action guides how the means to be deployed (the "ability-to-do") to effect the surmounting of these blockages and the implementation of the entailments harboured by this repositioning. As regards the implementation of the new ability-to-do, the regulatory mechanism aimed at by the collective actor's repositioning will remain incomplete unless it is equipped with an evaluation system designed to ensure that the operations performed do, in fact, allow for the desired repositioning through collective identity creation. See Table 6.3 for a comparative presentation of the specificities of the regulatory mechanisms related to the three main approaches to learning that labour unions can adopt in the case study of the electricity sector.

Table 6.3 Regulatory Mechanisms in the Case Study of the Electricity Sector

	Operation	Impact	Labour movement	Criteria for attention
Experimentalism	Pragmatization	Capacities	New defensive strategies	Quality of arrangements for learning
Reflexive learning	Reframing	Roles	New cooperative mechanism	Quality of participatory commitment
Genetic approach	Terceization	Identities	New type of civil society leadership	Quality of operators for translation of identity

The genetic approach seeks to accumulate the benefits of existing reflexive approaches to social learning while situating these benefits within a process of collective action likely to have an impact on the identity conditions (critical tests) and normative conditions (translations) for the self-transformation of that process. Thus the defensive and collaborative learning that has taken place in the situation in question are taken into account, but resituated within a more fundamental process of self-capacitation associated with the actors' transformation. What has been learned can thus be linked to the terceization mechanism that the redefinition of identity positioning entails and can explicitly confront the impasses that identity repositioning works to surmount, as a condition for the possibility of a new ability-to-do.

In comparison with the genetic approach, the major weakness of the pragmatist approaches is that they do not take into account the introduction into new contexts of interaction of behaviours already incorporated into identities of action. It is as if the mere fact of submitting to the rule of the shift towards a new *ability-to-do* sufficed to guarantee that identities of action should evolve in such a way as to warrant against any recurrence of defensive and regressive behaviours. The adoption of this perspective incurs a twofold danger. On one hand, no identification is made of the past risks linked to previous behaviours; and on the other hand, these behaviours are not subjected to questioning and no future-oriented work is done on them to prevent their possible recurrence. In such a perspective, attention paid to ability-to-do could actually thwart the identification of risks of recurrence and also foster regressive behaviours triggered by resistances.

Thus it appears that, beyond the summoning forth of a degree of ability-to-do in the groups of actors involved, the significance of the learning process necessarily resides in the possibility of transforming the groups' manner of identity-making, that is, transforming their identity relationship with the resistances that mobilized them and defined their relations with their normative expectations. It is a question, then, of recognizing the necessity for a specific kind of translation operation that would act on collective capacities and that would make it possible to articulate, in the process of action, the potential for a return along the trajectories of action already described, along with the needed projection of new positionings. Such an operation would aim at ensuring the true self-transformation of identities of action within the democratic arena and of the conditions for access to new role production, both of which factors are integral to the process of the social generation of the collective interest.

This operation consists of constructing a relationship with externality by a kind of "terceization" necessary for identifying and transforming resistances. Only such structures of reflexive frameworks for collective action would allow for accumulating and sharing the intelligence produced by the restructuring of political identities during the search for solutions undertaken by groups of actors. In dealing with their own vulnerability, governance processes lack the reflexive operators for translation that would allow them to expand the range of their possibilities to include a structuring that pays more attention to the collective-identity-making capacity of the actors involved.

Conclusion

The thesis we have sought to defend in this book is that current approaches to democracy have remained dependent on a conception of collective action that is deficient in the way it addresses two issues: the construction of the legitimacy of public authority and the mobilization of the actors concerned by the application of norms. This inadequate way of conceiving collective action has led to two blockages in current theories of democracy, including the most recent instances of the reformulation of these theories. The aim of this book has been to analyse these blockages in current political thought and to surmount and go beyond them.

In characterizing the first blockage, we have written of a persisting "representative belief" found in applied theories of democracy. This belief consists of the ascription of a self-sufficient nature to reference to the public authorities. To surmount this blockage, we showed in Part I that the positivist definition of the concept of law solely through reference to the practice of the public authorities is problematic and theoretically incomplete. This definition does not allow for an account of the set of conditions for possibility required as the foundation for the operation by which members of a social group adopt obligatory rules. In our view, *the normativity of a norm does not depend only on its conformity with some standard for recognition derived from a cooperative practice engaged in by the public authorities in charge of applying it. It also depends on its recognition, its practical acceptance, by its citizen addressees.* The "end purpose" for which a norm is intended depends, in its elaboration, on attention to the kinds of cooperative action by which its addressees—both officials and citizens—will be able to cooperatively construct their normative expectations, thereby participating in the shared construction of the norm.

The second blockage relates precisely to this issue of a more cooperative form of participation by citizen addressees in the procedures for producing norms. Addressing this blockage thus requires engaging with the current renewed work on the issue of "governance" being conducted in social science research. As it emerges from our reconstruction of the current debate on governance in the social sciences, the departure point for present-day research on the issue is a shared perception (that is, shared across disciplines and trends) of the weaknesses of forms of governance that are linked to a conception of law centred on a self-sufficient referral of the production of norms solely to the practices of the public authorities. This perception is the basis for the critique of what is too often given the (insufficiently conceptualized and developed) designation of "command-and-control" regulation. From this critique has flowed the search for more "decentralized" kinds of regulation and the questioning of the conditions for the desired "participation" by a normative intervention's addressees in the modes of the norm's production.

As we showed in Part II, it is the learning operation that is at the heart of this effort to improve the mechanisms designed to ensure the governance system's capacity for maximizing, to the extent possible, its addressees' normative expectations. In contrast to the externalist approach favoured by neo-institutionalist and evolutionary economists, the desired transformation of behaviours/representations is considered by adherents of the pragmatist turn to result from the very way the learning operation is organized at the level of the decentralized interaction. Of course, however, the form taken by the effort to internalize the conception of the learning operation varies depending on whether one adopts a deliberative or a pragmatist approach, or indeed a genetic approach of the kind we recommend. Further, as we pointed out, the various approaches that have emerged from the pragmatist turn can be ranked according to their capacity to define the operations necessary to fulfil and heighten the impact of the "internal constraints for organization" that it is desired thenceforth to impose on the decentralized interaction. This internalizing effort has, in fact, been taken progressively further, working its way from deliberative through "pragmatist" approaches to governance. The pragmatist approaches have been framed in two successive versions: a Deweyan version that is referred to as "experimentalist" (the democratic experimentalism advocated by C. Sabel and some others) and a version we have called "reflexive pragmatism", which is advanced mainly by D. Schön and C. Argyris. Despite the advance represented by both the view that the communicative competencies of actors in a collective action must be shaped deliberatively and the idea that interactions must be organized in an experimentalist manner, such that the actors will "allow themselves" to be taught by the process of the joint inquiry for solutions, the fundamental question of the transformation of the actors themselves during this learning process has not been adequately taken into account and elucidated. The error of the *experimentalist* approach as regards "internalizing the conditions for success of the learning operation" consists of not taking cognizance of the "obstacles" that may hamper the success of the operation if it is assumed that the "spontaneous capacities" of the actors suffice on their own to bring about the success of this "joint experiment". As is demonstrated by the furthered analysis carried out by D. Schön and C. Argyris, attention must be paid to the "defensive strategies" that the actors are at risk of deploying unwittingly and that would lead the actors to restrict the scope of their "representations" about what the maximization of the fulfilment of participants' normative expectations would require. Nevertheless, D. Schön and C. Argyris' proposals do not go beyond intervention mechanisms which, although designed to bring about reflective attention to the need for cooperatively surmounting defensive strategies, to some extent operate from the outside while presupposing a pre-existing rule that can be deployed in the actors' minds and that would guarantee the desired transformation in behaviour.

It is to compensate for this "pragmatic weakness" that our genetic approach proposes expanding the conditions for success of the learning operation by organizing a specific "operation" designed to lead actors to collectively build their representation of the new identity called for by change in their context for action. Since this operation of adapting their identity representation does not take place automatically, it must be organized! And it is precisely this adaptation of our identity representation (collective identity creation) that determines our grasp of the objectives for action that we set for ourselves and consequently the choice of methods for their fulfilment (ability-to-do).

As we have shown, the principal question left in suspense with respect to the evolution of modes of participation in public life is that of the possible resurgence of impasses in social interaction that derive from past experience. The concern of pragmatism is to orient the participatory process towards the "ability-to-do" of the actors involved in a process of solving shared problems. But this teleological concern does not sufficiently take into account the risk of repeating past behaviours in the context of new situations. As we have shown, only the genetic approach manages to highlight and explore the role played in learning processes by the taking account of identity transformations. This approach aims to determine how actors can transform their own involvement in learning processes into experimentation with the limits of their own learning processes.

The key to such a transformation of the relation to learning resides in an "operation of translation" that allows for identifying behaviours that are the sources of blockages of possible solutions and then producing one's own rules for learning (learning to learn or choosing how to choose); that is, *acquiring new capabilities for using the learning processes themselves.* The stakes associated with this translation operation are twofold: on one hand, identifying the internal limitations of the cooperative framework being tried out, from the perspective of the difficulties in transforming the blockages engendered by the positionings at play; and on the other hand, pinpointing the difficulties with reconstructing one's own positionings, to the extent that they themselves were involved in the blockages identified. An operation of this kind can only be implemented as such by the actors to the extent that the learning processes the actors are faced with are conceived in a way that allows the actors to build a relation to the external through a kind of terceization—supported by a "genetic practice" for intervention—that enables them to better identify and transform the resistances inherent in their relational matrix.

Thus the genetic approach invites us to radically question the forms of social intervention associated with learning processes. It suggests a change of practice in the way of incorporating the requirements for the actors' identity transformations.

This change must be of such a kind that, not only will the learning mechanisms inherent in applying the norms result in more capacities for choice, positioning, and influence in the actors involved, but at the same time the actors will be able to adapt their identities of action to the new relationships opened up by these possibilities.

Only a "genetic practice" of social intervention would be capable of guaranteeing such a change, because, in relying on the necessary recomposition of the identities of action in the search for solutions between groups of actors involved, it allows for the accumulation and sharing of the intelligence produced by the processes of social experimentation. Given the vulnerability of actors' identities, current governance processes based on social learning still fail precisely to identify (as the genetic approach proposes to do) the operators for translation that would enable groups of actors to reconstruct, within the very learning experience, the kinds of relations with the external that elicit forms of terceization of intergroup relations and thus break through the biases produced by defence mechanisms and mirror relationships. It would thus be possible, based on the genetic approach, to envisage a new conception of the generalizability of social subjects and of the role that could be played by the transformation of their relational matrix in a context of genetic intervention that has been rethought in the light of what is specific to the given collective action.

At the level of political philosophy, a research perspective taking this approach would surely result in re-evaluating the role of intergroup identity constructions that have resulted in the compartmentalization of the "public" and "civil society" such that they could become groups capable of renegotiating their roles and positionings in the social whole. Increased attention to the resources of psychoanalytic intervention processes should make it possible to further the terceization operation by specifying its conditions for implementation within a relational frame that would foster recourse to the external in order to transform identities of action.

This would represent a way to re-start the inquiry, in political philosophy and theory of the subject, about the conditions specific to that "action on others' action" that M. Foucault (1982) considered to be co-extensive with all social relations and to lead to always partial forms of reflexivity open to strategic instrumentation. The operation of terceization also makes it possible to question what is not thought about in new participatory ideologies, going beyond reliance on the aggregate impact of interactions between levels of power or between actors previously kept separate and in hierarchical relation to each other (like hybrid forums). In fact, the operation of terceization approaches the possibilities opened up by action on others' action as a *necessary* mechanism in identity transformation, while requiring going further than the mere placement face-to-face, mirror-style, of the actors caught up in the potentially repressive play of action on others' action.

Thus today, unlike what was thought in the 1970s (Foucault 1994), it no longer makes sense in political philosophy to begin from the hypothesis that we have made the transition from a society based on law to a society based on regulation, that is, from an order based on centralized laws, but nevertheless potentially revolutionary, to an order based on diffuse norms, but nevertheless potentially repressive—indeed reifying. Instead, the issue is the capacity to think through the consequences for political subject formation of the evolution in modes of the legal monitoring of practices, and in particular an increase in the reflexivity of these modes. It is not a "disciplinary society" that has arisen through governance practices but rather a neoliberal society that has adopted ever more refined frames for self-experimentation and that relies on social learning to optimize this approach.

The problem is that the adjustment of these governance practices in terms of their capacity for the defining and production in common of a new possible world was insufficiently reflected upon. Thus the capacity of this new form of social organization to take over the structures of the welfare state is still in shortfall today. True, inquiry into governance has done a good job of exposing the illusions and weaknesses in the thinking of neo-classical economists, who believed that the operation of adjusting and constructing the objectives of a collective action could be theorized in terms of natural selection. Nevertheless, as has been shown, the theory of learning that has since been developed in order to adequately theorize this operation of the decentralized construction of the collective too often rests on a black box. It is true that more and more emphasis is being placed on the necessary increase in structures designed to enhance the "reflexivity" of kinds of action on others' action, which is at the heart of any decentralized process of collective action. But the blind spot in this new operating frame, for which urgent action is needed, is the necessary transformation of the identities of action of the subjects involved, precisely at the level of the learning structures' practical teleology. And this blind spot accounts for the recurring inability of neoliberal projects to provide for the capacity of a system of collective action to satisfy the requirement for constructing a possible shared world, that is, a world that satisfies, to the extent possible, the normative expectations of its participants. What is needed here, in analysing the action of norms today, is not a focus on repression and suppression; but rather a focus on the power of a relation with the external in the processes of terceization and self-transformation undertaken by social subjects in order to emerge from reification. Social intervention mechanisms must accordingly be developed in this perspective; and their priority aim must be to shift collective actors' attention to learning mechanisms that make possible the true transformation of their collective identity creation into a kind of obligatory conduit through which the process of search for a solution must pass.

Social intervention, then, should manage to transfer to actors a critical capability with respect to the risks of repetition and blockage inherent in the mere multiplication and intensification of participatory processes. In intervention of a genetic kind, the primary issue is to shift the actor towards self-enabling positioning by introducing a requirement for the transformation of her or his positioning according to the external on which it depends. In this perspective, the theoretical critique that has been developed all through this book cannot be dissociated from a practical requirement for reflection on the conditions for social intervention and the ways of evaluating intervention. A reflection of this kind must be understood as constituting the implementation of the critique itself in the practice of intervention, in the form of know-how about how to engage in collective construction with the actors as they analyse their own positionings.

List of References

Alchian, A. 1950. Uncertainty, evolution and economic theory. *Journal of Political Economy*, 58, 213.

Arcq, E. and Aussems, M. 2002. Implantation syndicale et taux de syndicalisation (1992–2000), *Courrier Hebdomadaire*, n. 1781, Brussels: CRISP (Centre de recherche et d'information socio-politiques).

Argyris, C. and Schön, D.A. 1996. *Organizational Learning II*. Reading, MA: Addison Wesley Publishing Co., reprinted with corrections, 1996.

Arthur, W.B. 1994. *Increasing Returns and Path Dependence in the Economy*. Ann Arbor: Michigan University Press.

Baldwin, R. 1997. Regulation after command-and-control. *The Human Face of Law*, edited by K. Hawkins. Oxford: Oxford University Press.

Bentley, T. 2005. *Everyday Democracy*. London: Demos.

Bix, B. 1993. *Law, Language and Legal Determinacy*. Oxford: Clarendon.

Black, J. 2000. Proceduralising regulation, part I. *Oxford Journal of Legal Studies*, 20, 597–ff.

——2001a. Proceduralising regulation, part II. *Oxford Journal of Legal Studies*, 21, 33–ff.

——2001b. Decentring regulation: Understanding the role of regulation and self-regulation in a "post-regulatory" world. *Current Legal Problems*, 54, 103–ff.

——2002. Critical reflections on regulation. *Australian Journal of Legal Philosophy*, 27, 25.

Bobbio, N. 1961. Sur le positivisme. *Mélanges Paul Roubier*. Paris: Dalloz. vol, I, 53 73, 61–62, 67–68.

Braithwaite, J. and Ayres, I. 1992. *Responsive Regulation: Transcending the Deregulation Debate*. New York/Oxford: Oxford University Press.

Bratman, M.E. 1992. Shared cooperative activity. *Philosophical Review*, 327–41.

——1993. Shared intention. *Ethics*, October, 107.

Brousseau, E. 1999. Néo-institutionnalisme et évolutionnisme: Quelles convergences? *Economies et Sociétés*, HS 35, 1/1999, 189–215.

——2000a. Processus évolutionnaires et institutions: Quelles alternatives à la rationalité parfaite? *Revue Economique*, 51 (5) (September), 1185–213.

——2000b. La gouvernance des processus de coopération. *La Coopération Industrielle*, edited by C. Voisin, A. Plunck and B. Bellon. Paris: Economica, 29–43.

——2001a. Régulation de l'Internet: L'auto-régulation nécessite-t-elle un cadre institutionnel? *Revue Economique*, 52, hors série: *L'Economie de l'Internet*, 349–77.

——2001b. Processus évolutionnaires et institutions: Quelles alternatives à la rationalité parfaite? *Revue Economique*, 52, hors série: *L'Economie de l'Internet*, 1206–7.
——2002. L'auto-régulation des réseaux numériques: Quelques réflexions d'économiste. *Les Cahiers du Centre de Recherches Informatique et Droit*, 22, 127–32.
Brousseau, E. and Curien, N. 2001. Economie de l'Internet, économie du numérique. *Revue Economique*, 52, hors série: *L'Economie de l'Internet*, 7–36.
Brousseau, E. and Rallet, A. 1998. Une nouvelle pratique de l'interdisciplinarité? Quelques réflexions à partir d' "innovations et performances". *Revue Economique*, 49, 1601–11.
Brousseau, E. and Raynaud, E. 2005. *The Economics of Private Institutions*. Working paper on file with the authors.
Burris, S., Drahos, P. and Shearing, C. 2005. Nodal governance. *Australian Journal of Legal Philosophy*, 30, 30–ff.
Cafaggi, F. 2005. Organizational loyalties and models of firms: Governance design and standard of duties. *Theoretical Inquiries in Law*, 6 (2) Article 7. Available at http://www.bepress.com/til/default/vol6/iss2/art7.
Campbell, D. 2001. Ian Macneil and the relational theory of contract. *The Relational Theory of Contract*, edited by D. Campbell. London: Sweet and Maxwell, 3–58.
Carvalho, F. and Deakin, S. 2010 (forthcoming). System and evolution in corporate governance. *Law, Economics and Evolutionary Theory*, edited by Peer Zumbansen and Pieter Callies. Cheltenham: Edward Elgar.
Cefaï, D. 2007. *Pourquoi se mobilise-t-on? Les théories de l'action collective.* Paris: La Découverte/MAUSS.
Chayes, A. 1976. The role of the judge in public law litigation. *Harvard Law Review*, 89, 1281–316.
Cohen, J. 1989. Deliberation and democratic legitimacy. *The Good Polity*, edited by A. Hamlin and P. Petit. Oxford: Blackwell, 17–34. Reprinted in *Contemporary Political Philosophy: An Anthology*, edited by R. Goodin and P. Petit (2nd edition). Oxford: Blackwell, 159–70.
Cohen, J. and Sabel, C.F. 1997. Directly-deliberative polyarchy. *European Law Journal*, 3 (4), 313–342.
Coleman, J. 1995. Truth and objectivity in law. *Legal Theory*, 1, 33–68.
——2001a. Incorporationism, conventionality and the practical difference thesis. *Hart's Postscript: Essays on the Postscript to the Concept of Law*, edited by J. Coleman. Oxford: Oxford University Press, 99–147.
——2001b. *The Practice of Principle: In Defence of a Pragmatist Approach to Legal Theory.* Oxford: Oxford University Press.
Cooter, R. 1994. Structural adjudication and the new law merchant: A model of decentralized law. *International Review of Law and Economics*, 14, 215–31.

——1996a. Decentralized law for a complex economy: The structural approach to adjudicating the new law merchant. *University of Pennsylvania Law Review*, 144, 1643–57.

——1996b. The theory of market modernization. *International Review of Law and Economics*, 16, 141–72.

——1997. Normative failure theory of law. *Cornell Law Review*, 82, 947–79.

Coppens, P. 2000. *Normes et fonction de juger.* Brussels: Bruylant.

Cunningham, N. and Grabovsky, P. 1998. *Smart Regulation: Designing Environmental Policy*. Oxford: Oxford University Press.

Deakin, S. 2007. *Reflexive Governance and European Company Law*, CLPE Research Paper 20/2007, Special Issue: EU Governance 3, 4, 26–27. Available at http://ssrn.com/abstractid=1002678.

Deakin, S. and Michie, J. 1997. *Contracts, Cooperation and Competition: Studies in Economics, Management and Law*. Oxford: Oxford University Press.

Declercq, C. and Vincent, A. 2000. L'ouverture du marché de l'électricité, I. Le cadre institutionnel. *Courrier Hebdomadaire*, n. 1684. Brussels: CRISP (Centre de recherche et d'information socio-politiques).

Dewey, J. 1982. Reconstruction in philosophy. *The Middle Works, 1899–1924*, vol. 12, 1920, edited by J.A. Boydston. Carbondale: Southern Illinois University Press.

——1986a. The public and its problems. *The Later Works, 1925–1953*, 2, 1925–1927, edited by J.A. Boydston. Carbondale: Southern Illinois University Press.

——1986b. Logic: The theory of inquiry. *The Later Works, 1925–1953*, 12, 1938, edited by J.A. Boydston. Carbondale: Southern Illinois University Press.

Dorf, M. 2000. Legal indeterminacy and institutional design. *NYU Law Review*, 78, 875–ff.

Dorf, M. and Sabel, C. 1998. A constitution of democratic experimentalism. *Harvard Law Review*, 98, 284–ff.

——2000. Drug treatment courts and emergent experimentalist government. *Vanderbilt Law Review*, 53, 831–ff.

Dworkin, R. 1977. *Taking Rights Seriously.* London: Duckworth.

——1986. *Law's Empire.* Oxford: Oxford University Press.

ECOTEC. 2001. *The Effects of the Liberalisation of the Electricity and Gas Sectors on Employment*, A Final Report to the European Commission, ECOTEC Research and Consulting Limited, Birmingham.

Elhauge, E. 1991. Does interest group theory justify more intrusive judicial review? *Yale Law Journal*, 101, 31–ff.

Endicott, T. 2000. *Vagueness in Law*. Oxford: Oxford University Press.

Farber, D. 1994. Environmental protection as a learning experience. *Loyola of Los Angeles Law Review*, 27, 791–ff.

——1999. *Eco-Pragmatism*. Chicago: University of Chicago Press.

Festenstein, M. 1997. *Pragmatism and Political Theory: From Dewey to Rorty.* Cambridge: University of Chicago Press/Polity Press.

Fiss, O. 1978. *The Civil Rights Injunction.* Bloomington: Indiana University Press.

——1979. The forms of justice. *Harvard Law Review*, 93, 130.

——1983. The bureaucratisation of the judiciary. *Yale Law Journal*, 92, 1442–68.

Foray, D. and Zimmerman, J.B. 2001. L'économie du logiciel libre, Organisation coopérative et incitation à l'innovation. *Revue Economique*, 52, HS, 77–93.

Forester, J. 1989. *Planning in the Face of Power.* Berkeley/Los Angeles: University of California Press.

——1993. Learning from practice stories: The priority of practical judgment. *The Argumentative Turn in Policy Analysis*, edited by F. Fischer and J. Forester. Durham, NC: Duke University Press, 186–209.

——1999. *The Deliberative Practitioner.* Cambridge, MA: MIT Press.

Foucault, M. 1982. The subject and power. *Michel Foucault, Beyond Structuralism and Hermeneutics*, edited by H. Dreyfus and P. Rabinow. Chicago: University of Chicago Press, 208–26.

——1994. Les mailles du pouvoir. *Dits et écrits (1954–1988)*, vol. IV 1980–1988. Paris: Gallimard, 198–9.

Freeman, J. 1997. Collaborative governance in the administrative state. *UCLA Law Review*, 45, 1–99.

——2000a. The contracting state. *Florida State University Law Review*, 28, 155–214.

——2000b. The private role in public governance. *NYU Law Review*, 75, 543–675.

——2003. Extending public law norms through privatization. *Harvard Law Review*, 116, 1285–ff.

Friedman, M. 1953. The methodology of positive economics. *Essays in Positive Economics.* Chicago: University of Chicago Press.

Froomkin, M. 2002. ICANN's "Uniform dispute resolution policy"—Causes and (partial) cures. *Brooklyn Law Review*, 67, 605–718.

——2003a. Habermas@discourse.net: Toward a critical theory of cyberspace. *Harvard Law Review*, 116, 751–871.

——2003b. ICANN 2.0: Meet the new boss. *Loyola of Los Angeles Law Review*, 36, 1087–101.

Fung, A. 2001. Accountable autonomy: Toward empowered deliberation in Chicago schools and policing. *Politics and Society*, 29, 73–ff.

Fung, A. 2003. Deliberative democracy and international labor standards. *Governance: An International Journal of Policy, Administration and Institutions*, 16, 51–ff.

Fung, A., O'Rourke, D. and Sabel, C. 2001. Realizing labor standards. *Can We Put an End to Sweatshops?*, edited by J. Cohen and J. Rogers (for Boston Review). Boston: Beacon Press, 3–40.

Fung, A. and Wright, E. 2003. *Deepening Democracy: Institutional Innovations in Empowered Participatory Governance.* London: Verso.

Garrett, B. and Liebman, J. 2004. Experimentalist equal protection. *Yale L. & Policy Rev.* 22, 261–ff.

Grabovsky, P. 1995. Using non-governmental resources to foster regulatory compliance. *Governance: An International Journal of Policy and Administration*, 8 (4), October 1995, 529.

Green, L. 2003. Legal positivism. *The Stanford Encyclopedia of Philosophy*, Spring 2003, edited by Edward N. Zalta. Available at http://plato.stanford.edu/archives/spr2003/entries/legal-positivism/.

Guerrien, B. 2002. *La Théorie des Jeux*, 3rd edition. Paris: Economica, 54.

Habermas, J. 1993. *Justification and Application: Remarks on Discourse Ethics*. Cambridge, MA: MIT Press. Translation of the original text by C.P. Cronin, *Erläuterungen zur Diskursethi*, 1991. Frankfurt am Main: Suhrkamp Verlag.

——1996. *Between Facts and Norms: Contributions to a Discourse, Theory of Law and Democracy.* Cambridge, MA: MIT Press. Translation of the original text by W. Rehg, *Faktizität und Geltung: Beiträge zur Diskurstheorie des Rechts und des demokratischen Rechtstaats*, 1992. Frankfurt am Main: Suhrkamp Verlag.

——2000. From Kant to Hegel: On Robert Brandom's pragmatic philosophy of language. *European Journal of Philosophy*, 8 (3), 322–55.

Hajer, M. and Wagenaar, H. 2003. Introduction. *Deliberative Policy Analysis: Understanding Governance in the Network Society*, edited by M. Hajer and H. Wagenaar. Cambridge: Cambridge University Press, 2.

Hart, H. 1983. Kelsen visited. *Essays in Jurisprudence and Philosophy*, Oxford: Clarendon, 286–308.

——1994. *The Concept of Law.* Oxford: Oxford University Press (2nd edition).

Hart, H.M. and Sacks, A.M. 1994. *The Legal Process: Basic Problems in the Making and Application of Law.* Westbury: Foundation Press.

Helper, S., MacDuffie, J. and Sabel, C. 2000. Pragmatic collaborations: Advancing knowledge by controlling opportunism. *Industrial and Corporate Change*, 9 (3), 443–83.

Héritier, A. 1998. After liberalization: Public interest services in the utilities. *Preprints aus der Max-Planck-Projektgruppe, Recht der Gemeinschaftsgüter.* Bonn, n. 5. Available at http://www.mpp-rdg.mpg.de/publik1.html.

ICANN. 2002. *ICANN: A Blueprint for Reform.* Available at http://www.icann.org/committees/evol-reform/blueprint-20jun02.htm. Internet Corporation for Assigned Names and Numbers. California (ICANN).

ILO. 1999. Sectoral activities programme. *Managing the Privatization and Restructuring of Public Utilities (Water, Gas and Electricity): Report for Discussion at the Tripartite Meeting on Managing the Privatization and Restructuring of Public Utilities.* Geneva: International Labour Organization (ILO). Available at http://www.ilo.org/public/english/dialogue/sector/techmeet/tmpu99/tmpure1.htm.

Innes, J. and Booher, D. 2003. Collaborative policymaking: Governance through dialogue. *Deliberative Policy Analysis: Understanding Governance in the*

Network Society, edited by M. Hajer and H. Wagenaar. Cambridge, UK: Cambridge University Press, 33–59.

Karkkainen, B. 2000. After backyard environmentalism. *American Behavioral Scientist*, 44, 690–ff.

——2003. Adaptive ecosystem management and regulatory penalty defaults: Toward a bounded pragmatism. *Minnesota Law Review*, 87, 943–ff.

Kelsen, H. 1960. *Reine Rechtslehre*, 2nd edition. Wien: Verlag Franz Deuticke.

Klein, A. 2002. ICANN et la gouvernance d'Internet: La coordination technique comme levier d'une politique publique mondiale. *Les Cahiers du Numérique*, 3 (2), 93–128, 122–3.

Knight, J. and North, D. 1997. Explaining economic change. *Legal Theory*, 3, 211–26.

Kooiman, J. 1993. *Modern Governance: New Government-Society Interactions*. London: Sage.

Leiter, B. 1995. Legal indeterminacy. *Legal Theory*, 1, 481–92.

——2001. Legal realism and legal positivism reconsidered. *Ethics*, 111, 278–301.

Lenoble, J. 1994. *Droit et Communication*. Paris: Editions du Cerf.

——2006. Teoria della norma e teoria della governance nella filosofia del diritto: al di là dell' attuale dibattito tra ermeneutica e pramatismo. *Scientia e Normatività*, profili etici, giuridici e politico-sociali, Atti XXIV Congresso Nazionale della Società Italiana di Filosofia del Diritto, edited by A. Andronico and B. Montanari. Napoli: Scriptaweb, 95–144.

——2007. Beyond the judge: From hermeneutic and pragmatist approaches to a genetic approach to the concept of law. *European Journal of Legal Studies*, 1 (2). Available at www.ejls.eu.

Lenoble, J. and Maesschalck, M. 2003. *Toward a Theory of Governance: The Action of Norms*. London: Kluwer.

Lewis, D. 1969. *Convention*. Cambridge, MA: Harvard University Press.

Liebman, J. and Sabel, C. 2003. A public laboratory Dewey barely imagined: The emerging model of school governance and legal reform. *NYU Rev. L. & Soc. Change*, 28, 183–ff.

Luhmann, N. 1992. Some problems with reflexive law. *State, Law and Economy as Autopoetic Systems*, edited by G. Teubner and A. Febbrajo, 389–415.

Macneil, I. 1980. *The New Social Contract: An Inquiry into Modern Contractual Relations*. New Haven: Yale University Press.

——2000. Contracting worlds and essential contract theory. *Social and Legal Studies*, 9 (3), 431–8.

Maesschalck, M. 1996. *Droit et Création Sociale chez Fichte: Une philosophie moderne de l'action politique*. Paris/Leuven: Bibliothèque Philosophique de Louvain (44), Vrin/Peeters, LVI.

——2001. *Normes et Contextes*. Hildesheim/NewYork: Olms Verlag.

——2008. Normes de gouvernance et enrôlement des acteurs sociaux. *Multitudes*, 34 (4), 182–94.

——2009. Pour une approche génétique de l'action collective: Relations intra-groupes et relations exo-groupes. *Ethique et Gouvernance: Les Enjeux Actuels d'une Philosophie des Normes*, M. Maesschalck (dir.). Hildesheim/Zürich/New York: Olms, 19–36.

Marcus, R. 1988. Public law litigation and legal scholarship. *Journal of Law Reform*, 21, 647–57.

Marengo, L. and Dosi, G. 2005. Division of labor, organizational coordination and market mechanisms in collective problem-solving. *Journal of Economic Behavior & Organization*, 58 (2) (October), 303–26.

Maynard Smith, J. 1982. *Evolution and the Theory of Games*. Cambridge, UK: Cambridge University Press.

Mayntz, R. 2002. Common goods and governance. *Common Goods: Reinventing European and International Governance*, edited by A. Heritier. New York/London: Rowman and Littlefield, 15–27.

Misak, C. 2000. *Truth, Politics, Morality, Pragmatism and Deliberation*. London/New York: Routledge.

Morgan, B. 1999. Regulating the regulators: Meta-regulation as a strategy for reinventing government in Australia. *Public Management: An International Journal of Research and Theory*, 1, 50–ff.

——2003. The economization of politics: Meta-regulation as a form of nonjudicial legality. *Social and Legal Studies*, 12, 490.

Mueller, M. 2002. *Ruling the Root, Internet Governance and the Taming of Cyberspace*. Cambridge, MA/London: MIT Press.

Nelson, R. and Winter, S. 1982. *An Evolutionary Theory of Economic Change*. Cambridge, MA: Belknap Press of Harvard University Press.

Nonet, P. and Selznick, P. 1978. *Law and Society in Transition: Toward Responsive Law*. New York: Harper and Row.

North, D. 2005. *Understanding the Process of Economic Change*. Princeton: Princeton University Press.

Oakerson, R. 1992. Analyzing the commons: A framework. *Making the Commons Work*, edited by D. Bromley. San Francisco: Institute for Contemporary Studies Press, 41–59.

Offe, C. 2003. The European model of "social" capitalism: Can it survive European integration? *The Journal of Political Philosophy*, 11 (3), 437–69.

Ogus, A. 2000. Self-regulation. *Encyclopedia of Law and Economics, Volume 1: The History and Methodology of Law and Economics*, edited by B. Bouckaert and G. De Geest. Cheltenham: Edward Elgar, 587–8.

Ostrom, E. 1999. Coping with tragedies of the commons. *Annual Review of Political Science*, 2, 493–ff.

Ostrom, V. 1973. *The Intellectual Crisis in American Public Administration*. Tuscaloosa, AL: University of Alabama Press.

——1991. *The Meaning of American Federalism*. San Francisco: ICS Press.

——1997. *The Meaning of Democracy and the Vulnerability of Societies: A Response to Tocqueville's Challenge*. Ann Arbor: University of Michigan Press.

Parker, C., Scott, C., Lacey, N. and Braithwaite, J. (eds) 2004. Introduction. *Regulating Law*. Oxford: Oxford University Press, 10.

Patterson, D. 1988. Wittgenstein and the code: A theory of good faith performance and enforcement under Article nine. *University of Pennsylvania Law Review*, 137, 335–429.

——1990. Law's pragmatism: A theory of law as practice and narrative. *Virginia Law Review*, 76, 937–65.

——1996. *Law and Truth*. Oxford: Oxford University Press.

——2006. Reflecting on reflexive law. *Luhmann on Politics and Law: Critical Appraisals and Applications*, edited by M. King and C. Thornhill. Oxford: Hart, 13–35.

Perry, S. 1988. *Politics and Law*. Oxford: Oxford University Press.

——1997. Interpretation and methodology in legal theory. *Law and Interpretation: Essays in Legal Philosophy*, edited by A. Marmor. Oxford: Clarendon, 97–135.

——2000. Holmes v. Hart: The bad man in legal theory. *"The Path of the Law" and its Influence*, edited by S. Burton. Cambridge, UK: Cambridge University Press, 158–196.

Peters, G. 1995. The two traditions of institutional design: Dialogue versus decision? *Institutional Design*, edited by D. Weimer. Dordrecht/Boston: Kluwer, 133–79.

—— 1998. Managing horizontal government: The politics of co-ordination. *Public Administration*, 76, 295–ff.

Post, J. 2000. Moving from geographic to virtual communities: Global corporate citizenship in a dot.com world. *Business and Society Review*, 105 (200), 1, 27–46, 36–38.

Power, F., Higgins, A., Kohlberg, L. and Reimer, J. 1989. The just community approach: Democracy in a communitarian mode. *Lawrence Kohlberg's Approach to Moral Education*, edited by F. Power, A. Higgins and L. Kohlberg. New York: Columbia University Press, 989, 33–62.

Powell, W. and Dimaggio, P. 1991. *The New Institutionalism in Organizational Analysis*. Chicago: University of Chicago Press.

Prosser, T. 2005a. Competition law and public services: From single market to citizenship rights? *European Public Law*, 11, 543–ff.

——2005b. *The Limits of Competition Law: Markets and Public Services*. Oxford: Oxford University Press.

Prosser, T., Adlard, H., Eberlein, B., Britz, G. and Herzmann, K. 2010 (forthcoming). Neo-institutionalist and collaborative-relational approaches to governance in services of general interest: The case of energy in the UK and Germany. *Reflexive Governance*, edited by O. De Schutter and J. Lenoble. Oxford: Hart Publishing.

Putnam, H. 1988. *Representation and Reality*. Cambridge, MA: MIT Press.

——1990. *Realism with a Human Face*. Cambridge, MA: Harvard University Press.

——1992. *Renewing Philosophy*. Cambridge, MA: Harvard University Press.
——1995. Are moral and legal values made or discovered? Replies to Brian Leiter and Jules Coleman. *Legal Theory*, 1, 69–81.
——2002. *The Collapse of the Fact/Value Dichotomy and Other Essays*. Cambridge, MA: Harvard University Press.
Rhodes, R. 1997. *Understanding Governance: Policy Networks, Governance, Reflexivity and Accountability*. Buckingham: Open University Press.
—— 2000. Governance and public administration. *Debating Governance*, edited by J. Pierre. Oxford: Oxford University Press, Chapter 4.
Ricoeur, P. 1990. *Soi-même Comme un Autre*. Paris: Seuil.
Rorty, R. 1996. Moral universalism and economic triage. *Diogenes*, 44, 3–15.
Rosanvallon, P. 2006. *La Contre-Démocratie*. Paris: Seuil.
——2008. *La Légitimité Démocratique*. Paris: Seuil.
Rubin, E. 1996. The new legal process, the synthesis of discourse, and the microanalysis of institutions. *Harvard Law Review*, 109, 1393–438.
Rutherford, M. 1994. *Institutions in Economics: The Old and the New Institutionalism*. Cambridge, UK: Cambridge University Press.
Sabel, C. 1994. Learning by monitoring: The institutions of economic development. *The Handbook of Economic Sociology*, edited by N. Smelser and R. Swedberg. Princeton/New York: Princeton University Press-Russell Sage Foundation, 137–65.
——2006. A real time revolution in routines. *The Firm as a Collaborative Community: Reconstructing Trust in the Knowledge Economy*, edited by C. Heckscher and P. Adler. New York: Oxford University Press, 106–56.
Sabel, C., Fung, A. and Karkkainen, B. 2000. Beyond backyard environmentalism. *Beyond Backyard Environmentalism*, edited by J. Cohen and J. Rogers (for Boston Review). Boston: Beacon Press, 3–115.
Sabel, C. and Simon, W. 2004. Destabilization rights: How public law litigation succeeds. *Harvard Law Review*, 117, 1015–ff.
Sabel, C. and Zeitlin, J. 2004. Neither modularity nor relational contracting: Inter-firm collaboration in the new economy. *Enterprise and Society*, 5 (3), 388–ff.
Schön, D. 1963. *Displacement of Concepts*. London: Tavistock Publications.
——1971. *Beyond the Stable State*. London: Temple Smith.
——1991. Concluding comments. *The Reflective Turn: Case Studies In and On Educational Practice*, edited by D. Schön. New York/London: Teachers College Press, Columbia University, 343–59.
——1993. Generative metaphor: A perspective on problem-setting in social policy. *Metaphor and Thought*, edited by A. Ortony. Cambridge, UK: Cambridge University Press, 137–63.
——1996. *The Reflective Practitioner: How Professionals Think in Action*. Aldershot: Ashgate Publishing Limited.
Schön, D. and Rein, M. 1994. *Frame Reflection*. New York: Basic Books.

Schotter, A. 1981. *The Economic Theory of Social Institutions*. Cambridge, UK: Cambridge University Press.
Scott, C. 2006. Privatization and regulatory regimes. *The Oxford Handbook of Public Policy*, edited by M. Moran, M. Rein and R. Goodin. Oxford: Oxford University Press, 664.
—— 2007. How reflexive is the governance of regulation? Paper presented at the annual meeting of The Law and Society Association, Berlin. Available at http://www.allacademic.com/meta/p177403_index.html.
Shapiro, S. 2002. Law, plans and practical reason. *Legal Theory*, 8, 387–441.
Simon, W. 2004. Solving problems vs. claiming rights: The pragmatist challenge to legal liberalism. *William and Mary Law Re*view, 46, 128–ff.
Stewart, R. 1975. The reformation of American administrative law. *Harvard Law Review*, 88, 1667–813.
——1985. The discontents of legalism: Interest group relations in administrative regulation. *Wisconsin Law Review*, 655–ff.
——1990. Madison's nightmare. *University of Chicago Law Review*, 57, 335–ff.
—— 2003. Administrative law in the twenty-first century. *NYU Law Review*, 78, 437–ff.
Teubner, G. 1985. After legal instrumentalism: Strategic models of post-regulatory law. *Dilemmas of Law in the Welfare State,* edited by G. Teubner. Berlin: de Gruyter, 299–325.
——1989. *Recht als Autopoietisches System*. Frankfurt am Main: Suhrkamp Verlag (English translation 1993, *Law as an Autopoietic System.* Oxford: Blackwell).
——1994. *Droit et Réflexivité: L'Auto-référence en Droit et dans l'Organisation* (French translation by N. Boucquey and G. Maier). Paris/Brussels: L.G.D.J.-Bruylant.
Teubner, G. and Febbrajo, A. 1992. *State, Law and Economy as Autopietic Systems*. Milan: Guiffre.
Thomas, S. 2005. *The European Union Gas and Electricity Directives*. Public Services International Research Institute, University of Greenwich, September 2005.
Ullmann-Margalit, E. 1977. *The Emergence of Norms.* Oxford: Clarendon Press.
Vincent-Jones, P. 1999. The regulation of contractualisation in quasi-markets for public services. *Public Law*, 304–27.
——2000. Contractual governance: Institutional and organizational analysis. *Oxford Journal of Legal Studies*, 20, 317–51.
——2001. The reception of Ian Macneil's work on contract in the UK. *The Relational Theory of Contract*, edited by I. Macneil and D. Campbell. London: Sweet and Maxwell.
——2005. Citizen redress in public contracting for human services. *Modern Law Review*, 68, 887–ff.
——2006. *The New Public Contracting: Regulation, Responsiveness, Relationality*. Oxford: Oxford University Press.

Vincent-Jones, P. and Mullen, C. 2010 (forthcoming). From collaborative to genetic governance: The example of healthcare services in England. *Reflexive Governance*, edited by O. De Schutter and J. Lenoble. Oxford: Hart Publishing.

Vincent, A. and Declercq, C. 2000. L'ouverture du marché de l'électricité, III. Organisation et stratégies des acteurs, *Courrier Hebdomadaire*, 1695, Brussels: CRISP (Centre de recherche et d'information socio-politiques).

Vromen, J. 1995. *Economic Evolution: An Enquiry into the Foundations of New Institutional Economics.* London/New York: Routledge.

Wagner, R. 2005. Self-governance, polycentrism, and federalism: Recurring themes in Vincent Ostrom's scholarly oeuvre. *Journal of Economic Behavior & Organization*, 57, 173–ff.

Waluchow, W. 1994. *Inclusive Legal Positivism*. Oxford: Clarendon Press.

Weimar, D. 1995. Institutional design: Overview. *Institutional Design*, edited by D. Weimer. Boston/Dordrecht: Kluwer, 10.

Williamson, O. 1985. *The Economic Institutions of Capitalism.* New York: The Free Press.

——1987. Transaction cost economics. *Journal of Economic Behaviour and Organization*, 8, 617–25.

——1991. Comparative economic organization: The analysis of discrete structural alternatives. *Administrative Science Quarterly*, 36, 269–96.

——1993. Transaction cost economics and organization theory. *Industrial and Corporate Change*, 2, 107–56.

——1996. *The Mechanisms of Governance.* Oxford: Oxford University Press.

Winter, S. 1986. The research program of the behavioural theory of the firm: Orthodox critique and evolutionary perspective. *Handbook of Behavioural Economics*, edited by B. Gilad and S. Kaish. Greenwich, CT: JAI Press, 151–88.

Witt, U. 1997. Des présupposés sociaux de la rationalité. *Les Limites de la Rationalité, 2, Les Figures du Collectif*, edited by B. Reynaud. Paris: La Découverte, 68.

Zipursky, B. 2000. Pragmatic conceptualism. *Legal Theory*, 6, 457–85.

Index

For Product Safety Concerns and Information please contact our EU representative GPSR@taylorandfrancis.com Taylor & Francis Verlag GmbH, Kaufingerstraße 24, 80331 München, Germany